SPIRIT AND THE
POLITICS OF
DISABLEMENT

D1564581

SPIRIT AND THE
POLITICS OF
DISABLEMENT

Sharon V. Betcher

Fortress Press • Minneapolis

SPIRIT AND THE POLITICS OF DISABLEMENT

Cover art: "The Broken Column" by Frida Kahlo (1907-1954) © Banco de Mexico Trust. Photo © Schalkwijk / Art Resource, NY
Cover design: Danielle Carnito
Book design: Tim Parlin and Amy Anderson

Library of Congress Cataloging-in-Publication Data
Spirit and the politics of disablement / Sharon V. Betcher.
    p. cm.
  ISBN-13: 978-0-8006-6219-6 (alk. paper)
  1. Church work with people with disabilities. I. Betcher, Sharon V., 1956-
BV4460.S65 2007
259'.4—dc22

                                                                    2007027496

The paper used in this publication meets the minimum requirements of American National Standard for Information Sciences—Permanence of Paper for Printed Library Materials, ANSI Z329.48-1984.

Manufactured in the U.S.A.
11   10   09   08   07   1   2   3   4   5   6   7   8   9   10

CONTENTS

The following chapters were previously published as essays:

"Monstrosities, Miracles, and Mission: Religion and the Politics of Disablement." In *Postcolonial Theologies: Divinity and Empire*, edited by Catherine Keller, Michael Nausner, and Mayra Rivera. St. Louis, Mo: Chalice, 2004.

"Putting My Foot (Prosthesis, Crutches, Phantom) Down: Considering Technology as Transcendence in the Writings of Donna Haraway." In *Women's Studies Quarterly: Women and Technology*, edited by Lee Quinby (Special Issue, Fall 2001): 341–348.

"Wisdom to Make the World Go On: On Disability and the Cultural Deligitimation of Suffering." In *Word and World*, Supplement Series 4 (2000): 87–98.

PREFACE

The residue of Eden, spoiled fruit: such might metaphorically summarize how the Augustinian Lutheranism of my childhood prepared me to live into my own becoming disabled. Augustine—refusing to allow any pastoral indulgence to be extended to anything so pathetic as blindness, deafness, or being born with "as little wit as the cattle"—explicitly linked disability with humanity's "condemned origin," concluding his exposition with the rhetorical embargo, "God forbid we say this is done without its being deserved."[1] The fall, his version of an original, normal, and perfect world fouled by sin (a Christianity Nietzsche sarcastically called a simple "platonism for the people"[2]), would come to assume the shorthand hermeneutic of brokenness versus wholeness, stigmatically symptomatized in disfigurement and disability.

Today I, however, live disability on the streets of one of this planet's smaller, but still global, cities: Vancouver. One might presume this city, where Arcadian dreams fuse with chic cosmopolitanism, to be quite a step away from the quaintly nostalgic Augustinian Lutheranism of my rural Minnesota roots. Yet disability—which but for the inflection of cultural politics might be defined simply as that which happens to a body in a lifetime or a variant capaciousness within natality—nonetheless still appears even here as the residue of Eden.[3] The question comes at me, "What happened to you? What did you do to yourself?" It seems answering such questions is, for a so-obviously fallen woman, the admission price for a modicum of social inclusion.

These questions to which my body is asked to confess seem not unlike the question "Where are you really from?" pressed upon ethnic others in the West. As postcolonial theorist Ato Quayson observes, "the interest in surveilling otherness is dispersed everywhere, sometimes making itself manifest in the question, 'Where do you really come from?' constantly asked of newly arrived immigrants . . . and, most irritatingly, to those of mixed descent in the various postcolonial diasporas of the West." He continues, noting that "the question . . . is never an innocent one: it is a question of origin that, posed to particular subjects, and in particular contexts, also involves a question of return."[4] Within the postmodern, multiethnic carnival, the seemingly innocuous questions "What happened to you?" and "Where do you come from?" patrol so as to set up a containment wall within sociality. This surveillance system, as Quayson insinuated, continues to protect modernity's "origin." Like Quayson (and Frantz Fanon's phenomenological report on the experience of colonized persons left "amputated," "disarticulated," and "hemorrhaging" suggests the intersection between disability and postcolonial studies),[5] I find myself outside some kind of in/security zone—as if set outside a compound with an invisible, but palpable, electronic fence. But what Eden would I today—in this cosmopolitan city—despoil?

I.

Despite theological modernity claiming to have outgrown such purportedly archaic notions as sin, evil, and the fall, my body evidently remains—in the psychosocial cosmology undergirding what Guy Debord calls "the Society of the Spectacle"—marked as fallen. Debord drafts the concept of the society of the spectacle to name the way in which appearance has come to serve as the primary mode of social life and of economic hegemony during late modernity. Variously said, today "social relationship between people . . . is mediated by images."[6] Equally an outcome of the modern social contract as "the goal of the dominant mode of production,"[7] the spectacle is, Debord insists, "the negation of life that has invented a visual form of itself."[8] When we ask after this society's creative stimulus, Debord takes us back to the classical imaginary of Eden: "The spectacle is the material reconstruction of the religious illusion . . . . The absolute denial of life, in the shape of a fallacious paradise, is no longer projected onto the heavens, but finds its place instead within material life itself. The spectacle is hence a technological version of the exiling of human powers in a 'world beyond.'"[9] "A specious form of the sacred," the spectacle, Debord now emphatically points out, is "capital accumulated to the point where it becomes image."[10] Where anxiety about urban space ensued amidst early industrialization and urbanization,[11] modernity developed alongside its definitive Kantian dialectic of self/other, the cultivation of self-image and, more specifically, the image of luxury, whose material excess was appropriated from the colonies.[12] Developing technologies and advertising reinforced visual culture, reinforced the demand for a stellar performance of the ideal, now become "normal" self.

Given how easily persons living the Society of the Spectacle recognize me as broken, I suspect that the fall has been telescoped into that analytic—namely, wholeness/brokenness—wielded by modernity's clinical gaze and used to detect and to categorize pathology in this age of image. The theological analytic of brokenness—an analytic tool to assess sociohistorical conditions within the portfolio of wisdom theology—has instead been read through a morality attuned not simply to "obedience to transcendental command," but "to an intrinsic design of things."[13] As theologian J. Joyce Schuld explains in her volume *Foucault and Augustine*, "No longer action and social consequence, but nature and defect analyzed through rational quantitative study govern the relations of power to those falling outside expected norms, values and behaviors."[14] The analytic of the fall, releasing with it a voracious program of recovery and the reclamation of origins, here becomes social policy, meted out through the patrolling power of the norm.

II.

Whatever Christianity had meant by sin now d/evolves within this cultural frame to the practice of pathology, the culling out of defect, by employing the simple ego-invested outline—indeed (in a Lacanian sense) a "hallucination"—of "wholeness."[15] The fall, introjected more broadly into the privacy of every self, would then aggravate "modernization" or "progress" as we take responsibility for and excruciating pleasure in detecting defects in our self-image.[16] Disability appears to be, in other words, a symptom of a comprehensive, cultural optic. In the "specular spectacular" that is globalization, an ancient, still classical reading of the fall, shaping religious sensibility toward the world (as it did for Augustine), comes home to haunt Christianity—that is, as the inner logic of a social structure with which Christian theology would rather at this time assume to take umbrage. When Christianity mistakes its own ancient analytic of world brokenness as having something still to do with me and my body, treating my body as if it were defective and needed to be made whole, it substitutes the standards of Fitness World™ for the visitation of passion, which would unhinge us from the values of "the society of the spectacle" (Debord).

What makes deconstruction of this binary imperative is the way in which such idealization (and the pleasure of classifying its dysfunctions) metabolizes that vision of life now going global, the way in which the practice of transcendence has been, among the first-world class, subsumed in idealization. As rubbish heaps accrue and technology creates more and more obsolescent human lives, sociologist Zygmunt Bauman wonders if moderns, while enchanting ourselves with the ever new, the novel, might rather be reveling in "expelling, discarding, cleansing [our]selves of a recurrent impurity," in "stripping off, throwing away, setting aside."[17] In "pollution behavior," in other words. "'Eliminating,' Mary Douglas famously said, 'is not a negative movement, but a positive effort to organize the environment.'"[18] If "the production of 'human waste'" that is, the production of "'excessive' and 'redundant' [human bodies]", is an inevitable outcome of modernization, this is, "in the broadest of outlines," Bauman warns, "the setting for contemporary life."[19]

III.

So while the view of a fallen world may have helped Augustine's congregations achieve an objectifying distance from Rome so as to discern between the various proffered architectures of "the City of God," the pathologizing of brokenness does not today help us parse the conditions of flourishing. An enervating of the perpetual crisis of the modern self and its persistent need for Extreme Makeovers, including spiritual transformations, might rather occasion among Christians, called to responsible and compassionate living in the midst of economic imperialism—that is, globalization—a more capacious presence to life. But be forewarned: disabling the cosmic fall will also require a certain recalibration of divine efficacy, of the physics of Spirit. Because of the ways in which disabled persons have been seen as the epitome of The Cosmic Devolution, our bodies have been, since at least the time of Augustine, figural paradigms, used within biblical theologies to demonstrate a "strong"—miraculous, supernatural—notion of divine power and to counterprove the conditions of paradise, that is, confirming the redemption of the body to the status of cultural normativity.

Our contemporary notion of disability takes shape against industrialization and the demand for employability in a now consumer-based economy. But the Isaianic poetry, whose incantation sets up the miracle stories of the Christian gospels, that is, "the blind see, the lame walk, the deaf hear" (Isaiah 35:5-6, Luke 7:22, Matthew 11:4-5), will likely rather have had ancient empire and the colonization, indeed economic enslavement, of the body in mind.[20] If so, that changes one's reading of the miracle texts from an issue of perfect health and wholesomeness to an issue of sociopolitical critique—of the colonizing nation, its colonizing of bodies, of persons living under empire—like us, living in the Society of the Spectacle (Debord). Ironically, then, the concept of "Spirit" (as divine physics and then divine appellation) may have been conceived (conceptually speaking) by persons "physicalized" by and "hemorrhaging" under the impress of colonial forces (Fanon)—and coincidently those with a glee for "the weakness of God,"[21] which unhinges us from cultural preoccupations (See chapters 6 and 7).

In the early stages of the Jesus movements, persons, their bodies hobbled by slavery and not expecting to be reconditioned by biotechnology, nevertheless began assaulting the Roman Empire, its military legions, and its sociopolitically habituated realism with rumors of miracle, of the visitation of Spirit. Up against aristocratic rule, foreign occupation, the monetizing of the agrarian economy, the innovation of property rights, heavy taxation, and dislocating urbanization, Christians showed signs of, well, enchantment. The real world for them had somehow just admitted at least a psychic supplement to the Roman economy, had admitted a sense of wonder, a life enchantment not so delusional as Rome's free market felt to them. But imagine that: That persons at the bottom of the economic heap—and cripped at that—should become gripped to the point of enchantment, should fall in love with the world. Even more ridiculous, to think that the circulation of life love—witnessed by bodies who would never experience the medical miracle—would have any effect upon the way things were in the empire. Yet, having already fallen, the cripped may have broken that hold where idealism otherwise cannot be so deftly distinguished from ontological, become political, cynicism so as to take joy in a life from which pain cannot be cut away.

Comparably, philosopher Gilles Deleuze—like recent postcolonial writers and political theorists—set out "cripped" figurations so as today to invite us to conceive a new humanity, a new earth. Deleuze's figures of the schizo and of the "body without organs" were set within an energetic materialism that lives "without transcendence"—but also without "the God of Judgement" and the templates of order, form, and norm (see chapter 8). If transcendence or "strong theology," correlated with the cosmic fall, has set disabled persons under judgment, Deleuzean philosophy (even if I admittedly must dig behind Deleuze himself) might conversely help us understand what the Crip Nation might have wanted in their deployment of the fall and its correlative notion of Spirit. For Bergson, that vitalist predecessor of Deleuze, "Spirit arises . . . out of the very poverty of our conscious perception, that is, out of the fact that [our conscious perception] is highly selective and subtractive."[22] Contrary, then, to the impulse to think of the Spirit as disciplining us into the strictures of cultural ideology and a culture's politics of representation, Spirit may have been conceived in those times under imperial gaze, within a colonized zone, to swerve the colonial optic so as to open out spaciousness in the cultural imaginary—not then as a medicinal miraculously remediating impairment, that is, nature's lack.

So Spirit does not necessarily arrive on the scene free-wheeling from the pure netherlands of the two perfections—Never-Known Eden and Ever-Delayed

Parousia. Rather, Spirit might begin as an intensity, a vibration, within the zones of social assessment, where we admit our ease at falling into desire with the powers that be, with property and propriety, with the security of identity and with the glamors of image, all of which keep us from the freedom and responsibility of creating the new earth, if even subversively from within the belly of empire. Given the ingress of today's empire, that is, economic globalization with its accumulation of wasted lives and ecological discontent, this book ventures that a reconstruction of Spirit—by way of becoming disabled—can return Christians to the practice of "believing in this world,"[23] entrusting ourselves to a love of life within less than ideal circumstances.

IV.

This book has emerged from a chasm opened in my thirty-seventh year, a wrinkle in the anticipated trajectory of a life that nevertheless cannot be separated from the intensity with which I now find myself in love with life nor from a certain standpoint epistemology—a double-vision, for which I am not ungrateful. Around the traumas of a life, I have known the deepest humanity, that humanity that almost literally carries another in their thoughts and prayers and warms one back with the intensities of their most practical care and affections. That this book has come to the light of day, I owe in no small way to the faculty, administration, staff, and students at Drew University's Casperson School of Graduate Studies and its School of Theology during my residency there; members of the Episcopal Church of the Redeemer, Morristown, New Jersey; and to the medical staff of Overlook Hospital, Summit, New Jersey. In those challenging days, stretching into months, of my health crisis, I learned that surgeons, like Evan and Jerry, and physicians, like my friend, Maureen, were themselves also persons tending the mysteries.

I want especially to acknowledge several threesomes that have enfolded me and continue to warm my life to the intensity of vital life–love. First, the nestled household threesome formed with me by my daughter, Sarah, and my partner, Jeff. Sarah and Jeff, yours is a daily grace that suffers with me my humiliations and enjoins me to make the world go on with you and for you. Thank you. Second, to the other two members of the Three Sisters—my *doktor-mutter* and sister-friend, Catherine Keller, and my teacher become sister-friend, Virginia Burrus: I'm so honored by your intellectual companionship, by your mentoring, by the sisterly affection that has grown and endured among us. And finally, to my colleagues at Vancouver School of Theology, and especially to Principal-

Dean Wendy Fletcher, my thanks for feedback, for sabbatical time, and for the research support (which has included the skills, accompaniment, and not insignificant fits of giggles of research assistants Barbara Boruff and Jeffrey Preiss, as well as the skills and humor of independent editor, Bud Bynack) that allowed this manuscript to emerge, even during the initial years of my teaching at VST.

INTRODUCTION: TELLING IT SLANT

This book broaches a theology of Spirit incanted "on the slant," to borrow Barbara Kingsolver's improvisation on Emily Dickinson. In her postcolonial novel *The Poisonwood Bible*, Kingsolver includes among her chorus of narrators a girl named Adah, who is as morphologically asymmetric as her twin is perfect: "Tell all the Truth but tell it slant, says my friend Emily Dickinson. And really what choice do I have? I am a crooked little person, obsessed with balance."[1] Born in Bethlehem, Georgia, on Christmas Eve, Adah was the gift that legitimated her Baptist preacher father as missioner of mercy, but that hemisphere of meaning left Adah, a hemiplegic, "hemmed-in, hemlocked."[2] Moving to another hemisphere, the Congo, where "bodily damage is more or less considered to be a by-product of living," Adah finds "the prison house of her disposition shaken open."[3] There, her "two unmatched halves . . . add[ed] up to more than one whole": "In Congo I was one-half *benduka* the crooked walker, and one-half *bënduka*, the sleek bird that dipped in and out of the banks with a crazy ungrace that took your breath."[4] Hemming and hawing, she speaks in palindromes—playing hymns, sermons, proverbs backward and forward, as if truth might be found only when listing between hemispheres.

Like Adah, this theology of Spirit—that sleek bird—hems and haws, traversing hemispheres of thought so as to dissociate theology from a certain wholesomeness, all too sonorously synonymous with the perfections, virtual/osities, and immaterial technologies espoused by globalizing capitalism. Having found a capacious unhinging in the coincident, if distinct, hemispheres of disability studies and postcolonial theory, this pneumatology hopes to release Spirit from its prison house—from the transcendental enframement that structurally supports the hegemony of transnational capitalism.

I have been interested in recuperating the concept of Spirit for Christian theology for several reasons. Concepts, the philosophers Gilles Deleuze and

Felix Guattari suggest, are "centers of vibration."[5] Concepts should be capacious, should "summon forth 'a new earth and a people that does not yet exist.'"[6] In that vein, the theological concept "Spirit," as ancient as it is new—and theological readers may almost hear in Deleuze and Guattari's description of "concept" that creative vibration over the tehomic deeps of Genesis 1—allows us, perhaps even requires us, to speak about the divine immanently, from within the planetary or cosmic milieu. Further, the physics of or dynamic energies suggested by the Spirit concept may be much more conversant with the post-Einsteinian worldviews that we technologically inhabit. In parallel, Spirit helps us speak about the power of the divine in troubled social times, in crisis times.

Let me offer an example: The September 11, 2001, terrorism attack in New York City destroyed the waking horizon of what my family had called home for some ten years. Not only does the town of Summit, New Jersey, overlook the Big Apple, with its twinned navigational landmarks, but 20 percent of the adult population of Summit worked in the World Trade Center towers. My household, now living in Vancouver, B.C., spent the first week after 9/11, working across the width of the North American continent, accounting for old neighbors, parish members and, most poignantly, the parents of my daughter's friends. Two months later, now more reflective, my then-fourteen-year-old daughter turned to me and announced: "I don't believe in God."

But of course not. Who can? Who does, if by God we mean the comptroller of fates, of history, if by God we mean some providential agent of world causality? Theologian Elizabeth Johnson shares a similar sentiment: "The whole modern movement of protest atheism," she writes, "springs from this reaction" to classical theism's impassible, omnipotent God, whereas "language about the suffering God," the God who is wholly, incarnately given into the cosmic milieu, "has a particular affinity with the experience of Spirit."[7] If we are to think of the contours of divine activity after the twentieth century (considered the most brutal century in human history, despite the humanitarian and scientific strides that were effected), we might find it advantageous to think with the concept of Spirit. Further, given the judicious concerns of poststructuralism, which insists that we cannot guarantee our truth claims by resort to a presence outside history, and postcolonialism, which among other things necessitates respect for the truth claims of other religions, Spirit suggests itself as a viable referent. As theologian Jay McDaniel has observed, "Spirit is not reducible to Christianity," and yet it allows us to speak the particularity of our experience of the sacred.[8] Within that crux—the locus of protest atheism, the need to speak realistically, if faithfully, even fervently, of the divine within troubled times . . . well, Spirit may allow progressive Christians to reinhabit our religious commitments.

Here, I specifically want to think Spirit "on the slant," rather than on the up-and-up of philosophical idealism, materialism (philosophical idealism's twinned, Cartesian inverse), and "decency theologies."[9] Thinking Spirit from this location may disrupt certain colonizing vectors of globalizing capitalism—especially the one that I will call globally mediated Platonism, or normative idealism: The Western, idealized self, cosmetically and prosthetically enhanced, has become, according to Benjamin Barber, the most lucrative item for sale in the global market place.[10] Urban studies scholar Harlan Hahn echoes Barber's point: "A principal effect of the media has not been to sell specific products; they have sold imagery and, especially, an idealized image of the human body."[11] The posing and posturing of such "media/ted" representations inherently involves us, Thomas De Zengotita argues, in "a form of flattery," dares us to be "celebrities all." So the ideal self has become normative in such a way that the globalization of capitalist economics rides upon this figural ideation, our lives shaped by and toward "a culture of performance."[12] Globally mediated Platonism shapes desire and belonging, carving fault lines between rich and poor and within ecological systems.

In theology, Spirit has often been made the agent of such Final Perfection, telescoped in terms of the miraculous remediation of disabilities and magnified in the eschatological purging and purifying of the world's brokenness. Christianity has shaped its understanding of and practice in regards to divine power upon the dynamic trajectory it has read into miracle accounts, which Christianity has assumed in some way to remediate (via supernaturalism or compassionate inclusion) the disabled body. Consequent theological representations of the physics of Spirit (or of divine efficacy, then), including the trajectory of western Christianity's social mission and its politics of compassion, have been mapped in relation to defect and so assume the monolithic or sovereign power of Spirit and its representatives to effect remediation or tolerant inclusion of such difference. Such transcendentalist energies are rampant in economic globalization, in biotechnology, and in medical and humanitarian colonialism. This theological work, however, instead circles back to rethink Spirit in relation to bodies that refuse the "hallucination of wholeness."[13] Theology, which has been prone, given its ongoing relationship to metaphysical idealism, to teaching people to live by analogy, is not innocent, but dangerously inadequate to this situation. Thinking Spirit on the slant might, I hope, open up a different way of doing theology.

Intriguingly, historian of science Donna Haraway, in the philosophical essay conceiving a postmodern figuration, or condensed visual map, to replace the wholesome modern transcendental subject, "Ecce Homo, Ain't (Ar'n't) I a Woman, and Inappropriate/d Others. . . ," pivots the turn from modern humanism, with its cast of "coherent and masterful subjects[. . .], the bearers of rights, holders of property. . . ," to consideration of "The Human in a Post-Humanist Landscape" upon "the disarticulated bodies of history."[14] With no small irony, this new "figure of speech," this icon of new humanity, turns out to be those whom postcolonial theorist Trinh Minh-ha first called "inappropriate/d others."[15] Haraway explains: "My focus is the figure of a broken and suffering humanity, signifying—in ambiguity, contradiction, stolen symbolism, and unending chains of noninnocent translation—a possible hope." "It is," she concludes, "the very nonoriginality, mimesis, mockery, and brokenness that draw me to this figure and its mutants."[16] Haraway hinges "new turns of historical possibility" upon these cripped figures. (And do let it be noted that Haraway's sensibilities for innovation of such figural maps reach back so as to recuperate the Isaianic figure of the suffering slave-servant as forward to the cyborg.) In much the same way that Deleuze and Guattari's notion of the new philosophical concept resonated with the symbol of Spirit in its capaciousness to bring forth "a new earth and a new people that do not yet exist," Haraway turns to the Crip body as figural map for a postcolonial humanity and renewed earth. The Crip turns out to be a map of hope.

So thinking Spirit on the slant (through disability studies, that is) might, in other words, help bring forth an alternative way of minding the world—a world in which we are called to believe and to work out conditions of entrustment to this life in all its variations and vulnerabilities. Idealism, which has shaped Western Christianity's way of minding the world, is not well suited to complexly interdependent systems. Capitalist economics shares philosophical idealism's "loss of interest in the physical world."[17] Disabled persons are some of the fallout, the marginalized, of these complicit ways of minding the world. Disability may simply be defined as "the way the majority of folks is looking at you."[18] To denaturalize this cultural optic informing the [S]pirit of religious, economic and scientific speculation, I will work with poststructuralist convictions, asking what brings the physiological mark of disability into sociopolitical stigmatization—making it seem necessary thereby for differently abled persons to be redeemed by science and/or by Spirit.

Disability is produced by "the context of social power relations," theorist Rosemarie Garland Thomson writes.[19] Here, I combine disability studies with a postcolonial biblical hermeneutic to read biblical healing accounts within the politics of Empire with a capital *E*, as Michael Hardt and Antonio Negri call it. The psychologist of decolonization, Frantz Fanon, called the colonized subject "the slave . . . of appearance."[20] In his more famous text, *The Wretched of the Earth*, he observed that phenomenologically, the colonizer's "glance . . . shrivels me up . . . freezes me . . . turns me into stone."[21] It does not take much of a mental stretch for persons living with disabilities to hear a similarity between that and what we call "the stare" that "sculpts the disabled subject into a grotesque spectacle," "the stare . . . that creates disability as an oppressive social relationship."[22] The colonizing of bodies in both cases psychosocially manifests itself in terms of what Fanon called "epidermalization."[23] Fixed in the gaze or caught in the stare, the colonized and/or disabled body—thoroughly objectified and physicalized—takes place at the skin, threatening to collapse the psychic room of personhood. Such a coincidence of experience between what we now call postcolonial theory and disability studies will inflect this work.

Thinking Spirit with and through disability studies will have nothing much to do with ideals, perfections, and whole(some)ness. Quite simply, we who are disabled refuse to live as if broken and therefore refuse to discard the world as broken. While the view of a fallen world may have helped Augustine's congregations achieve an alienating distance from the Pax Romana so as to discern between the various proffered architectures of "the City of God," the binary of wholeness/brokenness—a shorthand hermeneutic for world engagement, stemming from the doctrine of the fall and iterated through modernity—does not today help us parse the conditions of flourishing. Rather, the binary of brokenness/wholeness aggravates modernity, including this latest phase sometimes referred to as hypermodernity. An enervating of this perpetual crisis of the modern self and its persistent need for extreme makeovers, including spiritual transformations, might actually occasion among Christians, called to responsible and compassionate living in the midst of economic imperialism (globalization), if not among North Americans at large, a more capacious presence to life.[24]

The Politics of Disablement

Admittedly, disability hardly seems, at least on first glance, a matter of national security or even anything remotely linked to the global economy such that a theology, taking in such a critique, might occasion any disruption of today's empire. In other words, to think about disability studies in relation to globalization, given cultural presuppositions about disability, can itself seem globalizing, psychologically speaking. Because we tend to think of disability in terms of an individual and unique morphology and, therefore, also tend to assume that we are speaking of a very limited population, the connection between disability studies and global issues, especially economic issues, can seem an incredible stretch—even a bit fabulist. Yet disability is "not so much a property of bodies as a product of cultural rules."[25] Consequently, this work analyzes the cultural optic—the way of looking at the world—that constructs disability over and against normative whole(some)ness, to serve as its economic and political perimeter. Disabled persons—and Fanon's phenomenological report on the experience of colonized persons left "amputated," disarticulated, and "hemorrhaging" suggests how this category stretches into the international economic scene of politics and mission[26]—live at the intersection of the messianic, soteriological aspirations of biotechnology, the benevolence of Christian social-justice practices, the mediated Platonism of the global market, the humanitarian concerns of nation-states, and the obsessive-compulsive hamster wheel of spiritual transformation or transfiguration toward wholeness.

While incanted on the slant, this is *not* intended to be in the mode of identity politics and liberation theologies (a disability theology). Rather, insomuch as "disability defines 'normal' by presenting its opposite,"[27] I want to stare back so as to "remov[e] the veil of ideology from the concept of the normal"—an ideology that serves as infrastructure for the hegemony of transnational capitalism.[28] Making of certain physiological variables a categorical deposit, a sedimentation, or a representation called "disabled persons" allows a culture to offload certain fears and anxieties as well as conversely to craft its ideal sense of self.[29] In other words, treating these physiological differences in this categorical, classificatory way does political and cultural work, generating a centripetal force called "normalcy."

Metaphors of disablement have been among the most perduring patterns of what postcolonial theorist Gayatri Spivak calls cultural "othering"—an intersubjective process of locating the self by excluding and then controlling difference. Creating the other as deviant object, often accomplished by psychically unloading and projecting upon him or her what one finds objectionable in one's self, conversely creates the self as sovereign subject. For example, Aristotle affected the hierarchies along the great chain of being by considering the female gender to be a disabled form of humanity. Indeed, something has been seriously overlooked if, when analyzing colonial discourse, it is recognized that the racial other was often figured as feminine and subordinate without also observing that the feminine was itself considered a form of *debility*. Because this politics of representing certain others as disabled often pulls the shades over conscience by cloaking "the weak and helpless" in pity and consequently inflecting the subject's actions as obviously benevolent, it has been easy to ignore the fact that the representation of disablement has been and continues to be a template for the colonizing interests of empire and must therefore be considered a form of "anti-conquest rhetoric."[30] Disablement, too, belongs among the gallery of representations that imperial forces use to rationalize as innocent, even compassionate, their own imperial interests and colonizing actions. Such imperial assertions are not wholly distinguishable from the "Mask of Benevolence"(Lane) worn when colonizing minoritized populations such as the Deaf World.[31]

Tropes of disablement have likewise been deeply embedded within Christian and Jewish religious discourses—as a spiritual diagnostic, for one thing, and as a somatic reference for expressing the phenomenology of psychosocial pain, among other things. Further, such representations continue to play upon religious sentiment and within spiritual discourse. With social justice in mind, Christians, for example, often are tempted to speak of themselves as the voice of the voiceless—asserting thereby the imperative to act as knowledgeable and benevolent representatives of another. While attempting to locate so as to remediate injustice, the assumption that the other is somehow not able to articulate his or her own needs and wants allows the proxy—the one who presumes to act as voice of the voiceless—to fill in the discourse using the proxy's own psychological imaginings. To be clear, humanitarianism is hardly at issue, but the ethical quality of a particular imperialist humanitarian interface is. What are questioned here are objectifications—displacement by the gaze, exclusion by attitudes and architecture, by economics and science—that divert discursive negotiation into mere rescue tactics.

Or, to draw upon an example of how the trope of disablement is used in other facets of religious practice, consider Henri Nouwen's not at all atypical use of the metaphor of deafness in his description of spiritual practice. After noting that, etymologically speaking, "'obedience' includes the word *obaudire*, to listen," Nouwen explains spiritual practice in this way: "Contemplative prayer requires us to listen, to let God speak to us. . . . Without this obedience, this listening to the God of our heart, we remain deaf and our life grows absurd. The word absurd includes the term *surdus*, which means deaf. The absurd life is the opposite of the obedient life."[32] So the deaf life is spiritually absurd? The only way that Nouwen's explanation of contemplative obedience works is by presupposing and carrying forward a prior cultural valuation of deafness as irrational, then reinforcing that with our own contemporary cultural projection that deafness lacks a receptive-discursive and cognitive modality and is therefore abnormal.[33] Given such presumptions, religiocultural identity and practices of compassion can easily get conflated with sociopolitical normalizing and imperial interests. This current theological work hopes to intercept and to analyze these projections (cultural, transnational, theological) so as to address the anxiety, the insecurities, the felt powerlessness, if also the productive pleasure of normative idealism, which I take to be the collective psychology, even psychotheology, and metabolic catalyst for economic globalization.

Spirit, the Politics of Disablement, and the Postcolonial: Three of a Kind?

So this book aspires toward a theology of Spirit that takes as its analytic consultant disability studies in its coincidence with postcolonial theories so as to swerve the technologies of embodiment that serve the interests of transnational capitalism. But hardly do these three—a theology of Spirit, disability studies, and postcolonial studies—seem like three of a kind. For me, in terms of this work, disability studies provide an analytical angle from which to undertake the work of dehegemonizing minds of first-world class persons. Hegemony, as Antonio Gramsci defined it, names the dominant class's persuasive view of reality. Given globalization, the dominant class tends not to be so simply coincident with any nation, continent, or country of origin as with economic assets that float their interests around the planet—hence, my term *first-world class*. This economic club tends to be "global in their capacity of being watched," observes sociologist Zygmunt Bauman.[34] Hegemonic views, rather than being militarily enforced or even promoted by propaganda tactics, move by influence. "Fundamentally, hegemony is the power of the ruling class to convince other classes that their interests are the interests of all."[35] This persuasive standpoint, the circulation of dominant-class ideas made intriguing by the political sociology, aesthetics, and authority that attach to them, becomes structurally inscribed in education, economics, science, media, and all other cultural venues, as if this were simply the way things are. Disability studies contests one particular hegemonic aspect of contemporary culture—that which constitutes the normal human self. In other words, disability critique is my way of working toward a postcolonializing theology for people of the first-world class and those caught watching, eying, espying, aspiring; a theology for those of us caught in the hegemony of transnational capitalism.

Intriguingly, images of disability have been borrowed by postcolonial literary authors, for example, Salmon Rushdie's Saleem in *Midnight's Children*, the amputee of Anosh Irani's *The Cripple and His Talismans*, as well as Barbara Kingsolver's Adah in *The Poisonwood Bible*, to denormalize the singular, wholesome subject of Western modernity, whose self-image continues to be invested with colonial, economic surplus. Postcolonial theorist Ato Quayson acknowledges this use of "tropes of disability in postcolonial writing," offering us a most astute mapping of bodies on the postcolonial landscape: "The presence of disabled people in postcolonial writing marks more than just the recognition of their obvious presence in the real world of postcolonial existence and the fact that most national economies [often now iterated through transnational capitalist interests] woefully fail to take care of them."[36] Even so, Quayson swings his lens wide to take in not only the suffering psyche of the colonized, but the "nightmare which is also as much a product of warped postcolonial national identities," the "proliferation of disability on the streets daily" in countries like Angola, Mozambique, Sierra Leone, and Rwanda.[37] Quayson, in so doing, catches us up in a number of disability's dizzying dimensions—its place in the history of war and brutality, in the vicinity of poverty, as a metaphor of psychological experience, as a physiological variable turned via the politics of representation and iterated through transnational economics into a dislocation of subjectivity, even as a concern impinging upon national self-image. But Quayson then concludes, explaining the "more than" of his opening upshot: "The encounter with the disabled in postcolonial writing is . . . a struggle to transcend the nightmare of history."[38] Despite this, postcolonial studies, a mode of critical theory developed in the wake of political decolonization and with awareness of the colonizing effects of imperial presence upon cultures, has not always found a way to apply the insights gained from textual analysis to the work of interrupting contemporary imperialist energies, has not always found a way to intervene within the impulses toward colonization "at the level of more general global developments" today.[39] Differently said, the activist or pragmatic immediacy of postcolonial theory has not always been featured.

Quayson has been trying to bring this theoretical discourse to the creative edge of worlding. Consequently, he speaks of this field of critical theory as a practice of "postcolonializing." With Quayson, I want to work postcolonial theory as "a process of coming-into-being and of struggle against colonialism and its after effects," as "a project to correct imbalances in the world."[40] In a world so full of economic and social injustices, that will mean crisscrossing the terrain defined by the theology of Spirit, disability studies, and postcolonial studies from a number of different angles, considering the status and lessons of disability in terms of a number of related topics; theological, political, economic, and cultural. In doing so, we may be able to reconsider wisdom for life, to remake justice, and to learn to practice spirituality without resort to an idealist and hallucinatory whole(some)ness. Learning from disability experience to revalue a life, we may one morning awaken refusing to make of life a production, to be productive (as if that were the value of a life), awaken to refuse to be broken, defective, and in crisis. If the grotesque body is "a body in the act of becoming . . . never finished, never complete,"[41] then our own hope for a generative, creative future (for becoming, that is) may be, given that we are now so sick of our selves, in becoming disabled becomingly.[42] Refusing the ways in which the body has been organized for efficiency, autonomy, and productivity, for example, we become minor, "widening the gap between oneself and the norm."[43] In this way, becoming disabled may creatively occasion acquisition of an exit visa from globalization.

Empire: The Disabled as Subaltern

Globalization names the vast assimilation of life to the images and values established in the marketplace.[44] It concerns Christians for the same reason that Quayson wishes to develop the practice of postcolonializing—because we are aware of massive global inequities, especially the foreclosing of access to life sustenance among a majority of the world's peoples and the foreshortening of the lifespan of species and ecosystems. Christians are concerned about the increasing economic divide and the ecological devastation while recognizing that those social ills that theorist Homi Bhabha names as the "social pathologies" of the "modern world order"—"loss of meaning, conditions of anomie"—already also infect our life region.[45]

Another way to name the processes at work in globalization, however, is a name that has resonated with the problematics of Christian theology since its institutionalization as a religion in the West—*Empire*. Marxist theorists Michael Hardt and Antonio Negri view today's forces of globalization as an empire without an emperor, per se. Characteristically, empires have been distinguished from occupying forces by their effectiveness at establishing cultural hegemony, their most potent force being the ability to influence the conceptual worlds of the colonized.[46] Globalization, like past phases of imperialism, is "not only a territorial and economic, but inevitably also a subject-constituting project."[47] Following Hardt and Negri, we might even say that globalization is *quintessentially* a subject-constituting project: Empire "seeks directly to rule over human nature. The object of its rule is social life in its entirety."[48] As a subject-constituting project, empire depends upon becoming deeply lodged or hegemonically hidden in people's everyday habits—in the ways people take in or see the world, in what becomes seemingly aesthetically natural and ethically, morally appropriate. As anthropologists Jean and John Comaroff point out,

> Colonialism has been as much a matter of the politics of perception and experience as it has been an exercise in formal governance. . . . The essence of colonization inheres less in political overrule than in seizing and transforming "others" by the very act of conceptualizing, inscribing, and interacting with them on terms not of their choosing; in making them pliant objects and silenced subjects of our scripts and scenarios; in assuming the capacity to "represent" them.[49]

Consequently, a pivotal intervention in the economy can be made by interrupting the politics of representation. Disability studies shares with postcolonial studies "arguments about the material efficacy of representations"—those culturally specific, figural maps of who or what counts as human, the various articulations and disarticulations of the body according to how we value life, according to what we make of a life.[50] Thus, analysis worked back from the locus of disability can unlock the psychotheology that keeps us within the hegemony of the normal and, therefore, economically complicit.

Disability studies is analogous to a subaltern speaking up. *Subaltern* designates those withheld from or with limited access to the circulation and implementation of ideas creating our world—today, namely, the capitalist bourgeois narrative. Disabled persons have historically been among the subalterns—those who have not been allowed access to narrating history. Caught in the webs of science, medicine, and paternalistic others who claim to know what's best for us, we have not been allowed to be critical interlocutors in even our own most intimate concerns. For Gayatri Spivak, "To make the place of the subaltern subject visible can therefore become a model for interventionist practice."[51]

Disability studies has found some space from which to speak. To that extent, disability studies theory marks its difference from Spivak's methodology while nonetheless being interested in turning the question toward critique of the controlling subject positions. To the extent that this space has been qualifiedly liberally endowed, we can both celebrate the generation of a modicum of justice, but caution that we can be complicit with liberalism's politics of identity. Nevertheless, if not in any way assuming to be uncontaminated, disability gives us a site from which to read back supernatural, transnational capitalism's body politics, its anxious insecurities, its transcendental physics.[52] Tapping what wisdom we can from this site opens out justice as something other than pity or charity for those less well-off, allowing us to justify our own lives in the face of knowing that we members of the first-world class live upon the "philanthropy of the poor."[53] To that end, let us inquire more deeply into the lessons that contemporary work on the politics of representation in disability studies has made available.

Reading Capitalism's *Body Politics*

Disability studies theorist Rosemarie Garland Thomson (*Extraordinary Bodies*, *Freakery*) situates the experience of disability within the cultural politics and literary practices of modernity. "Modernity," Thomson reminds us, "effected a standardization of everyday life . . . producing and reinforcing the concept of an unmarked, normative, leveled body as the dominant subject of democracy." Noting that scientific discourse depreciated particularity while valorizing uniformity, she enumerates the mechanisms of body discipline: "Statistics quantified the body and evolution provided a new heritage; eugenics and teratology policed its boundaries; prosthetics normalized it; and asylums cordoned off deviance." Attainment to this image of the "regularized body," she concludes, "was both an individual and national obligation." Social status accumulates to those who can obtain and perform the transcendent— that is, unmarked and unremarked—body within this patrolled space.[54] With the global mediation of Western culture through television, Hollywood, advertising, and the star cults of sports, music, and fashion, that regularized—now idealized—image goes global. Within such a visually patrolled culture, the categorical classification of disability falls upon those bodies that conversely are stigmatically marked, those bodies that cannot hope to become transparent, that cannot get access to the ethers of the transcendentalized star culture. We might simply, summarily conclude, then, that capitalism creates a simple two-class system (as is becoming evident with globalization): "Capitalism creates two completely different groups of people: those bound in radical ways to embodiment . . . and the privileged, who experience their bodies by means of objectification."[55]

Assuming similar social-constructionist perspectives, disability theorists Harlan Hahn, Harlan Lane, Marta Russell, and Lennard Davis advance disability studies discourse toward possible interruptive insinuations within the process of economic globalization.[56] Harlan Hahn, a theorist of urban policy as well as of disability studies, strikes at the aesthetic imagery pumping through the media arteries of globalization, daring us to recuperate an aesthetic of disability as beautiful. He observes that literature as well as human histories, for example, festival fools and the medieval carnival, attest that "disabilities could be perceived as valued characteristics."[57]

Author of *Beyond Ramps*, Marta Russell—a producer, photographer, and political activist—also situates the experience of living with disabilities within the body politics of capitalism, despite capitalism's much vaunted "purely economic interests."[58] Russell raises the question of "disability at the end of the social contract"—or more specifically, the questions "What does it mean to live 'in a society that places its focus on economic concerns rather than human ones?'" and, following that, "What does the desire to wipe out disability say about our culture?"[59] While her assumed sociopolitical context is the United States, given the dismantling of liberal American policies (from Franklin Delano Roosevelt's 1944 Economic Bill of Rights through the Great Society's welfare liberalism of the 1960s), her framing of the question takes its orientation from the earlier twentieth-century Euro-Western melding of eugenics and economics into capitalist social Darwinism, with its early, telltale Holocaust. Reminding readers that the "original victims of Nazi cleansing were . . . the German disabled," she scopes out the horizon against which persons with disability are defined: "It was man's [*sic*] 'civilized' world of dominant physicalist notions and the growing culture of wealth accumulation that would become our biggest adversary."[60] At the dawn of modernity, the Western world assumed that humanity would create systems of coordinated work so as to be free in all other areas of life. Since what each person could contribute was labor value, and since capitalism consequently assumed that all working bodies must be equal, the phenomenon of disability as we know it today "came to be defined in relation to a capitalist labor market."[61] In the wake of the collapse of communism and in the downscaling of human work due to technology, social welfare sensibilities can no longer curb economics and, consequently, capitalism, as a now globally mutating form of unmitigated social Darwinism, produces rampant social casualties, including persons with disabilities, as well as a new slavery.[62] (Disablement was in earlier periods of history correlated with slavery—the hobbling of a slave to prevent running, for example.) Insomuch as disability often results in poverty, and poverty often results in health crises, Russell's reflections on capitalism's body politics—its protection of the rich from the poor in the name of morality, that is, work as worth, and biological naturalism or normalcy, that is, the survival of the fittest—sound a harrowing warning amid economic globalization.[63]

While it has always needed a disposable population, capitalism—with its inherent duties to be healthy, fit, and spiritual—unloads itself of bodies too heavy or cumbersome for an economic system committed to growth. Persons with disabilities not only feel like but are treated as economic burdens, redeemable to the point that social and scientific technologies or charities turn our bodies into profitable industries. The social-psychic pressures that objectify and/or refuse disabled persons are tremendous: "America's disabled population lives in an economic straitjacket, squeezed simultaneously by current social, physical, and entitlement policy barriers to employment and a national ethic that equates human value with work."[64] This can result in a not unfamiliar impulse to suicide among persons with disabilities. Such an impulse does not insinuate that we are emotionally unstable, but that we are systemically—given this socioeconomic architecture—refuse/d. The tidal undertow of that collective psychology is remarkably tricky and unpredictable. The way in which liberalism then raises the question of our quality of life—on an individual basis, without reference to the systems either encompassing or failing to support bodies—tends to rationalize this trimming of the herd. The liberalizing of biology and the biologizing of economics covers up an ideology of normalcy as a "mechanism for social control," which Russell also refers to as a "subtle eugenics policy."[65]

Disability is an economically generated category, indicative of capitalism's "reservations" and its "tendency . . . to use physical characteristics as a basis for creating a cheap and docile group of workers," which are perhaps "the source of ethnicity itself."[66] As Russell's disconcerting, but truthful discussion of suicide indicates, disabled persons feel the effect of making society an adjunct of the market—hence, the psychic pain of the disabled as one of capitalism's waste deposits often echoes that of other poor, the formerly colonized, as well as localized communities that are evacuated of meaning through globalization. As markets go global, local communities experience the evacuation of value and of the power of voice, and people—suffering the lack of communal belonging, interdependence, and purpose—fear having no future. Disabled bodies represent the threat of what happens if a person were to fall down within such an economic system.

But disabled bodies have also often been exploited in the soft war of images and humanitarian prowess—soft wars within which Christian theology is also implicated. Military and biotechnology applications have often first been developed and tested in relation to disabled bodies, which then serve as humanitarian legitimation for applications that far exceed the interests of disabled persons.

Members of the Crip Nation become poster children for nationalistic and missionary acts of mercy and show ponies for the miracles of Western biotechnology and Christian humanitarianism.[67] Given that the ideal Western self is for sale on the global marketplace, the appearance to cure or to rehabilitate disabled bodies within empire's metropolitan centers may be as necessary to today's national or first-world-class appearance as were the invention of prosthetics to national self-image following the U.S. Civil War.[68] Our figural redemption to wholeness factors into the self-promotion of Western cultural superiority, including Western political and church-based humanitarianism. So thinking beauty otherwise, as Hahn proposes in "Can Disability Be Beautiful?" may not be a mere incidental in this venue.

It is only seemingly paradoxical that while tribes of the Crip Nation in empire's metropolitan centers work assiduously to interrupt eugenic tendencies within biotechnology and to kick open the padlocks on sociocultural and economic architecture, internationally (as also where the third world transpires within the first), other systemic pressures occasioning disability must be mitigated. While refusing simply to equate disability with lack of health within the metropolitan centers, I want to acknowledge that globalizing economic conditions exacerbate systemic poverty and violence—conditions that in turn aggravate ill health and a population among which life-onset impairments or disabilities unnecessarily multiply.[69] What encompasses both scenes, however, is the needed thirdness of "care for the environment of the body": We can no longer treat bodies as isolates, as modernity, especially capitalism, has demanded.[70] Analytically opening the psychosocial strictures that construct disabled persons as a physically disposable caste may also help first-world-class persons locate the systemic interconnection between and our responsibility for the international, neocolonial poverty zones—not to be resolved merely with charity, but by regenerating first-world-class lives and livelihoods, given the demands of planetary interdependence. If today the "far-away locals, . . . the millions incapable of being absorbed by the new global economy" are for us "the monstrous"—a warring, murderous, contagious, hungry, envious "subhuman world beyond ethics and beyond salvation," as Zygmunt Bauman puts it, mimicking an earlier colonialism, we can learn from disability and postcolonial studies about how our fears can often foreclose ethical accountability—about keeping our spiritual obligation "to respond to our environment and other people in ways that open up rather than close off the possibility of response."[71]

Looking into the *Mirror of Deformity*

Psychoanalysis—as a philosophy of desire—is also a theory of cultural power. . . . Decoding the psychopathology of this *fin de siecle* may well be one of the most urgent tasks of the critical intellectual. . . . [T]he intellectual [is] a technician of practical knowledge: an analyst of the complex and ever-shifting ways in which the technologies of control of the embodied self—the corpo-r(e)ality of the subject—intersect with the macro-instances that govern the production of discourses socially recognized as "true" and scientifically "valid."

—Rosi Bradotti, *Nomadic Subjects:*
Embodiment and Sexual Difference in Contemporary Feminist Theory

I write as a member of the first-world class who has had something of a falling out with this richly-resourced orientation to life.[72] I fell down and broke my crown. That is, I am now a person living with a disability, a sure promise of downward mobility. These two locations of first-world class and disabled hybridically modify each other: Disability definitely dampens transcendence among the aesthetic class, the residents of spiritually toned hypermodernity. Disability experience opens out into political geographies and social pockets with which I would have preferred to believe myself already in liberal, sympathetic solidarity. Then again, as I have come to understand, sympathy can be a very aggressive and self-protective form of energy. As a member of the first-world class, I recognize in myself the anxious aesthetic desire to wholesomeness as a way of belonging, the fear of falling out of the cycle of just making it, if also the social impulse to live justly. I don't doubt these attributes to be more or less true of this class. Yet our critical, creative know-how—given the global economic divide, the planetary ecological devastation, the technological undercutting of a working life, the evacuation of conditions of employment, and the "glocalization" of community, values, and rituals[73]—surely seems inadequate to life at this, our turn in the becoming spin of the universe. Our impulse to justice and compassion is caught between desire to belong and the fear of falling out.

Now going global, modernity—despite its staging of the "spectacular spectacular," if I may quote from the postmodern musical *Moulin Rouge*—has shockingly, surprisingly, left many of us in the first-world class feeling powerless (incapacitated, shall we say?). As Anishinabe organizer and political activist Winona LaDuke has observed, the unprecedented freedom from relations among the first-world class comes coupled with unprecedented civic and political incapacity. Resonating to the perception of one in her Native American community, she observes that "the difference between white people and Indians is that Indian people know they are oppressed but don't feel powerless. White people don't feel oppressed, but feel powerless." Seeing the political powerlessness evident among first-world-class peoples, she offers this challenge: If you want something to deconstruct, "deconstruct that disempowerment."[74] That sense of powerlessness has often been covered over by a certain mania for colonial mission, postcolonial theorist Gayatri Spivak would be quick to add—if not covered over by other heroic, salvific ventures of help for the presumed helpless, persons with disabilities might well add.[75]

So as to deconstruct this powerlessness, to develop the creative know-how appropriate to life at this time, to break with the power of idealization, this text methodologically imitates Carlin Barton's *The Sorrow of the Ancient Romans*. To map "Roman collective psychology," Barton simply asks, "What did the Romans see in the mirror of deformity?" and advises us that "To see the Roman monster, we must look into the gaze of the Roman spectator."[76] Like an ophthalmologist intruding upon the patient's gaze, Barton stares back into the eyes of the beholder and his or her category of deformity to observe the play of emotions shaping the onlooker's worldview. As Barton stares into the curious eye of the spectator, deformity loses its status as inherent and obvious defect and instead opens out upon "the strictures of civilization [that] create monsters," the psychology that orders and categorizes the world.[77]

Like the Roman category of the monstrous, disabilities constitute one of the ways in which what we call modern civilization sets aside a caste of persons. Creating the normal over against the disabled has been but "one aspect of a far-ranging change in European and perhaps global culture and ideology" consistent with modernization.[78] Disability is not, then, simply an instance of individual somatic difference. Or to put it another way, "disability is as much a symptom of historical and cultural contingencies as it is a physical and psychological reality."[79] The creation of a historical epoch, disability is not, then, an innocent or innocuous casting. For one thing, stigmatizing difference creates a diversion from and, therefore, protects official realities. Second, modernity's disabilities optic overlaps with colonial and neocolonial issues and transnational concerns to the extent that, as theorist Linda Tuhiwai Smith explains in *Decolonizing Methodologies*, "Imperialism provided the means through which concepts of what counts as human could be applied systematically as forms of classification," then "structured into language, the economy, social relations and the cultural life of colonial societies."[80] By looking into the mirror of disability as one of the psychic reservations of the "specular spectacular," the head-spinning marketplace of globalization, what might we learn about ourselves as the anesthetized, if anxious-feeling, selves of the first-world class? What do we hide from or reject about ourselves in that classification of physiological variations known as disablement? What fears do we anxiously cast upon the disabled? As I will address more fully in chapter one, fears and anxieties, as much as materialistically motivated desires, keep us in the centripetal power of the normal, under the sway of the ideal self.

Dismissively sidelined as but a peripheral issue of a small minority, the extreme measures of foreclosure taken against those become disabled—both rational means and irrational acts—suggests this mortal confession may be a more potent challenge to the hyperagency of biotechnoscientific reason than it might first appear. Seemingly but a fleabite of a concern given the big issues facing the world (terrorism, religious intolerance, global climate change, and so forth), the presence of disabled persons can nonetheless occasion extreme intolerance. As I write, I cannot help but have in mind a forty-seven-year-old man from East Vancouver, known to the community for his pronounced stutter, stiff-legged gait, and tendency for cultural irreverence, murdered in the street the day after Easter 2004—not unlike the beating and dragging death of James Byrd in Texas in 1998, disabled as well as black.[81] Such paranoia, such panic attacks, cannot be understood without regard to cultural aspirations to civilization, to high culture. Modern idealism, like earlier Platonism, takes perverse pleasure in "hunting down phantasms."[82] Postcolonial literature and disability studies' figural invitation to become disabled challenges an economy based in territorial enclosure, the first act of territorial enclosure being taking possession of and, therefore, managerial control over the body. The modern belief in transcendental subjectivity and agency has proved "functional, especially in helping us dominate and control our environment," if not also exhilarating in its wielding of power.[83]

Working through such a psychoanalysis as Barton proposed in regard to the Romans may allow us to inhabit our life desire differently, especially insomuch as economic globalization achieves its hegemonic status in and through—as Foucault earlier suggested—a "politics of health."[84] Since early modernity, what counts as official reality has stigmatized and marginalized its resistance—that is, other ways of minding life—through and in the name of medicine and science.[85] Given the proximity of the medical discourse to matters of religion, religious discourse can and has easily slipped into an unwitting collusion with a medicalized view of reality. This moral hegemony, as Harlan Hahn points out, has had a continuing effect on scientific research and on human behavior.[86] While neoclassical and orthodox theologies might want to claim a sharp deviation between their understandings of salvation and that of liberal theologies' intellectual kinship with science and medicine, I—as I hope will become clear—do not see that such views of transcendence are any more innocent of technological imitation than the technological progress supported by a liberal mentality.

Making the World Go On

> A monster is a species for which we do not yet have a name. . . . All history has shown that each time an event has been produced, for example in philosophy or in poetry, it took the form of the unacceptable, or even of the intolerable, of the incomprehensible, that is, of a certain monstrosity.
>
> —Jacques Derrida, *Points*

Postmodernity dawns with a huge question on our agenda: Might there be a "New Way to Be Human"? Or more forthrightly, as theologian Ivone Gebara puts it, "We feel the urgent need to refashion ourselves as a human species."[87] It is in that vein that Luce Irigaray and Gilles Deleuze have conceived of philosophy as "an integrative practice meant to bring about a transformation in corporeal morphology" as "continual confrontation with the limits of conventional perceptions and conceptions of life and the invention of new modes of being through the pursuit of the immanent unfolding of desires."[88] Philosophy, including in the form of cultural reflection, is done not so as to pass along consumer information regarding the current product line (modern, rational human), but so as to reconceive ethical self-other relations, to renovate and renew our selves, and, as even the biblical apostle Paul would add, so as thereby to renew the earth. "Insofar as we are able to engage in a practice of thinking, speaking, and writing that overcomes the [modern] mind/body split," Irigaray and Deleuze have contended, "we will be able to break out of forms of life that have already been lived and thought and to invent new forms of life more suitable to our present circumstances."[89]

A turn to popular culture suggests the already crowded theater of the popular imagination in this regard. Within television, movies, and cartoons, crips, gimps, aliens, monsters, X-Men, and rather surprising antiheroes (for example, the quirky depressive Andrew Largeman in the movie *Garden State* and the dwarf Fynn in

The Station Agent) join the inappropriate/d others of postcolonial literature and poststructuralist scientific reflection. But if the contemporary Christian rock band Switchfoot invites us coincidentally with this cast of the Crip Nation to remember an ancient Christological motif, that Pauline and then Irenaen notion of the New Way to Be Human, truly this is not the only power that today hails a new humanity. Biotechnology and the Human Genome Project, if also the specular and spectacular aspects of star culture, invite great affection for the perduring, if ramped-up, figures of modernism. Haraway impales the wisdom of the Human Genome Project and what it will count as human on her mimicry of its inherent metaphysics, that is, "with all its stunning power to recuperate, out of the endless variations of code fragments, the singular, the sacred image of the same, the one true man, the standard—copyrighted, catalogued, and banked."[90] But mock it as we may, modernity's figure of normalcy, its desirable self, has obviously not relented: Television series like *The Swan, Extreme Makeover*, and their normalcy lite versions, for example, *What Not to Wear*, still play in the celebrity sandbox of modern, if hypercapitalized and hyperrealized, views of the self. Within the cultural contestation over interpretation and articulation of what we will construe entering postmodernity as new humanity, "the discourse of 'monstrosity' . . . subversively . . . signals the fragility of [normative] boundaries."[91]

I place my work within this contestatory cultural discourse in the hope of "making the world go on."[92] The work of theological ethicist Kathleen Sands happened to intersect my own thinking just after the fall, the time when I felt my own life deconstructed by personal health trauma and life-onset disability. Sands's *Escape From Paradise: Evil and Tragedy in Feminist Theology* aspires to think—not surprisingly, given the title—after the fall. Her work challenges liberal, rationalist idealism as also its obverse, ethical, and religious dualism—both of which presume to locate religious values in and to orient sacred practice from a paradisiacal garden—from "there," that "nowhere." Sands admits that which an eschatologically driven ontotheology wallpapered over—namely, "irrecoverable loss and irresolvable contradiction, . . . the absence that is tragedy."[93] Whereas Plato felt compelled "to dispel the illusion of tragic conflict, lifting people beyond the world of corruption and change to contemplate the incorruptible, intelligible Good" postmoderns have been sobered by the inhumanity effected when making ourselves morally invulnerable by appeal to the Absolute Referent and a presumed, fixed meaning: "Living, complex, and delicate, humankind cannot partake of the more tenacious stability of the inorganic or the Ideal."[94] Seemingly of a like mind with Sands on this point, biblical scholar Mark Thompson observes that "the more we seek to return to Eden to make some judgments about the original cause of our malaise, the more we miss the point."[95] Rather than escaping back into Eden or forward into eschatology, "suffering forces us to be 'here,' where we are accountable to many forces," postcolonial feminist literary critic Laura Donaldson likewise insists.[96] If by escaping Eden we postmoderns may take a more humbled view of knowledge and of ourselves, yet life, consequently, given the complexity of forces, lacks the sheer resolve that we had found in origins and foundations. As Sands puts it, "in a world of suffering and radical conflict," given a plurality of truth and of values and vitalities, "making the world go on is not an innocent faith, but a *practice* of compassion" [*sic*].[97]

What can the Crip and our "discard[ing of] all those striving ambulist metaphors of power and success"[98] suggest about loving life, about what Irigaray calls "felicity in history"?[99] Keeping faith with the world may be among our greatest intellectual and psychic challenges as modern idealism meets up with the backwash of ecological and colonial devastation. Crips, to be sure, challenge the labor agenda, as well as modernity's wholesome subject and its cult of public appearances. But one of the more overt differences between modernity and postmodernity will be our acquaintance with suffering. Modernity held suffering as meaningless, and so modernity dreamed of eradicating it. Postmodernity will need a spiritual pedagogy for pain—will need to be able to tolerate anxiety[100] and "to think with pain."[101] If "to affirm life only in the hope of eradicating suffering is not to affirm this life," as Nietzsche put it, cripping our figural maps may be among the ways to imagine that love of life which can cope with suffering, which will find beauty—beyond idealism—in the midst of life.[102]

Deleuze, as well as the mid-twentieth-century Jewish philosopher Franz Rosenzweig, lived with disabilities. Each insisted on speaking an exquisitely poignant love for the world from a location that most of modernity has deemed insufferable, unlivable. But each likewise insisted that moderns were prone to a serious error named metaphysics (and, intriguingly, the attachment to metaphysics appears to be related to the refusal to feel pain). Idealist metaphysics—the insistence upon taking cropped photos of the world—is something of a psychological error, not reserved for theologians or philosophers, Rosenzweig observed. Metaphysical idealism is, according to Rosenzweig, "a kind of withdrawal from, a kind of fantasmatic defense against, our being in the midst or flow of life." During modernity "these defenses, this peculiar autoimmunity, ha[s . . .] assumed the status of the norm," writes Eric Santner, a theological commentator on Rosenzweig.[103] Consequently, our souls have been persistently disaffected with what is; to be satisfied, truly gratified, has become an impossibility.[104]

Being psychically attached to such an idealized fantasy is, for those of us called to love the world as God has loved it and in this sense to believe in it, a religious problem. The poignant beauty of our world cannot be severed from suffering and pain, even from the structural possibility for innocent suffering and gross injustices. Christianity as a philosophical deep materialism believes in *this* world, not in some other heaven beyond. If we are to be creative with the world, Deleuze insists, we need to wade into the painfully poignant midst of it all, into the muck or chaotic edge of world becoming. Where world wonder cannot be deftly cut away from rupture, there we find our only opportunity for becoming creatively different—as persons, as a world. There in the churning whirl, the creative vortex of always beginning again, we find ourselves gathered up into the capacious presence of the Spirit of life.

Using the critical lens of disability studies with and on behalf of developing postcolonializing conscientization, I work toward a constructive pneumatological theology resistant to the mediated Platonism circulating among and enveloping, inviting an emergent global citizenry. After this introductory chapter, I propose, in Part I (chapters 1 through 5) to work with disability studies, especially in its resonances with postcolonial conditions, to deconstruct the ideology of normalcy or whole(some)ness that uses the construction of the pathetic body to stimulate its culturally productive "fear of falling" (Ehrenreich) into empire's economic and physiognomic bottomlands. Because the symbolic economy of empire advances as a hegemony of public appearance, working poststructuralist theory with and through disability studies may help us formulate philosophical intuitions for living so as to disrupt colonizing vectors of globalizing capitalism. Gathering up such intuitions becomes the work of Part II, chapters 6 through 10.

A Falling Out with the Theological In-Laws

One might consider this book a meditation on that theological analytic we call "the fall." I will introduce two distinct readings of the fall, given how Spirit and its physics has been conceptually conceived in relation to it. I do not intend mere metaphorical play; I take the psychosocial critiques named by the fall seriously, even if I do not do so within the terms of classic ontotheology. We do fall into social significatory systems, such as our current construction of normalcy, the social physics of which are less than flourishing. That which culture compositely circumvents in invalid/ating and avoiding the disabled inflates its view of supernatural transcendence. Pain, flux, necessity, and interdependence, the ambiguities of the lack of fulfillment and the loss of control, all of which modernity has written out: None of these can be considered outcropping conditions of such geopolitical preoccupations as occasion the analytic of the fall. That's already to transcend—by hallucination—the ground conditions.

The fall, which I read within classical theology to be a traumatic refusal and objectification of pain, holds out and hopes for idealism. Making the fall a metaphysical foundation and thereby circulating a philosophy of nature as broken leads to serious sociopsychic and ecological problems (any of which persons with disabilities may feel pressing upon our bodies): First of all, materialist idealism informs scientific agendas, such as those of biotech. It is a temptation toward what feminist historians of science (Donna Haraway, among others) call "a second birth away from earth" or "reproduction without the mother."[105] Second, religious supernaturalism—like its rationalist twin, hyperreal transcendentalism—tempts us to ignore our role in circulating social constructs and our responsibility for the social depressions into which we fall. Reactive responses to pain—such as accomplishing Spirit by holding our breath and becoming dissociative—can splinter our attachment and our attention to the world. While Augustine may have been less at peace with empire than we seem to be powerless in its throes, I take seriously theologian Thandeka's analytic observation as concern for those of us living within the semiosphere of contemporary globalization: "The shame theology Augustine bequeathed to the Christian West is a doctrine that had made peace with a Roman world of pervasive human suffering framed by a profound sense of personal alienation," which effects a historical realism "without an edge of social criticism."[106] We know empire's divisive splits, but seem feelingly anesthetized, except for our anxious and private insecurities.

Finally, objectifying suffering and iconically setting it aside as the indigestible of disabled and/or disposable bodies, we lose track of the responsibility for social critique (as do narrative theologies) at precisely the point when, as Zygmunt Bauman notes, "the private . . . colonizes . . . public space, squeezing out and chasing away everything which cannot be fully, without residue, expressed in the vernacular of private concerns, worries and pursuits."[107] And when it comes to objectifying suffering, systematic theology has, theologian Marcella Althaus-Reid claims, made something of an industry of it: While "Christian dogmatics is built upon bodily struggles" theology has tended to expropriate and then dissociate suffering "from the system which . . . locates it."[108] I will be pointing to this phenomenon in terms of foreclosing the suffering of the colonized by instantiating an ontology of the fall, as well as theology's tendency to make meaning (not my own!) from the experience of disablement. Significantly, however, when suffering is objectified in others (the poor, the disabled, the helpless) as when it is "medicalized," members of the first-world class also are left without means of reworking life politics with and from our own pains. Pain may be intimately linked to prophetic critique.

Spirit, I suggest, might have been conceived not so much on the up-and-up of idealist metaphysics as in the midst of a colonial power (Babylon, then Rome) whose presence could only be described as incapacitating. If Spirit nonetheless inspired those who had fallen into the social depression of a colonizing power to make the world go on, what might we rub open on this conceptual plane to creatively cope with the awareness that we must learn how to "escape [the dominant order] without leaving it"?[109] If along with or beside a subjugated history of a tehomophilic Spirit, of Spirit fondly affiliated with the depths of cosmic becoming (Keller), some theological proposals considered Spirit to be a vibrating capaciousness, an ever newly emergent force for making the world go on even when preoccupied by empire, what could that mean for today's first-world class citizens? If we can surmise how the resonances of Spirit opened out the constricting space of colonization, would that translate in any way across geotemporal zones and philosophies? What might that suggest to those of us within the multiple metropolitan centers of the Pax Americana? Hardly can we claim ourselves to be the colonized. Then again, we have been found to be suffering "new maladies of the soul" (Kristeva), found to be anesthetized (Bauman, Holler) and even incapacitated by normativity.

In the end, then, this book desires nothing so much as analytically to open toward a constructive Spirit theology. While I work the deconstruction of a certain mode of Spirit, this too remains in the interest of promoting Spirit as a theological concept supporting multiple, diverse forms and habituations of corporeal flourishing. If Spirit "summons forth 'a new earth and a people that does not yet exist'"; and if Spirit is here relative to the Crip Nation, then what on earth might be creatively forthcoming?[110] How would we conceive to practice Spirit if articulated by persons who do not find physical disablement a cause for cursing God or hating nature and who do not spend their time waiting for cure?

C H A P T E R

THE FEAR OF FALLING

"What happened to you? What did you do to yourself?" I wonder why answering such questions is the admission price for a modicum of social inclusion. What explains this inquisitional prelude, given that I do not get to ask the same question in turn? Do I, though apparently hanging open, seem to have something to hide? Why should I confess myself? To

Imagining the degeneration into which human- ity could fall was a necessary part of imagin- ing the exaltation to which it could aspire. The degenerate classes, defined as departures from the normal human type, were as necessary to the self-definition of the middle class as the idea of degeneration was to the idea of progress . . . . Normality thus emerged as a product of deviance . . . . The poetics of degeneration was a poetics of social crisis.

—**Anne McClintock,**
Imperial Leather

what should I confess? And once you know, what difference will it make? So one day I tripped, I fell, I lost a leg. In the trauma to my leg, group A beta-hemolytic Streptococcus—the flesh-eating disease—found an opportunity. Like a grain wagon toppled in the middle of a wheat field in the path of a tornado, it was nothing personal.

What happened to me? How did I also fall out of grace? My world fell apart not with the medical scenario of my health crisis and amputation, but when I reentered social life. Already self-conscious of my hill-clan origins, first amid the cosmopolitan ethos of the New York City region and now in Vancouver, my psyche still occasionally trotting out homely memories of "my first bought'n clothes," my stigmatic disability forces me through the wringer, dropping me out of high culture. The size four to which I had once mercilessly reduced myself in suburbia will never return, mobility now requiring of me sleeve-splitting and unfeminine biceps, while my single thigh thickens like a tree trunk, my abdomen loses its muscle tone.

Again the question comes at me: "What happened to you?" Answer: I fell. I fell from the stratosphere of gracious virtuosity. I fell into social class, gender-sex oblivion. No, rather, let me put it this way: I was tripped up by a social depression in the surface of the human interface and dropped down a rabbit hole of refusal. It's a very odd place to be, where transcendence transpires at such low voltage. I am not expected to be wise, interesting, funny, beautiful. The love of life, the call to be a lover and defender of that territory of ambivalence we call human nature: it is much harder after ten years of this to want to make the world go on.

I am on public display: always seen, always overlooked. The toxicity of the social staring wearies and wears down the psyche, as other writers of the disability experience have also noted. Activist and poet Eli Clare, for example, simply observes, "I store the gawking in my bone."[1] I likewise resonate to the poetry of First Nations poet Chrystos, who explains the psychosomatic effects of being held in the gaze: "We, People of Color, are stared at so much that we have high blood pressure, ulcers and alcoholism."[2] While once upon a time before the fall my extroversion seemed to be a major link in circuits of sociality, I feel today as if I am inside a glass chamber made of fears not my own, that an undertow has taken me down into a falling dream in which I can never hit bottom, that I can do nothing to waylay the palpable fears that hit me like a storm surge as I walk into a room. Not infrequently I swallow the social abjection and refuse myself.

A farm kid born and raised, I hear childhood poverty's haunting refrain yet again: "She's just ugly and stupid, just ugly and stupid." Is it just me, psychologically toppling from one abject position into another? Or do I telepathically overhear the crowd? If revoked along with other civil rights legislation, do the ugly laws nevertheless—like racism—remain psychically but barely underground?[3] I read the cosmopolitan magazine thrown on my doorstep, describing the downtown club scene. One interviewee observes, "It's like Hitler's master race out there. They've got the beauty-o-meters going, and if you can't measure up you don't get in."[4] Amen! Though to be sure, I haven't tried getting into the club scene. It's just that, well, I could swear those beauty-o-meters were in operation even at the local PTA meetings. Even when I am just walking down the street. When people at a social occasion make their decisions about whom they might find interesting.

Now I likely may be perceived as antisocial, given that I must often turn eyes downward to scope out the lay of the land I am about to traverse. And to be sure, I have learned not to look at passers-by. I simply do not want to see the shudder of dread that passes upon our encounter, to swim through the social abjection yet again. I increasingly find it tempting to avoid social events where the idea is to circulate: Spending time sitting with me seems to threaten to swallow up others in (my?) desperate straits.

But if you should ever want to find me, here's where to look—in the office next to the bathroom, in the parking space next to the dumpster. Not atypically, I enter a building through the back door, access other levels of a building by proceeding to the farthest, darkest, loneliest back corner. I ascend and descend with the maintenance or supply elevators, with garbage and food. No more Cinderella grand staircase entrances.

So the question comes at me: "What happened to you?" Answer: I fell into a zone of vulnerability, the dimensions of which I'm still trying to plot. I can be harassed, stared at, and overlooked simultaneously. When I walk out on the street, it seems so easy, given that I carry nearly everything in a bag born 'round my neck (how else?), to misconstrue me as a bag lady. Not that street people aren't sometimes the most conversant, friendly, even the most intimately knowledgeable interlocutors of my daily life: "Honey, you don't look so good today; you okay? You should be in your chair. You're looking too tired to be up on those crutches." I could be displaced from a nation in which I am but a landed immigrant, if my economic contributions do not exceed the drain I may be perceived to be on national health resources.

And then I, of course, must qualify what I just described to you, because I can pass in certain venues. And I do have access to the middling class by education and income. And there are, of course, theatrical roles for persons with disabilities in the marketplace of globalization—among them the spirited athletic crip who overcomes, the medical miracle, the cyborg with a sixth, mutant sense, the daily inspiration. And sometimes, in a world in which you "bleed just to know you are alive" (The Goo Goo Dolls), I may even be envied my heroic entanglement, my apparent wrestling with life. Such an enthusiasm modernity has taken away from most personal lives.

Yet walking the gauntlet of cultural humiliation as an amputee on crutches without cosmetic, prosthetic veil: well, there's a cultural cost to refusing to seem altogether. It's paid every time I answer the question, "What happened to you?"

In an interesting parallel to my experience, postcolonial theorist Ato Quayson makes the following observation:

> But the interest in surveilling otherness is dispersed everywhere, sometimes making itself manifest in the question, "Where do you really come from?" constantly asked of newly arrived immigrants, to second – and third-generation children of immigrants, and, most irritatingly, to those of mixed descent in the various postcolonial diasporas of the West. For, the question "Where

are you really from?" is never an innocent one: it is a question of origin that, posed to particular subjects, and in particular contexts, also involves a question of return.[5]

Quayson, too, has found a surveillance system still at work within the postmodern, multiethnic carnival. This surveillance system, Quayson insinuates, continues to protect modernity's homeland, or origin. While verbally directed by the questions "What happened to you?" and "Where do you come from?" this surveillance system confronts the minoritized as something like a tidal surge of dread and fear. This dread and fear sets up a fire ring, a containment wall within sociality. Like Quayson, I find myself outside some kind of in/security zone—as if set outside a compound with an invisible, but palpable fence. But what fiery angels keep me on the outside of what Eden?

Being Seen: Globalization's Specular Spectacular and the Fear of Falling

The postmodern age dawns as a bombardment of images and spectacle: Take the stars of music, sports, fashion, and business, or even just the tasteful first-world citizen at home in his or her L.L.Bean, Tommy Hilfiger, or Polo Ralph Lauren casuals. Mirror them by satellite, through movie, Internet, and advertising across the globe. Branding the star styles in transnational markets exponentially multiplies this cult of public appearance and its spellbinding powers of idealization.[6]

Although for ancient Platonism, the ideal was not considered humanly achievable, but was ascribed to the gods alone, the ideal has now become the expected standard of and for public performance.[7] Cut away from the cloth of nature by scientific objectification, the modern self was subjected to the powers of statistical and philosophical idealism. For empire, this ideal self—brought to health by biotechnology, cosmetically augmented so as to achieve a more natural look, and fashionably coutoured in the global marketplace—has become normative. With MTV as its "most compelling . . . catalog," this idealized (and Western) self-image has gone global.[8] "For the first time in history," observes urban studies scholar Harlan Hahn, "women and men are inundated with physical images of others who can only be found outside the confines of their immediate vicinity."[9] Any citizen of the globe cannot but imbibe the sublimity of Western technologically enabled, aesthetically toned, and enculturated idealism.

Quayson himself traced "the pressure of images of luxury under late capitalist image culture . . . back into the period of colonialism."[10] That postcolonials now find themselves "at the mercy of an image culture" has to do, Quayson suggests, with the way in which aspects like blue eyes (as traced by Toni Morrison in *The Bluest Eye)* or a woman's blush "shift epistemologically from a human domain through a quasi-theological one and into an area of aesthetic commodification." Even within the specular spectacular that is globalization, then, there remains "a certain discursivity . . . that places the desired objects within cycles that define a nebulous but regulative capitalist or Western or white area of power." While the postmodern, Quayson reminds us, would have us celebratively "settle on the economy of the image" and its generative multiplicity of subject locations, post-colonial theory insists that "the next step has to be [consideration of] how such images ought to be subverted or how . . . their effects are to be challenged with a view to setting up a better order of effects."[11] Simply put, cultivating self-image, as this work now arrives in our lives, serves as a substitute for communal inter-dependence, the holds of kin and the folds of trust. That we live "at the mercy of image," in the transcendental zone of the first-world class, is an aspect of "proto-colonialism," of imperialism as effected among the metropole of modernity.[12]

The Cult/ure of Public Appearance "Kant's *Critique*, which set off at extreme poles things-in-themselves from the Transcendental Ego," Bruno Latour explains, "is what made us believe ourselves to be 'modern.'"[13] In one sense, the mod-ern transcendental ego generated by material objectification "stands outside of the flesh"—as does its offspring, the consumer self.[14] But where philosophical modernity aspired to such transcendent heights, image became the basis of social negotiation: The transcendental self, belying its claim to birth from within the extraterrestrial ethers, assumed "the iconography of social status."[15] Within the "changing demographics of cities in the West, . . . modernism relentlessly defined the individual against an engulfing urban background," even as "it also succeeded in producing an important opposition between interiority and exteriority."[16]

Where anxiety about urban space ensued, modernism developed alongside its definitive dialectic of self/other the cultivation of self-image, that free-float-ing identity, and, more specifically, the image of luxury, whose material excess was appropriated from the colonies.[17] The capitalist enhancement of self-image subtly reenforced the felt superiority of imperialism's mission-oriented relations. As developing technologies and advertising reinforced visual culture, modern transcendental subjectivity aspired toward transparency—that is, a stellar per-formance of normalcy. "Whereas in previous centuries the powerful were dif-ferentiated from the lowly by markers of privilege (wigs, insignia, crowns, etc.)," today power assumes, Thomson explains, the "undistinguished" or "indistinguishable, . . . while otherness is elaborately visible."[18] But morphology could go unremarked only in relation to "a moral order of the body" established by ruling elites—an idealism, enhanced by colonial capital, become normative.[19]

Situating modernity's transcendentalization of the self in the realm of Kant's philosophical ideas has frequently ignored the play of ground conditions upon ideation itself. For even as transcendentalizing the ego occasioned the objectifying and then commodifing of the body, Western modernity's push toward urbanization came to relate persons through image. "Economic forces are an invisible army of occupation, forcibly evicting whole communities from settled ways of life, from their sole means of survival" into a cash-only nexus, Jeremy Seabrook explains in relation to globalization, that contemporary transmutation of imperial power. Dislocation by capitalist forces, Seabrook adds, "extirpate[d] all previous ways of answering need," including the need for cultural identity, belonging, and purpose. Such needs, he suggests, were replaced during earlier stages of modernity by shopping for the acceptable image.[20] Urbanization, adds Hahn, writing between his fields of urban and disability studies, increased the striving or pressure to mold appearances in a manner that would enable one to fit into a community of strangers. "Through the persuasiveness of the media, the aspirations of elites and masses have been joined in narcissistic striving for a shared vision of a flawless physical appearance."[21] The unmarked or non-stigmatic body, equally generating fall-out in terms of class as also disability, proved the price of social acceptance and circulation in the culture of public appearance.[22] Since for modernity "class was considered disability,"[23] the Cult/ure of Public Appearance likely patrols compulsory normalcy with shame in the same way that Thandeka has suggested we create whiteness.[24]

Even as consumerism replaces "feeling together with feeling the same," one hears in the modern aspiration toward cultural image the human striving for social belonging.[25] "All these dislocations [of modernization] create anonymity, forcing people to rely upon bodily appearance rather than kinship or local memberships as indices of identity and social position," concludes Thomson. "In addition," she continues, "secularization deemphasized the condition of one's soul, while an intensifying market system spawned the anxious display of status, and technologies . . . located identity in one's exterior image." Consequently, she concludes, "the way the body looked and functioned became one's primary social resource as local contexts receded, support networks unraveled, and mobility dominated social life."[26] While appearing a multiethnic carnival, globalization's specular spectacular of the marvelous and of the image also then has its sad history, its colonial interior, an exacting platonic template patrolled by the heights of exhilaration in belonging and the depths of public humiliation and self-censor when one fails to comply.[27]

At least for Christian theologies, the call to become declassified, thereby disabling our transcendentalized cosmesis, may be imperative. To be sure, poverty is not an identity to be assumed where class division is a "by-product of unequal access to resources."[28] Rather, I am suggesting deconstructing the conflation of theology with authoritarian decency, moral order (also known as "uprightness," a very difficult virtue for those among us who are "Waist-High in the World," quips disabilities writer Nancy Mairs), and economic assumptions about gracious living, all of which hide a fear of falling.[29] Such a cosmesis of colonially enhanced decency refuses transcendence to lived-in flesh and worn bodies. But taking our leave of the transparent class requires us to ferret out the anxieties through which culture creates over against itself the class/ified body. Relevant to the psychological process involved in creating its colonial others by projection, postcolonial theorist Homi Bhabha has observed that "the colonial stereotype is a complex, ambivalent, contradictory mode of presentation, as anxious as it is assertive. . . . 'The fetish or stereotype gives access to an "identity" which is predicated as much on mastery and pleasure as it is on anxiety and defence.'"[30] But could that anxious pleasure, that defensive mastery, also straitjacket us into acting with empire? (Don't such energies surveil me?)

The Fear of Falling Given such pressures, the pleasurable exhibition of image, of bodily appearance, can, not surprisingly, become desperate in its alienated transcendence: "As the world takes on a more and more menacing appearance, life becomes a never-ending search for health and well-being." The state of health within the skin line becomes an all-absorbing concern.[31] The marvelous tugs on desire and challenges us to aspire, but also threatens us with the fear of falling—falling out of economic viability, out of the sociality of likeness and appearance, into the physiognomic bottomlands. "Disability has functioned as a marker of where the bottom is in American society," theorist Paul Longmore explains, helping us understand the shudder of dread which persons with disability encounter.[32]

Given "the total subordination of the real under the irreality of the images generated by visual culture under capitalism," the fear of being found physically unfit—a fear projected upon persons with disabilities—haunts sociality.[33]

"Constructed as the embodiment of corporeal insufficiency and deviance, the physically disabled body becomes a repository for social anxieties."[34] Addressing the ways in which "the fear of collapse" attends the Western image of disease, Sander Gilman continues:

> But the fear we have of our own collapse does not remain internalized. Rather, we project this fear onto the world in order to localize it, and, indeed, to domesticate it. For once we locate it, the fear of our own dissolution is removed. Then it is not we who totter on the brink of collapse, but rather the Other. And it is an-Other who has already shown his or her vulnerability by having collapsed."[35]

So, like a buoy or flare, the word *disabled* marks the drop-offs, the tidal channels, in the social order—the insecurities and anxieties that influence, among other things, global politics.

While empire may have learned to capitalize upon the multicultural carnival of racial and ethnic diversity, disability—insomuch as it often is or becomes coincident with class—appears to be something of a perimeter for empire. Disability appears along the baseline where empire still dialectically works out its worst fears. Disabilities are differences situated too uncomfortably proximate to the self. What, after all, is to prevent any of us from one day tripping up and sinking that low? Whereas ethnic and racial differences were experienced as external to the self, degeneracy has to do with otherness felt to be intimate to a shared semiosphere, threatening—via the contagion of bad karma—to pull one likewise into the bottomlands. What shall we make of the fact that the presence of disabled bodies inevitably raises the question of the quality of life? Why lay that question against this physiological incarnation of difference? Within what politics of representation does that question make sense? Whose paradise do we despoil?

Of Metaphysical Fantasies and Science Fictions

Disabilities, even as they now mark the bottomland into which postmoderns fear falling, have often theologically been considered evidence of the brokenness of nature pursuant to the fall, the presumed cosmic devolution. Paradigmatically, disabled bodies have been borrowed in the religious imaginary conversely to prove a notion of absolute transcendence, a concept of divine efficacy connected with metaphysical idealism. So Augustine, for example, writes that "this heaven and this earth . . . shall pass through a universal change. . . . Then (as I said) shall the world's corruptible qualities be burnt away, and all those that held correspondence with our corruption shall be made for immortality."[36] Creating the metaphysical fantastics of transcendence as a power outside of this world deposited the pathetic residue of the corruptible. Disabled persons have often been, as Augustine makes clear, construed as the epitome of corruptibility—even as but a lump of matter without spirit. But where we still find disability serving as the physiognomic bottomlands, we might also then suspect reliance upon a metaphysical fantastics of nature itself.

Despite theological modernity claiming to have outgrown such purportedly archaic notions as sin, evil, and the fall, in the psychosocial cosmology undergirding globalization, my body evidently remains unavoidably marked as fallen. That ancient analytic has eventuated today into persons being treated as but a medical condition, similar to the case of colonial subjects being regarded as mere physicality, as handicapped—each in their own ways appearing to the Self (that member of the Cult of Public Appearance) as a densely heavy or material and, therefore, unassimilable body.[37] Ethically foreclosed, decisions continue to be made about us, but not with us.

Given how easily persons recognize me as broken, I suspect that the cosmic fall has been telescoped into that analytic—namely, wholeness/brokenness—wielded by the clinical gaze and used to detect and to categorize pathology in the age of image, within the purview of globally mediated idealism. the fall, interjected into the privacy of the self, aggressively continues to aggravate modernization or progress as we take responsibility for and excruciating pleasure in detecting defects in our self-image.

Deconstructing Brokenness Basic to much Christian theology, where it has been contemporary shorthand for dogmatic teachings about the fall, has been the modern binary of wholeness/brokenness. If one finds this analytic pervasively displayed in popular culture's many versions of Extreme Makeover™, it continues to inform Christian spiritualities and even ethically progressive Christian communities. William Stringfellow, for example, defines spirituality as supporting the development of our full humanity; but he then defines being fully human not in terms of being humane or compassionate, but as being whole, even perfect.[38] The United Church of Canada's recent teaching document on ecumenism, "Mending the World," makes the assumption that the world is broken, an assumption we trace back to the Augustinian tradition, but which (as I am arguing) received a particular pathological tilt during Western modernity: "We are residents of a place created and owned by God, who came in Jesus and who works still, through the Spirit to bend the broken creation back into the unity and wholeness for which it was made." In its recent 2005 statement of faith, "Faith Talk II," the United Church seems, in the face of ecological challenges, to have stepped up the use of this analytic, repeatedly resorting to rhetorical notions of a broken world, while evoking wholeness as eschatological hope.[39]

Poststructuralist theorists challenge us to cull out binaries, such as nature/culture, body/mind, self/other, because they are reductive, if also violently hierarchizing means of managing difference and suppressing ambiguity. Brokenness/wholeness remains an active binary, inherent in our modern technological incarnations, our globalizing of immaterial technologies, our way of taking place within and among the transcendental idealism of the first-world class. What makes deconstruction of this binary imperative is the way in which such idealization (and the pleasure of classifying its dysfunctions) metabolizes that vision of life now going global, the way in which the practice of transcendence has been, among the first-world class, subsumed in idealization.

"The encounter [between a person with a disability and a normate] is always overdetermined by stereotypes of wholeness," Quayson acknowledges. But, he rather surprisingly concludes, moving into a Lacanian psychoanalytic, "Paradoxically, the notions and stereotypes of wholeness are grounded on the repressed *imagos* of the fragmented body'" [*sic*].[40] Modernity's transcendental ego, and thus its cult of public appearance, might be said to be fixated at the developmental mirror stage—the initiatory stage of subjectivity when the self first recognizes itself in the mirror. But the mirror self, a specular image, appears whole, with intact boundaries, whereas the body feels pulled and tugged by frustrations and tensions. "The baby [the onset of the mirror stage purportedly transpires between six and eighteen months of age, this but initiating a life-long aspect of subjective formation] develops an attachment to this specular image," writes Quayson, explicating Lacan. "Reflecting a unified object back to it, [the mirror] is actually deluding the baby with a sense of wholeness."[41] When cathected to the placid serenity and pleasurable display of the mirror or specular image ("a counterfeit paradise," adds Robert Murphy),[42] the subject—confined to the mind and patrolling the perimeters of the specular image—avoids or evades awareness of the pulsions of the body, avoids awareness of systemic interdependence and sentient enfoldment, avoids insight into its own heterogeneous and ambivalent desires. All such psychic avoidances will then be overwhelmingly brought to mind in the encounter with the apparently fragmented or partial body, that body which refuses specular wholesomeness, that egresses firm boundaries, that of the disabled.

Modernity has been stuck in the mirror stage, concluded postcolonial theorist Homi Bhabha, after studying Lacan: "The *surveillance* of colonial power . . . function[s] in relation to the regime of the scopic drive" [*sic*].[43] "According to psychoanalytic interpretation," feminist philosopher Rosi Bradotti explains, "the scopic drive is linked to both knowledge and control or domination," adding that "modern science is the triumph of the scopic drive."[44] Lacan simply termed modernity "the paranoid 'ego's era.'"[45] In its psychological, indeed egoistic, immaturity, the era aspired to living as real this specular spectacular or idealized relationship: "A modern and profoundly Western economy[, the objectification and commodification of nature evolving out of this same psychic complex,] has made omnipotent fantasies into realities."[46]

If others have, in a philosophical vein, identified this fantasy with metaphysical idealism, whatever Christianity had meant by sin now d/evolves within this cultural frame to the practice of pathology, the culling out of defect, by employing the simple ego-invested outline of wholeness.[47] The image-based template represented in the term *wholeness* refuses ethical and affective negotiations within the heterogeneous flux of nature. Biology makes the interest of the ego appear innocent: "Modern scientific-medicalized paradigms of knowing and perfecting presume to stand at a safe remove from traditional disputes over what constitutes the good. . . . Such discourses tend[, nevertheless,] to ignore the moral and social biases of those who decipher information and the moral and social consequences of their determinations."[48] In this way, "biological images of disease and contagion [have] served . . . 'the institutionalization of fear.'" Indeed, disease images, historian Anne McClintock has noted, earlier "provided the Victorian elite with the justification it needed to discipline and contain the 'dangerous classes.'"[49] In sum, as Foucauldian scholar and theologian J. Joyce Schuld explains, "No longer . . . action and social consequence, but nature and defect analyzed through rational quantitative study govern the relations of power to those falling outside expected norms, values and behaviors."[50] Normalcy consolidates "the power of the bourgeoisie," the empire of the ego.[51]

Intriguingly, even Luther had differently parsed the dissuasive dread persons report in encounters with disablement, suggesting that this anxiety should be considered to have been roused by Satan to occasion the sin of avoidance.[52] But as the horizon of salvific concern shifts toward salvation as well-being in late modernity, Christianity's analytic awareness that we at birth inherit structured ways of being in the world that occasion our involvement in injustice (hence, theological notions of brokenness, or original sin) easily gets conflated with the emergent biological categories of pathology and humanistic aspiration (namely, brokenness/wholeness). Michel Foucault traced the development of the clinical gaze, which patrols the borders of self-image, to the modern period, where it evolves with and beside the churchly inspired technologies of the confessing self within which "desires [had] become sliced up into manageable pieces and analyzed in isolation."[53] "The modern[, "scientized"] version of confession consists," explains Schuld, "in using a variety of techniques[, "a whole battery of tests, observations, categorizations, recordings, and chart notes,"] that purport to provide an unclouded knowledge of ourselves and others through 'the rarefied and neutral viewpoint of science,'" that which ruptured or disfigured the idealized, if the colonially enhanced image was pathologized. "Once moral and religious discourses are transposed into a scientific key, a whole range of human frailties and fallibilities . . . are 'no longer accounted for simply by the notions of error or sin, excess or transgression, but [are] placed under the rule of the normal and the pathological.' . . . Today we strive to be autonomously well-adjusted, high-functioning, productive members of society. That is the vision of a redeemed life under this paradigm."[54] Reading the disabled body as broken conflates these two quite distinct analytic moods—that is, structured sin and pathology, making it nearly impossible for contemporary Christians to get our bearings on the critique of normalcy.[55]

Biology became, explain postcolonial anthropologists Jean and John Comaroff, "explanatory of relations already laid down in society, economy, international relations," thereby justifying "natural distinctions."[56] Quayson's analysis helps us assess the dread attending the encounter with the broken or the fragmentary, and Foucault's pleasurable sense of certitude and safety gained from clinical analysis and categorization of defects. But as Seabrook noted, the growth of asylums and the swelling population of the ill had not only to do with the development and refinement of the clinical gaze and the technologies of confession, which Foucault so adeptly analyzes, but with the effects of protocolonialism. Seabrook sets his reflections on the development of the modern middle class in purview of the way in which colonial surplus worked upon the psyche: While "the application of some of the surplus gained from overseas served to attach the British working class both to its betters and to acquiescence in the necessity of empire," the "creation of a working class" also "involved a breaking of the sensibility of an agricultural population, the reworking of the psyche of a people whose lives were articulated to the rhythms of the seasons." Modernization, in other words, inflicted great psychic violence, resulting in psychological conditions not unlike those in the colonies.[57] The scientific and medical moves to perfect the body then but propped up, without a nod of cognizance, the social conditions generating distress.

As with ancient Platonism, so here in the televisionary mediation of normative idealism: We transfer our affections to an image, rather than feelingly creating in and with a vital, energetic cosmos. Where the cultivation of life's flourishing gets singularly, narrowly attached to culling out somatic pathology, there results the cult of public appearance, an idealized body then presuming to occasion civic respectability, even responsibility. Globalizing capitalism has all humans bearing our suffering, whether alienation or dislocation, as personal and pathological defect—and in such a way silences prophetic critique of social structure. Whereas the fall analytically named the geopolitical storms of life as experienced by Jews during the Pax Romana,[58] this analytic of sociocultural devastation, which modern liberal theologians assumed to have outgrown, has been introjected and turned upon the individual body. Exposing defects to the light (of the speculum) generates the prurient power of ego-mastery, sustaining the specular spectacular.

If there are physical, psychic, and relational ramifications that ripple endlessly out from simply tripping myself up one day, I want rather to address—in terms of the fall—those "social depressions" that "hemlock" (Kingsolver) persons with disabilities. Social depressions, like potholes in the road, trip us up and threaten to disappear persons with disabilities. But unlike the surveilling of bodies aggravated by the transcendentalist metaphysics of the cosmic fall, social depressions of the sort into which I now fall develop because Christianity has long perpetuated a falling out with planetary life, because Christianity forecloses nature as itself lively and flourishing.

In constructing a "theology of becoming" (Keller) by one presumed somewhat unbecoming, someone unraveling toward death (or so it has appeared to some), I want to admit the existence of "life-denying taxonomies" (Wallace), among which I include globally mediated Platonism, without conflating these with the fall of which deviant bodies have often been assumed to be proof-text. Social depressions can be admitted without turning them into "the vanity of metaphysics."[59] Culturally speaking, this cosmotheological revision is no trivial matter.

Decolonizing Spirit One might say that deconstructing the binary of wholeness/brokenness is an attempt to decolonize Spirit—or more specifically, to decolonize how Spirit has been conceptualized as agent of the final perfection, as salvific solvent erasing the material effects of cosmic devolution. The fall has named for classical theism an ontological break or rupture between a past and future perfect nature. Spirit has conceptually been made to collude with the powers of normalization and, therefore, has been read as a totalizing, colonizing power. Not surprisingly, given postmodernizing and postcolonizing sensibilities, Spirit has come to something of an impasse.

Spirit so conceived stands implicitly accused by postmodern and postcolonial discourses. Jean-François Lyotard ushered in postmodernity by denouncing the "transcendental illusion" of G. W. F. Hegel, the nineteenth-century philosopher of Spirit. As Lyotard saw it, Hegel's illusion of Absolute Spirit had worked out its totalizing and terrorizing "nostalgia of the whole" with the effects all too apparent: "The nineteenth and twentieth centuries have given us as much terror as we can take."[60] Mapping it geographically, feminist philosopher Uma Narayan, in *Dislocating Cultures*, draws attention to how Hegel's Absolute Spirit was specifically projected across the hemispheres so as to emplot the trajectory of colonial modernization: "Even history-intoxicated philosophers like Hegel . . . could complacently place entire colonized regions of the world 'outside' of history . . . Hegel proclaims that Africa 'is no historical part of the World, . . . What we properly understand by Africa, is the Unhistorical Undeveloped Spirit'"—at least "until the advent of colonialism."[61] Additionally, as Gayatri Spivak critically observes, Hegel's Spirit consolidated itself by affectively, then also ethically, foreclosing the site and speech of the "native informant."[62] How can the conclusion be avoided that any "Phenomenology of Spirit" would then but be in and of the history of imperialism?

So I want to think about Spirit after [t]he [F]all, if you will. Obviously, I play ironically here with my own experience, with what happened to me. But I want more so, given the theological and social inflections that label my subjectivity as broken and disabled, to work with the concept of Spirit after enabling its epistemic falling out with colonization and modernization, which also means writing after the fall—after razing the scaffolding of metaphysical idealism and its concomitant materialism, after knocking down the cultural scaffolding of transcendence as a power of the ideal by deconstructing its religious legitimacy, an authorization gained, at least in part, by making disabled bodies exemplary (as if this power were sympathetically inclined toward us!). Spirit, when put in metaphysical play with the cosmic fall, was construed as the power of the ideal and transcendence or divine efficacy as a matter of unlimited power over the material world—with totalizing and colonizing effects, as Lyotard and Narayan have insisted that we recognize.

This scaffolding of metaphysical idealism has been and remains deeply materialized in Western culture. Nietzsche, for example, recognized that "science was just one more version of Christian Platonism."[63] Likewise, Heidegger saw technology as the most advanced theater of Western metaphysics. One might even read such a hard wiring for the virtual transcendence of matter as the enthusiasm behind the power grid of transnational capitalism, as Naomi Klein seems to insinuate in *No Logo*: Transnational companies eject the warehouses of physical stock, sell image and culture rather than durable goods, while corporate heads, like a class of absentee landlords, disappear into the ether. Globalization is constructed of the immaterial technologies—the ether of cyberspace, image, and the supernatural flow of money.

We overdraw transcendence, that physics of Spirit, when we lose track of the sociopolitical conditions of religious articulation. Pulling transcendence into a vertical scaffolding that supersedes the terrestrial, we anesthetize ourselves. Idealism, and its stress-induced deformation, dualism, are, as Sands puts it, "amnesic strategies."[64] We habituate ourselves to our cordoned off in/security zones, rather than take responsibility for that which opens off the edge of our present. The hyperreal of late modernity—not an unreal or merely virtual, but a virtuality that has been materialized—may be quite consonant with the creation of the Western religious notion of the supernatural.[65] And both may hide our worst fears. Such trajectories overstate the claims of transcendence, given life on the plane of immanence. Effectively, they are, unfortunately, no little miscoding.

A move to decolonize or to "dismodernize" (Davis) the concept of Spirit and to deconstruct the binary of wholeness/brokenness will undoubtedly require not only hemming and hawing between various hemispheres of meaning, but is also likely to involve confronting just how pervasive and powerful the fear of falling remains within globalizing capitalism's ideology of infinite growth and given the hegemony of normative idealism.[66] If modernization implies the compulsive making new—implies renovation as innovation, as ever-new creation—doesn't that compulsion get its anxious energy for renewal from a persistent problematizing of existence, from aggravating a sense of crisis, whether writ small and personal (presumed physical and character defects that must be cured or transformed, for example) or writ large, transcontinental, and englobing? Modernization played off of the fall, the fear of everything defective—hence, even spiritual practice was identified with the pursuit of wholeness, fulfillment, perfection.[67]

In religion, this fear of falling was manifest in a biblical and theological hermeneutic in which nature was construed as degraded, depraved, and powerless insomuch as it was evidently transitory. According to Hegel's philosophy of religion, religions evolved from those "tied to nature," a disposition that he presumed still evident in African and Asian religions and that he consequently valued as deficient, into a religion of humanity in history. In religions celebrating human history, Spirit was said to overcome or transcend nature with and through the establishment of [civilized] culture. That philosophy of religion and the phenomenology of Spirit were turned into a biblical and theological hermeneutic for reading Spirit as dialectically absolving Nature. Insomuch as the conceptual world of Hegelian idealism informed most modern biblical scholarship, a certain fear of falling away to nature was theologically instantiated and continues to be circulated exegetically.[68]

Refusing to be Alive to the World As a theologian, I want to think analytically about this fear of falling mobilizing the first-world class in relation to modernity's wholesale absolution from suffering in human existence. Disability has been assumed to be inherently a suffering—though for most crips it is what is, the ground condition of our liveliness. Our medicalization toward normalization is linked to this cultural project and its cult of public appearance. Further, in a certain cultural, iconic sense, disability remains the final frontier in returning to Eden. As an epoch, modernity—according to ecofeminist historian and philosopher Carolyn Merchant—was imagined to be the time of the earth's "redemption from the fall"—from the curses of time, toil, and troubles: "Indeed, the story of Western civilization since the seventeenth century and its advent on the American continent can be conceptualized as a grand narrative of Fall and recovery. The concept of recovery . . . not only meant a recovery from the fall, but also entailed restoration of health, reclamation of land, and recovery of property."[69] Serious and appropriate analysis—both cultural and theological—has begun to open out the repressions and compressions of time and space and their economic, ecological, and human sociological ramifications. Yet side by side with these agendas, modernity promised remediation of suffering, pain, disease, and disablement, such that, gathering together the insights of Baconian science, medicine, and technology, modernity assumed an "unquestioned commitment to technological control of the body for the sake of eliminating 'misery and necessity.'"[70] Consequently, Dr. Francis S. Collins, director of the National Center for Human Genome Research in the United States, can simply assert without rippling the eyebrows of popular dissent that "the mandate to alleviate human suffering is one of the most compelling of all expectations of humanity."[71]

While modernity has slated pain for wholesale demolition, pain, throughout much of our religious history, has been treated as a resource that, pricking us with its impingements, can be the occasion for personal, egoistic, or cultural deconstruction and reconstruction. Could it be, insomuch as pain is a psychophysical gauge of our being in the world, that "the attempt to render our bodies free from suffering . . . is morally impoverishing"?[72] Pain has been culturally projected upon the visibly disabled so as to be dislocated from culture. But to tell the truth, David Morris observes, we are as a culture experiencing massive levels of chronic pain. And we no longer have the religious and cultural know-how to tap into or open out such pain for social analysis, no longer know how to use it as a motivational force for either personal or sociocultural change.[73] The fear of falling includes our aversion to pain, and hence a fear of being alive to the world, a fear I believe to be culturally more pervasive than the fear of death (Ernst Becker). Since, as disabled persons, we have been carrying that cultural project and we wish to return it to its prophetic sites, this theology of becoming needs to recuperate pain as a valuable means of perceiving and making cultural wisdom.

The fear of falling can keep one from taking the risk of living. That one day I simply fall and lose a leg makes the first task of physical therapy a psychological nightmare: My physiotherapist tells me that I must learn to fall down, that I must throw out my crutches and fall to the floor, that I cannot leave the rehab room until I have completed this act a significant number of times. But such practice leads me, after reflecting upon the psychological trauma this therapy presents me, to ask whether theological reification of the cosmic fall left us in a similar traumatic relation with the cosmos. Does not such a traumatic relation also contrarily secure perfection—in Dr. Collins's sense—as realistic? Does theological reification of the fall lead us to conceive of sacredness as a hallucination of wholeness, of nostalgia for security and fulfillment, rather than compassion for incongruities, for living amid arbitrariness, and for tying off loose ends? Wouldn't we theologically call that disordered desire? Does it (not) lead us to a persistent problematizing of existence, starting with our own bodies, such that empire has us in its grip by playing with our anxieties—with our somatic, social, and psychic insecurities? The fall itself continues to aggravate the globalizing of capitalism, continues to aggravate the pleasure in classifying and overcoming defects.

A reminder seems in order: Treating deterioration or falling as a threat works back upstream in a subcritical flow to exact cultural formations, cultural normalization, cultural superiority. If the fire ring of dread withholds or forecloses some, it also simultaneously holds out belonging to those made in its mirror image. We can and have made of our fears certain technological, transcendentalized cyberspheres. America, Jean Baudrillard asserts, functions like a "power museum for the whole world." Rich or poor, through the wonders of our media/ted and tele/visionary realities, we can live most of our waking hours in virtualized stratospheres without accounting for ground conditions per se. That is to say, our heads, our dreams, our consciousness, our idealizations can and often do take place in a zone of hyperreality—not at all unreal, because it has materializing effects.[74] Christianity's current evocation of Spirit, its ethereal transcendentalisms already taken up into modern science and its vision/version of new creation, may not then emancipate us from globalization: While our words speak resistance, our embodied psyches succumb to the transcendental insecurity zones, our anxieties still too unresolved to find our sea legs along the plane of immanence.

Consequently, I should warn you, given that I suspect that the cosmic fall (as accounted for within metaphysical idealism) and our consequent fear of falling may be a psychic refusal "to be alive to the world" (Rosenzweig): This pneumatology, incanted on the slant, may seem somewhat more modest than the promised fantasmatics of idealism or its cyberrealism. But if we are to exit the vexing vectors of globalization without taking leave of our love for the planet, then the movements of Spirit might be something more schizo-like, something like "the crazy ungrace of the breath-taking dipping bird," who shares territory with the one who comes up crooked just as a by-product of living (Kingsolver).

Writing Spirit Over/After the Fall: Trajectories of Transcendence

Given the encompassment of globalizing economics, based in its catalyzing of mediated ideality, supernatural capital, and technologies of the immaterial if also technobiopower, Christian theology must pass through the critique of metaphysical idealism if it is to provide capacious imaginaries for the flourishing of life. Opening out the foreclosure that has marked disability in relation to Spirit may help us ferret out another way of holding life sacred, of creating the conditions of entrustment to and for life as distinct from the transcendental imagination powering empire. If transcendence might be construed as the physics of Spirit, the Spirit of modernity acquired its overpowering transcendentalist and idealist arch from the way in which, at least as its been told, Jesus demonstrated miraculous divine power over the monstruous body—the body turned toward death (Augustine), just as Spirit also, in classical theism, was made responsible for resurrecting Jesus, as an individual, from death. That modernity moved the interpretation of disability from religious mystery to medical theater does not necessarily negate my concern. The Christian imaginary has resourced modern cultural enterprises and Christian spiritualities; as well, its' social-justice discourses loop back through a medical-type conversation.[75] Indeed, Hahn suggests that, during modernity, religion and medicine joined forces to form something of "a moral hegemony."[76] If so, then religious practitioners would be well-advised to heed Ivan Illich's warning that "medicalization is the tranquilizer we take to put our social problems out of mind."[77]

Without thinking Spirit after the fall and on the slant, Christian views of transcendence, of wisdom for entrustment to life, may not at this time be able to pose an interruptive variable to empire. Christians, tempered by modern realism, have been guilty of not respecting the difference between doxological evocation and propositional claims to truth, which may too often, then, leave our thinking conflated with cultural ideals. So, for example, we sing, "Hosanna, blessed is the one who comes in the name of the Lord. . . . Power and might belong to our God," forgetting that this Passion Sunday refrain was a mocking parody—not an imperial imitation—of the power of Caesar. The power we celebrate, riding on the back of the donkey, was a nonviolent power of solidarity with history's humiliated.

In the same vein, I distinguish a transcendentalized Spectral Spirit—an eschatologically oriented, if now obviously colonizing Spirit overcoming the fall—from Spirit after the fall, from Spirit that arrives on the slant. Interpretations of Genesis 1–3, consolidated into an analytic we now call the cosmic fall, began to circulate through the intertestamental writings in the centuries surrounding the turn into the Common Era.[78] Reminding ourselves of the truism that all philosophy responds to local conditions, any or all of the following may be viable social, political, cultural situations that might account for such local interpretations—the fall into the englobing powers of Rome, the fall of bodies into the subjectivating desires of the Pax Romana and away from presumed religiocultural values, the fall of the Temple in 67/70 C.E. While Irenaeus, in the second century C.E., begins to construct doctrine as historical emplotment, Christian theologies since the fourth century have been sequenced into an ontotheological history of creation-fall-redemption, which disappeared local conditions and social critique. Such theological dehistoricizing leaves us with a philosophy of nature as ontologically, inherently, fallen, and broken. Similar to the way in which our culture avoids its responsibility in the construction of disability, this construal of nature's essential brokenness also offers us a way of staying unconscious to the fact that a good part of history depends on human responsibility.[79]

But if Genesis were not so much about beginning, as "beginning again" (Keller), then the creation story of Genesis was told not so much "once upon a time" as into those times when people suffered colonization and exile—when they became increasingly "pre-occupied by other's demeaning definitions. . . , transmitted through the violence of structures of exploitation and abuse of power."[80] If various geopolitical storms—and not the fall—were the occasion for theologizing with Spirit, Spirit—that brooding intensity—itself appears to have been conceptually conceived amidst so as to lend its resolves to the ways in which bodies fall into such social depressions, into social conscriptions that leave us less than human. Theological innovations on *rûah* first generated by Ezekiel and the priestly writers of Genesis were later appropriated by Christian communities—themselves forming in the wake of the razing of the temple, in the horizontal violence occasioned under the impress of an imperial, colonizing presence, amidst the social architecture of the Pax Romana. Spirit does not arrive on the scene freewheeling from the pure netherlands of the two perfections—Never-Known Eden and Ever-Delayed Parousia. Rather, Spirit begins as an intensity, a vibration within the zones of social assessment where we admit our ease at falling into desire with the powers that be, our falling out with nature as less than ideal.

So Spirit, conceptually speaking, may have had a life before the fall. Indeed, the concept of Spirit was apparently conceived in these times under imperial gaze, within a colonized place, to swerve the colonial optic so as to open out spaciousness in the cultural imaginary. Ironically, Spirit, as a divine physics and then divine appellation, may have been conceived by bodies on the slant, which means that Spirit's "hoodoo disposition" (Kingsolver) has likely broken loose in hemispheres and semiospheres—meaning-making regions of life—besides that one in which it has been put to work as an agent of progress, that one in which it has been worked to weave the final perfection.

To think Spirit in relation to the social depressions and life-denying taxonomies in which we find ourselves will be quite distinct from thinking Spirit in relation to a fallen nature. Because of the way in which disability has been related to the cosmic fall, persons with disabilities may, like canaries in a coal mine, recognize certain aversions that Christianity hides from itself and that it has reified as Spirit's transcendence of the conditions of life. Persons with disabilities are equally likely to feel a physics of Spirit that, recognizing us as among the multiple forms of life's flourishing, refuses to overwrite or to idealize transcendence.

Rhetorically inflecting the differences of disabled bodies has been one of the key means for speaking about sacred or spiritual presence in the biblically informed Christian imaginary. Figurally, sacred texts move from the limping Jacob who wrestled with God to the stuttering Moses to Israel's national designation as God's "limping people," and on to the pivotal positioning of the broken body of Jesus.[81] The miracle stories, for example, the healing of the blind, the lepers, and so on, appear as early and pivotal narratives informing Christian communal formation. But to bring this genealogy to light does not yet suggest in what ways these differences were taken into the negotiation of sacred value in and for various life regions. For that, we must rely on theological archaeology.[82] At minimum, however, we might acknowledge that how we make religiocultural meaning using disabled bodies today is likely to be grossly distinct from how meaning was made at the turn into the Common Era: Today, among the first-world class, physiologically stigmatic disablements—and what counts as disabilities for this culture tends to be visually overdetermined, given the body politics of capitalism—are relatively rare. Contrarily, at the turn into the common era, physiological disablements proliferated, perhaps even to the point of being the ordinary condition of humanity, at least among the perimeter social strata, given the presence and pressures of imperial Rome.

Ironically, since at least the time of Augustine, for Christianity, disabled bodies have been figural paradigms illustrating the extremes to which Spirit must go to reclaim wholesomeness and, therefore, are indicative of the Holy Spirit's capacity for resurrecting life.[83] While I might not in principle wholly disagree with Augustine (given that I am trying to recalibrate how we think Spirit and transcendence with and through the experience of disability), I am refusing to carry over his cosmological conviction that in a universe, pneumatically visited, resurrection names the remediatory normalization of my body. In that hemisphere of meaning, the Easter liturgies—"The body has risen from the grave all-glorious"; "Life has conquered death"—become, ensuent to my own health crisis, nearly unpalatable. Each year I know, especially since the anniversary passage of my health crisis often occurs quite parallel to that of the liturgical calendar, that Easter morning will be among my most psychologically agonizing days—my body pummeled by the overstrident choruses and uncritical pronouncements. I can imagine singing these refrains in other hemispheres or semiospheres of meaning. But that's the point: I suspect that Christians have become habituated to singing them within the hyperreality, the rarefied stratosphere, of technotranscendence and of a Christianity that, whether liberal or conservative, has been habituated to God as "the celestial double of the powerful" and to this way of seeing the world.[84] In the sacred imaginary of Christian theologies and in our culture's science fiction, disabled bodies have become an iconic hinge, a pivot, a theatrical pallet, for misreading a doxological evocation, for making of the refrain life conquering death into what Oona Eisenstadt calls a "voracious dialectic."[85]

According to Eisenstadt, the twentieth-century Jewish theologian Franz Rosenzweig insisted that in Luther's Bible, the Pauline Easter cadence of "the death of death" served as a primary hermeneutic lens, releasing a "voracious dialectic" that prevented the culture from making room for Jews. This same dialectic,

through which "perfect conditions overcome present conditions"—a fairly straightforward expectation of the eschatological potency of Spirit within classical theism, by
the way—cannot make room for persons with disabilities, either. It promises, via the
miraculous power of God—or of scientific technobiopower—to do the impossible,
to work against nature.[86] That voracious dialectic, a reading of the physics of transcendence, has been aggressively pinned against differently abled bodies—not just
punishing by pitying our difference, but thereby accomplishing among the population
at large a certain obligation or submission to centralized morality, decency, virtuosity,
the gracious living of the transparent class.

Holding such a voracious dialectic as life conquering or overcoming death within
the religiocultural psyche releases an aggressive energy, even if or perhaps especially
when cloaked in pity for those who carry our anxious projections. Brokenness names
the pleasurable-problematic aversive for which Spectral Spirit has been made the
transcendent solvent. If, in classical theism, brokenness denoted the effects of the
ontological devolution of matter from the fall, today it pertains to a body and that way
of life loaded down with abnormal or defective—over against transparent, flawless,
or unmarked—physicality. "By suppressing materiality," patristics scholar Virginia
Burrus observes of the fourth-century Fathers, "they push spirit to new heights."[87]
Could that be true of a culture that, while immersed in materialism, nevertheless
creates technologies of transcendence by pushing against defect? Indeed, might that
be something of the nature of that "*cybernating* space" we now call globalization?[88]
Have we sacralized a fear of presence to life that remains, like a virus, in our hard and
soft technologies, even if/as postcolonial and postmodern theorists cull Spirit and its
foreclosures from the pages of our history?

In his "Answer to Julian," Augustine, responding to the question pressed upon
Jesus in the narrative of John 9 concerning the man born blind, situates physiological
differences occurring with birth not as random differences of nature, but in relation
to humanity's spoiled origin: "Tell me, then, because of what wrong are such inno-
cents sometimes born blind and other times deaf? . . . [F]rom its beginning when
it [humanity] abandoned God, the human race contracted from its condemned origin a sinfulness fully deserving all these punishments."[89] Contracting the doctrines
of Creation-Fall-Redemption into a hermeneutic lens for reading defective bodies,
a normative reading of John 9:3 (The Gospel author reports Jesus as saying, "[T]his
man . . . was born blind so that God's works might be revealed in him") now marks
the miraculously remediated body as definitive of the transcendent omnipotence of
Spirit. Augustine—at least in the generous reading of contemporary theorists Hardt
and Negri—may have held up this version of transcendence to help people discern cit-

izenship between "the two cities"—one of God and the other of Rome, both of which appear interwoven on Earth.[90] But we must be aware that, given modernity's liquidation of relations (kinship, locality, loyalties, obligations), which serve as the constituting condition for the individual's freedoms, and given the materialization of virtual realities, relieving us further of finite limits and conditions, endowing such readings of John 9 with metaphysical force or supernatural power today can leave us much more exposed or prone to fantastical, dualistic notions of absolute transcendence.[91] Hardly, then, would Christianity meet philosopher John Caputo's definitional assumptions about religion: "Religion disturbs our sense of reality and leaves us a little unhinged."[92] (Limping, even?) Indeed, Christianity has not simply failed to inhibit the spectrality of capitalism and of technobiopower, but has lent our authorization to their (shared) imaginary, so that we as Christians are at best momentarily slightly confused and bewildered by our doppelgänger.

Iterated through the conditions of late modernity, the voracious dialectic of transcendence leaves but marginal living room for the physicalized, for all of those marked invalid. Christianity, wed through Spirit with eschatological idealism, refuses to speak the truth of tragedies, to grieve its losses, the losses that life engenders. A Spectral Spirit likewise promises fulfillment. Each promises to satiate the past. Transcendence circulated as idealization lays the psychic track that takes profitable pleasure in the obsession with pathology, with defect and, thus, with curing and fixing. But idealization, as Spivak has insisted, forecloses an ethical relation with those whom it objectifies. Ethicist Kathleen Sands likewise warns that "idealism remains history's eschatological backdrop," even within certain strains of scientific materialism and as the imaginary of biotechnopower.[93] But "nature idealized is not nature at all," Sands continues, concluding that "To long for the death of death is to long for the death of life."[94] And could we not also say, "a body idealized is no body at all"? But what, then, would happen to the body spectacular that is the glue of belonging within empire?[95]

What might the fallen ones—the limping and unhinged, working life on the slant—have to say about Spirit? Could these provide Spirit a new lease on life? Then again, how would Spirit signify if articulated by bodies resistant to cure? And how would we think theology if not against such a clear horizon as offered by eschatological resolution? What could Spirit mean if not the promise of a clearing, an eschatological absolution, an ideal, a higher power, a wholesomeness? How would we story the self if not triumphantly, redemptively—if not enhanced from above, from the beyond?

CHAPTER 2

MONSTROSITY, MIRACLE, AND MISSION:
RELIGION AND THE POLITICS OF DISABLEMENT

"Was Blind But Now I See," the headline sang from a special issue of *Newsweek* magazine devoted to "The Next Frontiers" in medicine and technology (June 24, 2002). This article specifically announced the development of neural prostheses to remediate blindness, deafness, voice, and balance loss.

All my life . . . / I have felt there is something/ more wonderful than gloss—/than wholeness— / . . . Every morning on the wide shore / I pass what is perfect and shining / to look for the whelks, Whose edges / have rubbed . . . against the world. . . .

—Mary Oliver, "Whelks"

But its echo of the genre of the miracle story to which it alludes feels uncomfortably familiar to many disabled persons. The story unfolds like this: Position a disabled body as evincing a humanitarian necessity; resolve the riddle of suffering, which appears to imprison the disabled body, and all will enter the promised land of perfection.

To be sure, most faith-healing accounts have another stock character—the Holy Spirit, which has frequently been construed as that power that heals by curing disabled bodies and resurrecting dry bones. Yet Spirit is not restricted to religious appeals: "The 'hardest' science is about the realm . . . of pure spirit," science historian Donna Haraway observes.[1] Science historians like Haraway trace the genealogy of modern (Western) science not only to its cradle in European Christianity, but through the Western Christian imaginary and its generative assumptions about Spirit. So we might well wonder whether the remarkable transcendence accruing, even as of a fabulous nature, to the scientific ledger, imbricates the transcendent potency of the Holy Spirit of Christianity in late modernity's attempt to materialize what Foucault ironically called "the original state of health."[2]

Foucault's ironic quip challenges a culturally operative picture of health that assumes that, either in the past or in the proximate future, an Edenic zero point—a state of human wholeness, absent disease and genetic mutation (whatever that would mean in a Darwinian-informed world)—can be identified, even now achieved. Further, Foucault tracked the rise of modern medicine to a certain materialist assumption: Medicine would be "a lay carbon copy" of the Church, thereby assuming a parallel "spiritual vocation."[3] Indeed, doesn't the reproductive competency of biotechnopower resemble a certain redemptive Christian imaginary in which Spirit rebirths bodies into a "nature enterprised up," a nature where there is no suffering, no toil, no death?[4] Biotechnology might then represent the latest secularization of certain Christian hopes for a transformation of nature.

Empire, the name theorists Michael Hardt and Antonio Negri give to the postnational phenomenon of the globalization of capitalist economics and Western culture, advances through what Foucault called "biopower," the cultural phenomenon of intensifying social integration and control through the politics of the body, health, and "the production and reproduction of 'life' itself."[5] Biotechnology—not just in its actual effects, but in its culturally purported sublime capacity to materialize the incredible—supports the emergence of this ideal self of the market economy. Its miracle stories with disabled bodies still firmly positioned on the theatrical pallet—as the *Newsweek* article attests— dare all humans to "wake to the dream of human perfection," as Dr. James D. Watson (one of the founding fathers of modern genetics) puts it.[6] This dream, this Western vision of the perfect, the whole and wholesome body, should worry Christian theology. Theology needs to consider the way in which secularized forms of the miracle story and its evocation of wholeness, this picture of health, play into the hands of late capitalist and neocolonial conditions.

If yet but "the stars" traverse the transcendental ethers with the many watching enviously (Bauman), certain other bodies have been socially construed as lacking full humanity—thus, as less than whole. In modernity, these were the degenerate types, a conflation of what we today distinguish as disability, race, and gender. The notion of degeneracy operates in tandem with modern scientific anthropology, complementing its ideal of the autonomous self-made, self-mastering individual. To be sure, race and gender, which were earlier considered degenerate conditions, have been raised as primary analytic vectors for decolonizing and then postcolonial theory, extending from Frantz Fanon's *Black Skin, White Masks* through Anne McClintock's *Imperial Leather*. Yet modernity's overarching trajectory of degeneracy has not been analytically deconstructed, despite these recuperated subjective locations. Following theorists Wendy Brown and

Lennard Davis, I would suggest that this leaves in place a subjective idealism, even within race and gender identities, which is epitomized by the marginalization of disabled persons.[7]

I am suggesting that debility has served as a heretofore unstudied vector of imperialism. If this is so, then we understand why both disabled persons and colonial subjects have been conjointly marked as the territory of mission and objects of social pity. So marked, disablement has been read as necessitating (humane) intervention. Consequently, Sherene Razack, following upon postcolonial theorist Gayatri Spivak, critiques "the politics of [colonial] rescue," which is also known as "the politics of saving," just as disability studies critiques the mentality of fixing or curing.[8] Neither critique has yet been taken up within theologies concerned with social justice. Such theologies will thus find important clues to the postcolonial within this emerging disability discourse.

Further, the territory or space of degeneracy has generally been socially patrolled by what the psychoanalytic philosopher of decolonization Frantz Fanon identified as "the gaze" and what disability studies refers to as "the stare." Psychosocially, this colonizing of bodies manifests itself in terms of what Fanon called "epidermalization." Fixed in the gaze or caught in the stare, the colonized and/or disabled body—thoroughly objectified and physicalized—takes place at the skin, threatening to collapse the psychic room of personhood.[9]

In this chapter, I therefore consider how the metaphor of disablement, when imbricated with Spirit, figures into Western Christian and cultural eschatology and modern social, even scientific and economic, practice. Absorbing the theological plot line of the fall as the cultural dialectic of wholeness overcoming the broken, modernity affectively canceled out the possibility of ethical relation with those it saw in terms of brokenness.[10] The anxious exercise of caring concern has consequently been mediated or seen through an ideal form. Hence, Spirit was made into a dominant, controlling power that comes heroically to rescue, to occupy and to fix, those construed as disabled—as physically or culturally handicapped. This practice of Spirit's physics of transcendence is about as effective as American attempts to rescue and fix the nations of Afghanistan and Iraq. Comparably, bodies—and not just bodies of disabled persons—are dominated by a scientific view of the original state of health, just as Iraq and Afghanistan experience domination by a globally mediated ideal. So the pneumatology toward which I deconstructively work here promotes Spirit not as the power to rescue and repair according to some presupposed original state or ideal form, but as the energy for unleashing multiple forms of corporeal flourishing.

Globalization's "Body Silent"

Amid the media/ted postmodern society of spectacle, surface, image, and icon, I want to pose the question of "the body silent" (Murphy) at the heart of biotechnology's miracle and of cultural public performance. I want to ask, wheeling myself up next to Derrida, "What if what cannot be assimilated, the absolute indigestible, played a fundamental role *in the system*, an abyssal role rather?"[11] Derrida asserted that what is excluded may actually play a key role in systemic construction and stabilization. With his thesis in mind, I want to advance the suspicion that "the ubiquitous unspoken topic of disability in contemporary culture" may sustain empire's artery of normative idealism as well as its economic organization.[12] With Lennard Davis, I share the surmise that disability may be the "specter haunting normality in our time."[13] If ideation mobilizes economics, then disrupting the representational economy, the cult of public appearance, might itself begin to diffract not only the global media/tion of the ideal self, but the economics and social cultural politics thereby metabolized.

If empire, as Hardt and Negri claim, has learned to metabolize and capitalize upon the new racial, ethnic, and sexual subjectivities brought into being during the decades since the 1960s, then thinking disability studies together with postcolonial theories, in their confluences and disagreements, might allow us to begin to track those who are today being "written out, written off" (Spivak), given the prevailing ideology of the normal.[14] It was theorist Homi Bhabha who recognized that "the objective of colonial discourse is to construe the colonized as a population of degenerate types . . . in order to justify conquest and to establish systems of administration and instruction."[15] Bhabha's theoretical subversions, however, have tended to assume that difference was productively generated into a dialectical and externalized encounter of the same and the other, such that hybridity unsettles colonial power. But as cultural theorist Robert Young points out, colonialism "operated both according to the same-Other model and through the 'computation of normalities' and 'degrees of deviance' from the white norm."[16] While liberal humanism has through the past several decades developed race, gender, and sexuality as available identities, the threat that one might degenerate and perish— the obverse of social and evolutionary Darwinism (and therefore perhaps also the specter haunting growth economics)—remains a potent physical anxiety. In other words, empire may still foment, if not a dialectical divide, then a bottom line below which people are afraid to fall. In an economy in which image sells and looking good is everything, the disabled body may not be at all irrelevant, but may rather be a needed, if abject, other—a silenced body of evidence serving up the ideal.

While a certain creative room for what feminist theorist Susan Friedman calls "play" or "performativity" makes the postcolonial strategies of mimicry and hybridity feasible in dereifying race and ethnic absolutes or other assumed authenticities, the scaling of normalcy/deviancy—more intimately internal to and developmentally archaic in the colonizing psyche—shuts down the transcendent energies of desire. Whereas the feeling of lack of vitality can occasion what bell hooks calls "eating the [ethnic] other," the ideology of normalcy as "whole(some)ness" construes itself in rigid abjection of the pathetic (deviance, disease, degeneracy, disability, poverty,and so forth), such that these are linked into class prejudices as well as private anxieties. Disgust, as Martha Nussbaum explains, "pervasively constructs social hierarchies" and can blend with what we in earlier eras called "aristocratic disdain."[17] But such disgust blended with disdain, keeping us from the anxieties and vulnerabilities of the animal body, keeping us imagistically cathected to "an aspiration to be a kind of being that one is not," may also today float the specular spectacular of globalization.[18] If, as Zygmunt Bauman theorizes, modernity "means the compulsive critique of reality"—and today, given the liquidization of social systems and relations, that critical compulsion is turned upon the self—then extreme makeovers or other such remediations to normalcy might be something of the impulse of modernization itself in this time.[19] Thus, it seems that something like the colonial management of normalcy may continue productively to serve the imaginary of empire.

Yet, as the earlier reference to miracle stories has insinuated, I suspect such silencing of bodies transpires not merely in and through culture at large. Rather, Christian theological use of the metaphor of disablement and its purported remarkable healing accounts informs and reinforces the transcendence—by remediation or avoidance—of disability itself and thus supports empire's bioregime. Within sacred texts and spiritual practice, the metaphor of disablement has been used to establish over against disability the terrestrially transcendent quality of sacred power—Spirit—and the contours of spiritual bodies as whole(some). Rather than blessing corporeal flourishing in all its multiple forms, even when it limps, wheels, and winces, even progressive, liberal theologies focused on Jesus as Healer might be included under what theologian Marcella Althaus-Reid designates as "decency theologies"—theologies that, given the impetus of modernity, became conflated with middle-class morality and, consequently, begin to discipline bodies into the status quo. Given the history of colonialism and the trajectory of empire, we need to consider the possibility that theologies of healing can get caught up into the imaginary anticipation of remediation to normalcy in the same way that psychoanalysis has, in the eyes of philosophers Deleuze and Guattari, facilitated adjustment to the machinery of capitalism.[20] Indeed, looking at disability metaphors as the converse of whole(some)ness brings to conscience those sites where the West could recognize itself as simultaneously engaged in "civilizing mission and a violent subjugating force."[21]

Monstrous Races: Disablement, Degeneracy, and the Geography of Mission

Disablement, in all its physiological variations, including blindness, deafness, and muteness, has been a politically and religiously deployed metaphor of boundaries and their trespass. As a metaphor deployed along the boundaries of international politics and economic practice, as well as within Christian eschatology and social mission, disablement metabolizes remediatory impulses. While physiognomic handbooks of the second to the fourth centuries clearly figured God and Jesus as beautiful, with spiritual formation itself focused on becoming more Godlike in this regard, the construction of monstrous races, from the fifth-century Greco-Roman teratological traditions to the Euro-Western colonial centuries espying degenerate races and continents, have limned the Christian eschatological imaginary.[22]

Augustine displayed a somewhat intriguing and respectful reserve in his curiosity about monstrosities, which included cyclopses, cyneocephali or the "dog-faced," pygmies, sciopods, androgynes, antipods, and hermaphrodites, among others. This same encyclopedic imaginary of monstrous races was set as a figural horizon at the ends of the earth for seventh – to tenth-century Christian evangelization, these frightful curios being presumed to populate the uncivilized territories.

Augustine, relying on Pliny's *Natural History* to supplement regional tales and encounters, believed the monstrous races to be continuous with the monstrous births known among any populace. It would be best to assume God knows what God is doing in the generation of monsters, Augustine advises, adding that "it would be utterly wrong for anyone to be fool enough to imagine that the Creator made a mistake." God is not an "imperfectly skilled craftsman."[23] If Augustine, in the first breath, insists that monstrosities, too, are therefore descendants of Adam, taking a second breath, he calls into being the force of the majority of the self-same: "However, it is clear what constitutes the persistent norm of nature."[24] So how, then, does Augustine explain the divine's apparently purposeful craftsman-ship in the generation of abnormal members of the human race? "The name 'mon-ster,'" Augustine writes, evidently comes from *monstrare*, "to show," because they show by signifying something. . . . Now these signs are, apparently, contrary to nature and so they are called "unnatural.". . . For us, however, they have a message. These "monsters," "signs," "portents," and "prodigies," as they are called, ought to "show" us, to "point out" to us . . . that God is to do what he prophesied that he would do with the bodies of the dead, with no difficulty to hinder him, no law of nature to debar him from so doing.[25]

In other words, the monstrous demonstrate or serve as a stage set for the display of divine power, specifically of the power of Spirit to resurrect life, to make whole.

Augustine's confidence that heaven holds the miracle of remediation to normativity for such bodies allows him to demarcate their temporal presence as ontological proof for the resurrection: Earthly monstrosities were paradoxically signifiers of the wonder-working power of the divine—seen not for who they were, but through the power of the contrary, for what God's power would do with them. While Augustine did not construe miracles as supernatural, but assumed rather that their transformative energies were in contiguity with the miracle of everyday life, he nevertheless naturalizes remediation of physiological variances in the Christian imaginary: be assured that heaven normalizes the human body.[26] Such spectacles of daily encounter, Augustine insinuated, reawaken human wonder and respect for "the vigorous power" of God.[27]

As the ecclesiastical historian Bede constructs his eighth-century historical account of the Christianization of the known world, these monstrous races became more figurally foundational for Christian eschatology. Christian evangelization takes shape (at least in the understanding of Bede) as an act of pastoral concern, but a concern vested with the self-interested, internal urgency to extend the Gospel to the ends of the earth so as to occasion the end of time. As historian Ian Wood puts it, "Mission at the geographical limits of the earth could thus be related to the eschatological end of the world."[28] Laboring ever outward to the edges of earth's limits, missionaries turned the eschatological key to saving time—to the time of salvation. But the ends of the earth were peopled or at least populated, such that between Christians and the promised-land time of the *parousia* lived the other, the monstrous races. Wood comments on Bede's positioning of the monstrous at the limits of the earth: "More than a simple geographical limit was being established: the limits of humanity were being scrutinized."[29]

If for Augustine the monstrous were clearly "bodies of evidence" in and for divine power, they now became something more of an eschatological keystone. Missionaries' felt need to proselytize required them to discern the edges of humanity: If human, the monstrosities were to be prosthetically supplemented or rehabilitated—that is, fitted with the Gospel. If not human, they were to be eliminated. The decision regarding the humanity of the other was based upon the evangelist's self-referential discernment regarding what made one human. As it was historically configured in the eighth to tenth centuries, evangelical mission proceeded as repair to the ends of the earth, which simultaneously necessitated remediation of the edges of humanity. If the task of mission was not yet replete with the notion of improvement and progress or the annexation of territory, nevertheless the colonization of time already had begun to aggravate against the anomalies or morphological alterities peopling the horizon of the Christian imaginary—a scenario not unlike the relationship between the human genome project and globalization today.

Modern colonialism, assuming in its own way this evangelical, eschatological need, advanced with a psychosocial map of zones of degeneracy. The notion of degeneracy was based upon the Enlightenment's biological and evolutionary notion of the Family of Man. This biological mapping of the evolutionary tree of humanity presumed the progressive biological development of the civilized modern European human, descendant from the so-called earlier primitive races of distant continents encountered in the Age of Discovery. Degeneracy here categorically encompassed the spoiled others of the emergent modern self, "those groups whom Foucault describes as the 'internal enemies' of the bourgeois male—women, racial others, the working class, people with disabilities, in short all those who would weaken the vigorous bourgeois body and state."[30] The moral propriety of the middle class and also the moral superiority of the colonizing nation depended on spatially confining degeneracy, both geographically (whether to a specific country or neighborhood) and socially, for example, to a particular class. The stigmatic markers of debility also then denoted the spatial confinements to which such bodies must be returned—for example, to slums, housing zones, the streets, and asylums. That is to say, as transnational feminist Sherene Razack explains, disability—and also, therefore, race and gender, because these were categorical variations of disability—have been *terrritorial* markers. Because "physical, mental and social defects pulled people down . . . [i]t was therefore necessary to avoid this pull downwards by maintaining rigid boundaries between those prone to decay and those who were to participate as citizens in the new social order."[31] The rights and benefits of liberal humanism, as Razack observes, then apply only in the zones of cultured civility.[32] Limited employment options or social isolation, one of the most frequent confinement strategies in regard to disabled persons, also effect social containment.[33] That even today a person in the West who becomes disabled often drops down in status in their professional as also their social class might well suggest the continuing habit of strategic quarantine of disablement.[34]

In modernity then, the Western world's sense of itself as an advanced civilization obversely depended upon the delimitation of degeneracy. Yet given the anxiety around contamination, there needed to be both confinement of the despoiled and, as Razack goes on to explain, "controlled excursions" across the boundary between the respectable and the degenerate: "It was not enough to seal off the disorder and the disease. It was also necessary to repeatedly affirm that bourgeois subjects could journey into those regions and emerge unscathed in order for those subjects to deny the permeability of their body politic and to position themselves as invincible."[35] Among the means of allowable transgression, Razack includes not only prostitution (the primary subject of her research article), but also touch and rescue work. Thus, for example, the salvation armies of Christians, as well as science and medicine and medical missions.[36] Territorial transgress could thus be worked to establish a dominant culture's sense of superiority.

Miracle stories, read in the mode of modernist realism, likewise have served as training manuals in sympathy. In novels, Davis explains, the disabled character "is placed in the narrative 'for' the nondisabled characters—to help them develop sympathy, empathy, or as a counterbalance to some issue in the life of the 'normal' character."[37] But sympathy or pity, unlike compassion, can be an incredibly aggressive energy.[38]

The metaphor of disablement as connoting deficiency marks off for modernity a presumed zone of human insufficiency; the metaphor has also been read to authorize entry or access. The notion of degeneracy—with the disabled body as somatic and geographic template—thus invites the imperial dynamic of a superior helping a deficient person or population. It mobilizes the imperialist to act as savior.[39] The metaphor of disablement, in other words, geographically maps out a politics of rescue. What has been conceived of as social mission plays upon the sentiment of moral uplift of the previously spatially confined. Or as Mitchell and Snyder put it in another context, the metaphor of disablement "acts as a shorthand method of securing emotional responses."[40] Whether in international politics and economics or in Christian missions, the metaphor works by subverting the need for conscious reflection.

So employed, the metaphor has invited what Ashis Nandy has called the second wave of colonialism. "Its carriers," Nandy explains, referring to the Christian, humanitarian, social and medical mission, "were people who, unlike the rapacious first generation of bandit-kings who conquered the colonies, sought to be helpful. They were well-meaning, hard-working, middle-class missionaries, liberals, modernists, and believers in science, equality, and progress." This second wave of colonialism, Nandy nonetheless observes, "released forces within the colonized societies to alter their cultural priorities once and for all," principally because these soft technologies worked on the everyday life habits of the book.[41] Emotionally leveraged by a metaphor that had become shorthand for "saving action urgently required," an emotional shorthand that then avoids critique of one's own ideological investments as one seeks to exercise compassion, humanitarian concern misfired into eradicating alterity, into prosthelytizing the bodies on its horizon. That the lenses of modern theologians have revealed a culturally unique Jesus coming into contact with the untouchables, for example, presumably transgressing Jewish religious prescriptions as well as territorial boundaries, will need to be reread in light of both the gaze of the modern to see over against him or herself the untouchable, pitiable, disabled degenerate and the cultural ascendancy gained by trespass, especially that portrayed as humanitarian rescue.

The cultural construction of disability as we specifically inhabit it in the twenty-first century emerged within the modern regime of the biologizing of differences and alongside the industrial and economic normalizations of modernity. Within the modern regime of biopower, "bodies of individuals and populations are now measured against norms related to utility, amenability to profitable investment, capacity for being usefully trained and prospects of survival, death and illness."[42] Given these terms, which are both terms of employment and determinants of civil society and culture within empire, more than two-thirds of disabled persons in North America have been left unemployed and, therefore, with limited access to the global capitalist economic structure. Not surprisingly, Western society's commitment to the elimination of suffering through advancing biotechnopower forms subjects according to the needs of this society for productive and efficient bodies and populations, such that, as bioethicist Gerald McKenney observes, "what appears to be a moral commitment to . . . the elimination of suffering is also a way of producing ['the societally desirable, normative'] body."[43] According to the politics of representation that encodes relations among citizens of the globalizing culture, disablement metaphorically works to contain physiological variance. By mapping the bodies of those to be pitied, medicalized, socialized, rescued, fixed, rehabilitated, or contained, the metaphor of disablement also simultaneously occasions a sense of and the power of the normative as that toward which citizens should strive.

If both formerly colonized peoples as well as persons with disabilities may be found on the margins of today's empire, and if both have been cast as deficient and degenerate, the multiple inflections thereof must nevertheless be acknowledged. From the stage of the metropolitan theater of the public performance of the Western wholesome self, I address my critique of globally mediated Platonism. Living among the potentially "GenRich" or biotechnologically enabled, I challenge the fixation on ideal image, the excessive regime of health that avoids recognizing the social construction of normalcy as well as the traces of economic colonialism that attend "images of luxury under late capitalist . . . culture."[44] Elsewhere, however, even where the third world is present in the first, economic globalization creates a whole cast of disposable persons—often people of the formerly colonized countries whose bodies bent toward menial labor and consigned to the wastelands continue to buffer first-world class citizens from industrial, environmental fallout and who exercise what essayist Barbara Ehrenreich sardonically calls "the philanthropy of the poor." Given the lack of health care and of environmental and industrial protections, physiological disablement proliferates among this class of worked-over bodies—as it perhaps always has at the edges of empire. Indeed, the proliferation of stories of disablement within the synoptic Gospels may in some way, I suspect, have to do with how the Roman Empire effected the bodies of the colonized.

The demarcation of disability—again, if differently inflected and with various pressures—nevertheless remains, like an electrified fence, highly activated as Western culture goes global. As globalization of the Western economy sweeps the planet and as countries are brought into the patterns of industrial and postindustrial capitalism, the body count swells. Because of the way in which the capitalist economy reorients relational communities, "leaving solely the 'cash nexus' of the many bonds underlying human mutuality and mutual responsibilities," it has been estimated that upward of 90 percent of persons with disabilities worldwide are unemployed.[45] This is not necessarily an issue of humanitarian backwardness in non-Western countries, but a sign of how Western-style economic globalization shifts the patterns of relational interdependence, which bodies with disabilities often require. Even given the mixed and confluent world classes of the planet, somatic stigmata—the morphological difference established by the gaze of the dominant—remain as much in use today to prevent border crossings as during earlier stages of modernity.[46] Indeed, if empire today enjoys the chromatic carnival of formerly colonized hybridities, if cultured civility now flows across formerly racialized borders, a certain map of stigmatic debilities—a purported lack of wholesomeness—seems to remain firmly in place at the borders. To be sure, biotechnology, just like Augustine's God, circulates theatrical postings for its demonstrative others, offers its miraculous remediations to normativity, stages its power over the body silent. But refuse that script, or take the script and invent a prosthetic erratic, or behave with anything less than aspirations to wholesomeness and obeisance to the cult of public appearance, and one finds one's self subject to pity—if also very occasionally its obverse, envy, when the assumption is made that a person with a disability has at least a heroic relationship to suffering by which to emplot the self.

Religions Use the Metaphor of Disablement "to Think with"

To wrap some conclusions around this short religious and cultural history of the metaphor of disablement, I would first of all suggest that Christianity has used disablement "to think with."[47] From the Greek reading of monstrous births for messages about that culture's social character to contemporary culture's scapegoating of disabled persons, disabilities have remained philosophical commitments to idealism—disablement psychically registered as social disruption, an exception proving the rule, the normative form. If religion can be said to be the substance of culture as culture is the form of religion, Christians recognize themselves in the social, colonial impulse to saving missions catalyzed during modernity by the metaphor of disablement.[48] Without forgetting that the metaphor of disablement appears to mark the eschatological edge of the world for Christianity, let me also suggest that Christianity—implicitly reading disablement as degeneracy—has laid down the metaphor "as a . . . signifier of social and/or individual collapse" and as a spiritual diagnostic.[49] The metaphorical use of disablement as a spiritual diagnostic is in no way somatically innocent, but in fact always already presumes the need for redemptive prescription. For example, a people blind or deaf to the ways of God must, we have learned to presume, require remediation, since blindness and deafness must be obstacles.

Christian ethicist Cynthia Moe-Lobeda's *Healing a Broken World: Globalization and God* provides a relevant case in point. This book presents a lucid analysis of the institutional and transnational aspects of globalization and its subjective effects, including the short-circuiting of ethical agency and democratic voice among Christians, if also among the middle class and/or citizens of the first world in general. Moe-Lobeda's theoethical text deserves to be celebrated for taking up what Marcuse called the very difficult and unwelcomed work of liberating the majority from "a relatively well functioning, rich, powerful society."[50] Nevertheless, Moe-Lobeda, despite her awareness of the prevailing ideology of normalcy at the heart of globalization, hinges her whole theoethical analysis upon the metaphor of disablement and its remediation. She writes: "I argue that the prevailing model of economic globalization normalizes and dictates political-economic relationships that cripple human capacity to make decisions. . . . [M]any people, insulated by privilege, remain blind to the suffering and ecological devastation created by current global trade and investment regimes. Others, while aware, feel muted, dwarfed by the situation . . . . As a society, we are . . . morally malformed by and into ways of economic injustice."[51] Her use of the metaphors seems not at all inadvertent, but intentional. In fact, her book is neatly divided into Part I, which "explores . . . the disabling of moral agency," and Part II, which "explores . . . the enabling of moral agency by relationship with God indwelling creation."[52] A miracle story—the healing of the paralytic, I would assume, based upon Moe-Lobeda's rhetorical refrain—provides the not so covert scrim for the remediation of this incapacitation of Christian agency in the face of globalization. By her use of the physiological variations classified as disabilities, she necessarily equates disability with occlusions in character development, in our assumption to full humanity.[53] In the end, she, by relying upon the rhetorical resort to the disability metaphor to incite spiritual action, unwittingly bases her remediation of Christian agency upon the desire toward wholeness with which globalization girds itself up.

Seemingly ever the problem in need of a solution, disablement always already evokes resolve. To expose and to label a body as disabled is always already to determine to correct the deviance, to assume as natural the transformative transcendence thereof. Strategies of resolution have typically included the remediation of deviance through cure or cosmesis, including prosthesis, extermination of the deviant other, and keeping deviance at bay and under control via strategies of confinement or containment while maintaining rights of allowable trespass.[54] But please note: Thinking with the body of persons with disabilities requires silencing persons with disabilities. Such egoic cogitation presumes physiological disablement to be lack, then leaps over the testimony of persons with disabilities to repair and to rescue.

Harlan Lane, a psychologist who has practiced among the Deaf World and who has as such also been consultant within the Belgian protectorate of Burundi, calls this colonizing move "an extrapolative leap, an egocentric error" of "imposing the familiar on the unfamiliar."[55] Among disability theorists, Lane has most explicitly laid open the parallel between imperial acts of territorial colonization and the colonization of persons dominant culture has considered disabled. He insists in *The Mask of Benevolence: Disabling the Deaf Community* that terms of colonization fit both scenarios: "I call deaf communities colonized, using the term in an extended sense—as when French philosopher Michel Foucault speaks of the 'colonization of the body' by the state—because deaf communities have suffered oppression in all its forms and consequences, in common with other cultures that were literally subjugated by imperial powers."[56] In an effort to mediate the contemporary social struggle between the Deaf World, in which congenital deafness is treated like ethnicity (that is, as a linguistically distinct culture), and the technologies of normalization, for example, cochlear implantation, prescribed by biotechnoscientific and medical communities that view deafness as deficiency, infirmity or disability, Lane writes: "To imagine what deafness is like, I imagine my [hearing] world without sound—a terrifying prospect, and one that conforms quite well with the stereotype we [hearing persons] project onto members of the deaf community." The hearing person, thinking him or herself into deafness, can only imagine it to be something like the silent treatment, a sociological form of punishment, driving toward despair, even threatening the stimulation of and cognitive growth of the mind.

Swallowed up in such existential, if egoistic dread, colonizers consistently refuse to change their frame of reference to take in the world of the other. Rather, saturated in dread and consequently imputing their own egoistic frame of reference as standard, they override the alternative structures and values of the colonized. Caught in the swirls of their own existential anxieties, the colonizer is unable to see, other-wise. Yet, such dread and consequent benevolent paternalism proves economically and psychologically beneficial to the colonizer—placing and keeping its beneficiaries in a dependent relation.

While physiological variations categorized as disablement—for example, blindness, deafness, being crippled, to name but a few—may be among the most frequently employed metaphors of difference in scriptural, theological, and liturgical evocation, simply deploying the metaphor of disablement does not then insure that the lives of disabled persons have been taken into consideration: The reverse has, in fact, been true. So, for example, Augustine's demarcating of monstrous bodies did not enable Christians to see the person, but trained the imaginary to overlook and to speculate upon the other without actual engagement of and appreciation for her or his life. Reflecting on the use of the metaphor within literature, David Mitchell observes what may also be true for religious communities: "Disabled peoples' social invisibility has occurred in the wake of their perpetual circulation throughout literary history." As a "master metaphor," Mitchell continues, disablement "provides a means through which literature performs its social critique while simultaneously sedimenting stigmatizing beliefs about people with disabilities."[57] Building upon the assumption that disability is naturally obvious to everyone and, beyond doubt, a deficiency at that, the use of the *metaphor* of disablement actually participates in the dynamics of socially constructed exclusion of disabled persons. Reading back from the purportedly diseased heart of Africa, modern Christianity's deficient other, anthropologist Jean Comaroff warns that "metaphors of healing"—and given the Protestant need for scriptural legitimation, modern Christian healing practices have almost always, at least textually, relied upon the display of disablement and miraculous remediation—"have justified 'humane imperialism.'"[58] Again, this is not, to be sure, a blanket indictment of humanitarian concern or compassion, but a critique of the optics evidenced by making a spectacle of disability. A disabled person can, after all, be the picture of health but for the exclusionary social gaze and the consequent social, architectural, and economic structures of exclusion. So deploying the metaphor of disablement creates the crisis of and for redemption, rouses the anxieties, warrants the redemptive intrusion.

Could disablement be a keystone in Christianity's eschatological assumptions? in its soteriological economy of what bodies need and desire? And, thus, also in Western presumptions to culture and civility? While perennially posed as a problem in need of a solution, disability is no more natural nor innocent as a social construction than race or gender. It is, writes Rosemarie Garland Thomson, "a representation, a cultural interpretation of physical transformation."[59] For disabled persons, physiological disablement is not existentially a suffering: It is what is, the condition and possibility of our livingness, even our liveliness. But if it is a living and lively condition, then what happens to the Christian eschatological imagination, which has from Augustine through biotechnology turned upon the felt need for remediation to wholeness, on the dream of normative resolution, even now scientifically configured as the dream of human, indeed even humane, technical perfection? The eschatological teleology of Christianity, in other words, also has harbored the power of social construction of the disabled as marginal and therefore alien other.

Razing the Theaters of Cultural Power

From charity telethons to *Reader's Digest* and *Chicken Soup for the Soul* moralisms, from freak shows to biotechnology labs, from evangelical evocations toward missionary colonialism to repeated readings of Gospel miracle accounts, disabled persons have been made the show ponies of monstrosity, miracle, and mission. The stories are formulaic: Set up the image of the disabled as weak and handicapped, then valiantly rescue with superior power (which may be but evidenced by the supercrip's own amazing inner spirit)! Such scenarios expect persons with disabilities to give evidentiary testimony. Evidently, then, miracle stories or medicine shows—the fantastic of technobiopower, for example—actually serve as theater for imperial or dominant cultural power.

While miracle stories have typically been read as stories of miraculous remediation of the pitiful body (or, if not remediable, then as inviting humane imperialism), I suggest we turn our focus around: Might not these stories contribute to the dramaturgy of power necessary to and for imperial presence and for dominant cultural self-image? The dominant, observes James Scott, "have a collective theater to maintain which often becomes part of their self-definition."[60] While the public transcript of the colonizer or dominant power may "awe and intimidate [subordinates] into adurable and expedient compliance . . . [i]t may well be" Scott explains, "that insofar as the public transcript represents an attempt to persuade or indoctrinate anyone, the dominant are the subject of its attention. The public transcript [may serve] as a kind of self-hynopsis within ruling groups to back up their courage, to improve their cohesion, display their power, and convince themselves anew of their high moral purpose."[61] I am suggesting, in other words, that we read what have come to be called (following the history of Western biblical scholarship) the miracle stories—the stories that have been normatively framed for us as the healing of various disabling conditions—as discourses vying for and consolidating social power. This would equally include stories coming out of today's biotechnology labs, for example, "Was Blind But Now I See," as well as out of our theological texts.

If miracle stories, then, on the one hand, establish the incredible as a power of and among the dominant, their success must be equally, on the other hand, that of training a way of looking at the world, a way of being in it. That is, the function of miracle stories is to pass on the prevailing normativities. Disability is a social construct. It is a certain read of "bodily particularities in the context of social power relations."[62] An indisputable morphological condition, a somatic particularity, allows culture to assume that "difference . . . reside[s] in the person rather than in the social context." This is especially true in Western culture, where disability is medicalized and scientific rationalism prevails, such that, as regards persons with disabilities, "we are able to ignore our role in producing it."[63] But produce it a culture does, particularly as a containment strategy for what troubles the cultural ideal. As Thomson asserts, "The 'disabled' emerged . . . in tandem with its opposite: the abstract, self-possessed, autonomous individual" of and for industrial, now global, capitalism.[64]

To raze the theaters of cultural power, we might recall this observation: These miracle stories have insistently kept the body displayed upon the pallet silent. Disability is not allowed to speak, to narrate, but is used instrumentally. By definition, those in this condition have been assumed not able to speak up, such that representative others step in—like ventriloquists—as the voice of the voiceless. Spivak noted that in relation to territorial colonialism, Hegel's Absolute Spirit both required and foreclosed the presence of "the native informant" to mark the unconscious of nature. Spivak's argument suggests that, like disabled bodies in the history of literature, colonial natives are both discursively situated and silenced. They carry, she writes, "the mark of expulsion from the name of Man."[65] As Spivak puts it, following Freud and Lacan, the rejection of an incompatible idea—the full humanity of the displayed other—together with "the rejection of affect served and serves as the energetic and successful defense of the civilizing mission."[66] Using the shortcut of these rejections, Spirit has been turned into a dominant, controlling—indeed, colonizing—power. To promote Spirit as a practice of multiplying forms of corporeal flourishing, Christian practice must come to include an ethics of alterity where it has previously inscribed transcendence—a transcendence that now appears to cover over an affective, ethical lapse.[67] Such an ethics, then, will begin to swerve us from the heroic, redemptive path often taken in relation to one of modernity's "others."

Releasing Spirit from Effecting Normativity

To answer the question "from what must we be saved," Christianity has often borrowed against the lives of disabled persons. Within Christian discourse, Spirit has been the divine contour vested with the power to make things whole, to heal. But this turns Spirit into an aggressive energy of final causality. In modern theology, Spirit has been construed as the eschatological agent of the end and, therefore—as Wood observed in reflecting upon Bede—of the edges of humanity. Spirit has, as was already true for Augustine, been gaining its religious credibility by its treatment of disability—its textually performative ability to cure, to miraculously remediate, to solve and resolve the loose ends and ragged edges of the human body. We indeed must now consider the likelihood that wholeness is not only a psychological illusion, but the extent to which wholeness might also be an archeological and therefore eschatological illusion.

Consequently, Christianity's *doxological* hymns to Spirit—that, for example, life conquers death, that the body rises from the grave all glorious—have often been confused with *propositional* claims about the fabulous power of Spirit and its capacity for making whole. Yet, turning toward the thick texture of life, "it becomes apparent," as theologian Michael Lodahl puts it, commenting on Christian claims regarding the "[S]pirit" of the Easter account, "that the triumphalist claim of eschatological presence is overblown. . . . While Christian faith rightly holds, and holds tightly, to the answer of resurrection," Lodahl continues, "it cannot be glibly bandied about as though it represents the unambiguous manifestation of divine presence, or the irresistible in-breaking of the eschatological fulfillment."[68] No body knows this more keenly than the body of evidence at center stage of miracle stories—what Augustine already read as paradigmatic of the resurrection accounts. But if the miracle spectacle, with the disabled body at its theatrical center, consolidates a way of looking at the world (a perspective that I have variously called globally mediated Platonism or normative idealism), then Spirit has become an agent amenable to companioning imperial power.

To develop theologies of Spirit and healing praxes that can disrupt the ideation subjectifying the culture of globalization, which I earlier called the cult of public appearance, continuing conversation with disability studies in its convergences with postcolonial theory is needed. Interface with disability studies may disquiet the prevailing normativities of the body and, more particularly, the way in which those normativities have been soteriologically embedded in Christian theology. "Wholeness is in fact," as Davis counsels us, "a hallucination, a developmental fiction" attached to the mirror stage.[69] As Christian theologians, we must, in turn, consider the extent to which wholeness might also be an eschatological illusion. Turning to the liturgical evocation of wholeness at the heart of the religious imaginary, I apprehensively ask: Might the fact that we construe wholeness as the epitome of sacred encounter itself collude with the ideation of global empire, given the way in which wholeness is equated with conformity to cultural images disseminated as ideal self?

Insomuch as transcendence might be construed as the physics of Spirit, rethinking Spirit in its familiar, if contrarian correlation with disability—again as physical or cultural handicap—may help us ferret out a way of holding life sacred, of creating the conditions of entrustment to and for life as distinct from the transcendental imagination informing biotechnopower.

In her *Postcolonial Feminist Interpretation of the Bible*, Musa Dube recommends that women in decolonizing zones open out what she calls *"Semoya* space" (*Moya* means "Spirit")—a critical discourse zone supported by the biblical hermeneutic of "listening to what the Spirit says."[70] Pneumatology has been singularly definitive in the formation of African Independent Churches—churches seeking, that is, independence or liberation from "colonialism, capitalism, racism, and cultural chauvinism."[71] Describing these capacious new spaces attuned to Spirit, Dube explains that this new spatiality comes about by defining "new frameworks of imagining reality and building social, economic, and political structures that do not espouse patriarchal and imperial forms of relationships." If, in Dube's postcolonial reconstruction, Spirit both demands "the courage . . . of critical assessment of social structures" and occasions viable, new cultural imaginaries that can be feasibly incarnated or inhabited, then disability studies would insist that Spirit's physics (or divine efficacy) need not split transcendence from need, from relational interdependence.[72] Whereas Augustine separated transcendence from necessity, because necessity distracted the rational mind, necessity, given the liquidation of relations during modernity, can magnetically regenerate collectivities—communities of interface, that is. "It seems to me," writes Dawn DeVries, regarding the doctrine of creation through a disabilities perspective, "that the 'new creation' could be understood not in terms of a restoration of the 'old' order [i.e., nature as cosmic plenitude or Edenic paradise and thus as the cure visited upon persons with disabilities], but as the fashioning of a new order in which pain, exhaustion, and death are inducements to a new understanding of community."[73]

Refusing the modernist crises of personal defects, the plot of brokenness to wholeness, and therefore refusing to make life a capitalist production, persons with disability might give Spirit a renewed lease on life. To improvise upon the thought of Robert Murphy, author of the memoir *The Body Silent*: As the presence of the poor betrays the American dream, persons with disabilities constitute the refusal of not only the American ideal, but also Christian eschatological idealism.[74] We refuse to be resolved, saved, made whole, thereby invalid/ating eschatological idealism and, hopefully, some of its aggressive pity, preferring our histories of flesh, even as functionally enabled by technology. As the poet Mary Oliver puts it, "there is something more wonderful than gloss, than wholeness."[75] Strikingly, then, while the decolonized may hold strategic wisdom for dehegemonizing the citizens of global empire, crip culture may be key to unlocking its imprisoning normativities and mandatory public appearances.

MEDICINE SHOWS:
HUMANITARIANISM, HEALING, AND THE PHYSICS OF SPIRIT

> *Those whom modern disciplinary power would destroy it first makes visible.*
>
> —Michel Foucault,
> **Paraphrase by David Halperin,**
> *St. Foucault*

Recently, I had one of "those" moments: According to the rotation of faculty leadership for Anglican-Lutheran morning worship at the school of theology, it was my duty and delight to be wide-awake and prophetic at 7:00 A.M. I sat to prepare with the assigned lectionary texts: Ezekiel 47, the sacred river (this is looking promising for one ecologically minded, I thought!); Psalm 46, with mention of the city set on the fresh-flowing stream (too good to be true for a Vancouverite!); and, finally, the designated gospel account—John 5, the healing of the paralytic at the pool of Bethzatha with its well-known refrain, "Pick up your bed and walk." That did it: No way out now, I knew. Given my disabled body as unavoidable backdrop for this text, I would have to address the glaring perceptual incongruity of how I sat there leading morning worship—from a half-lotus position on the floor of the chapel—while trying to inflect my reading of the miracle account with, well, spiritual authority.

But must we assume a perceptual incongruity between my body and this text? If not, why did the gathered community intuitively, sympathetically panic—gasp, clench their guts, silently scream with their eyes, as if caught in the glaring headlights of a psychic dilemma—as I read the familiar narration? Many in the purview of persons with stigmatic disabilities euphemistically position themselves as having been visited by the grace of God—as in "there but for the grace of God go I." We Christians surely know better than to mean anything theological by it, and yet something got challenged into the open because my body was felt, even with attendant sympathy, to be posed in contradiction to the effectiveness of sacred power represented by the text. But what, pray tell, would be thrown askew as I—sitting half-lotus—read such a miracle account? Then again, what kind of spiritual authority can such a text possibly hope to perform if read by one on the slant?

In this chapter, I consider biblical, theological representations of the efficacy of Spirit as related to bodies exhibiting disabilities.[1] So that these readings and our consequent practices do not become unwitting agents of the ideals of global-ization, I bring critical theories to bear upon the optics through which we have read the biblical narratives assumed to authorize our theologies of healing and, by extension, social justice. The optics with which we have read spiritual power from healing narratives and in relation to "the sick and handicapped" have, in turn, come to inflect social-justice practice. Liberal Christian communities, for whom healing suffering—more than Word-based evangelism—constitutes our primary cross-cultural practice, have often rhetorically invoked our humanitar-ian responsibilities by way of a certain "prosthetic ventriloquism."[2] But assum-ing a representational responsibility to serve as voice of the voiceless suggests that certain assumptions about disability have been correlated with the impera-tive of Christian social justice—as, for example, the assumption that the voice-less or mute lack communicative capaciousness, or that oral speech, despite the preference among some peoples for the sign capacity of bodies, must be indica-tive of imago dei. Humanism assumed a particular somatic organization, in the Deleuzean sense—specifically valuing order, regularity, rationality, productivity, power as causal force, independence, and symmetry. And Western Christianity has not distinguished our understanding of healing from the cultural appropria-tion of bodies into this socioeconomic system of value.

By concentrating on our reading of biblical theologies, especially our reading of Jesus as one with the monolithic power of Spirit reaching out and healing the blind, the cripple, the outcast, I attempt to deconstruct our psychic cathection to normalcy. If "perfect love casts out fear" (1 John 4:18), including the fear that we hide in our structures of exclusion of persons with disabilities and the correlative assumptions about the pathetic passivity of the needy, devitalized other, then the work involved here has more to do with removing an affective mechanism of exclusion within liberal humanism than with fixing or curing the disabled. A truer humanitarianism opens out hospitable, generous psychic spaciousness—free from horror, fear, pity, disgust and avoidance, free from insisting upon one's own way, especially the way in which economics lodges its demands in the image of the self.

Returning finally to the theological theater, the question must be asked: Because "power has been central to any discussion of divine efficacy," what the-ology of Spirit—since Spirit's efficacy has somehow been configured over against its body of evidence, the de/monstrative, disabled body—emerges consequent to the end of the apartheid of disabled bodies?[3] In regards to disabled bodies (given the medical materialism of Western culture), Spirit has, I suspect, been made to cooperate with "the conventions of representation" in this later stage of mediated Platonism within which the ideal itself has become normative.[4] If, on the one hand, that suggests Spirit has become complicit with, even been used as, agent of the cultural colonization of the bodies of differently abled persons, it, on the other hand, might suggest that thinking Spirit on the slant could "disrupt the hegemonic way of seeing through which subjects make themselves dominant," veiled as this hegemonic discourse has been within liberal humanitarian works of mercy.[5] Transvaluing Spirit from guarantor of miraculous remediation (with its overinflated ideals of what makes life livable) toward the recognition of persons living the variability and vulnerabilities of bodies with real presence to life can allow Christians to get inventive about subjectivities that take their leave of contemporary, englobing capitalist economics.

From Jesus as Healer to Science as Savior

For those of us who live with disabilities, miracle stories such as John 5, because of a certain cultural preunderstanding with which these texts tend to be approached, might best be designated "texts of terror," to borrow here Phyllis Trible's famous feminist phrase, referring to stories such as the rape of Tamar and the sacrifice of Jephthah's daughter in the Hebrew testament. Such healing accounts, with their purported promise of miraculous remediation to normalcy, often contribute, not to the well-being of differently abled persons, but most frequently to our social and spiritual segregation.

Stephanie, a recent student, who moves through life with a wheelchair, told me of one of "those days" in her life. While waiting at the bus stop, a zealous woman approached and asked why Stephanie allowed herself to remain in the wheelchair when but a willing heart and the name of the Lord could get her on her feet. Trying initially for reason, Stephanie finally turned her head in a move intended both to try to break with the woman's intense fervor and to check for her bus. In that moment, the woman swatted Stephanie's arthritic knees with a newspaper and uttered with a cry, "In the name of the Lord, be healed!" Stephanie admits, now able to laugh, that her knees did in that moment tremble, but not for the reason for which the woman had hoped.

In the vicinity of such stories I, like other disabled bodies no doubt, begin to feel the walls of Christianity closing in. The stigmata of disability flushes red with shame and fury. The Spirit and its healing efficacy? Believe me, most disabled persons have been exposed to the fervor of its promise and the bite of its rejection when our bodies proved heretically resistant to cure.

Modern liberal theologies have not, to be sure, presumed that lightening bolts of supernatural power would work our instant remediation, and so those of us living with disabilities do not tend to be visited in this theological vicinity with inestimable expectations of a miraculous cure. Liberal theologians rather have tended—like the late Albert Schweitzer—to appreciate a modern worldview, both in terms of the demythologization of supernaturalism and of gratitude for modern medicine. During the nineteenth and twentieth centuries, a "major difference in paradigms of the body and in healing modes became itself an index to what was seen as the uniqueness and superiority of Christianity," explains William LaFleur. Appreciation for the medical miracle was consequently seen "as an index to . . . a civilization with 'enlightened' religion."[6] If I were forced to choose between creationist supernaturalism and such an enlightened view, my theological sentiments would not necessarily be located elsewhere than with a civilization with enlightened religion. Nonetheless, even in the vicinity of modern reason, a certain "reflexive patrolling function" gets effected by our reading and presentation of spiritual authority as exhibited in and through these healing narratives, such that those of us with modalities differing are nonetheless still left chilled to the bone and terrified.[7] Surely God wants me to be normal, right? That is, with two little eyes, two little ears, two little hands, and two little feet? While liberal theologies set aside supernaturalism, our close alliance with the miracle of modern medicine leaves us with a comparable anticipation of health as normalcy. But to wish me normal is no kindness, no generosity of spirit.

Normalcy, disabilities theorist Lennard Davis explains, developed as a sensibility within modern (nineteenth-and twentieth-century) Euro-Western science and is "less a condition of human nature than it is a feature of a certain kind of society."[8] With the development of statistical mathematics came the notion of an average person. Anyone who knows mathematical statistics could, of course, tell us that, given a select population that is then averaged, no person from that population may, in fact, fit the description of the norm. But this construct of the norm or average, used in relation to industrialization and also in turn to public health, led to utopian ideas of—here in the words of the French statistician Quetelet—"the perfectibility of the human species," such that "defects and monstrosities disappear more and more from the body."[9] The eugenic commitment of early statisticians was reinforced with an interpretation of Darwininan thought, Darwin's ideas being read to deposit disabled persons "along the wayside as evolutionary defectives to be surpassed by natural selection."[10]

When psychically inhabited, this cultural cathection to normalcy generates in the onlooker to disability a ridge of abjection, displacing the fear of and containing the variability and vulnerability of somatic life elsewhere—in that disabled body over there. A primal terror emerges along with the psychic commitment to the norm—an anxiety of dissolution or of losing control, perhaps something like the fear of falling off the flat edge of the earth. This fear can reasonably be dealt with by locating one's fear in the body of the disabled other. Naming this encounter with one's own denials now projected upon the surface of another as *unheimlich* or "uncanny," Freud observed that "this uncanny is in reality nothing new or alien, but something which is familiar and old—established in the mind and which has become alienated from it only through the process of repression."[11] When unhinged by the forces of fear, anxiety, and repulsion, an onlooker—consequent to an encounter with disability (the disabled encounter being but an encounter with one's own psychic abject)—can then move to insist upon reorganizing the body of the other in a prescribed and familiar way—even thinking, thereby, to be benevolent.[12] "The fear evoked by the presence of people with disabilities," theorist Paul Longmore writes, "has produced two simultaneous and predictable responses: they have been stigmatized, and they have been subjected to relentless exertions to fix them."[13]

Even where architecture and social geography may have been reworked toward greater inclusion of persons with differing modalities (still very rare), a psychological apartheid preserves a sociocultural preference for appearing wholesome and functionally integrated, for being like everyone else, or so it is said. Rather than admitting how differently abled we all are and how the ingress of time, environment, and work affect the life of the body, we protect a certain transcendentalized version of the body and of life as average or normal. In this way, disability, "like so many other [modern binary categories]—straight/gay, male/female, black/white, rich/poor—is part of an ideology of containment and a politics of power and fear."[14] To be valued members of society, persons must assume or resume normalcy. They must organize themselves toward the values of publicly acceptable appearance, independent function, and productivity, the key values of capitalist economics.

The template of normalcy and its contrary—lack, deficit, deformation, deviation, degeneracy—were deployed as maps of Western Christianity's social mission of the nineteenth and twentieth centuries. The constituting of the disabled as also the wretched of the earth were outcroppings of this utopian, scientific hope of normalcy. Viewed as aberrations or deviations, these bodies were fixed in an objectifying gaze and subjected to salvific social cures.

We have learned to call this concern for the aberrant other "compassion," but have not dared to question the modern medicinal and economic organization of the body itself. Yet wrote the twentieth-century philosopher Theodor Adorno, "A psycho-analysis of today's prototypical culture . . . would . . . show the sickness proper to the time . . . to consist precisely in normality."[15] Such an ideology of normalcy, a psychopathology so important to the economic flows of capitalism, has become hidden in our theological anticipations, especially in relation to the healing of suffering and, thus, in our theologies of Spirit. Spirit has been conflated with the scopic dynamics that generate the bourgeois—whole and idealized—body. Spirit, in this vein, generates a zone of respectability, propriety, and civility.

Meanwhile, however, scholars of the historical Jesus quest, including Marcus Borg and John Dominic Crossan, have insisted that (and I quote Borg) "it is virtually indisputable that Jesus was a healer and exorcist."[16] Again in a subsection titled, "The Power of Spirit," Borg reiterates his point (with a slightly more provocative uptake): "That Jesus was a 'wonder-worker' is historically very firmly attested."[17]

Jesus, the Healer: this is one of the winsome pictures that has been reemerging, given the relaxation of the most intense grip of twentieth-century Bultmannian demythologization and the Western hope for religious reenchantment. Borg and Crossan have been working against merely symbolic readings of the purported healing accounts in the synoptic Gospels, insisting that these Jesus stories must have some reach into historical practice in order even to have been memorable.[18]

Although disavowing the scientific positivism of the historical Jesus quest, Rita Nakashima Brock goes on in her now classic Christology text *Journeys by Heart* (if a fifteen-year-old feminist text can begin to disturb the notion of the classic) to suggest what may be the rationale behind this historical recuperation—that healing be "understood as a normative statement about the sacred within [contemporary] Christian community."[19] In other words, the recovery of these purported healing stories may prove to be models of christological praxis in a time in which, as Brock puts it, "our very survival depends upon how we come to terms with our pain."[20]

For Brock, as for the scholars in the Jesus quest (though quite differently construed), this recuperation of healing praxis seems inconceivable without the conjoint recuperation of Spirit, of pneumatology. Thus, Borg writes: "The mighty deeds of Jesus, exorcisms and healings alike, were the product of the power which flowed through him as a holy man. His powers were charismatic, the result of his having become a channel for the power of the other realm, that which Jesus and his contemporaries also called Spirit."[21] On the surface, at least, there does appear within the synoptic Gospels to be an interesting coincidence of emergence among metaphors of disablement, the practice of healing, and the construct of Spirit. Read what we have increasingly learned to call the resistance literature of the Christian testament, and we find that what have been called miracle stories make up much of the synoptic content.

"Go and tell John: The blind see, the lame walk, the deaf hear": As we have already seen, these banner headlines of the synoptic gospels Matthew (11:4) and Luke (7:22) were penned amid conditions not wholly unlike our own—within an englobing empire. And yet, if Spirit might have emerged as a construct of sacred activity within resistance literature (although one cannot necessarily assume any ratio of resistance to accommodation suggested thereby, or how a colonized culture can use empire's discourse for its own well-being), what is to prevent this renewed figure of Jesus the Healer, filled with the power of Spirit, from becoming Doctor of and for "the Great Dream of Normalcy," that dream being proffered via contemporary globalizing media and technobiopower?[22]

"To make healing normative within Christian community": if I do not disagree with the temperament and trajectory of this recuperative and reconstructive commitment, which Brock has named for us, perhaps you can nevertheless sense my dilemma. Will differently abled persons be subjected to yet more terror or pity or technological redemption? The Spirit of the historical Jesus quest, the epic tale of Jesus the Healer, shrouded in all its purported historical realism (and whether evangelically or liberally voiced), is all too similar to the spirit of Western science and culture.

For example, although persons with disabilities have been the curios of much religious and scientific speculation, we have historically been refused discursive voice in either of these regards (Did anyone ask us if or, more likely, how we want to work with science? Did anyone ask us if we need to be made whole in order to be spiritual creatures?). What formation of power, religious and/or scientific, does this curious suppression, this religiocultural perimeter of silence into which disabled persons are discarded, make up and make culturally real? If healing were to become the epitome of sacred praxis of Christianity, then persons with disability should, I would insist, finally be allowed to speak back to this normalizing spirit, which has until now mobilized scientific and even Western Christian healing practice as well as Christianity's social-justice mission.

Of Miracles and Medicine Shows

In Adolf von Harnack's early-twentieth-century reconstruction of Christian origins, Christianity "deliberately and consciously . . . assumed the form of 'the religion of . . . healing.'" Whereas "religion had . . . been intended originally . . . for the sound," von Harnack surmises, Christianity—"a religion for the sick"—won over the Roman Empire. To be sure, "Into this world of craving for salvation the preaching of Christianity made its way," von Harnack writes, but "long before it had achieved its final triumph by dint of an impressive philosophy of religion, its success was already assured by the fact that it promised and offered salvation—a feature in which it surpassed all other religions and cults." Von Harnack's portraiture of Jesus resonates with his construction of Christian origins: "Jesus proclaimed a new message . . . but . . . did his work as a Savior or healer." Indeed, "Jesus appeared among his people as a physician . . . as the Savior or healer of [persons]." And as to Jesus' bedside manner, von Harnack observes that "Jesus says very little about sickness; he cures it. . . . [Jesus] sees himself surrounded by crowds of sick folk; he attracts them, and his one impulse is to help them . . . . No sickness of the soul repels him. . . . Nor is any bodily disease too loathsome for Jesus. In this world of wailing, misery, filth, and profligacy, which pressed upon him every day, he kept himself invariably vital, pure, and busy."[23]

Hardly can one ignore the likelihood that Roman colonization in those centuries surrounding the Common Era, like the colonial contact of Europe with the Americas or Africa, left in its wake a devastating rampage of diseases, the razed clear-cuts of the trusts of kin and clan, as well as ruptured systems of care giving. And hardly would I want to dismiss a materialized, therapeutic Christianity, as von Harnack has envisioned, which "formed a permanent establishment for the relief of sickness and poverty."[24] Rather, what concerns me here is von Harnack's particular construction of a binary dichotomy between a "vital, pure and busy" Jesus set over against the miserable wash of humanity—all of whom, he notes, Christianity assumed to be "in a state of disability."[25] Why this portrait of a Jesus so singularly morally virtuous, energetic and industrious, when other children born "Upon a Midnight Clear" tend, like Salman Rushdie's *Midnight's Children*, to be mutilated, hybridized, cracked enough to have radiolike telepathy and foreknowledge, and of more compromised genealogies than would please Freud? Take note, too, of that silent, penetrating, knowing look that accompanies Jesus' impulse to heal in von Harnack's portraiture. Does not Jesus' bedside manner seem amazingly resonant with that "silent and gestureless" clinical gaze Foucault discerned as emergent with the birth of the clinic and the modern bioregime?[26] Obviously, von Harnack's Jesus would not himself have been among the Crip Nation of the blind, lame or deaf, despite the predominant Hebrew testamental inflection of the portrait of Jesus as one "unseemly" (Isa 53). Looking into the mirror of this Jesus portrait, do we not find a liberal consciousness, filled with all-knowing compassion, yet framed itself in bodily perfection? A Jesus that, as biblical scholar Stephen Moore found elsewhere in God's [twentieth-century] beauty parlor, seems incandescent even?[27] The dichotomy upon which von Harnack pivots his recuperation of origins, a dichotomy between the vital and the disabled, might rather be the optic named modern realism.

What von Harnack found in the origins of Christianity is a socially constructed way of viewing the world, a cultural optics specifically generated during modernity. The literary genre of modern realism, disabilities theorist Leonard Davis explains, emerged in the late eighteenth century "as an ideological form of symbolic production whose central binary is normal-abnormal." Further, "This dialectic works in a fundamental way to produce plots," such that deviance is encountered and "cure as closure is the rule." Or variously said, modern realism, where "real means average," emplots itself as "strategic abnormality overcome." Observing that modern novels seem to feature a multiplicity of disabled bodies, but set only as stage or plot props over and against the central protagonist, Davis concludes that "narratives involving disability always yearn for the cure, the neutralizing of the disability. . . . [T]he fantasy of normality needs the abjection of disability to maintain a homeostatic system of binaries." This narrative commitment to the redemption or cure of deviance—whether by repair, by rescue from social censure, or by extermination—supports the development of the modern subject, Davis argues, training the subject to desire "the ideological fantasy of" and "the comfort of bourgeois norms" by denigrating disability.[28] When reading miracle stories as events of healing, especially as events of cure, are we not performatively reinforcing the modernist epistemological optic?

When read through the optics of modern realism, encounters between the protagonist Jesus and a person with a disability become medicine shows, scenes in which disability read as degeneracy seems to have but a bit part, in which disabled characters are but stage props in the constituting of modern, even postmodern or transcendental globalized subjectivity. The miracle cure—miraculous remediation—can be, according to the redemptive plot line of modern realism, the only viable conclusion to such a story. Given these optics, we indeed assume the account to be about miracles—about either supernatural or medicinal interventions in nature. Read in this way, these narratives echo the commitment of modern science to normalcy, that of modern medicine to the redemptive cure, and that of modern culture to the bourgeois, aesthetically wholesome, and productive body.

What persistently disappears behind the stage of modernist realism as it lodges itself in a biologized and medicalized commitment to the normal are the socioeconomic determinations of the ideology of normalcy—the utility and desirability of the body according to the dictates of capitalist economics. The belief that disability is an intractable physicality, that to be healthy is to be other than disabled, that normalcy excludes variations in physical modalities: These contentions also allow the emergence of the category miracle, even as we have come rationally to dispute it or scientifically to qualify it (as medical miracle, for example). If we remove our modern realist optics, miracle (in its supernaturalist register) appears as a built modernist, theobiblical category comparable to what postcolonial biblical scholar R. S. Sugirtharajah identified in terms of the "Pauline missionary trips."[29] As Eric Eve notes in opening his study of *The Jewish Context of Jesus' Miracles*, "In relation to the Bible, 'miracle' is a potentially misleading term. . . . No biblical writer shows awareness of such a view."[30]

Incanting the Foucaultian truism that "power operates—and therefore can only be opposed—discursively,"[31] Davis elsewhere notes that "this normalcy must constantly be enforced in public venues (like the novel), must always be creating and bolstering its image by processing, comparing, constructing . . . images of normalcy and the abnormal."[32] But the public venues of the medicine show of remediation are by no means limited to the novel. Such shows are staged throughout both the discourses of Christology, including its liturgical venues, and the discourse of biotechnoscience.

Since no medicine show is complete without a smooth-tongued practitioner selling miracle cures, evoking that scene no doubt leaves persons of faith uneasy when sham is so suggestively situated next to Christology. It is by invoking the concept of the medicine show, however, that I critically examine the optics of modernist historical realism which generates the fascinating spectacle and biographical portrait of Jesus as healer with Spirit as cure-all. Addressing earlier stages of historical Jesus realism, theologian Martin Kahler (1835–1912) lamented the propagandistic purpose thereof: "When Christology appears in the form of a 'Life of Jesus,' there are not many who will perceive the stage manager behind the scenes, manipulating, according to his own dogmatic script, the fascinating spectacle of a colorful biography."[33] To be sure, as Barry Henault acknowledges in his essay "Is the 'Historical Jesus' a Christological Construct?" the construct of the historical Jesus has at times and in certain contexts had "an implicit antidogmatic" function. Nevertheless, it is the way in which Christianity does look to the historical Jesus as a model or pattern to support "ego consciousness," as Henault puts it, especially as that modern project of character development makes use of persons with disabilities, that concerns me here.[34]

The real illusion of the medicine show happens among the audience: The theater of geeks, freaks, and grotesques, all needing to be cured, seem but the prompts for the inner subjective theater of crisis, lack, and repression that churns in the guts of most modern persons. The technology of subjective normalcy punishes not only persons with disabilities, as we have noted; but this theatrical performance becomes introjected as anxiety, shame, or fear around how normal bodies should perpetually remediate their deviances, which multiply under speculation. As sociologist Zygmunt Bauman repeatedly observes, capitalism requires subjects in perpetual crisis: "Privatization of the ['modernizing'] impulse means compulsive self-critique born of perpetual self-disaffection."[35] The deviations of bodies and subjectivity opened out in the name of health has become the consuming crisis of postmodern subjectivity—literally, a consuming crisis, in terms of personal (as opposed to political) attention and appropriation of resources.[36]

Christianity has disseminated miracle stories to justify this cultural processing or sorting of bodies. Our readings, even liberal readings that expressly deny the supernatural, nevertheless induce a certain performance of the body and of moral life. Recourse to such narratives as miracle stories discursively establishes a cultural boundary among bodies. When viewed through the optics of modernist realism, disability locates the boundary where bodies join modern, capitalist culture—or are otherwise stamped "invalid." What Foucault called "the advance of bio-power," along with its "proliferation of the modern categories of anomaly," seems to have gotten lodged within Christianity's understanding of Spirit and practice of healing.[37] I wonder if liberal Christianity, finding relief in the intellectual concomitants of modern science, nevertheless has handed over its theological anthropology to modern medicine.

Certain readings of Christian biblical narratives discursively operate to stage or legitimate the performance—in both religious practice and biotechnoscience—of the medicine shows of miraculous remediation. That the miracle or healing stories have had culturally performative and determinative power, comparable to what Davis identifies in the modern novel, suggests that we have inhabited this binary of the average/disabled or normal/abnormal and its eliminative closures by cure, assuming them to be of the physics of Spirit. Despite the fact that "disabled persons are very visible in the Gospels," as Elizabeth Stuart acknowledges in an essay titled "Disruptive Bodies," they seem nevertheless consistently to be disappeared from stage, to be "rendered invisible by the healing touch of Jesus."[38] Persons with disabilities tend miraculously to evaporate or to be disappeared into the law of the average.

In that vein, biblical scholar Gerd Theissen, a leading researcher on New Testament miracle stories, maintains that "the miracles of Jesus . . . were unique because of their manifestation of divine power."[39] In Theissen's own words, "The narrators know that where all doctors . . . have failed . . . Jesus heals."[40] Though I find Theissen tripping unconsciously over some of his best insights around the social power of the miraculous (to which I will return later), he returns again and again to the modernist theme of the intractability of physical deviance and its need for divine, rehabilitative corrective. So he writes, for example, that "the central feature of the miracle stories is an experience of limitation, which challenges the human being . . . to transcend this limitation. . . . Miracle stories are symbolic actions of human subjectivity in which the real negativity of existence is transcended."[41]

Theissen seems to assume that, as was true of modernity, the somatic-material or biological must be the limit to be transcended. Theissen concludes his study:

> The structure of the sacred has left its mark on the miracle stories. . . .
> This is the final implication of the miracle stories: they will rather deny
> the validity of all previous experience than the right of human suffering
> to be eliminated. They proclaim this right as a sacred law, as something
> absolute. In symbolic actions they make a radical refusal to submit to the
> experienced negativity of human existence.[42]

Such an explanation repeats modernity's tendency to visit such frustrations of the flesh as limit, finitude, and nature, as if these were oppressions of a life. Cured of such apparently gross negativity, disabled persons supposedly slip into the crowd of the validated—our difference miraculously remediated (not!). There's something about that healing touch of Jesus and its ability to disappear us that persons with disabilities have come to suspect, especially in terms of using us for its own narrative conclusions: Theologically speaking, the unique Spirit power of Jesus appears to prove out the cultural law of the average.

Western biotechnoscience seems to possess something of the same ability to disappear persons with disability. I am sitting in the chair of my physiatrist's office. He is trying to offer comfort after yet another round of prosthetics has failed. Two years of physical rehabilitation so as to learn prosthetic choreography and five years of technological labor have come to this: The stronger I get, the more unlikely the prosthetics fit. A prosthesis is generated at a cost of approximately U.S. $45,000. Before the end of the ninety-day warranty period, I have literally gained enough strength to kick off my own leg. Don't worry, Sharon, my doctor assures me. In your lifetime, science will develop permanent limb replacements that are surgically fused to your skeletal frame. You'll fall asleep with it, shower with it, make love with it—24/7! For me, this sounds but the latest science-fiction fabrication, the most extreme version of which greeted me while I was yet in intensive care and on full life-support systems—the promise of cloning. As diametrically opposed as this biotechnoscience fiction might seem to what we have by convention called faith healing, both scenes presume some transcendent cure-all—as if that were the only way we could make peace with existence.

This spirit cure-all augurs for persons with disabilities nothing so promising as healing, but smacks instead of social entombment, the socioeconomic death sentence—the refusal of our body-selves as living and lively and capacious as is. Every time persons with disability turn around, the wholesome spiritual body and its demanding cultural corollary of normative wholesomeness (even technologically, prosthetically incarnated) taunt us from one direction or another—promising us, cajoling us, demanding us to conform, to be made whole, to pick up our bed and walk. While I address this more directly in a subsequent chapter, "Putting My Foot (Prosthesis, Crutches, Phantom) Down," let me note in passing here that the cure and restoration of the disabled body has been as necessary a foundational fiction for the technological sublime, for the cultural belief in the wonder-working power of science, as it has been for modern belief in the power of the Spirit in Jesus. Nor should the spirit of biotechnoscience be construed as anything but religiously inspired, since science did assume, as feminists have noted, the power of second birth. While Western science and Western Christianity pretend to have nothing in common at this late stage of modernity, they have shared at the very least the imagination of transcendent efficacy. Even as I concentrate here on the optics of engaging biblical texts, we'll need simultaneously to keep our minds on technobiopower and its spiritual imaginary, its aspirations to eradicate all suffering. In each medicine show, persons with disabilities find this cure-all to be visited against our bodies—with which if we have our grumbles (like the rest of you!), persons with disabilities nevertheless have no inherent death wish.

Voice of the Voiceless?
Christianity's Prosthetic Ventriloquism

For those of us raised in the ethos of liberal, social-justice-oriented Christianity, Jesus' hosting of the banquet of outcasts, that is, "When you have a banquet, invite the poor, the crippled" (Luke 14), has been paradigmatic. That John Dominic Crossan, one of the principle scholars in the contemporary historical Jesus quest, has identified Luke's parable of the banquet for "the poor, the maimed, the lame and the blind" (14:15-24) as exemplary for what it meant to "render . . . the Jewish God of justice present on earth" would hardly shake, rattle, or level any of our presumptions.[43] While many of us have developed an uncomfortable awareness that these Jesus portraits may have their supersessionist elements, such commitments as evoked by this banquet scene have been staged over the last several decades against sociopolitical scenarios that had previously legalized their disgust against the humanity of any number of the rest of us—women, gays, blacks, and so on. Fearing similar socioeconomic structures of exclusion based on the theologizing of disgust elsewhere, we in the Christian justice communities, taking such a scene to heart, assume to speak to economic and political systems as if we were the vocal prosthesis of a marginalized group, as if we were, that is, the voice of the voiceless. But as anthropologist Jean Comaroff warns from South Africa, retrospectively prophetic: "Colonial relations found an alibi in the ailing human body."[44] As soon as disability studies begin to disrupt the passivity and cure associated with miracles and healing, we must also consider the colonial deployments of the metaphor of disablement and its purported cures.

Disabled persons have often been read, I have suggested, following Davis' literary analysis, as stock characters in biblical narratives, as bodies that aggravate and then illustrate the redemptive plot line. In the modernist mode, such characters equally serve to locate that other massive objectification, the oppressed, the outcast, or, simply, the other. Consequently, Christianity's social-justice practices have often presumed to effect the redemption of the oppressed, the poor, the sick, and the handicapped. While Western Christianity's assumption of social mission suggests an earnest attempt to move out of self-preoccupation, even (as already with Albert Schweitzer) to amend the ramifications of first-stage colonialism, postcolonial theories of recent years have been extremely critical of Christianity's social mission. Gayatri Spivak, for example, has consistently maintained that "the gravity of imperialism was that it was ideologically cathected as 'social mission.'"[45] Presumed needy, the objects of pity and therefore of mission, disabled and—inevitably, rhetorically—poor bodies have been used in no small way emotionally to motivate what theorists have called the politics of rescue or the politics of saving, politics informed by the eugenic science of normalcy.

Early decolonizing theorist Ashis Nandy, critically observing that "colonialism minus a civilizational mission is no colonialism at all," indicted missionary

zeal—shared among Western development and religious forces—as more destructive, because more psychologically insidious, than the earliest phase of conquering robber barons. Observing that "genocides, ecodisasters and ethnocides are
but the underside of corrupt sciences and psychopathic technologies wedded to
new secular hierarchies," Nandy goes on specifically to name "the ideology of
normality" as among the psychopathologies informing modern technology and
science, further noting that the polarity of "the normal and the abnormal" and
"the liberated and the savable" developed in the wake of such sciences.[46]

At least as much as offering remediation, what has been effected by the discursive cultural implementation of the dialectic of vitality over against disability is the
fixing of cultural boundaries, including acceptable socioeconomic boundaries, of
the body, all within a discourse that appears to be interested in, indeed invested in,
personal and social health. As Foucault noted, "these [modernist] modes of classification, control, and containment" of the body, within which "the mediation of
a science . . . and the practice of exclusion" are yoked, come equally enthusiastic
about "a distinctive tradition of humanitarian rhetoric on reform and progress."[47]
Further, as disabilities theorists David Mitchell and Sharon Snyder observe, "disabled populations [have] been used to solidify and secure definitions of the altru-
istic service and moral commitments of diagnostic disciplines."[48] Consequently,
the social-justice pathos and politics of Spirit have often resembled what culture
theorist Rey Chow calls "sentimental sponsorship of 'the oppressed'"[49]: While
presuming to heal or redeem the life of the other, thinking "the wretched" or "the
oppressed"—like thinking "the handicapped" or "the disabled"—truncates the
physics of love, yet again depositing Western culture's ego-abject, that is, what we
cannot tolerate about ourselves, in the place of the other.

Assuming to speak as the voice of the voiceless, an act of "prosthetic
ventriloquism,"[50] reflects—conversely, of course—Western assumptions of self-
hood and cultural values. Warning us about the power of representationalism,
anthropologists Jean and John Comaroff write: "The essence of colonization
inheres less in political overrule than in seizing and transforming 'others' by the
very act of conceptualizing, inscribing and interacting with them on terms not of
their choosing; in making them into pliant objects and silenced subjects of our
scripts and scenarios; in assuming the capacity to 'represent' them, the active
verb itself conflating politics and poetics."[51] Rather than saving or healing the
other, our love may then actually end up insisting upon its own way, insisting
upon our own psychopathological orientation toward normalcy, that is.

The Spirit of the Contemporary Historical-Jesus Quests

Insomuch as Christianity's social mission has often presumed to map itself by analogy to the life of Jesus, consideration of recent christological theologies from the quest for the historical Jesus would seem appropriate. While considering both Marcus Borg and John Dominic Crossan's Historical Jesus, my focus will be upon the divine character that haunts the premises of this medical practice—namely, Spirit (or Jesus, to the extent that he has been christologically configured as a unique vessel of ineffable transcendent or pneumatic potency). Under the sign of Spirit, a presumed cure-all when read through the lens of modern realism, rides—I am contending—the legitimating of a socioeconomic discourse that has become for us an unexamined regime of theological truth about bodies. Again, the optics of modern realism include the modernist dichotomy of normal/abnormal, its redemption or narrative closure by way of cure, and the tendency to inscribe "biology, rather than social institutions, as the causal agent of physical aberrancy."[52] While the physics of Spirit as miraculous remediation to normalcy was perhaps more overt in early stages of modern christology, within the most recent historical Jesus quest the impulse to cure has, it seems, been transmuted into the politics of compassion, engendered upon analogy to the agency of the Jesus exegetically and archeologically discovered.[53]

For both Borg and Crossan, Jesus was a paradigmatic Spirit practitioner, a healer. Borg, for example, insists that Jesus was "grounded in the world of the Spirit," that "Jesus' relationship to the Spirit was the source of everything that he was," and that, consequently, "Christian life is not about believing but about entering into a relationship with that to which the Christian tradition points . . . [namely,] the Spirit. . . . The most crucial fact about Jesus was that he was a 'spirit person,' a 'mediator of the sacred,' one of those persons in human history to whom the Spirit was an experiential reality," Borg claims.[54] As "a channel for the power of the other realm," Jesus' mediatory work was principally as healer and exorcist, Borg claims. Hence, "Jesus' healings were the result of 'power'"—namely, the power of the Spirit. But just as he has established this pneumatic aspect of Jesus ministry, Borg qualifies such miracle, healing, and exorcistic works, noting that these were culturally common at the time of Jesus.[55]

Borg is consequently driven by the demands of his Christological suppositions to locate the uniqueness of Jesus elsewhere—specifically in what he comes to call the "politics of compassion."[56] Explaining that the synoptic healing narratives should be seen not as exhaustive, but as typical, he offers this summary: "Sometimes Jesus healed by word. . . . Most often touching was also involved. When a leper came to him, Jesus was 'moved with pity' and touched him."[57]

Extending inclusive touch across the ridge of abjection apparently serves as a conduit of Spirit. "For Jesus," Borg writes, "compassion was the central quality of God and the central moral quality of a life centered in God."[58] Among the Jewish renewal movements spawned under Roman occupation, the politics of compassion were, as Borg sees it, uniquely innovative: "Whereas the first-century Judaism spoke primarily of the holiness of God, Jesus spoke primarily of the compassion of God."[59] And elsewhere: "In the message and activity of Jesus, we see an alternative social vision: a community shaped not by the ethos and politics of purity, but by the ethos and politics of compassion."[60]

Borg gathers up what he considers to be the import of Jesus' politics: "The stories of his healings shatter the purity boundaries of his social world. He touched lepers and hemorrhaging women."[61] Jesus' practice of "open commensality"—Borg here notably agreeing with by borrowing Crossan's terminology—exposed him to impure people, to "'dirty' people" as for example "women, the untouchables, the poor, the maimed, and the marginalized."[62] Here, Spirit has morphed into a community-logic of "boundary-subverting inclusiveness," a political vision relevant, Borg insists, for today's Christians.[63] Yet as transnational feminist Sharene Razack has observed, sympathetic touch can, across hierarchical social boundaries, accrue as social and/or spiritual superiority to the supposed helper—while applauding Jesus' and our supposed heroic transgression.[64] Despite the familiar theological sway mapped by this biblical exegesis and historical recuperation, might Razack's insight into the supposed boundary subverting trespass occasion at least further reflection on the culturally rutted physics of our movements?

Meanwhile, John Dominic Crossan, author of *The Historical Jesus* and *Jesus, A Revolutionary Biography*, identifies Jesus as a cynic philosopher at the hub of what he programmatically calls "open commensality"—a "social program" intended "to rebuild a society upward from its grass roots . . . on principles of religious and economic egalitarianism" by way of reciprocally exchanging "miracle and table" or, variously, "free healing and common eating."[65] In Crossan's reconstructive imagination, itinerants—whether peasant Jewish cynics, who were something like "hippies in a world of Augustan yuppies," or displaced householders, now among the world's expendables —carried "free healing . . . directly to the peasant homes" where their thaumatological work was received with "free sharing of whatever [the peasants] had in return."[66] This program of "open commensality," Crossan asserts, undercuts—not in theory, but in practice—the universal human tendency to make and maintain discriminations: "The deliberate conjunction of magic and meal, . . . free compassion and open commensality, was a challenge launched not just on the level of Judaism's strictest purity regulations, or even on that of the Mediterranean's patriarchal combination of honor and shame, patronage and clientage, but at the most basic level of civilization's eternal inclination to draw lines, invoke boundaries, establish hierarchies."[67] Indeed, in a world where the table functioned as "society's mesocosmic mirror," where "the very social function of table . . . [was] to establish a social ranking by what one eats, how one eats, and with whom one eats . . . ," the logic of Spirit, Crossan asserts, precisely precluded "distinctions and discriminations."[68] Spirit, quite simply, levels caste and class presumptions.

Contrary to Borg, Crossan undercuts Jesus as a mediator of the divine, insisting that "He was neither broker nor mediator but, somewhat paradoxically, the announcer that neither [broker nor mediator] should exist between humanity and divinity or between humanity and itself. Miracle and parable, healing and eating were calculated to force individuals into unmediated physical and spiritual contact with God . . . and . . . with one another."[69] Insisting that even human-divine relations had to be "without hierarchy," Crossan underlines his point: "And I emphasize that it involved not so much Jesus' personal power as communal empowerment."[70] In regard to the itinerants: "They share a miracle . . . and they receive in return a table and a house. Here, I think, is the heart of the original Jesus movement, a shared egalitarianism of spiritual and material resources. I emphasize this as strongly as possible and I insist that its materiality and spirituality, its facticity and symbolism cannot be separated."[71] The physics of Spirit for Crossan, then—at least in terms of where he wants to point us—are to be located as trajectories of communal economies, especially where there is effected material resource sharing, but also where spiritual energies—including sharing without distinction, if also healing—effect the well-being of bodies.

Yet let it be noted that there's something of a conspicuously perfect Jesus, a hero, in the midst of Crossan's communalist politics—one preserved from Hellenistic Platonism's spiritualizing tendencies, one who was sarcophilic, one who was enough of an insider to be able to reach to the outside and yet enough of a Robin Hood to earn the seal of approval from those who were raised to question authority. Crossan's recovery of Christian origins—like Borg's—celebrates a socially ingenious Jesus and his unique "religiopolitically subversive" touch, a touch that reaches across so as to dismantle caste boundaries, to overturn spiritual and social hierarchies, to erase somatic distinctions.[72] That presumed extension of inclusion that presses flesh across a psychic ridge of abjection clearly still moves from a body on the clean, intact, and superior side to touch upon the mutilated and dirty. Crossan, for example, claims Mark as a more politically radical gospel than Luke, for Luke—despite having ten lepers in his variation of this healing account—never asserted such a socially transgressive and redemptive touch as did Mark.[73] Although Crossan recognizes Mark's use of the story as a confrontation with the temple, he insists upon "the first or original level" of bodily healing, as if touch breached Jewish social regulation and, further, as if touch of outcasts were not only illicit, but consequently subversively redemptive.

In their various propositions, Crossan and Borg have similarly swept bodies differing into a pool of permanent social outcasts—namely (here in Borg's words), "women, the untouchables, the poor, the maimed, and the marginalized."[74] Yet this sociological categorization of the marginal suspiciously resembles modernity's designation of degenerates—"those groups whom Foucault describes as the 'internal enemies' of the bourgeois male" (namely, "women, racial others, the working class, people with disabilities, in short all those who would weaken the vigorous bourgeois body and state").[75] Within ancient classical and medieval to early modern European culture, however—and thus I am assuming the synoptics to be within the broader philosophical purview of this concern—the ideal body toward which we aspire in the name of health could never, by definition, be found in this world. While the category of "the grotesque . . . was inversely related to the concept of the ideal," Davis explains, "the grotesque was "a signifier of the people, of common life." Contrary to the way in which disability today names the cultural stigmatization of an indisputable morphological condition and thereby singles out its victims, the grotesque in earlier eras, Davis concludes, "signified common humanity."[76] Both Crossan and Borg, in other words, assume what has been obvious to moderns—that healing and miracle stories were written about cure of or compassion for individuated disabled or diseased bodies, that touch and inclusion across social boundaries proves religiously and sociopolitically redemptive of alterity, especially of bodies evidencing degeneracy.

Based on modern sociological organization, both Borg and Crossan discover a Jesus who, whether a pneumatically infused magician or grass-roots organizer, was a healer-hero. As with Crossan, so with Borg: each—in spite of what they state as their intentions—assumes the superior privilege of the eye of the beholder, the one—Jesus, as the practitioner of compassion—who surveys and judges, if even in the name of health. The commitment to the impressive body remains hidden within the invocation to reach out—from the locus of the culturally superior and intact—to the defectives. Crossan, to be sure, imagines much greater communal interaction and mutuality as constitutive of healing practice, and his notion of healing comes coupled with socioeconomic import; but even he retains a Jesus who seems not to have been counted among his list of outcasts.

Performatively reading the normal as set over against the abnormal, even so as to countersuggest inclusiveness, does not disperse social dominance, despite Borg and Crossan's best hopes. Inclusion does not undo the hegemony of normalcy, nor does it participate in transvaluation. Rather, such politics can preserve a normative, if nominally multicultural community as a dominant base within which the different are paternalistically accommodated. Further to the point, as feminists have insisted since the first wave thereof, touch—compassion being an extension of touch for both Borg and Crossan—can objectify, especially when the rules of touch have been hierarchically authorized. Because persons with disabilities have been the touchable and specular object of experimental study and demonstration, and indeed are subject to domestic abuse as an outcome of relating with our differing modalities and vulnerabilities, being touched might not necessarily be experienced as socially liberating.

An insidious conflation of sympathetic humanism with superiority, indeed with economic colonialism, can transpire, as Edward Said's now famous postcolonial essay on "Jane Austen and Empire" insinuated, under the cloak of the development of spiritual sensibilities.[77] Compassion, as both Razack and Said have analyzed its physics, actually inversely continues to support the character development of the transcendental self by posing it in sympathetic relationship to disabled or degenerate bodies, which are assumed to lack and are assumed, therefore, to need help.[78]

Persons of liberal suasion, convinced to take up the politics of compassion, often lose awareness of the socioeconomic world in which bodies transpire. Repairing ever and again to help the helpless, that deviant, diseased individual so caught in the eye of the modern, avoids larger systemic critique, assuming already to understand—by biologizing—suffering. Disability has caught on modernity's eye because of the economic demands for a fit body and ideological notions of self-sovereignty. Assuming epistemological privilege, assuming the eye to measure deficit and to scale the body for productivity and public appearance and health, the modern self also unconsciously presumes as health the values most conducive to capitalism. Rather than challenging the identification of the body with labor value, or challenging the subjective representation of wholeness or somatic intactness, which inform this division into normalcy and aberrance, the politics of compassion seems to conjoin itself to current economic principles of industrial, become consumer, capitalism. Compassion can then glibly assume and reinforce identification with our own location.

This results, I contend, in a critical problem in Borg and Crossan's exegesis itself: Assuming disability to be physiologically or psychologically self-evident, they have not archaeologically considered the political valences of health, disease, disability. What neither Borg nor Crossan has asked is, within what culture, within what socioeconomic systems and theocosmological orientations did "blindness, deafness, lameness" come to mean in the earlier century of the Common Era?[79] If Christians are to act, as each presumes, by analogy (a dangerous game, which runs the risk of looking into the mirror of our own projections!) to their unveiled portraits of the historical Jesus, their particular politics of compassion—insomuch as Crossan's as also Borg's exegesis seems to continue to assume the abjection of degeneracy and the centripetal pull of normalcy—may have ethically questionable, because colonial and/or colonizing, effects.

Medicine, Jesus, Degeneracy, and Spirit

Even amid the earliest quests for the historical Jesus, "Kahler saw clearly," writes Henault, "that many . . . lives [of Jesus] were in fact social programs and little more than propagandizing tracts."[80] In the mode of modernist realism, the extraordinary Jesus, the unique Jesus, takes as his dialectical undertow the psychosocial constitution of degeneracy—a point already established by Suzannah Heschel in regard to Christianity's modernist construction of Pharasaic Judaism as "degenerate."[81] The supernatural power presumed of Jesus has, in liberalism, been dampened and transmuted to higher consciousness, now carrying the power of the miraculous as pathos for the outcast, the spoiled. To what extent, then, have Christian communities, who likewise aspire to be among the helping professions, gained a sense of our spiritual, communal, and cultural selves via a compassion that is only secondary to the primacy of categorical mechanisms of fear and exclusion? Compassion, too, can be performative, a medicine show of sorts. A critical intervention, given the only seeming paradox between the possibility of being a helper and the political triumphalism of a nation yielding its energies to the economics of empire, must include a critique of the dramaturgy or spectacle of power effected among those at the center of this cultural ideology of helping the helpless.

Given that the "life of Jesus theology," as Christian testament scholar Dieter Georgi speaks of the historical Jesus quests, "developed . . . in close interplay with the socioeconomic and ideological evolution of the . . . bourgeoisie, as one of its motors as well as its conscience. . . not just as an ideal but as an expression of a socioeconomic and political momentum," should we not spend more time looking behind the curtains of today's theater of miraculous remediation—the contemporary historical Jesus quest?[82] Postcolonial feminist theologian Kwok Pui-Lan plants a parallel, inductive suspicion:

The need to present a historical account of early Christianity came as a response to the emergence of historicism in the eighteenth century, the challenge of the scientific worldview, and the construction of the superiority of Western culture. . . . The quest for Jesus went hand in hand with the quest for land and people to conquer. From a postcolonial perspective, we must plot the quest for the authentic Jesus against the search for knowledge of authentic "natives" for the purpose of control and domination.[83]

Given the popularity of this form of Christology at this time, she bares the directness of her challenge: "Is it mere coincidence that the newest quest for the historical Jesus is taking place in the United States, when the United States is trying to create a Pax Americana?"[84]

To be sure, the advent of biomedicine in the nineteenth century came to complement (again, as in the model of Albert Schweitzer), even to supplant the soul salvation of Christian missionary efforts. Schweitzer "represented the high point in the West's confidence that historic Christianity could be successfully repristinated in a modern medicine dispensed with moral concern."[85] But as First Nations scholar Ronald Niezen charges in an essay titled "Medical Evangelism," science, especially biomedicine, has been comparable in ethos and effect to a fundamentalist Christianity insomuch as it, too, assumes an orthodox belief commitment to a foundationalist, philosophically essentialist, and locationally abstract worldview. "Among the indigenous peoples of North America," Niezen asserts, "the dissemination of Western biomedicine has paralleled the development of missionary religion. . . . The synergy of missions and medicine derives in part from their foundations in belief, in the acceptance of basic convictions that serve as strong influences on perception, judgment, and motivation for reform and improvement."[86] In the spirit war between indigenous healing systems and Western fundamentalisms (both absolutist religious truths and scientific-medicinal paradigms, according to Niezen), the field of human communal trust gets disrupted, such fundamentalisms conditioning us to "coercive power" (by imploring us to forsake subjective affect so as to trust an outside authority) and therefore to control, if also subjectively immobilizing us, in fear.[87] Whether, then, the medicine show is set within fundamentalist rhetoric and a cosmotheological theater of absolute transcendence or in terms of the theater of biotechnology, the politics—as seen from the objectified other—seem similar. This is also the case with respect to the biotechnology of prosthetics, as we will now see.

CHAPTER

PUTTING MY FOOT (PROSTHESIS, CRUTCHES, PHANTOM) DOWN:
TECHNOLOGY AS TRANSCENDENCE

The "hardest" science is always about the realm of pure spirit.

—**Donna Haraway,**
"The Promise of Monsters"

"In the era of techno-biopolitics," writes feminist historian of science Donna Haraway, "prosthesis becomes a fundamental category for understanding personal and political" embodiment. For technonatural bodies, she concludes, "embodiment is . . . prosthesis."[1] This chapter considers Haraway's prosthetic technology, especially as figurally established in the cyborg, from two perspectives: the witness of prosthetically enabled disabled persons and via a critical examination of the Christian incarnational or embodiment practices to which Haraway herself alludes.

Haraway recognizes that Western technoscience has been motivated by Christian millennialism—a "salvation history" or metanarrative of Edenic, pastoral innocence, its loss, redemption, and re-creation. As Haraway realizes, this mytheme, a potent narrative node that has colonized modern time and space, can be divorced neither from the genocidal, ecocidal horrors nor from the modest remediations of suffering that have prevailed within modernity. Attempting to reprogram this "time machine" so as to commit ourselves to the midst of history (not its end), Haraway calls upon the figure of the cyborg to generate new practices of embodiment and, therefore, also new configurations of world-making practices that will embrace mortality and finitude. This mutant figure, she maintains, confuses the naturalist categories of Christian salvation history and can therefore mutate its incarnational technologies and salvific matrix.

The term *incarnation*, following upon the work of Merleau-Ponty, who phenomenologically located the corporeality of the soul, has been employed in philosophical discourses to name the practice of embodiment.[2] This usage has specifically prevailed within feminist philosophy in an attempt, I believe, to subvert the biologic that has repressed women's lives by consciously evoking the phenomenon of spirited corporeality. While Haraway uses the term sparingly, I choose to frequent the term *incarnation* here because I contend that it is precisely Spirit's relation to mortality and finitude that Haraway fails adequately to calculate. Haraway's cyborg figures, despite her feminist and ecojustice commitments to morph the edges of the second Christian millennium, have been metabolized by Christianity's discourse on Holy Spirit. As we have seen, Christian pneumatology, or the doctrine of Spirit, has been an idealist discourse that floats upon Christianity's abjection of all things transient. Its transcendentalist currents—quite easily, if surprisingly, fused with Western technological aspirations—inflate Western technological infatuation.

"Embodiment is . . . Prosthesis"

Postmodern philosophies, hoping to disrupt totalism, sport allusions to the morphological fragmentation of disabled, apparently totaled, bodies. Among such philosophies, Haraway's "socialist, feminist, and anti-racist environmentalism" seems most promising for one such as myself who has unwittingly joined the Crip Nation.[3] For one who has found it difficult to walk the line of ecological commitments with anything but my phantom foot, her insistence that, when considering survival hopes for the next millennium, practices of embodiment must learn to incorporate material technology seems helpful, hopeful even. Given that and her avowed commitment to a future that includes monstrous, mutated, and dismembered bodies, Haraway's figural "cyborg for earthly survival" would seem a natural *affiné* for the prosthetically enabled disabled.[4]

Haraway's "embodiment is . . . prosthesis" seems finally to invite those of us who each day don our prostheses, plant our feet, and/or spin our wheels into discourse. Until this time, disability has remained the province of healing professions and public benevolence. Despite the liberative humanitarian agenda of the past four decades, disability has not yet been "privileged . . . as a foundational category of social experience or symbolic investment [within the humanities]."[5] Consequently, Haraway's poststructuralist allusion to our experience of body feels like an open door, the possibility for a discourse in which we might have something authoritative to offer. Such an agenda as Haraway sets out might even generate affinity between the able and the disabled, could possibly open out an affinity circle in which we, the disabled, could contribute our constructive witness. Insomuch as incarnation presumes to be a prosthetic technology, surely disabled persons could finally garner some subjective respect. Who, after all, has spent more time in prosthetic labs than the disabled? If anyone knows how to don a prosthesis, it would seem to be one of us, who, like Herman Melville's Ahab (*Moby Dick*), has "one leg standing in three places"—a prosthesis planted in the material eternity of prosthetic titanium and carbon-fiber, a phantom thick with the sinews of memory, and a set of crutches or wheels to prop up the other two.[6]

Such a discourse as Haraway proposes is not, then, to be ignored as the disabled—the last identity group in the politically correct catechism—attempt a subject position. As the disabled, we need an allied philosophical discourse that can enable the emergence of a shared political agenda among those whose bodies are, as Haraway correctly notes, "irredeemably specific."[7] That the identity politics and rights legislation of previous liberative movements will not work for us is attested by the fact that, during the first five years of the Americans with Disabilities Act, the unemployment rate for the disabled rose from an already scandalous 66 percent to 71 percent.[8] Further, even though technology has promised to be the great equalizer for the disabled and, despite the obsolescence of the human body to the way of life within the information age, we, the disabled, find ourselves positioned on the edge of a sociocultural precipice.[9] Having served as high technology's poster children (thereby giving it figural legitimation while disguising its hidden militarism), we now find ourselves to be socially expendable: Given the socioeconomic burden we are perceived to present, genetic breakthroughs on one end of the life spectrum, like euthanasia on the other, promise easy, if merciful, eradication. Given this, how can we not accept the hand of friendship from a cyborg?

Although the disabled represent one of the earliest, most intimate facilitations of human and machine, the disabled have typically been made figuratively to speak *for* a cyborgian existence without being allowed to *speak up* or, in Haraway's terms, to "witness." This, oddly enough, also pertains within Haraway's prosthetic practice of incarnation. Despite her explicit rejection of discourses in which some represent themselves as the voice of the voiceless (a discourse practice that, despite its social-justice commitments, has itself gained its transcendence from the marginalization and suppression of disabled bodies), Haraway chooses as her witnesses not the actual lives of disabled persons, but characters from the pages of sci-fi literature.[10]

Haraway has consistently contested the coconstitutive technologies of modern gender and science that originated with Robert Boyle's demonstration of the air pump, the infamous experiment of suffocating a bird under glass that required the exclusion of women from the laboratory. But inasmuch as gender was in the making as that experimental way of life built on the exclusion of actual women, I must ask, what are these discursive disciplines of scientific theory and postmodern philosophy now making up that should require that we, the disabled, be wallflowers rather than witnesses? As long as the disabled remain the bird under glass of scientific theory and postmodern philosophy and, therefore, of social and material technologies, one must ask whether there still remains something this incarnational technology is choreographed to keep silent. When one person becomes the object of vision (as Haraway herself notes), someone else gets to play at transparent, transcendent objectivity.[11] So, what transcendentalizing move would be disabled by our presence in this discourse? Because I do not choose to slight the hand she extends to the family of abjects in solidarity, I want to challenge Haraway's discourse—not so as to refute it, but so as to find a "prosthetic territory" where I can put my foot (prosthesis, crutches, wheels) down.[12]

Inasmuch as the tenacious rhizomes of Christianity's salvation history sprout up like crabgrass in disabled bodies, enticing us to try to master its old grave-to-glory and tragedy-to-triumph plot lines, I personally couldn't be happier than to work beside Haraway to dispense with the "bracing discourses of salvation history."[13] Haraway, however, seems to assume of the term *prosthetics*, as she does of the figure of the cyborg, that by simply coupling human flesh with machine, we have generated politically agile transgressors who "trouble kind and force a rethinking of kin."[14] Haraway consequently presumes that the cyborg—theoretically now a mixed breed—has already put its foot down on and walked away—as if a fugitive—from Christian salvation history, that the cyborg has entered as agent into a new prosthetic territory that eludes the demarcation of the next Christian millennium.[15]

Sounding out the suspicious silence exacted of the disabled and the reluctance of the disabled community to embrace either the cyborg or postmodern prostheticism, I would suggest that Haraway's cyborg may not be quite the positive perversity Haraway imagines.[16] I suspect, rather, that the cyborg's prostheses represent a condensed referent of what has been construed as the most natural in a certain trajectory of Christian discourse. Specifically, I am suggesting that in the cyborg, we encounter totalistic holism parading as technological hybridism. If that proves true, then without some interpellation, the cyborg may not prove demonstrative for postmodern humanity. Postmodernism's incarnational prostheticism would then need to be reconfigured, since—as Haraway herself has said—anything that figures itself as "natural knowledge" is readily and covertly "reincorporated into techniques of social control instead of being transformed into sciences of liberation."[17]

Given that the studies that led to Merleau-Ponty's theoretical conjecture of the corporeality of the soul were conducted with amputees, perhaps we, the disabled, can swerve incarnational technology once again.[18] I will proceed by first reviewing the social and material technologies currently motivating prosthetics and continue by critiquing Haraway's arguments on behalf of the fugitive status of the cyborg. Finally, can we—without discarding prosthetics as a hopelessly totalistic technology—reconfigure prosthetic incarnationalism on behalf of a "mutated experimental way of life that does not issue in the New World Order, Inc.?"[19]

"She Thought She Was Getting the Chair": On the Social and Material Technologies of Prosthetic Sciences

That prosthetics in common language refers only to artificial limbs and not to my wheelchair or crutches gives you some preliminary idea of the disciplinary power operating in prosthetic sciences and, by extension, within our culture itself. To illustrate this disciplinary power, I refer you to ad copy in the fall 1998 issue of *Enable*, a magazine with the express mission of empowering the disabled to reach our full potential. An ad for Universal Institute, which describes themselves as "rehabilitation and fitness specialists," features an elderly Caucasian woman seated dejectedly beside a square, chrome, orthopedic wheelchair. In successive phases, moving from parallel bars to an independent walker, she is lifted from despondency. The caption reads: "She thought she was getting the chair. Instead we gave her life."[20]

As this ad suggests, prosthetics is most often socially motivated by the "pick up your bed and walk" philosophy. Prosthetic technology seems to have one goal in mind: the uprightness of bipedal existence, whether or not this proves the most empowering possibility for a particular body. Because my body has refused to concede to this technological solution with anything much more than cosmetic seemliness, I have become—socially speaking—a somatic heretic of our cultural belief in the power of technoscience. While learning consequently to piece together a prosthetic multiplicity of shape-shifting forms; for example, crutches for daily distance, wheels when chasing my preteen daughter through the mall, prosthetic limb when it's raining, I have been construed, from a social and medical perspective, as failing to adjust.

Material technology can bedazzle us with its claims for culturally endowed transcendental transparency. Perhaps it is only when you stub your (prosthetic) toe on the doorjamb to eternity that you figure out technology's habitus—that is, how our social beliefs and values functionally energize or articulate the body in relation to its world—and eternity's perimeters.[21] It might appear, when adding cybernetics to organic bodies, that, as Haraway ascribes to cyborgs, bodies no longer "end at the skin."[22] And to be sure, a disabled person can, in fact, learn to incorporate the machine into his or her body image. Nevertheless, it is also the case that prostheses may materially consolidate skin-deep oppressions. Greeting my first terrifyingly exuberant steps in a prosthetic leg, my prosthetist emitted a troubled, if cryptically prophetic scream: "You walk like an Indian!" I toed into the earth, having been raised in the rolling farmlands of southeastern Minnesota, where only city slickers would be fool enough to dig their heels into the undulating surface of a hay wagon while being rocked to the methodical push-pull of a hay baler. Because my hydraulic knee is activated by a firm heel strike, however, my prosthesis demands that I dig my heels into the earth. What story generated this habitus? Is not my prosthesis demanding somatic belief in the Christian story of the fall from the Garden of Eden? According to normative readings of the story, from henceforth, humanity would accomplish its salvation by exercising animosity toward the earth—figurally communicated by the human heel crushing the head of the earth serpent, Tiamat (see Genesis 3).

Once that little lesson in orthodox soteriology began to unravel, other revelations were quick to follow. If the prosthesis demands a clean heel strike, descending hiking trails would clearly prove problematic. I was destined for the flatlands of the Flat Earth Society—hardwood floors, cement sidewalks, parking lots, life on the level. Not only must I dig in my heel, my leg has been built with a heel-to-toe differential that demands I wear a shoe. Since my family and, therefore, our friendship circles have been built multiracially, this presents a bit of a problem when I am invited to the home of Korean friends. What social propriety prevails at this threshold: Shall I take off not only my shoe, but also put my foot down on their doorstep?

In donning a prosthesis, any such incarnation can be shown to demand consent not only to a certain ethnic, but also to a class and gender, posture. Inasmuch as artificial limbs are specifically built to fill in for what a body lacks, feminists should get a bit edgy.[23] "Cyborg technologies," write Gray and Mentor, "have the potential to reify in material bodies class and caste distinctions that were only social constructions up to now."[24] As habituated as we might be to certain social technologies, once they are incarnated in prosthetic machinery, they prove insidious, leaving precious little room for forgiveness, for free-flowing mimesis, for re-incarnations. Haraway seems, at times, to be cognizant of this point, for example, when she observes that "prosthetic devices . . . build in translations and specific *ways* of seeing, that is, ways of life."[25] In fact, Haraway proceeds to argue that our technological prostheses can therefore provide ethical critique in a way more objectively revelatory than "primate vision." Obviously, I may be illustrating Haraway's point precisely: I understand the habitus of the Western body better than ever before. However, my question to Haraway remains: Now that I know, how do I "intervene in this pattern of objectification"?[26] Where do I put my foot down? Once I don that prosthesis, it stipulates that I plant my heel on Tiamat's head. It is committed to that salvation history and demands my obedience.

More insidiously, compulsory bipedism demands that we consent to the social amelioration of suffering by hiding it, under the veil of the prosthesis, within the individual body. Contrary to Haraway's contention that the cyborg is no longer defined by the public/private split, the staunch individualization of suffering enabled by prosthetics enforces just such a split.[27] Prosthetics, as historian David Yuan's research correlating its use with national self-image following the Civil War has also shown, can be as much about offering an aesthetic and aseptic social response to suffering as it may be about the actual personal amelioration of such. "One of the most injurious wars in history," the Civil War, Yuan reports, "produced more amputees than any other war Americans have fought in."[28] A young nation was suddenly confronted with the problem of self-image: One hundred and thirty thousand of its most virile young males had been left "stumping" around. So as to avoid "the scorn that a critical Europe might have for the struggling United States," the physician, inventor, and statesman Oliver Wendell Holmes called for the politics of reconstruction to be applied to this grotesquery of amputated virility. Holmes, in an essay in the *Atlantic Monthly* (May 1863), praises the Palmer leg, one of the first cosmetically shaped prostheses complete with an articulating knee, for "counterfeiting [Palmer's injury] so far as possible."[29] In the process of making itself appear presentable and more aesthetically refined than the Old World, American society, specifically American technology (Holmes insisted), had an obligation to "raise the coarse and vulgar to the plane of symmetry and refinement." Putting the nation back together required "a new technology," "an artificial limb that [would] convincingly disguise the intolerable fact of the incomplete body"— the body social, the body personal.[30]

In my own experience, the day that I donned a prosthesis was the day that everyone else breathed a sigh of relief and I lost my sense of humor. For some of us, the psychic repression that belief in the cure of the prosthetic limb can entail may be comparable to that of a gay or lesbian being forced into the closet and the psychic relief, but social retaliation, when one refuses the cultural solution comparable to coming out. So what does the cyborg and her prosthesis keep in the closet?

While Haraway suggests that the cyborg figuration can, like the science-fiction wormhole, "cast travelers into unexpected regions of space," the wormhole in my cyborgian complex appears for public view when I take off my prosthetic foot.[31] What forces reconsideration of the question "And Aren't I a Woman?"—Haraway's meditative reflections on the question of what figure will gather up humanity so as to exit the second Christian millennium—appears to be the etchings of futility upon my mortal form.[32] That this unveiling (of the donut hole of my limb loss), rather than the curious, cosmetically covered endoskeletal structure standing in for my leg, should throw off the light switch of desire is a clue for me that Haraway's analysis may be slightly off course. When considering inclusion among the human community, the cyborg's machine/human interface seems not to be as troubling as a prosthetically unprosthelytized body—a disabled body refusing social comeliness or seemliness.

To be sure, by presupposing a feminist audience and inasmuch as Haraway specifically intends to resituate women in a technostrategic discourse, Haraway may presume that the mixing of kinds is actually not merely "cybernetics/organism," but machine/female.[33] Yet even this I do not find sufficiently disruptive, since Ivy, though an above-knee (AK) amputee, can simply don one or the other of her dozen or so prostheses and go back to work as a New York fashion model with nothing jarred loose in the social psyche. There is a point at which the machine/female interface may be transgressive—when, for example, showing my thighs of steel, the black-reptilian carbon-fiber endoskeletal frame as opposed to veiling the machine with a cosmetic cover. To a degree, then, I could agree with Haraway that there is an issue of cross-dressing here. A machine/female can never be as transcendentally transparent as a machine/male interface. A woman with her technological interfaces does not generate the same acceptance that a man and his machines do (see, for example, John Hockenberry's *Moving Violations*). This does not, however, refute my point that these machine/female interfaces can still provoke transcendence, whereas removing the machine interface inevitably shuts off the light switch of desire. In fact, given woman's identification with decaying flesh in the Platonic trajectory, when a woman becomes disabled, doesn't prosthetics—like some version of the chador—become even that much more socioculturally mandatory?

Thus, my suspicion: The science of prosthetics, in particular, and consequently of cyborg incarnations, may actually veil a discourse on compulsory holism. If so, it is not only on behalf of disabled bodies that we need to disrupt such composite holisms. Without disruption, postmodernism's "embodiment is prosthetic" may merely replicate idealism, all the more subtle because of its purported hybridism.

Without interruption, our prostheses—for "we are all cyborgs" now—may carry this totalism, like a zebra mussel, into the next millennium.

Considering Cyborg Incarnations

Haraway begins her political project from a theoretical position not unlike that of the philosopher Luce Irigaray, by theorizing from what Irigaray calls the catastrophic fold and what Haraway herself comparably calls the split—sites, in other words, that yield neither to radical severance nor to reductive fusion. "Splitting, not being, is the privileged image for feminist epistemologies of scientific knowledge," Haraway insists, concluding that "'splitting' . . . should be about heterogeneous multiplicities that are simultaneously necessary and incapable of being squashed into isomorphic slots or cumulative lists."[34] Whereas Irigaray "tends towards subversive figurations based on female *morphology*," for example, the two lips, Haraway, given the extensive and inescapable, even preferable dimensions of technonature, formulates political resistance from what she, in countering organicists, assumes to be the transgressive couplings across taxonomic lines—the machine-human.[35] She writes:

> Located in the belly of the monster, I find the discourses of natural harmony, the nonalien, and purity unsalvageable for understanding our genealogy in the New World Order, Inc. Like it or not, I was born kin to PU239 and to transgenic, transspecific, and transported creatures of all kinds; that is the family for which and to whom my people are accountable. It will not help—emotionally, intellectually, morally, or politically—to appeal to the natural and the pure.[36]

Given that it is my unprosthelytized rather than my prosthetically enabled body that haunts the social psyche, I am wondering whether these "trannies" of Haraway's—these transgenic, transmutated, and transsubstantiated creatures— are as transgressive as Haraway makes them out to be. In what follows, I want to consider whether Haraway's cyborg incarnation has in fact escaped "salvation history," as she claims, or whether the technonatural cyborg, though it disclaims all origin stories, might itself be born of the (S)pirit.[37]

I would like to pose the theoretical possibility that, while refuting the organic essentialist, Haraway has actually backed herself into the closet of another naturalist discourse. Haraway claims that the cyborg "has no truck with seductions to organic wholeness," and I have no doubt about that.[38] Haraway, however, seems to assume that by escaping organicism, she has also escaped millennial interests in wholesomeness. Yet, no more than the term *organic* does the term *prosthesis* refer us to a territory uncontaminated by the mythemes of the second Christian millennium. Haraway's primary argument on behalf of the fugitive status of the cyborg is that, looked at from the perspective of Christianity's interest in preserving the purity of kinds, the cyborg appears to be a taxonomically troublesome extraterrestrial.[39] Haraway reads Christianity as offended by this "mixing of kinds" and as consequently invested in patrolling the borders between humans and animals, between the races of humans, between the sexes, and now, in terms of both the debate surrounding genetic engineering and ecological organicism, between human and machine or between earth and technology. Read in this way, "embodiment is prosthetic" would appear to be syntactically transgressive.

However, if certain trajectories of Christianity have been invested in maintaining clearly distinct taxonomic kind-ship (as they indisputably have), this does not sum up the Christian project. One of the earliest baptismal formulas known to Christianity articulated a commitment to the formation of a heterogeneous community held together with pneumatic energy, that is, "In Christ there is neither Jew nor Greek, slave nor free, male nor female" (Gal 3:28). Baptismal commitments to an adopted spirit family—an affinity group, certainly not a nuclear family or any form of biological kinship network (see Matt 10:34-37)—specifically precluded soteriological exclusivism based in the delineation of kinds. In fact, the key salvific figure here—Jesus as Christ—was considered a hybrid. Jesus, it was asserted, hybridically merged two natures, such that he could be both "true God, begotten of the Father from eternity" and "true [hu]man."

According to the fourth-century theologian Athanasius of Alexandria, whose writings became Christianity's creedal gene pool, the eternal realm, ontologically distinct from the earth, is the most natural, while the finite world is a mere artifice. As a produced artifact and therefore likely to degenerate, the material porosity and solubility of corporeality had to be prosthetically stayed by fusion with the unchangeability of what was considered the most natural material, the incorruptibility of pure spirit. "Setting his sights upon the model of a re-creation performed by [the incarnation of] Christ," scholar of late antiquities Virginia Burrus explains, "Athanasius expects the human subject to supersede his own natural mutability through the granted stability of divine incorruptibility. . . . The divinization of humanity thus comes in the (dis)guise of a put-on, a cover-up, a veil, shrouding the ebb and flow of bodily existence."[40]

If the mixing of kinds is—as I would therefore submit—paradigmatically Christian, what has made this heterogeneous human community possible has been the commitment to live in the spirit—to live, that is, beyond the skin, by psychic divestment of the carnal body, by donning or putting on the prosthetic spirit body. This process of becoming a virtual somatic agnostic required Christians psychically to disarticulate sexuality and to disavow territorial ties and ethnic markings, thereby becoming—it was supposed—a generic, transcendent, if also hybrid human. In this vision of universal human solidarity, what has been at issue is not so much the mixing of kinds, of apples and oranges, Jews and Greeks, male and female, as what has to be kept out of the mix, the worm in the apple, the foot in the grave, the female-engendered body, the body "close to death," as Levitical laws seem to have construed disabled bodies (see Lev 21:16-24.).[41] Psychic delibidinalization of the carnal, female realm undergirded the practice given over to achieving Christological hybridity.

Haraway appreciatively reads Irigaray's mimetic critique of Plato's cave as the womb for man's second birth out of the body and into the mind.[42] Western Christianity, however, has had its own "breeder reactor," the Holy Spirit, through which men have given birth to "nature 'enterprised up.'"[43] Prior to the coming of the Spirit, writes theologian Jürgen Moltmann, "transitory time and the mortality of all the living was held to be the 'natural' condition of created things."[44] The Spirit, however (Moltmann continues), exposes finitude as a sickness amenable to remediation. Transience, in other words, is what appears most *un*natural in terms of Christianity's doctrine of the Spirit. Just as living in the Spirit has required Christians to live beyond the flesh, so here: The Spirit moves Christians into a territory beyond the reach of finitude—in the name of the most natural.

Given Christianity's commitment to break the bondage of transience or futility so as to restore the possibility for universal, human community (see Rom 8:20-21), (material) technology has itself been greeted as an evolution of the Spirit. That the Holy Spirit has not been at all averse to the evolution of material technology can be read in the work of the early twentieth-century philosophical theologian Nicholas Berdyaev. In the process of "liberat[ing] man [*sic*] . . . from his immersion in elemental nature," Berdyaev observed, Christianity was "obliged to mechanize nature" so as to keep humanity from the "danger of communing" with the earth.[45] Our Christological machinations have led us straight into prosthetic territories.

"Any transcendentalist move is deadly," writes Haraway.[46] When looking around for transcendentals, however, one cannot ignore their technological materialization, since, as theologian Catherine Keller has pointed out, when Columbus set sail, he bent the trajectory of Christian transcendence from the vertical thrust to "the horizontal, horizonal."[47] The Age of Discovery turned upon a new theological impulse that sought the transcendent not in the heavens above, but on the cusp of the next horizon—the horizon of scientific as well as of colonial discovery. Technology, begotten in the womb of Christian apocalyptic and modernist hopes for the New Creation, the New Heaven and New Earth, in and through the discovery and reclamation of the Garden—has been among the primary modern modes for Western Christianity's transcendence of transience (see Rev 21:1-4).[48] Consequently, what appears to be a transgressive technonatural hybrid from one angle may from another angle—specifically from what Haraway's own hopes for communities of abject, "dismembered," un-"kind" persons, bonded in solidarity . . . well, from that, angle the cyborg and her prostheses, rather than "subvert[ing] what counts for nature," may be all "most natural."[49] Haraway herself seems poised on the edge of such insights when she observes that "the 'hardest' science is about the realm of pure spirit" and that "science made was nature undone."[50] Even going so far as to greet cyborgs as "ether, quintessence," she nevertheless fails to recognize the import of her own words: as incarnational figures, cyborgs appear to have been born of (W)holy Spirit, animated by Western Christian salvation history, and quite at home in the Garden of modernity's New Earth.[51]

As she concluded her essay "The Promise of Monsters" with a rendition of the cyborg, so throughout her 1997 text, *Modest Witness@Second_Millennium*, Haraway has enfolded the work of artist Lynn Randolph. A review of these iconographic figures (inspired by, but also reflectively woven back into Haraway's text), suggests to this disabled person Haraway's consistent overestimation of the transcendent capacities of technoscience and her consequent unwitting commitment to a "summing and subsuming" holism.[52] In each figuration—from the Cyborg to OncoMouse, La Mestiza Cosmica, and the Millennial Children—the aesthetic loveliness of these supposedly dismembered and "disarticulated" figures stands out against their overtly contaminated landscapes. (Ironically, among the disabled, disarticulation refers to a radical amputation severed through a joint, whereas nothing comparable visibly disables the somatic innocence of Haraway's and/or Randolph's figures.) Remarkably, the biotech figures remain visually immune from the consequences of four decades of petrochemically and pharmaceutically enhanced life.

If "situated knowledges require that the object of knowledge be pictured as an actor and agent," why has the oil-polluted bayou not yet acted back—in the form of allergic rashes and asthma, at the least—upon the millennial children, who are figured instead as "whole, firm"?[53] Clearly OncoMouse, replete with a crown of thorns, serves as a christological figure, specifically a figure of substitutionary atonement. Yet, why has OncoMouse—"born" of the hybridic implosion of women with biotechnology's little "warrior princess," the rodent order used to wage humanity's war against cancer—remained so, well, well-endowed? Frankly, I would have expected her appearance among "the clan of one-breasted women."[54] Likewise the interpolation of the Virgin of Guadalupe straddling the Texas-Mexico border: Neither migrant labor nor work in a *maquiladora* leaves a body this pristine. Many of us who have been "gestating in the amniotic effluvia of terminal industrialism" spawn tumors; we wear the infamous necklace scar of thyroid cancers.[55] Some among us enter the postgender world of the cyborg through dismemberment (for example, the loss of breasts and testicles), others by developing a compensatory musculature, for example, bulging biceps from working crutches and/or a wheelchair, a morphology that henceforth refuses fashionable feminine seemliness. If these icons represent "cyborgs for earthly survival," if these are figures meant to gather up irredeemably suffering bodies at the end of the second millennium, why aren't their "freak flags" flying?[56] If the cyborg is to serve in any way as an incarnational figuration to get us out of the second millennium and back into the middle of history, wouldn't we see at least *three* feet sticking out from under the computer table? (I mean that question only figuratively, of course.)

On Prosthetic Erraticism: Reconsidering Technology as/and Transcendence

Haraway's evocation of incarnation as prosthetic constitutes her attempt to calculate the ratio of mortality imploded with the immortal or eternal—for her, the Promethean contours of the likes of PU239, or, in my case, the nondisintegrative prosthetic textures of titanium, carbon fiber, bioelastic, and silicon. In a footnote to her essay "Situated Knowledges," Haraway reviews the science-fiction literature of John Varley, affirming his ongoing exploration of the way in which prosthetic technologies remands a cyborg to finitude "despite their extraordinary transcendence of 'organic' orders."[57] In other words, by evoking prosthetics, Haraway intended to remand us—most appropriately, I would say—to the decisive split that Kate Soper simply writes as "Nature/'nature.'" As we "rethink . . . our conditions of flourishing," Soper advises, we can discursively do without neither an awareness of our dependence on and the independence of various strata of the ecological terrain nor an awareness of how cultural technologies reconstrue what counts as nature.[58] Yet, I would suggest that as Haraway has fit the cyborg with prostheses, these have actually seamed up the split of ethical, figurative accountability all too well. Prosthetics, as currently socially and theologically motivated, have not been about split subjectivity, but about its cure—about wholeness or, variously, holiness.

While Haraway has pointed to this decisive disjuncture figured in prosthetics, her own sci-fi enthrallment overwhelms a more "constructive ambivalence" toward technoscience.[59] If, as Haraway rightly puts it, "severely handicapped people can have the most intense experiences of complex hybridization," disabled persons also have the most exquisite awareness of the abrupt edge and shocking disparity between the organic and the machine.[60] Unlike the able-bodied, who may imagine the technologically endowed body as somehow bionic or indestructible, the disabled person becomes even more acutely aware of the need to take up what Irigaray calls "the life-death watch." Disabled persons must psychically wrestle with the exquisite loveliness of and frustration with one's own transient tissues at the same time as she or he wrestles with the physical and psychic cumbersomeness, the severe rigidity, if also acquired grace, of the technologically endowed body.

Further, what may appear to an outsider as the natural constraint operatively reducing disabled bodies to the bondage of natural immediacy reads far too repressive. It assumes, in my experience, a tremendous transcendentalist inflation about what makes life worth living. The exquisiteness of transient occasions and passing moments, even quite indeterminate moments—Did the child in the stroller recognize me with the waving of her hand?—are why some of us put on our feet, pick up our crutches, and spin our wheels every day.

Despite the fact that prosthetics do not generate the "reciprocational excess" or "extraordinary transcendence of organic orders" that both technoscience and an able-bodied culture want to believe in, we, the disabled, are also not likely to put down, that is, lay aside or give up, our prosthetic feet, wheels, or crutches.[61] For me, prosthetics, and consequently, incarnation, are about tipping the fierce ambivalence that is mortality toward a love of the futility of it all—toward a love of the flesh and of finitude, I mean.

If embodiment is prosthetic and is meant to remand us toward finitude, then I would like to propose the figure of the prosthetic erratic—the one who, self-admittedly, has her or his foot in at least three places. Barbara Hillyer, author of *Feminism and Disability*, takes the first step toward the production of this figure. For women with disabilities, Hillyer writes, "the issue is not whether to use technology but how best to integrate it with self-concept and with body awareness." She bases this observation on several studies, including "the experience of mothers of 'thalidomide babies,' who came into conflict with rehabilitation specialists about the use and interpretation of prostheses for the children's deformed or missing arms." While the professionals, assuming that a missing limb signified a somatic deficit, insisted on early initiation into and integration of prosthetic appliances, "the child's body image was already whole," Hillyer reports, "so the prosthesis was experienced as a deformation." Given the discrepancies between the professionals' and the child's own apparent, healthy body image, the mothers' response, Hillyer concludes, was "to frustrate the professionals by using the prosthesis erratically and at random in terms of tasks to be performed."[62] Interrupting the social demands for composite holism, the children and their mothers chose the path of prosthetic erraticism.

The prosthetic erratic would be a fugitive from the habitus of the upright— perhaps one like Mary Verdi-Fletcher, principal dancer of the Cleveland Ballet Dancing Wheels, who "stopped walking" and "started dancing."[63] At the least, the prosthetic erratic would not be socially constrained, under the threat of the death sentence, to veil him or herself and would, consequently, give us a better figure of what it means to be "stitched together imperfectly."[64] It is from the likes of Verdi-Fletcher that I have found the courage to admit to the world my heretically unprosthelytized body, to shift demonstratively the kind-ship relations thereby, and to discover for myself—offstage of that performance named "seeming/seaming so together"—the physics and psyche of a triped existence. Now I, with studied calculation, shape-shift through my cyborgian incarnations, prosthetic foot, wheels, and crutches. I suspect only the closest of friends can imagine how difficult it has been to resign from compulsory, social holism and join the erratics.

Spinning my wheels with five sixth-grade girls on rollerblades clinging to the back of my wheelchair handles, I crest the hill and, careening wildly, we "crack the whip." Exhausted, I kick off my leg. My daughter tickles my phantom silly; it is the only location on my body where I am ticklish. Now I'm getting my sense of humor back. Comedy, as Haraway knows, can be quite instructive regarding what carries us from here to elsewhere.[65]

CHAPTER 5

CONSPICUOUS COMPASSION: RACE, "DISABILITY," AND SALVIFIC IMPERIALISM

Whatever the issue, [natives] are entrapped in a circular dance where they always find themselves a pace behind the white saviors. . . . Natives must be taught in order to be anti-colonialist and de-westernized; they are, indeed, in this world of inequity, the handicapped who cannot represent themselves and have to either be represented or learn how to represent themselves. . . . Gone out of date, then revitalized, the mission of civilizing the savage mutates into the imperative of "making equal."

—**Trinh Minh-ha,**
Woman-Native-Other

A First Nations woman has made her way to a microphone, following a guest lecture at the school of theology. Her parents, she notes, were survivors of the residential school program, a Canadian government sponsored, church-run project assumed to bring First Nations peoples into the developmental patterns of settler culture, which has now been charged with occasioning cultural genocide. A number of teachers, religious workers, and priests in the residential schools were also charged with physical and sexual abuse of the First Nations children in their care. "Tell me," the First Nations woman now demands of the speaker, "What do you mean that what you have to say tonight might also offer healing for First Nations people?" As she proceeds to express how she no longer wants to hear about healing First Nations persons, the audience recoils at her obvious anger, if also its underlying weariness.

Admittedly puzzled and listening hard now, I hear the speaker describe how her parents' generation was told they needed to be saved from paganism, from the primitive, from underdevelopment. Now, in a second stage, she and her generation—reminded every day by church and government that they need healing from the traumas of cultural decimation—have been yet again found defective. Now her frustration finds an echo, resonating through me, a body so tired of being examined, so tired of medical appointments and social stares: She's describing the ongoing pathologizing of a people, the label

of "pathology" passed from one generation into the next. Though the diagnosis changed, those who had the power to judge had not changed seats. Despite
the ethical culpability of church and state and despite profuse apologies, those
who held the power to judge have retained that power, that superiority—have
remained immune from serious ethical self-examination of our cultural constructions. Stuck in what decolonizing theorist Albert Memmi called "the
dependency duet," the minoritized will never be allowed to be the provider or,
therefore, to suggest alternative cultural values.[1]

The power to judge has taken up residency inside Western cultural notions of
healing (health care and education have been nearly synonymous with compassion
in colonial contact), social justice, and even, as Gayatri Spivak would remind us,
the idea of human rights. Conflations of this power with healing and justice practices have made it difficult for Christians to discern why Franz Fanon insisted that
colonialism be considered, foundationally speaking, a "theological violence."

Making the Redemptive Plot Move

Multiple essays from the genre of postcolonial studies echo this First Nations'
woman's sentiment. In an essay titled "The Language of Nativism," postcolonial
feminist theorist Trinh Minh-ha insinuates that Western humanism has maintained itself precisely by propping itself up with "the perception of the outsider
as the one who needs help." While this perception has been worked through a
successive history of forms, for example, "the barbarian, the pagan, the infidel, the
wild man, the 'native,' and the underdeveloped," yet ever again it revolves so as to
stabilize the well-intentioned Westerner. "Thus, the invention of 'needs' and the
mission to 'help' the needy," Trinh concludes, "always blossom together."[2]

Comparably, Spivak, bemoaning what she calls in specific the "ferocious standardizing benevolence" of most U.S. and Western European scientific discourses
and of the salvific mission of imperialism more generally, repeatedly confronts
the way gender, color, and class have been used as signifiers of the need for emancipation, most famously with sarcastic reference to the plot of "white men saving
brown women from brown men"—a trope that proved not incidentally analytically insightful in reference to the U.S. invasion of Afghanistan consequent to
September 11, 2001.[3]

Canadian-based theorist Sherene Razack, moving more intuitively than by
specific theoretical argument, brings this critique into the field of disabilities
concerns in her essay "From Pity to Respect: The Ableist Gaze and The Politics
of Rescue." Pity, the emotional response most often summoned up in relation

to persons with disabilities, Razack notes, avoids facing the general vulnerability of embodiment and "fundamentally preserve[s] the pattern of relationships in which some people enjoy the power and position from which to consider—as a gift or act of benevolence—the needs of others without having to encounter their own implication in the social patterns that assign the problem to these others."[4] If "colonial power produces the colonized as a fixed reality which is at once an 'other' and yet entirely knowable and visible,"[5] for example, women as weak, persons with disabilities as in "dire need," or veiled brown women as the "absence of freedom," such racial stereotypes yield to the colonizer, who is the source of these psychic projections, a "certitude in the necessity of intervention."[6] Even where well-intended, "ferocious standardizing benevolence," as Spivak terms this helper complex, presumes the transparency of defect and assures helpers of being superiorly civilized, of living within "a good society."[7]

As we have noted before, Fanon's *The Wretched of the Earth* is, of course, the predecessor of such insights. His text suggests how easily the language of degeneracy and disability, itself the categorical undertow of the discourse of humanitarism and Western notions of progress, would slip between surveilling the colonial site and the bodies in the metropole of humanism: "The native is . . . the corrosive element, destroying all that comes near . . . the deforming element, disfiguring all that has to do with beauty or morality."[8] Fascism and its holocaust of the disabled, gays, gypsies and Jews, in mid-twentieth-century Europe evidenced the extreme of this always virulent logic turned upon bodies in the home region of western humanism. Yet aberrance, as disabilities theorist David Mitchell noted in regard to the literary genre of modern realism, has been consistently required in order to make the plot of modernism move. The optics of modern realism treat the presence in the narrative of persons with stigmatic disabilities as the problem to be overcome, as the obstacle to be transcended—not, then, as a subject to be engaged.[9]

Whether literary genre or modern humanist politics, this construction assumes an epistemological privilege and cloaks therein an absolute will to power.[10] "There is nothing more consistent than a racist humanism," Sartre wrote, reflecting upon Fanon's insights, "since the European has only been able to become [hu/]man through creating slaves and monsters."[11] Constructions that assume the invalidating displacement of stigmatic bodies, that is, slaves and monsters, also conversely assume a certain sovereignty of and for the active, protagonist self—the helper, the benevolent, the savior imperialist. Whether inside the literary imagination or within the skin of modern selfhood, one trained in modernist epistemological optics acquires the clinical gaze in the

name of redemption—to heal brokenness, to struggle against disease, to motivate one's own struggle against deviance from the norm.

So, for example, the human-rights agenda, Spivak contends, likewise borrows the
speck in the eye, aberrance, to make the plot move. "The idea of human rights . . .
may carry within itself the agenda of a kind of social Darwinism," Spivak writes, then
explaining that "the fittest" have been expected "to shoulder the burden of righting
the wrongs of the unfit." The impulse to "make it right for others," the duty of the
assumed fitter and superior self to act for and on behalf of the presumed interests of
the less fortunate, likewise presumes a superior base of knowledge. Responsibility,
assuming "the power to judge," becomes conflated with duty, short-circuiting any ethically deliberative interchange.[12] Stigmatic bodies have been presumed incapacitated,
according to Western standards of knowledge. Comparably, contemporary reality
television, even if presented with an ironically self-deprecating laugh and self-aware in
regard to its own triviality, continues to cultivate such surveilling logic of the modern
subject in relation to his or her own body within contemporary, global culture, with
shows like *What Not to Wear* and *Queer Eye for the Straight Guy*. Consciousness of
one's own inadequacies serves the interests of consumerism, but also then reenforces
the judging eye. With reference to the helper-savior, a modern subject so in touch
with her or his own shortcomings, poststructuralist theorist Kelly Oliver calls this
"the position of dominance, the position of the judge of others who confers or withholds recognition . . . without regard for the desires of those without power."[13] Noting
that "raced bodies" are not allowed to do critical thinking, to pose values, Oliver concludes, "those human abilities are reserved for bodies posing as disembodied neutral
forces of nature or truth."[14]

That Fanon dared to suggest that colonialism transpired in the service of theology stems from just such an intuition: "The primary violence of colonialism is
theological," Fanon insisted, "the semiotic violence of constructing the colonizer
(believer) as a spiritual being and the colonized (unbeliever) as a material being."[15]
Christianity having invented for itself "the power to judge," as D. H. Lawrence
put it, modernity built subjectivity upon the theo-logic of "the believer."[16]

Within the modernist milieu, redemptive practice, from healing repair to
compassionate inclusion, proceeds by attempting to fix the deviance or deviation—to cure, in other words. Our reflexes have been conditioned to hunt down
deviance. If that seems common knowledge about modernity, consequent to
Foucault, this critique has hardly shifted theology: The historical Jesus accounts
just reviewed continue rather to employ this in the name of historical realism.
Assuming at base the unerring ability to recognize defect, lack, need (hence, the

violence that Fanon charges against theology), modern theologies of redemption proceed from the point of recognition through its remediation. The modern emplotment of redemption does not vary: Expose a flaw, bring the deviance from periphery to center stage, and remediate the aberration—all to the credit of and in accord with the propriety of the protagonists, who are (need it be said?) never disabled or wretched.[17]

The demand for cure lurks even within the redemptive strategy of social inclusion. In modernist realism, as Mitchell points out, "repair of the deviance may involve an obliteration of the difference" via "the rescue of the despised object from social censure" as much as through supernaturalist or biotechnoscientific cure.[18] So with the historical Jesus quest, the modernist epistemological determination of deviance remains caught on scholars' eyes. These texts pivot upon what Ashis Nandy has called the modern polarities of "the normal and the abnormal . . . the vanguard and the led, the liberated and the savable."[19] Redemption—and thus the progress of morality, as one would expect within works of modernist realism—has been emplotted as rescue from social censure. Marcus Borg's politics of compassion presumes a dominant base, virtuously and tolerantly practicing inclusion, but inclusion into what values? And which persons then constitute the dominant base? The bodies of marginalized persons with disabilities (again, "women, the untouchables, the poor, the maimed, and the marginalized"), persons who are not necessarily seen as members of the base Christian community, still orient and map Christian mission.[20] How did these raced bodies come to be so stigmatically lodged in perception?

While John Dominic Crossan's "open commensality of healing and eating" aspires to be differently motivated, the superlative performance of Jesus the Healer (I have suggested)—of Jesus as a gloriously able, compassionate humanitarian who judges what makes for life—still lurks behind his goal of reconstructing interdependent community among just such persons. The celebration of heroic action, feminist theologian Rita Brock warns, tends to reinforce a notion of "a power outside ourselves that . . . transcend[s] the concrete realities of our lives," occasions displacement of trust into unilateral power, and consequently encourages us to act "by analogy"—just, in fact, as Crossan has commended.[21] Acting by analogy not only proves a dangerous game of entering the circuit of our own psychic projections, but "breeds . . . insensitivity to the presence of the other."[22] Rather than affectively engaging the other, persons acting by analogy presume to know what's needed, presume to know what's best.

Hence cure—although not by supernaturalist remediation, yet by inclusion or transcendent tolerance—remains the only acceptable outcome: Aberrance sets the redemptive plot in motion. Naming this conditioned response to deviance "compassion" convinces us that we are doing the right thing. Without compromising the sovereignty of the self, modern subjects enjoy the confirmation of being humanly needed, enjoy the fantasy of noble graciousness. The politics of compassion appears to mean helping persons into normalcy, into our definition of well-being and our definition of what makes for a good life. But undoing that, as we can deduce from Fanon's critique, will require us to theologize redemption without emplotting the redemptive encounter as the remediation of defect, remediation that hides the power to judge.

The Dramaturgy of Power and the Theater of the Miraculous

Extreme Makeover: Home Edition aired as a television show focused on the architectural and aesthetic makeover of American homes for persons under the duress of circumstances. While in one vein a variation upon the home and craft shows, such as *Trading Spaces*, currently on popular television, in *Extreme Makeover: Home Edition* the theatrics involve a display of more ostentatious, if hybrid humanitarianism and the presumed makeover of human lives. So the focus over the last weeks of the summer of 2005, for example, turned toward more decisively disabled bodies within particularly sympathetic scenarios: A young black basketball player in Los Angeles suddenly becomes a quadriplegic due to a drive-by shooting involving a case of mistaken identity; a young Caucasian father is blinded in yet another shooting.

While inadequate structures of refuge are razed and replaced with enlarged facilities and technologically sophisticated equipment (on the same lot, in the same neighborhood), tapes of the 9-1-1 phone calls are played back, family members interviewed, and cast members, weeping openly, are led (as if on sacred pilgrimage) to the crime scenes. But what, I wonder, is happening here—in front of the camera, to us as viewers? Why do we participate in this? That the show invites community participation and corporate donation (not always that conspicuously) remains subtly secondary to the display itself—that of providing an extreme intervention in the architecture of home, if also the economic future, of a person whom cast members extol as a model of inspiration and courage. But why air such a show? Why should we, the viewers, also find ourselves professing the privilege of being allowed to participate in this person's life? While miracle stories have been typically read as stories of miraculous remediation of the pitiful body, here I want to turn our focus around: How might these stories, including such versions as *Extreme Makeover: Home Edition*, contribute to "the dramaturgy of power" necessary to and for imperial presence and for dominant cultural self-image?[23]

The dominant, observes James Scott, "have a collective theater to maintain which often becomes part of their self-definition."[24] In the theater of race relations, as well as in that of medicine, the normative reading become rhetorical portraiture of Jesus as Healer, as effecting miraculous remediation and transgressive compassion, once again participates in the creation of a transcendentalizing sociopolitical power with profound implications for issues of both social justice and the physics of Spirit, in how we understand divine efficacy, in other words. While the public transcript of the colonizer or dominant power may "awe and intimidate [subordinates] into adurable and expedient compliance . . . [i]t may well be, " Scott explains, "that insofar as the public transcript represents an attempt to persuade or indoctrinate anyone, the dominant are the subject of its attention. The public transcript [may serve] as a kind of self-hypnosis within ruling groups to back up their courage, to improve their cohesion, display their power, and convince themselves anew of their high moral purpose."[25] In other words, what we have come to call miracle stories—whether in Western biblical scholarship, out of biotechnology labs, or riding the waves of contemporary, televisionary culture—function as discourses vying for and consolidating social power.

Conspicuous Salvation

Biblical scholar Gerd Thiessen's work on the miracle stories that we have been interrogating throughout supports Scott's notion of reading these transcripts as part of a "dramaturgy of power." Thiessen, although convinced that "there is no doubt that Jesus worked miracles, healed the sick and cast out demons," nevertheless also observes that "the miracle stories reproduce these historical events in an intensified form." However, he goes on to suggest that "this enhancement of the historical and factual begins with Jesus himself," as Jesus (according to Thiessen) brings together eschatological apocalypticism with prophetic miracle-working such that miracles evidenced the "episodic realisation of salvation."[26] The notion of eschatological fulfillment doubles back upon and intensifies the cultural weight of prophetic charism. By the time the synoptics were written, Thiessen observes, there have been several further developments around Jesus and the miracle stories: the eschatological-apocalyptic eccentricity of Jesus had been smoothed over via "popularizing adaptation," and the unique miracle-working power of Jesus has been heightened as the miracles themselves became more and more difficult to credit.[27] On this last point, Thiessen simply proposes that [the miracle stories] "contradiction of normal experiences becomes more and more prominent."[28]

Theissen's conclusion that "in order to do full justice to this sense of being something unique as regards miracles, primitive Christianity had to tell new miracle stories, elaborate old ones and out do any rivals" would seem to insinuate the miracle stories into the strategies of rivaling discourses of power within even the early centuries. While miracle stories establish the incredible as a power of and among the dominant, their success, however, must equally be that of training an optic that is both the catalyst and effect of this way of looking and being. These miracle stories, these social spectacles that objectify deficiency, observes Jean Comaroff, digging through the social effects of missionary colonialism in Africa, give "a definition of person, of body, health and society."[29] Within this ideological theater, the drama has to do with who holds the power of judging not just what makes for a life and what constitutes quality of life, but how we think what is of sacred value.

The physics of Spirit are, if you will, made conspicuous, according to the dictates of this optic. Where health and fitness come culturally to be seen as "the appropriate exercise of the sovereignty of the self," disabilities theorist Paul Longmore explains, "the ritual display of charity verifies the social and moral validity of individual givers and the moral health of . . . society by dramatizing compassion toward those socially invalidated by disability or disease."[30] Further, a "contribution must be conspicuous for it to demarcate the radical difference between socially valid Americans and their counter-image, the invalidated, disabled Others."[31] While the ritual display of compassion suggestively spotlights the remediation and/or inclusion of deviance, the performance of giving, of making place for the socially invalidated, accrues instead as moral, spiritual prestige and class status to the giver.[32]

Indeed, conspicuous giving does confirm the autonomy, mastery, independence, and fitness of the giver. But perhaps at least as important today, persons find in helping their own redemption. Humans do require interdependence, despite the prized autonomy of the modern individual. Given the sheering of kinfolds and the promotion of personal choice, humans feel increasingly socially alienated. Charitable action allows the subject to be needed but, even as it does so, it takes place on terms that don't compromise self-sovereignty.

Conspicuous salvation is a form of conspicuous consumption. Digging through the ways by which colonizing Christianity replicated the transcendental self of modern liberalism, postcolonial feminist theologian Kwok Pui-Lan identifies the Christological discourse as primary: "Christology reflected the demarcation of the . . . margins and boundaries of the bourgeois social body."[33] In a horribly ironic twist, a biblical folk utopia celebrating decolonization—Isaiah 35:5-6—has been reversed. Now read with enlightened, if objectifying eyes, it has been employed as a wager of imperial control. Earlier community pragmatics of rumor and resurrection "give way to the figure of Jesus himself" such that new system has been "conceptually. . . superimposed and ultimately fused" upon liturgical and catechetical practices of the community.[34] Turning the critique of the specular optics back upon the central protagonist, Christian testamental scholar Marianne Sawicki observes with ironic bite that "what hinders our comprehension" and leads us to assume "that the textual delivery system that packages 'Jesus' means to deliver over 'Jesus himself'. . . is our preoccupation with commodities."[35] The economics of modernist realism shape not only the bodies on the margin, but the presumption of what we see as the center of the text and the agential power of history.

In this regard, Dieter Georgi, summarizing his lifelong "interest in the life of Jesus," warns that "our modern market economy with its orientation toward performance has much in common with the cult of the extraordinary in Hellenistic-Roman society and its market economy. . . . Those missionaries of Jesus who propagated the extraordinary qualities and performance of the man from Nazareth and claimed similar strengths for themselves," Georgi asserts, "competed and collaborated within the conditions of the Hellenistic-Roman market." The portrait of Jesus as a strong, gifted, and charismatic man played well in the urban "missionary competitions" of Rome's religious market, Georgi notes. What was effected thereby was, as consequent redeployments of the historical Jesus from the eleventh to twelfth centuries and again throughout modernity would also prove, the "superhuman individuality" of the bourgeois class.[36] "Locat[ed] within the evolution of bourgeois consciousness, not just as an ideal but as an expression of a socioeconomic and political momentum,"[37] historical Jesus theology seeks to "re-establish our [sense of] superiority by noticing difference"—as if difference resided in the needy, weak, pitiable other.[38] Miracle spectacles cannot now be separated from that synoptic spectacle of representation—of the many watching the few, the star cult—that is media/ted globalization.

Rehabilitating the Colonizing Psyche

And then the occasion arose I had to meet the white man's eyes. An unfamiliar weight burdened me. . . . In the white world the man of color encounters difficulties in the development of his bodily schema. Consciousness of the body is solely a negating activity . . . . I took myself far off from my own presence. . . . What else could it be for me but an amputation, an excision, a hemorrhage that spattered my whole body with Black blood?

—Frantz Fanon, *Black Skin, White Masks*

Now "looking white people in the eye," Razack, an Indo-Canadian, situates herself analytically at that location where "powerful narratives turn oppressed peoples into objects, to be held in contempt, or to be saved from their fates by more civilized beings."[39] Christologies, using modernity's classification of disabled and degenerate bodies to mark their perimeter and mission, have acted as such powerful narratives, and may, without intervention, continue to do so. However, for a Christianity shaking off Christendom, Razack may suggest a starting place: "Disrupt the hegemonic way of seeing through which subjects make themselves dominant."[40] That hegemonic way of seeing has mapped social mission, traveled the circuit of compassion, and been proffered with works of mercy. Razack herself, citing Fanon, posits this "hegemonic way of seeing" as the founding optics—or pathology—of colonialism. It is, she writes, "the condition that enables the story of Western civil progress to be told, the bedrock upon which the emergence of bourgeois society is founded."[41] Razack's insights, like the intuition of McClintock, lead us back to the seething psyche as among the places within which we can hope to intervene so as to disrupt these powerfully productive narratives.

Ashis Nandy, working most intently on critique of the civilizing mission, which he has warned us was a colonialism that could survive the demise of empire, said much the same: "Colonialism is a state of mind."[42] Setting among his goals consideration of "the cultural and psychological pathologies produced by colonization in the colonizing societies," Nandy named the "isolation of cognition from affect" as an imperial pathology. Liberal critical morality, Nandy surmised, has been effectively truncated, such that the superiority of the colonizer may be as pathological as the inferiority of the oppressed. Triggering "'banal' violence" among colonizers as well as the colonized, this psychological impasse lodged between ideas and feelings becomes, a "religious and ethical theory and an integral part of a cosmology," Nandy cautioned.[43] Consequently, social missions cannot occasion a publicly effective and ethically deliberative space, which we might name compassion, but insist rather on recognition of their own [Western] way.

Postcolonial and disabilities literatures have identified several psychological trajectories that this pathological missional superiority tends to follow: pathological narcissism; the sanctifying of the subaltern, behind which helpers hide their own self-pity; and displacement of affect into a signifier, such as the lamentable "Third World." In terms of the first trajectory, as the colonized (those deemed degenerate, disabled, diseased, and/or deviant) get caught in the West's hall of mirrors and are consequently deemed to lack (wholeness, civilized aesthetics, development, fitness, and so forth), this hall of metaphysical mirrors also plays tricks with the psyche of persons trained in the Western subjective economy. If what passes for compassion within liberalism can be heard in the wish for me to be normal, equally that mirror catches up the psyche of my beholders (as well as me) in the presumption of wholeness. This cathection to wholeness has, following Lacan, been analyzed as a psychopathological hallucination: "Wholeness is in fact a hallucination, a developmental fiction."[44] Such a cathection to our mirror image, to wholeness, will not only occasion perpetual disappointment and anxious repair, because a body (like reality itself) constantly changes, but it will also occasion the transfer of our affections to the mediated image—rather than feelingly, ethically creating our present. Caught up into the world of images (as happens also with metaphysical idealism), helping behavior remains conflated with the narcissism of a person's world and/or idealist projections. Compassion, despite its inherent promise, does not here transcend the ego.

If compassion in the first instance has been distorted through the hallucination of wholeness and contorted by primary narcissism, compassion can be and has equally been distorted in practice by a resort to rhetorical righteousness with and through the "sanctifying of the subaltern," which turns out to be something of a shrine of self-pity or a way of pulling the shades on conscience—for example, lamenting the pitiable third world, while refusing to recognize the systemic nature of injustices.[45] In this latter passage, the third world becomes, cloaked in pity, a "signifier that allows us to forget that 'worlding'" process of imperialism, that disguises, naturalizes, and legitimates Western discourse.[46] Rhetorical invocatory resort of "the poor and the handicapped" or "the oppressed" works comparably: Assuming to be in solidarity with these locations, helpers, saturated with pity, avoid recognition of these loci as systemically constructed differences. A world heavily invested in pity toward the poor, the handicapped, the third world, and so on tends to privilege nondisabled norms, to identify power and success with ambulist metaphors.[47] A Christian theology that memorializes death, spoilation, and disease as structures of oppression will not unlikely be engaged in self-pity—even when historically projecting the pitiable elsewhere so that it can presume to remediate it, although now in the name of development, democracy, and/or justice.

Attempts at solidarity with subaltern or otherwise marginalized persons can also be an occasion for the sanctification of a person's own hurt, for our inability to measure up to the white, masculine, middle-class ideal. A step back from the founding fantasy of wholeness, we—now recognizing our own pain of incompletion, but projecting hurt elsewhere—mistake our own indulgence of life resentment for compassion for the systemically displaced or structurally excluded.[48] In a somewhat parallel development, quite recognizable (I suspect) to liberal-minded, especially religiously affiliated social-justice advocates, persons may hone, theorist Rey Chow suggests, a moral, intellectual rectitude, whose "claim to . . . truth . . . can only be made from 'a position of powerlessness.'" By rhetorically aligning ourselves with, so as to take cover behind, justice discourse, while renouncing political and relational power, the "protestant" makes him or herself into "the power of words alone." "Lying at the core of Anglo-American liberalism" and "the flip side of Western imperialism's ruthlessness," this rhetorical representational shelter provides persons with intellectual (though not ethical) exemption from participating in the systemic injustice each has come to recognize, but in a way that identifies with "the lack" as "powerlessness" of "the oppressed."[49] Not only does this misrepresent those for whom it claims to speak (this discourse typically misrepresents the disabled's capaciousness of voice, for example), but it continues to inhabit the dialectic of power versus lack in the modernist paradigm.[50] In the name of salvaging the wretched of the earth, it does not yet exit nor even necessarily intervene in the systemic production thereof. It has done nothing, for example, to swerve the hegemonic way of seeing that objectifies the oppressed. And given to reproaching rather than aspiring to power, even if differently articulated, it specifically disavows its own agency.[51]

In each of these psychological scenarios, saving the wretched of the earth is an affectively truncated critical morality that does not take leave of empire, but remains reactively, rather than transformatively, attached to imperialism. If so, Spirit, like a pall, covers an affective occlusion, and compassion aligns itself with the coercive power of superiority—either with the fiscal and military nationalist forces behind it or with an infinitizing, if sometimes cynical, despairing and ethically empty liberal consciousness. If Christianity might be at heart a philosophy of desire, as I trust it to be, that is, "God is Love," "For God so loved the world," then truncating the psychophysics of love into a moral modality hardly allows for the expansiveness definitionally attributed to compassion—compassion that would reflect a desire to connect with a larger sense of being and purpose, rather than with the interests of the self having its own way; compassion that would promise an exit from the jurisdictions of the marketplace; compassion that would allow us to breach our allegiance to privilege or status, to extend ourselves even into hostile affective zones (to love our enemy, in other words); compassion that might be deemed as acting out of awareness of life's basically communal ground, instead of remaining cathected to the optical illusion of consciousness, the ego-self.

In this regard, Spivak reminds us that compassion doesn't move from a well-fed world to one undeveloped, from the epitome of high culture, where persons' reflexes have been trained in human-rights discourse, to the helpless. "A desire to redistribute is not the unproblematic consequence of a well-fed society," Spivak observes. "In order to get that desire moving," she advises, "you have to fix the possibility of putting not just wrong over against right . . . but also to suggest that another antonym of right is responsibility."[52] When Spivak advises that "we need to suture [human] rights thinking into the torn cultural fabric of responsibility,"[53] she reprises the subaltern cultural wisdom that recognizes that to be human is to addressed by, to be called before, others.[54] In Spivak's words, we are "because the other calls us." Or variously, "the human being is human in answer to an 'outside call.'"[55]

Spivak would have us distinguish the notion of responsibility that has become synonymous with duty and that presumes the ideational template of metaphysical idealism from her notion of responsibility as affective and mutually capacious relations. This may be equally spoken of as "the difference between ethics as imagined from within the self-driven political calculus as 'doing the right thing' and ethics as openness toward the imagined agency of the other," including the agency of nonhuman earthlings and societies. Refining yet again her meaning, Spivak qualifies that she means "not a sense of being responsible for, but of being responsible to, before will."[56] Such response-ability to the imagined agency of the other precedes and cannot be derived from the language of rights, Spivak advises us. Finally, reminding us that "ethics are a problem of relation before they are a task of knowledge," Spivak concludes that "being defined by the call of the other—which may be a defining feature of [precapitalist] societies—is not conducive to the extraction and appropriation of surplus" as "living in the rhythm of the eco-biome does not lead to exploration and conquest of nature."[57] Spivak thus identifies as the aggitant opening out today's worldwide class apartheid what first appears as a subtle verbal difference between responsibility as the notion of moral duty attached to individual freedom (as embedded within human-rights discourse and including the moral duty to be a dispenser of human rights, that is, helper of the helpless and voice of the voiceless) as distinct from and over against the ethical responsibility of staying always open for the call of the other, of response-ability.[58]

"We are obligated to respond to our environment and other people in ways that open up rather than close off the possibility of response," theorist Kelly Oliver writes, putting this sensibility into something of a "golden rule," a wisdom teaching.[59] Alleviating objectification by engaging affective attention becomes imperative, given a sacred commitment to love.[60] But affect, Oliver quickly notes, must be distinguished from how the Western subjective economy has hinged desire on lack, deficit, deficiency—all of which behave reductively with difference and, of course, presume a hidden idealist template. "While desire is a lack in relation to the other that is born out of a primordial alienation," Oliver advises, "affect is a movement toward the other that is born out of love." "Affect," she continues, "is an alternative to a sacrificial economy that puts either the self or other in the place of lack or alienation." Where modern realism shaped our attention to difference through the logic of recognition, through the oppressive logic of superior/inferior, affective attention welcomes and, in that way, enables agency. Extending that thought, Oliver marks this affective, relational zone with an Exit sign from colonial spaces: "Opening a public space of love and generosity is crucial to opening a space beyond domination."[61] Compassion then flows "in opening myself to be 'othered' by the subaltern."[62]

Shall we then stop human-rights interventions and all current social missions? Not necessarily. "The enablement [of colonial violation] must be used even as the violation is renegotiated," Spivak advises.[63] It isn't as if "the liberated/savable" dialectic has been wholly and simply destructive, as if colonized persons haven't sometimes found ways to double-cross its logic so as to open out cultural strictures, as if liberation movements haven't been spawned from the margins that the dialectic itself in part generates, as if some persons with disabilities haven't gotten architectural access to public space and economy, given recognition by this optic. But as persons with disabilities have learned, there comes very quickly a point where liberation theologies will not work for us: While other liberation or civil-rights movements (feminism, queer, and black, for example) have been able to deconstruct the mark of lack as a phantasm of discourse, disabled bodies—because of the seeming facticity of incapacity—have thus far been theoretically not amenable to such discursive remediation, disclosive, perhaps, of the somatic wholesomeness and the economic individualism upon which other liberated subjectivities have depended.[64]

Persons with disabilities, interdependently capacious, may thus sit at the crux of rejoining response-ability with its propensity toward interdependent human collectivities, with the human rights of this passing modernist era. In that vein, Spivak insists on "ab/using" the Enlightenment episteme and its human rights agenda—just as a person with disability often works with science and medicine, and colonial subjects work with social missions, not in wholesale rejection, but "as a hacker enters software," as Spivak puts it. In terms of the human-rights agenda, for example, such ab/using of the episteme transpires by opening it out, supplementing it, rearranging it, changing its foci, recuperating dormant wisdom, while also "giving up convictions of triumphalist superiority."[65]

But that "cultural fabric of responsibility" as also this "public spaciousness of love" has intriguing and promising resonance with what has in nondominant Christian theologies been marked with the sign of Spirit. Addressing first the notion of public spaciousness, I turn to theologian Jürgen Moltmann. In a subsection of his *The Spirit of Life* titled "The Discovery of the Cosmic Breadth of Divine Spirit," Moltmann reclaims "the politics and ecology of the Spirit" within Christianity.[66] Deconstructing "anthropocentric pneumatology," he revisits the Hebraic sense of Spirit as "the power to live enjoyed by everything that is alive." Revisiting the Hebraic onomatopoetic play of *ruach* [spirit] as breath, he notes its connection to "breadth"—the space to breathe, the space of freedom, living room. Spirit, he then concludes, may be "experienced as this broad, open space for living."[67] It is a place of hospitality to difference, I would conclude, if one can open one's chest and breathe.

Comparably, "the 'spirits' of an indigenous culture" bear some resemblance to Moltmann's deduction of Spirit as animating energy of all that lives. "Spirits," David Abrams writes, referring to indigenous contexts, "are primarily those modes of intelligence or awareness that do not possess a human form"—the affective energies of other presences that surround and influence daily life to which every adult in the community must attune him or herself.[68] Within cultures that purport such responsibility and reciprocity, healing, which seems to lock Christianity's notion of the sacred into a world-transcending arch, has had precisely to do with adjudicating or balancing relations, both within the community and between the community and the larger field of forces in which it is embedded.[69] Exegeting Romans 8, Gerard Winstanley, leader of the Diggers of the English Reformation, similarly connected Spirit to "those who work together": "They that are resolved to work and eat together, making the earth a common treasury, doth join hands with Christ to lift up the creation from bondage and restores all things from the curse."[70]

Spirit does not appear in any of these scenarios as an intervening power or even as a supernatural, supercharged ether that causes changes such as miraculous remediation in others. Rather, Spirit names an inspirited or affective relational milieu with a hospitality to difference. That disability demands interdependent human collectivity makes the metaphor of disablement an intriguing postcolonial icon when connected with the metaphor of Spirit.[71]

Decolonizing Spirit

Theologies of healing—and inherently therefore theologies of Spirit—have been and can be unwitting agents of imperial ideals. We have been living Spirit as the potency of miraculous remediation and its offshoot, the politics of pity and rescue. Without critical, ethical reflection, a renewed theological emphasis on healing and the politics of compassion could but continue to participate with the interests of empire's bioregime. Without critical engagement of the orientation to normalcy that informs modern Western anthropology and medicine, if even also, then, theology, we may continue to carry the ideology of normalcy within our theology of Spirit. Spirit has, I suspect, become conflated with the scopic dynamics that generate normalcy and wholeness—the bourgeois body, that is. Spirit has become something of a prosthesis, we might say, of respectability and wholesomeness.

As experienced even in the rhetorical resort to a dramaturgy of miraculous remediation of disabilities via technobiopower, Spirit may—at least in this late stage of media/ted Platonism within which we live—cooperate with the conventions of representation within this cult of public appearance, that is, normalcy, efficiency, independence, productivity, wholesomeness. Healing practice—whether through technobiopower as also in certain incarnations of the politics of conspicuous compassion, or even in our liturgical performances of these texts—would not then necessarily ameliorate, but could exacerbate empire. If we are to creatively resist the anxieties occasioning our easy resort to the compunctions of normalcy, leaving us compliant with the ideals of globalizing capitalism, proceeding to reconstruct a theology of Spirit seems necessary.

Given that we have tended to read the efficacy of Spirit as correlated to our understanding of resurrection, if also miraculous remediation, feminist theologian Rita Nakashima Brock may begin to help us break through the power that has been paraded as transcendental realism, of the Spirit as Wonder Worker and Cure-All. Brock, in *Journeys By Heart: A Christology of Erotic Power*, notes that in regard to the colonized subjects of Palestine, "the resurrection did not cause the downfall of powers of political oppression." And, she adds, "no one heroic or divine deed will defeat oppressive powers and death-delivery systems."[72] Rather, resurrection was "just enough erotic power . . . to withstand and integrate tragedy," while redemption might name the communal restoration of the structures of the human life-world.[73] Now those are definitions of the efficacy of Spirit with which a differently abled person can live.

In a text that similarly reconstructs a theology of Spirit and healing, postcolonial feminist Musa Dube's *Postcolonial Feminist Interpretation of the Bible* situates events of healing within the politics of structural forces where people take life into their own hands. Healing names a "discourse for confronting social ills, not as helpless beings who are neglected by God, but as those who are . . . capable of changing their social conditions," Dube writes.[74] Brock adds, "The point is not Jesus' sole possession of power, but the revelation of a new understanding of power that connects members of the community. The power of reversal comes from those perceived as weak [by the imperial standard of power] who reveal the divine way of power, erotic [or empathic] power." Later, Brock concludes that "what is truly christological . . . truly revealing of

. . . salvific power in human life must reside in connectedness and not in individuals."[75] In that vein, "trust in [empathic] power . . . in the face of oppressive systems" is difficult but "crucial . . . to a community's survival."[76] In this regard, Spirit might be considered a personal and/or communal passion for life, a passionate equanimity that refuses the chokehold of trauma and terror, the daily grind of anxiety, so that life can be resurrected or inspirited within that life region.

The pronouncement that "the blind see, the lame walk, the deaf hear" (see Isa 35:5-6, Matt 11:4-5, and Luke 7:22) has been read as proof text of the supernatural power of the divine to remediate physiological conditions, a reading that, when visited through the politics of compassion as through discursive, religious and/or biotechnological performance of the supernatural, then turns 'round to marginalize and stigmatize bodies that prove resistant to cure. But what if miracle and supernatural metaphysics, or even healing and the supernaturally fueled imagination of biotechno-science were not so much the import of these stories as we have presumed to find there? Further, the question needs to be asked whether biblical miracle and healing stories would be in any possible way about us—about persons we see as living with disabilities, that is. After all, what we treat categorically as disability developed with modernity, between the eighteenth and the twentieth century—as a binary correlate of normalcy.

Somatic intactness, the fit body, has been much more important to the contemporary western world as a symbol of well-being than it was to the ancients. The synoptic Gospels portray Jesus as advising that the integrity of the body has nothing so much to do with its physiognomic wholeness: "If your hand causes you to sin, cut it off" (Matt 5:30). Amputation was simply basic medicinal wisdom. Further, disablement from disease, war, and malnutrition were, quite unlike today (at least in the North American and Western European regions) culturally pervasive, given limited medical remediation, the state of war technology, and the nature of physical labor. And as Martha Edwards observed in "Constructions of Physical Disability in the Ancient Greek World," "a physically handicapped person earning a living would not have been a remarkable sight."[77] Indeed, living to old age in the ancient world was hardly gratifying, but rather was dreaded, such that finding ways to throw oneself virtuously, heroically at death—not longevity—was culturally valued.[78] Whatever health was then, and consequently the apparent biblical liturgy of disabilities reversed, in which, "the blind see, the lame walk, the deaf hear," it likely did not have the biological enframement of a life in our world as its template. What, then, might a postcolonially invested reading of these same texts suggest?

CHAPTER

A CRIP NATION

Several of us mill around backstage, waiting to make our appearance for the new prosthetics conglomerate. Among the nervously prancing lot of us, considered to be stellar examples of the exceptional skills of the company's prosthetic design teams, are one veteran of the first Gulf War and myself. The CEO of the prosthetics firm, an inventor of one its leading technological breakthroughs and whose name now serves as that of the conglomerate itself, hearing of my athleticism and persistence as well as the difficulty of design that has gone into my latest prosthetic incarnation, has come backstage to meet me. In that gratuitous exchange, he promises to teach me to run on my prosthesis that evening—right there, in front of his gathered audience. Offstage and out of ear, the veteran rolls his eyes, signaling his reassurance in a collusion of disbelief. He confides in a whisper that his health care patron is Ross Perot, then a U.S. presidential candidate. His lower-limb prosthesis, given Perot's generosity, has been carefully cosmetically toned to his ebony skin and equipped with the latest prosthetic innovation, the ability to feel—restoring, so the literature claims, neurological sensations such as hot and cold. The veteran confesses that he isn't "a believer." No, we are "show ponies," he instructs me. That night, two show ponies play with the optics of being a living miracle, just doing what we have to do to get the best medical care we can while silencing our disbelief in the rhetorically inflated claims of the medicine show.

In an anthology titled *Staring Back*, poet Lynn Manning draws us into the tent of his own medicine show, a "world turned upside down" where, with the wave of a magic (white) wand, he miraculously turns from fearsome black man to pathetic blind man:

> No matter how powerful the image, it can be shaped and altered to fit within a particular cultural order. Furthermore... it is not simply the creator of the image doing this, but the spectator necessarily shifts and contorts the image.... From a clichéd and mass-produced painting to the body of Christ, there is a constant force of relations between image and culture.... Images do not simply exist—they must be made visible. This rendering visible of the image is part of the creation of a spectator.
>
> —**Patrick Fuery and Kelli Fuery,**
> *Visual Cultures and Critical Theory*

Quick-change artist extraordinaire,
I whip out my folded cane
and change from black man to blind man
with a flick of my wrist.

To account for his "profound metamorphosis" "From rape driven misogynist / to poor motherless child," Manning offers this explanation: "I only wield the wand; / You are the magician."[1] Such play with the optics of disability and miracle leave me interested in how the wondrous or the miraculous plays back upon the colonizing forces exercised upon bodies and what persons living with disabilities—the Crip Nation—make of miracle traditions.

Indisputably, in terms of Gospel texts and also early Christian icons and reliefs, miracles—the multiplication of the loaves of bread, the resurrection of Lazarus, the blind man healed by clay, the encounter with the hemorrhaging woman, the transformation of water to wine at the wedding in Cana, the three men in the fiery furnace (from Daniel), the cure of the paralytic upon the bed—appear to be "the core, the mainstay of Early Christian imagery." This is in contradistinction, for example, to today's emphasis on the life of Jesus from nativity and palm-strewn procession into Jerusalem to Golgatha and Easter.[2] "Like advertising slogans, [these images of miracle, in story and art, were] repeated to the point of saturation," concludes art historian Thomas Mathew. These images appeared on everything from dinner plates to textiles to amulets and iconography. In the war of imagery and representation, "What was the urgency that a Christian should need to have them on the hem of her tunic, on the ring on her finger, on her husband's tomb?" Mathews wonders, concluding that, surely, "miracles were repeated not because the artists ran out of things to say, but because these subjects said what they wanted to say, and said it perfectly."[3] But what precisely was being said?

"A convincing argument for inferring miracle working activity from miracle stories has been difficult to find," biblical scholar Burton Mack confesses.[4] And medical anthropologist Gary Ferngren, having studied patristic texts and church liturgies and noting the dearth of any references to healing in the Pauline Epistles, has concluded that "healing enjoyed little prominence in the first two centuries [of Christianity]; that it began to assume more importance in the third; that there is evidence of a major shift in emphasis—in which healing secured a prominence . . . during the fourth century."[5] In other words, miracle accounts likely did not, at least initially, correlate with Christian practices and liturgies of healing. And if Mathew's study leads him to suspect that these miracle images, representing "the standard repertory" of Christian art up through the fourth century, were "distinctively pacific, non-military, and non-imperial," why were people winging, flinging, wielding rumors of miracles against the powers of empire?[6] How might miracles have functioned within colonizing conditions, especially considering the rumor mill of miracles was run by a rather unwholesome lot, at least as measured by our standards and statistical norms?

Using Disability "to Think with"

Karen King once quipped that "men use women to think with."[7] Biblical texts themselves comparably evolved several ways of thinking analogically with and through the experience of disablement. Disability was, perhaps quite surprisingly, sometimes deployed to suggest paradoxical strength, for example, Moses' stutter (Exod 4:10-12) and Paul's power made perfect in weakness (2 Cor 12:9). Paradigmatic in this regard, the story of Jacob, as the one who wrestled with God and limped away, served the nation of Israel as its own event of naming (Gen 32:28, 35:10).[8] The nation of Israel carried in its own name knowledge that the interface with the divine could propitiously incapacitate. As biblical scholar Simon Horne points out in "'Those Who are Blind See': Some New Testament Uses of Impairment, Inability, and Paradox," "in ancient literature . . . paradox is associated with inability in a particular way: within inability is striking capability. . . . As if to underline the axiom's truth, the authority held in greatest respect in ancient society for his insight into human and divine affairs was a blind person, the epic poet Homer."[9] Even Jesus' death on the cross might be configured within such shades of meaning.

Disability sometimes has served within biblical passages as a rhetorical diminutive wagered to point to spiritual occlusions, for example: You Pharisees are more disabled than the disabled (See John 9). This resonates with the ancient paradox that the blind may be wiser than the sighted. Sight was never a guarantor of insight. Consistent with this, conditions of disablement served to name impediments within the liturgical practice of the spiritual body—barriers to hearing, seeing, walking by faith, such that spiritual blindness, for example, names "attachment to material goods" in Luke.[10] Though seemingly meant to remove physical disability as a relational stumbling block within the community by suggestively pointing to the spiritual impediments in those who refuse differently abled persons the energy of transcendent human relations (as, for example, in John 9), this metaphoric deployment has, of course, frequently been visited against the somatic or organic incursion that we now name disability—as if we culturally still believed sin were physiognomically evidenced.

That some were "born blind" (John 9) could also be read in a similar vein as the limp of Jacob—that is, as the mark of a capacious visitation, not requiring healing, but communal discernment. Monstrous bodies, bodies born differently abled and capacious, were in antiquity at times considered portentous. These bodies were reminders of cosmic surplus that was not and could not be captured within social order. The excessive quality of such bodies was not to be cured—either miraculously or by inclusion. Rather, their existence was the epiphenomenon of the miraculous—the visitation of the excess, the outside, the wisdom that comes from another place. To table with these portentous, if also socially marginal, bodies might invite derision—the positive, rhetorical art of social critique.

Taking us into the infamous Roman "monster market," Carlin Barton, in her study titled, *The Sorrows of the Ancient Romans*, suggests that the deformed or monstrous were cultural derisors, invited to perform at banquets and courtly events. If sometimes simultaneously also the target of derision, these "licensed fools" were the "professional," if also "envied" scoffers, mimics, and satirists who opened out political and social critique and broke through the resentments circulating under hierarchy, who, being considered outside the social limits, were authorized to deride or mock the emperor and the elite to their benefit and pleasure.[11]

Certainly such a system used freaks to allow resentments to be cathartically opened out and absorbed without social revision. And yet the scoffer might have enjoyed a certain power pleasure. A freak might have been making a communal contribution of social critique, and not just as the class clown who feels some measure of affirmation in rejection. Freaks may have had the double vision of the oppressed and the privilege—if complexly perverted—of saying so. "It is not surprising," Barton concludes, "that, in a period where Romans themselves complain of being debilitated by excessive refinements and distinctions, when the wealthy build 'pauper's huts,' sleep on boards, eat the black gruel of the despised rustic, and write bucolic poetry, they would be attracted to the virile wilderness of grotesques."[12] Barton's insight here suggests an assumed relation between wilderness and grotesques that was culturally appropriated to rehabilitate the wealthy, who had been weakened by overrefinement. We might ask whether a similar ethos might have been enfolded within Luke's charity banquet: Given that Luke's gospel was apparently addressed to a more intensely urban scene, might his audience have included those considered corrupted by leisure, those needing to be restored to nature?

To this list of insights regarding the metaphoric deployment of disability within biblical literature, I would like to propose yet another: What if—as unthinkable as it might have been in the mode of modern realism—the main characters, the assumed populace telling and hearing the stories, considered themselves cripped? What if these persons were playing with the power of a stigmatic difference across the lines of race-class oppression in the vein of Manning's play with race and disability? Then, far from assuming miracles to be about a repair to normalcy, might we rather have behind or within miracle and healing accounts a Crip Nation playing against empire, fighting fire with fire, through the powers of something like magical realism?

Not as a biblical scholar, but as a theologian practicing disability and postcolonial theories simply to insinuate other possible insights into these ancient texts and, therefore, into the imaginary of our future, I will ask two questions. First: How might these texts have effected or generated meaning in their life regions? In other words: What could Spirit have constructively induced in this hybrid zone, if not miraculous remediation? That Christianity has shaped its understanding of and practice in regard to divine efficacy upon the trajectory of power it has read into miracle stories, as theologian David Ray Griffin has noted, makes this question all the more important: "The 'argument from miracles' was usually the chief pillar of the Church's evidence for its authority."[13] Second: What does one do with such texts at this juncture in the twenty-first century? Reading with postcolonial and disabilities sensibilities, might Spirit suggestively sign for us a way of creatively living within so as to get an exit visa from empire?

Rather than focusing on any one healing story in particular, I take as my starting point the broad, liberative, if familiar banner headline in the synoptic Gospels of Matthew and Luke that appears to address the status of disabled bodies—"the blind see, the lame walk, the deaf hear." My reason for this choice has to do with the way this particular refrain gets carried forward into Christian and, especially, Advent liturgies, into our Christological portraits, and into the imagination of biotechnoscience. Consequent to the report of several healings, resurrections, and exorcisms performed by Jesus, John the Baptist purportedly sends several of his disciples to Jesus with the question, Are you the great prophet whom we were expecting, or are we to wait for another? Jesus purportedly retorts, "Go and tell John what you have seen and heard: the blind receive their sight, the lame walk, the lepers are cleansed, the deaf hear, the dead are raised, the poor have good news brought to them" (Luke 7:22 NRSV). Biblical scholars trace this refrain back to Isaiah 35:5-6 and 61:1, as well as through the intertestamental literature of the Sibylline Oracles. Parallels also appear in several of the Dead Sea Scrolls.

Not Disability, but Slavery

The recitatives of miracle cures, the liturgical refrain carried from Isaiah to Luke, "the blind see, the lame walk, the deaf hear," have sometimes been read as part of the Persian "World Made Wonderful tradition."[14] "It was the prophet Zoraster who as early as 1500 B.C.E. challenged the inevitability of social injustice [and "the imperial mythologies of an eternally hierarchical and oppressive status quo"] with a "vision of a coming time . . . the 'making wonderful.'"[15] Isaiah appears canonically to be the first to liturgize this refrain. But this suggests the reversal of empire—not necessarily of an individual disability per se, but of economic colonization and the body politics that go with them. Consequently, disabilities as poetically liturgized in Isaiah need to be read in terms of resistance to that political affliction—not on their own individualistic and medicalized terms of health, but in terms of life under empire and within economic straights.

In the surrounding region of the ancient Middle East, this particular refrain of impediments—blindness, lameness, and deafness—suggested ways in which debt slaves and prisoners of war were prevented from fleeing their captors. All such disablements have to do with preventing the flight of slaves or with the humiliation of prisoners of war or, where not directly and aggressively exacted, with the ways in which colonialism undercuts sufficiency, aggravating disease. "There is overwhelming historical evidence," observes historian Gerda Lerner regarding the earliest records of enemy survivors in Mesopotamia circa 2500 B.C.E., "for the preponderance of the practice of . . . mutilating male prisoners and for the large-scale enslavement and rape of female prisoners."[16] Indeed, there are "some references in the texts to blinded war captives, who were set to work in the orchards," she continues, citing additional evidence from the Neo-Assyrian period.[17] In a similar vein, historian Timothy Taylor, while writing of the slave trade in the second half of the first millennium B.C.E., incidentally notes that the annals of the fifth-century B.C.E. Greek historian Herodotus mention that "the Scythians blind all their slaves" so as to become "the principal workforce in horse dairying."[18] In this case, blindness seems to have been intended to prevent nomadic persons from escaping the drudgery of this repetitive labor, occasioning insurrection, or absconding with portions of the herd. Other ancient citations suggest that blindness, most frequently inflicted on males, led to labor in milling and in music.[19]

Moving from slave and prisoner practices in the broader Middle East to focus on our primary document, Lerner points out that the Hebrew testament itself testifies to such practices: "The Old Testament mentions a number of cases of the blinding of prisoners of war: Samson (Judg 17:21), Zedekiah (2 Kgs 25:7), and the story of the men of Jabesh (2 Sam 11:2)."[20] To put but one of these biblical examples in mind, consider 2 Kings 24:17–25:7: "Zedekiah rebelled against the king of Babylon. And in the ninth year of his reign, in the tenth month, on the tenth day of the month, King Nebuchadnezzar of Babylon came with all his army against Jerusalem and laid siege to it" (24:20b-25:1). After an extended besiegement and famine, King Zedekiah attempted an escape, but was captured and brought back to Nebuchadnezzar. Of the scene when Zedekiah was brought before the King of Babylon, the priestly writer reports that "they slaughtered the sons of Zedekiah before his eyes, then put out the eyes of Zedekiah; they bound him in fetters and took him to Babylon" (2 Kgs 25:7). Especially high-ranking prisoners of war—kings and officers of the defeated armies, for example—most frequently, though not solely, were subjected to blinding, to putting out the eyes, as a public act of humiliation.

Various other ancient texts similarly record the hobbling of slaves and of their amputations. In Kirghiz practice, "an incision [was made] in the sole of a captive's foot" and "a horse's hair [was inserted], so that after the wound is completely healed walking is very painful."[21] Citing sources like Seneca, Jewish scholar Shemuel Rubinstein explains the amputation of various appendages, including of a slave's ears, among slave-control practices in the ancient world: "For some wrongdoing in his work, or for breaking some vessel, the slave's fingers or hands could be cut off. . . . The amputation of a slave's ears was so commonly practiced that it was established as a punishment for slaves. The Hammurabi Code stipulates: 'If a slave strikes a free person on the cheek, his ear is to be cut off.'"[22] Like the rape of women, something that often occurred alongside these practices, such acts of intentional mutilation were about warfare by way of psychological humiliation.[23] Still other sources suggest that circumcision may also have arisen "as a mark of defilement or slavery."[24] That the males of the nation of Israel might then have assumed this as the sign of their solidarity queers their signs of enslavement or humiliation while generating an affiliative network, assumedly in the name of Yahweh, that expressly renounces slavery as an acceptable sociopolitical practice.

Such miracle scenes, which have been interpreted by biblical scholars to hold promise of eschatological reversal, may not have so much to do with supernatural cure or technobiopower's reversal of disability as with the destabilization and leveling of empire, an economic and sociopolitical situation in which poverty and ideological colonization and/or sociopolitical enslavement occasion injuries to corporeal flourishing and communal well-being. Various biblical passages, in fact, consistently yoke these conditions in appositive phrases—Psalm 146, for example

("The Lord sets the prisoners free; the Lord opens the eyes of the blind"), and also Luke 4, where Jesus' missional charge, assumed (although enhanced with the disabling images of captivity) from Isaiah 61, links "the setting at liberty" of debt prisoners with the erasure of such economic conditions. Jewish scholar Rav Elchanan Samet insists that for Israel "slavery in itself [was] considered an improper social situation" that "should not exist within the Jewish nation." While the people of Israel were invoked as slaves or "servants of Yahweh," this self-designation precisely "nullified the social practice of slavery."[25] Were these images of disablement, captured in liturgical refrain, then but expansive metaphors for recalling the broader Hebraic theme of Yahweh's peoples as expressly brought "out of" slavery? Jeremiah most explicitly memorializes the return of the exiles in terms of their stigmata: "See, I am going to bring them from the land of the north . . . among them the blind and the lame . . . for I have become a father to Israel" (Jer 31:8-9).

The first biblical instance of an image that will be built into the specific metaphoric refrain under consideration appears to be that embedded in an Isaianic unit on the redemption of Judah from Babylonian exile, specifically Isaiah 42:10-17: "I will lead the blind along the way, guide them in paths they have not known, turning the darkness to light before them, the rough spots into even ground" (v 16). The invitation to "sing a new song" (v. 1) appears addressed to the oceans and territories surrounding the Arab lands of Kedar and Sela, where Cyrus the Persian had been greeted as Israel's redeemer from Babylon (45:13). A second instance of the language, now more poetically stylized and complete, occurs in Isaiah 35:1-10: "Then the eyes of the blind will be opened, the ears of the deaf unstopped; then the cripple will leap like the deer, and the tongue of the dumb shout for joy" (vv. 5-6). This unit, assumed by scholars to have drawn on the themes in Isaiah 40–48, appears to have been composed—perhaps by Deutero-Isaiah after his return to Palestine—together with chapter 34 so as to conclude chapters 1 through 33.[26] This refined composition celebrates the conjoint human and ecosystemic restoration of Judah, the land itself—parallel to the human—having been imaged as scarred and scorched: "The parched land [will turn into] gushing streams; the haunt where jackals crouched will be a place of reeds and rushes" (Isa 35:7). Whatever had transpired to human bodies was also recalled as having exacted devastation on the land—more precisely as practices that have dried up wetlands and streambeds, occasioned desertification and the evisceration of the animate life of forests. With this latter occurrence, scholars suggest that the scene has clearly shifted to Judah, with "the glory of Lebanon" (Isa 35:2, 60:13) in view.

In short, these songs of Isaiah 42 and 35, with their enticing promises of ecological restoration, of divine sovereignty and spiritual endowments (dreams, prophesies), of human longevity and political reversal, appear to be borrowing Persian traditions, the philosophies of Israel's new colonial savior, to extricate or dislodge persons from its existing colonizer, Babylon. Reintroducing a cosmic or creation dimension "to a Yahwism languishing under an interpretation of divine activity which limited divine action too severely to historical events," the prophet's "making wonderful" embellishments "stop[ped] short of an escape into the purely visionary realm of myth."[27]

Yet as beautiful as the poetry is, as strong as its image may be and as enticing as was the Isaianic hope, Israelites, especially the elite, did not necessarily come jubilantly streaming out of their exilic holds at the beckoning of the hymn. The metropolitan cities of the empire, that of the Assyrians as also that of Babylon, had grown familiar, comfortable—especially when set over against the realia of that tiny, rural, and impoverished, twenty-five-mile-long subprovince of Judah, forced to "scrap[e] an existence from a land that had been repeatedly devastated by war, conquest, taxation."[28] So if the liturgical refrain yet again were chanted, as it would be later amid the Pax Romana (Matthew and Luke), might the refrain not always be a welcome rallying cry, but something more like a prophetic call to conscientization, a call to wake to the ideological, if not sociopolitical powers in the hands of which people found themselves, a call to renounce such enslaving, colonizing conditions insomuch as these servants of Yahweh had been called out of precisely such conditions?

In unfolding eras, people might have found ways, using this metaphorically loaded refrain, to remind themselves that they were but "docile bodies" (Foucault), socially constructed by regimes not resonant with their own cultural sense of life and wellbeing, constructed by regimes that hobbled their flourishing. This refrain, "the blind see, the deaf hear, the lame walk," whose metaphors we have presumed to announce miraculous cure of an individuated body, might instead have functioned as a persistent ideological interruption of the prevailing regime of constructed meaning when again liturgically evoked.[29] A world made wonderful needed not so much miraculous remediation of a disabled body as sociopolitical reconstruction.

One must wonder what conflations of these and likely other varied meanings get attached to the metaphors of disablement in biblical use. Intriguingly, there remains a metaphoric knot yet to unravel—"the strange fact that Passover, the Jewish holiday celebrated every spring to commemorate the Exodus from Egypt . . . is called *pesach* in Hebrew, and *pesach* is cognate with the root verb that means lame or limping."[30] Further, a spring ritual involving a limping dance, likely an imitation of the mating dance of the partridge, has been recorded in the Book of Kings (1 Kings 18:26). The dancers in this pericope belong among the worshipers of Baal, who leap around so as to appeal to Baal to "light the Spring bonfires and burn up the corpse of the old year." But yet again "the original Hebrew word [has been] formed from the root PSCH, which means 'to dance with a limp,' and from which Pesach, the name of the Passover Feast, is derived."[31] In cultural hybridization, how does that dance come to gather up Jacob's wrestling match and resultant limp and empty into the annual ritual of Passover? And how shall we know in the midst of it the reference for what limps? Does it not remember a certain way of living the body in pain, such that at such tensive interstices pain, even mutilation, might be simultaneous with knowledge, with especially spiritual knowledge?[32]

Does the limp have anything to do with Israel itself—as a nation, as a people who dance with God? Does this people wrestle with, ever and again succumbing to, that condition that they must refuse as a people—slavery or colonization? Micah 4 seems to suggest that this metaphoric disablement figuratively marks them as a nation: "In that day, says the Lord, I will assemble the lame. . . . The lame I will make the remnant and those who were cast off, a strong nation" (4:6-7). Rather than proving to be a perimeter of exclusion, the stigmata of disablement marks out these people. These people make meaning and value in relation to the marks life carves on their flesh.[33]

A Crip Nation remembers that it was but a slave in Egypt, refuses humiliation, and casts the cloak of shame back upon its colonizers. Isaiah 42 likewise either seems to suggest the servant leadership of one who had been blinded (42:19) or once again puts such metaphors of blindness and deafness, which I have connected with economic and political practices of enslavement, at the pivotal heart of being a covenant people. Given the presumptions of modernity, especially modernity's social group-grid overlay of normal/deviant, that a self-asserting Crip Nation proves the subjective center of the narrative named the history of Israel comes as quite the surprise.

In *Milagro* ("Miracle") Valley

The destruction of the Second Temple by Rome in 67/70 C.E. set the stage for the composition of the Christian Gospels.[34] While Israel had been living under various empires for six centuries (since the fall of the First Temple in 587 B.C.E.), the presence of the Roman Empire had provoked more Jewish resistance in the century surrounding the Common Era than any previous imperial presence.

Whereas in the earliest decades of the Common Era, Rome had worked on Palestine through the generations of the Herods, its client rulers, for example, Herod Antipas, whom Luke portrays as a "jackal" (Luke 13:32), the destruction of the temple proved Rome's all-determining grip. Rome's world encompassment must now have seemed rather complete, especially given its refusal, unlike earlier Persia, to allow for the rebuilding of the temple. Our Gospels, authored at such a point in history, thus constitute what Toni Morrison calls "acts of re-memoration"—that is, the "recreation of popular memory" among persons living in a land that has been "reterritorialized, even terrorized by another."[35]

History has a way of foreclosing the narratives of the conquered, as postcolonial theorist Homi Bhabha notes, of territorializing even the historical memory of the colonized.[36] "Acts of re-memoration" interrogate the haunts, the absences, the excisions and evictions of such persons, becoming "for that very reason . . . the *unheimlich* space for the negotiation of identity and history." "Suddenly from the space of the not-there emerges," explains Bhabha, "the re-membered historical agency 'manifestly directed toward the rediscovery of truth which lies in the order of symbols.'"[37] While the mood of modern historical realism has led readers into thinking of the Gospels as representing the decades of the middle of the first century, the Gospels may rather create a popular memory of that time so as to empower the last decades of the first century. The Gospels as later popular culture presume the need to live within the belly of the beast of the Roman Empire and its history.

Within the purview of the crushing devastation of the loss of the Second Temple and the now rather emphatic show of force of Rome's imperial presence behind the Herods and the economy of Israel, Christians recall the Isaianic blueprint of a temple not made with hands as a template for their "theology of subversive cohabitation."[38] "Save for the Psalms, the Book of Isaiah is the most frequently quoted Hebrew source in the New Testament."[39] Both Matthew and Luke—the Gospels that carry the liturgical refrain that "the blind see, the lame walk" most straightforwardly—display heavy reliance on Isaiah, a text that biblical scholar Paul Hanson claims had been pretty well quarantined within Second Temple Judaism, given its rejection of the stone-block temple-rebuilding project in favor of "the true temple," the community of Yahweh.[40] But how could the disfigured slave, the suffering servant, of Isaiah 53, which figures so prominently in the Gospel traditions, entice desire to obtain an exit visa from empire? On top of that, Second Isaiah was an appeal to "reluctant exiles . . . to come home to Jerusalem," which must be something like convincing persons to return to their economically decimated countries of origin after university training and time within North American culture.[41] How could an invocation of the Crip Nation be expected to appeal to the already reluctant? "He had followers," scholar Norman Cohn hypothesizes of Second Isaiah, "but there are no grounds for thinking them numerous. And if, as is more than likely, the fourth of the 'servant songs' is about him, he paid for his prophetic role by being scourged and killed—whether by the Babylonian authorities, alarmed by the political implications of his message, or by the deportees, disillusioned when Cyrus [initially] failed to carry out the prophesied destruction of Babylon."[42] Yet it would be the "body in pain," as scholar of late antiquities Judith Perkins puts it, that would serve as the iconic locus of early Christianity, despite the fact that we cannot presume any wide-scale persecution of Christians prior to the mid-third century.[43]

But not just the body in pain: If it is the crip body that catches the eye of speculation, that body has always already been caught up in the liturgical refrain of miracles. In the popular re-memoration of the Gospels, miracle stories parallel the redeployment of this crip figure even though, as Ferngren would surely remind us, "healing enjoyed little prominence in the first two centuries [of Christianity]," and it is this convergence of the symbol of disablement, of the Crip Nation, with the lore of miracles that concerns us here. Miracle stories were told by and among bodies performatively engaged in the body in pain. But that remembered agency, "those signs by which marginalized or insurgent subjects create a collective agency," then moved in the late first century through the Crip Nation.[44] Here we have what could only fall to modern realism as paradoxically impossible: The crip body tells miracle stories, and miracles support the emergence of a decidedly renovated and rereleased Crip Nation.

Making Something of the Body in Pain

"In the discursive climate of the early Roman empire . . . groups of Christians in the Greco-Roman world chose to foreground their own suffering," writes Perkins in *The Suffering Self: Pain and Narrative Representation in the Early Christian Era*.[45] Texts of the second century, Perkins contends, and the scholarship of Peter Brown and Gregory Riley corroborate this, contain an innovation in the technologies of self: Christians "represented the human self as a body in pain, a sufferer."[46] Before a culture innovates with healing practices, there arrives the performance of the sick and suffering body, the acting out of a body that needs to be tended. It is this representational performance of the body in pain that Perkins situates within the early centuries of and as the cultural innovation that was Christianity. But this new representation, Perkins further contends, had an explicit agenda: "This representation challenged another, prevailing, more traditional Greco-Roman image of the self . . . as a rational mind/soul exerting control upon a body whose needs and desires inhibited the mind/soul's attaining the perfection that was imaged in the rational order of the cosmos." Indisputably, such a philosophical orientation then as now sustained the emergence of a charmed life, of a romantic life immune from pain, if socially buffered and secured by other body castes.[47] What we name Christian movements formed as a broad-based, polylocal resistant protest, as a new representation of the self within that milieu—explicitly as "a mind/soul joined to a body liable to pain and suffering."[48] To wield the symbolic power of the body in pain amid "the reality of the second century where status was being increasingly delineated in law, and contempt for the common . . . by the well-born was nearly universal" was to offer sociality a great equalizer:[49] Just as the Wisdom of Solomon noted that death equalizes king and commoner (7:3-5), so this "cultural shift towards the body" performed by Christian movements "worked to downplay differences of class and gender," because "the body was one aspect of human being where all shared equally the need for external help—whether slave or emperor, man or woman."[50]

"The body in pain," as literary theorist Elaine Scarry titled her study of the phenomenology of pain in relation to war and torture, has long been used to give evidence of the power of a dominant regime. Hence, the strength of a nation has been assumed to be equivalent to the power of its military arsenal and standing armies—and inherently therefore equivalent to its ability to inflict injury and pain and to threaten or exact death during wartimes.[51] But Christian discourse in the early centuries of the Common Era, Perkins argues, inverted pain's authorizing power: "Christian discourse reverses this equation and thus redefines some of the most basic signifiers in any culture—the body, pain and death."[52] The body in pain now speaks back—not giving evidence for the dominant regime, but as a culture critic. Christians come to wear pain as a sign of their rejection of contemporary society, of its relational or cast geography and values, and most explicitly of how it constructed political power, that is, as the ability to inflict pain, injury, or disability.[53] It was in that socially prophetic vein, of course, that Christianity situated the body in pain—the body crucified at the juxtaposition of social forces—as its central icon.

"Christianity as a social and political unity," Perkins concludes, "would form and ultimately achieve its institutional power . . . around . . . the suffering self."[54] Within a basin of cultural discourse that did not have such social classificatory categories, that was searching for language to open out new vistas on its experience, Christianity wielded "this new knowledge of the self as sufferer."[55] Daring such a reversal of signatory power for pain, "Christianity offered converts a useful function for pain and a structure for understanding human suffering"—suffering "as powerful and redemptive."[56] Bodies in pain, whether of persons diseased or of those having thrown themselves at death in martyrdom, demanded social attention, rattled the calm of the charmed ones, not because these bodies in pain were pitiable, but because pain no longer acquiescently authorized the political and economic regime of the Pax Romana or its aesthetic calm and control.[57]

Like Perkins, Gregory Riley notes the inversion of the meaning of suffering in the late decades of the first century, rolling into the second: Suffering was no longer to be viewed as the punishment of God, as it was in the early Hebraic pastorals of the time of the covenant. Instead, the righteous, given the consequent interface of Judaism with empires (Persian, Greek, Roman), were now seen to suffer due to the malfeasance of the unrighteous.[58] "There was [in Hebraic thought]," observes Riley, "no provision for the suffering of the righteous on such a scale as national destruction." With the relentless march of empires, it had become obvious that "the idealistic [pastoral] covenants assuring long and pleasant life had failed."[59] Christianity, forming within the milieu of the razing of the Second Temple, then mobilized these bodies in pain by democratizing the hero journey, Riley suggests in *One Jesus, Many Christs: How Jesus Inspired Not One True Christianity but Many*. "The immortality promised the hero was in Christianity promised to all," writes Riley, adding that "this was the advantage of Christianity in dealing with ancient pessimism about death, in so far as all were invited to take up the life of the hero."[60] The Gospels may resemble *The Iliad* (43), as Dennis MacDonald and Marianne Bonz have also claimed; the Christian testaments did not, however, produce just one hero, but rather made the hero's path an available life narrative for persons at all social strata.[61] In a world where Greek romances envisioned marriage as the conventional happy ending, Christians pitted hagiography against romance. Christians threw themselves into the path of a heroic and virtuous death as a way of effecting judgment on their contemporary society, seen as "unjust and lawless."[62]

But to be sure, in a world in which old age was synonymous with being a host for diseases and within which there was no medical care, finding a virtuous or sacrificial death in what we might call the midst of life (the decades of the twenties and thirties) was the better part of wisdom. Consequently, Christians, like the ancient hero, cultivated the "choice to die for principle and with honor," to effect "a death of principle, commitment and integrity."[63]

Insomuch as a sacrificial life, a life of suffering seen to be induced by "opposition by superior powers" became "the very point of human life," crips and the poor were "central players in this cosmic drama."[64] If Isaiah chapters 53 and 54 give us a portrait of the prophet Isaiah himself, of one who dared ideological critique of Babylon's habituated comforts (as Norman Cohn presumes), perhaps it is not now so surprising that Isaiah's suffering servant figuration, the homely, disfigured servant, the crip of Isaiah 53, prominently informs the template of synoptic Jesus portraiture, the blueprint (given the razing of the Second Temple) for the corporate body of Christ.[65] Perkins, while writing more explicitly from confirmed texts of the second century, echoes Riley's deductions: Christians as a people wore their suffering as a sign of their rejection of existent human society, as a judgment upon their society's values. In that situation, suffering, whether from diseases and disabilities or from martyrdom, served as "the means of achieving real selfhood." Pain was no longer viewed as punitive, but as "a school of discipline," and death was ultimate victory insomuch as dissolution of the body represented ultimate release from sociopolitical authority and control.[66] "In the representational calculus of hagiography," Perkins concludes, "suffering was the new riches. The body wasted by suffering had become more desirable than one covered in jewels. . . . The goal, death, that [Christians] presented as a transcendence of human society was, in effect, a repudiation of their contemporary society." Martyrdom worked in that vein "to signify the end of contemporary power systems."[67] A Crip Nation, in other words, performatively judged dominant culture, wearing pain, whether etched in the body by disease and debt slavery or as self-selected sacrifice, as prophetic critique of Roman values. With neither longevity nor physical integrity nor intactness (wholeness) as values of what constituted a life, and with the hero journey allowing them to escape stoic criteria of normalcy, Christians in the earliest centuries found the courage to throw themselves into the constitution of a new creation.[68]

Taking this revaluation of suffering into the fourth through seventh centuries, historian Peter Brown, in his volume *Poverty and Leadership in the Later Roman Empire*, addresses one of the ways in which Christianity's vision of "the suffering body provided a new basis of power and enabled the formation of new institutions incorporating this power."[69] Arguing that classical notions of care for society implored the wealthy to practice civic virtue, but within an undifferentiated cultural system, Brown then traces the development by Christians of the notion of the category of the poor, who were often chronically undernourished and therefore susceptible to disease and disablement, as deserving justice. "In a sense," Brown writes, "it was the Christian bishops who invented the poor. They rose to leadership in late Roman society by bringing the poor into ever-sharper focus."[70] Institutional structures formed in the wake of this new representation, its occasion for knowledge, and its categorical attention to persons now identified as the poor, the sick, the suffering. While the civic power of bishops as well as a health care institution grew out of this virtue of being "lovers of the poor," the poor did find in the church a channel for sociopolitical criticism not before available, albeit already and only paternalistically voiced. At the same time, in "a world of persons who considered themselves, and often with good reason, to be vulnerable to impoverishment," giving to the poor assured one of a social trust, if one should fall into economic troubles.[71]

If today we recognize the problematics of prosthetic ventriloquism and the politics of rescue, which have developed within the outcroppings of Christianity's social-justice practices, an objectification of persons that was already evidenced in the earliest Christian practices, this should not be read simply so as to eviscerate the practices of justice created by Christianity, but with appreciative ambivalence toward them:[72] The creation of the category of the poor called for new forms of social justice. Neither should Christians avoid, by self-justification, the incredible sacrificial demand and also economic redirection encompassed in these early phases. The poor, including the sick—not biological families—were the inheritors of accumulated estate wealth. As Perkins also noted, "Wealth was no longer for the family or the state but was to be given for sufferers, for those poor and sick introduced into cultural consciousness through the narration of the saints' lives."[73]

In the percussive ripples and warps of empire, amid which "bodily suffering . . . provided Christians with their community identity," people discovered a new innovation upon the concept of a Crip Nation, an improvisation upon the dance of a limping people—one perhaps satirically or prophetically wielded in relation to the Pax Romana. This new performance was played ironically, not only with the memory of being called out of slavery (thus the metaphoric memorialization of disablements), but also as a people called to be slaves of the kingdom of God. Christianity, as Perkins and Riley have suggested, played innovatively into the optics of a culture, using Christians' decided limps to draw attention to itself, to recall itself to a spiritual pedagogy of wrestling the sovereign of the universe and wielding its crip bodies, its bodies in pain, to critique dominant culture. Of this period Perkins herself concludes that "through the work of Christian narrative and its construction of the notion of the 'self' as sufferer, the social community of late antiquity had come to include, conceptually, the mute and the paralytic. . . . [T]he poor and sick [became] treasure, an object of cultural desire."[74] Far from forming a pool of permanent social outcasts, as Marcus Borg and John Dominic Crossan have surmised—"women, the untouchables, the poor, the maimed, and the marginalized," to whom compassion was owed[75]— crips, these bodies wearing their pain in public demonstration and political protest, were the building blocks of the new temple not made with hands. If Isaiah was opposed to the reconstruction of the stone-block temple, insisting instead upon the people being a living temple, then those impure bodies, the colonially disarticulated, were its foundation.[76]

Because, phenomenologically speaking, "pain resists language," Western society has tended to subsume pain in and to biologize the pain of an individual body.[77] But pain can be not just biologically given, but socially constructed: that is, political and socioeconomic structures themselves generate different psychological dispositions, as well as structure susceptibility to illness. So, for example, late-twentieth-century poststructuralist philosophers Gilles Deleuze and Felix Guattari insisted that capitalism, with its oedipal infrastructure, demands we be depressed, while Harvard doctor Paul Farmer has relentlessly asserted the relationship between political and economic injustices and the susceptibility to disease of the structurally disempowered.[78] Similarly, psychologists have noted the increasing diagnosis of borderline personality disorder within our increasingly mediated culture. As Perkins reads the early centuries of Christianity, persons turned upon the sociopolitical structure as the cause of pain: Bodies in pain served as a prophetic critique of that structure. The new people of and for a new earth were those who performatively, by way of the limping dance, dared to rouse social consciences, to generate new economic and political arteries. At least at this point, Spirit and the body in pain were not obverse disjuncts, as they were to become in the age of the modern miracle and the medical mission. If Torah replaced land as the base of the covenant during the Second Temple period (as per Boyarin), Spirit—in relation to and animating this Crip Nation, this living temple—now sets Torah on the slant.

7

RUMOR MILLS:
SPIRITUAL PRACTICE IN THE CRIP NATION

With all of this talk of the stirring of the event, I do not mean to stir up expectations of power. For however much prestige and power a name may accumulate, an event is a more wispy and willowy thing, a whisper or a promise, a breath or a spirit, not a mundane force.

—John Caputo,
The Weakness of God

"Miracle stories were miracle stories. Greeks told them, Jews told them, and Romans told them," Biblical scholar Burton Mack observes. So with Mack I ask, "What could be the point of Christians telling them as well?"[1]

Miracles were an anticipated aspect of all hero journeys, hence of any ancient novel, Riley reminds us, insisting that we attend to the Greco-Roman influence upon, not merely Jewish heritage of, the gospel.[2] So if miracles were not at all unique accounts, then our question must be: How were Christians using miracle stories within their performance of the body in pain and in the colonial contact zone—that zone where politics played inequitably, but where worldviews also became entangled, even improvisational?[3]

If miracles were rumored and were iconographically and symbolically prominent among these Christian movements, it would seem logical that we must understand miracles in relation to the revolution in subjectivity just established. Given that disabled, diseased bodies would likely have been but prevalent, considering the wake of diseases from imperial interface, mass migrations, slums, and so on, how might these rumors of miracle have played with Roman hegemonic discourse, or at least as important, among the populace? In other words, if miracle stories might not necessarily have related personal accounts of somatic and/or psychic healing, then what did they effect?

Regarding miracles, Mack, reviewing the work of Paul Achtemeier, nods assent to Riley's contention regarding Greco-Roman influence, then qualifies: "The individual [miracle] stories were Hellenistic in form and style, but the narrative themes pointed to familiarity with the epic of Israel. . . . The miracles of the ten plagues were also still very much alive in the Jewish imagination and, of course, Moses had been reimagined in every conceivable posture of importance as the leader of the people out of Egypt towards the promised land."[4]

Biblical scholar David Frankfurter writes, echoing Mack's thesis: "In Greco-Roman Palestine (and undoubtedly beyond), there was a 'lore' concerning the signs and the course of events which would distinguish the age of redemption . . . from the ordinary chaos of history." "The particular focus of this lore of signs," he continues, "was the prophet after Moses, 'promised'. . . to arise and lead the people in a new exodus and the re-establishment of Zion."[5] Midrash, based on Deuteronomy 18:15-19, had suggested that another like Moses would occasion a new exodus. So the Gospels within which this liturgical refrain has now been set seem to presume a Moses *redivivus*, given that in Hebrew legend Moses was considered the first miracle worker among his people (Exod 4, 11; Num 12: 13-15).

"Pre-Christian sources," Frankfurter continues, "give strong evidence of a circumscribed tradition of miracles (predominantly healings) associated with the age of redemption"[6]—a tradition that James Scott, given his book *Domination and the Arts of Resistance*, might label a folk utopia. "The millennial theme of a world turned upside down, a world in which the last shall be first and the first last, can be found in nearly every major cultural tradition in which inequities of power, wealth, and status have been pronounced," Scott explains. "Most traditional utopian beliefs can, in fact, be understood as a more or less systematic negation of an existing pattern of exploitation and status degradation as it is experienced by subordinate groups."[7] In regard to our Jewish and Christian biblical texts, the world reversal (and here my concern remains with the metaphoric reversal of disablement, a world in which the blind see, the lame walk, and the deaf hear) has been configured with reference to the exodus, as a general resurrection of a world fallen under the powers of chaos, the powers that be—the power of empire and its economic patterns. From Isaiah to the Sibylline Oracles to the synoptics, miracles, saturated with exodus expectation, circulated in a strophic form of folk utopia,[8] now told (as I remind myself and the reader, so as to disperse the mode of modernist realism from our reading of the Gospels), after the razing of the Second Temple, as an act of what decolonizing theorist Ashis Nandy might call "anti-memories at that level [that] allows greater play and lesser defensive rigidity."[9]

This lore of signs, fused with the Elijah-Elisha cycles, as well as with the prophecy of Ezekiel concerning the resurrection of the dead and despairing, had already been set into poetic refrain, Frankfurter suggests—specifically, in the well-honed rhythms of Isaiah 35.[10] But to call this lore—something in the air—

differently sets the stage for miracles and how miracles might make sense within popular religiosity, especially within the strictures of colonial domination.[11] Within Matthew's and Luke's Gospels, this folk utopia appears as something like a hidden transcript within the narrative drama, a purported report to be passed along to John the Baptist: Each author now puts the utopia on the lips of Jesus, pressed by John's disciples to divulge his messianic status, that is, "Go, tell John, the blind see. . . ." In such a setting, "Go, tell John" may intimate or preserve the practice of communal rumor, which Scott calls one of the voices of the dominated and "the second cousin of magical aggression."[12] "Whatsoever be the real history of the event, the political purpose of rumour," Bhabha adds, "is to 'keep alive much popular excitement.'"[13] Such rumors keep open a certain ambivalence of causality and history, which of course otherwise belong to empire. As well, rumor generates a circulatory system of communication and communal adhesiveness.[14] If in any way portentous, rumors—rife with all sorts of ambivalence and energy, including panic—can be felt by a colonizing presence to destabilize their imposed calm, to leave them uneasy, to lay the groundwork of insurgency. Folk utopias, in other words, are socially productive, but the power of miracle likely then operates other than as miraculous remediation. That this folk utopia was yet again set to music—as the song "Go, Tell John"—and released during the 1960s civil rights movement in the United States may suggest something of its symbolic power and sociopolitical reference.

When looking at Isaiah 61 ("The Lord has anointed me . . . to bring good news to the oppressed, to bind up the brokenhearted, to proclaim liberty to the captives, and release to the prisoners"), a text that has been enhanced with the metaphoric reversals of disablement to serve as Jesus' prophetic call in Luke 4, scholar Eric Eve surmised that this liturgy was not so much a prediction of individual healing miracles, or even necessarily about eschatology, the "Wonders of the End Times." Rather, the text, become liturgical refrain, resembles something of an appositive to the resurrection scenes in Ezekiel 37:1-14, the valley of dry bones, as well as Hosea 6:1. "What may be in view," Eve concluded, "is not so much a literal . . . healing of the mortally wounded as the revival of God's hard-pressed people," "a poetic description of . . . return from exile."[15] If miracle accounts were themselves something like resurrection appearances, only more precisely of bodies that had come off the bone heap in the valley of despair, the miracle accounts may then have functioned to counter—whether through open resistance or through conscientization regarding the desires that Rome circulated—what Frantz Fanon called "the occupied breathing" of colonized, subjugated bodies.[16]

Comparably, while the specific iconographic scene of the crossing of the Red Sea appeared only late in fourth-century Christian art, the earlier miracle scenes can be read in the light of this latter, enframing narrative—connecting miracles to exodus, to national deliverance—at the very least, tying the Christian movements to Moses, "the Jewish figure through whom the greatest miracles were worked."[17] As Mack's earlier statement paradoxically insinuated regarding "the miracles of the ten plagues," what Egypt experienced as plague, Israel experienced as miracle.[18] "This insistence on a 'face-off' between Moses and Pharaoh," explains Mathews, "is the one constant in all of the Early Christian representations of the miracle."[19] Intriguingly, Pharaoh was now iconically garbed like the Roman emperor, in a military tunic, wearing the beard traditional to Roman emperors, his hair bound with a diadem.[20] "The politics of the scene," Mathews comments, "are extremely important and they could not have escaped the viewer of late Roman times. The salvation of [humanity] is represented as a deliverance from the power of the Roman emperor."[21] Thus, stylized miracle lists, transmitted as lore and carried by rumor and iconography (upon rings, tunics, plates, and the like) play with magic like Moses' showdown before Pharaoh.

The preeminent biblical scholar of the miracle accounts, Gerd Thiessen, himself locked in the mode of modern realism, nevertheless trips over the social value of miracle stories and perhaps then an alternative trajectory of Spirit. Thiessen went so far as to point out that "miracles functioned constructively for the lower class, not only providing help, but becoming a form of political critique and resistance to oppressive institutions."[22] He finds he cannot deny that "the conflict between wish and reality is one of the existential sources of the miracle stories."[23] But given his presumption of historical realism in regard to the accounts involving Jesus and his assumption that the miracles of Jesus must be unique, Thiessen can hear such a definition only reductionistically and as a reductionism—that is, as infantile and unconscious wish projection, as a futile and impotent protest. Consequently, Thiessen counters that miracles in the Christian tradition must rather be construed as "a revelation of the holy [and] . . . its power to break into the normal course of the world" in "a protest against human suffering."[24] Again, "The miracle stories point to Jesus's redemptive action . . . Jesus defeats disease and demons."[25] But the definition of miracle as conflict between desire and reality to which Thiessen, although sure that there must be more to the sacred than this, nevertheless does consent resonates with the literary genre of magical realism, which often arrives on the scene as a form of anticolonial or antihegemonic literature, and within which we often see resort to miracles as an assertion of value and power countering that of the dominant cultural strata.

The fantastical, the magic of magical realism, may be "more than anything else, an attitude toward reality." It is the telling of stories and experiences that challenge the hegemonic tendencies of any version of realism, pummeling it with dreams, smells in the air, unusual sightings, intuitions, visitations and the like, while nonetheless admitting the pervasive reach of the dominant power.[26] In this context, miracles appear like "wrinkles in time" (Madeline L'Engle)—like warps within a too tightly stitched causal structure or as "an unexpected alteration of reality."[27]

In magical realism, the magical or supernatural "happens as part of reality": Rather than being superimposed upon reality, it arrives as experiences of what exceeds the dominant, orderly worldview.[28] Anthropologists Jean and John Comaroff, referring to the play of magic among the colonized, likewise observe that "the whimsical 'unreason' of such movements . . . stems from precisely this conviction. These movements . . . are early efforts to capture and redeploy the colonialist's ability to produce value. And they are often seen as enough of a threat to elicit a punitive response."[29] Even the lore of magic, in other words, can be enough to threaten the sleep, to haunt the comfortable univocity, the definitional closures, and the declaration of rights of the colonizing culture, as well as to spark the remaking of the world among the colonized.

In Milagro Valley, Take 2

The Milagro Beanfield Wars, written by John Nichols in 1974 and then released as a movie in 1988, serves as an illustrative example of magical realism and, specifically, of the ways in which miracles play through a subaltern, politically and economically dislocated, population while also poking us in our ribs with theological satire. For nearly a century, Mexican-American farmers of northern New Mexico have resisted the water and land-use policies of the Middle Rio Grande Conservancy District with little success. Such conservancy plans as were typically proposed tended to favor development and agribusiness interests while occasioning new taxes and then displacing local, financially marginal citizens by foreclosure when such taxes could not be paid. Taking the finally successful 1971–75 resistance of the farmers of Taos County to the construction of the Indian Camp Dam as his inspiration, Nichols gives us a fable of communal resurrection equal that of the prophet (Prophesy to these bones!) Ezekiel.[30]

In Nichols's fable, the Devine family, with Ladd Devine III now in charge of the multimillion-dollar Miracle Land Development Corporation, with its vision for a Miracle Valley Recreation Project (trout streams, golf courses, and tourism) has held a century-long tenure by gaining the political ear of

the state in the dirt-poor Milagro Valley of New Mexico. Caught in the decimating crunch of the corporate and governmentally supported development
plan have been the small farmers, extended families, and native and mes-
tizo cultures of the Milagro Valley. Consequent to the 1935 Interstate Water
Compact that reallocated the flow of Milagro's Indian Creek to big-time
farmers, many sold off their land to the development corporation, which
was, in turn, touted as the only way to save a dying culture and to bring
wealth and security to the valley. Having fallen into generations of hard
times, the promise of economic development felt as compellingly realistic
and simultaneously dehumanizing to citizens of Milagro as it can seem to
any of us living within the values of turbocapitalism—even when that meant
for them increased taxes for infrastructure and only jobs without tenure
offered by a development corporation that merely appeased enough folks
enough of the time to prevent communal resistance.

One day in a fit of desperation, unable to find work and prevented from farm-
ing by the government's appropriation of water rights, Joe Mondragon, teen hood-
lum turned miracle handyman of all mechanical things for sheer survival's sake, acts
up and kicks open the water diversion at the edge of his father's former bean field,
starting what would seem to be a strategically underwhelming, if ultimately communally redemptive war. If the Coyote Angel of Milagro, who is said to protect
the valley, remains disappointed to the point of disgust with the small-scale action
("'Jesus Christ,' the angel whimpered. . . . 'Three hundred years, and just about all
you old farts got to show for it is seven-tenths of an acre of frijoles. And I hadda draw
the assignment.'"), the Anglo water barons and power brokers downstate in the capital immediately recognize the symbolic depth of Joe's miniscule bean field. [31] That's
when mundane miracles begin proliferating so as to prod the reluctant citizens of
Milagro into assuming their own resurrection. A sense of fatalism and futility had
sapped the citizens of Milagro into routine malaise and, with Joe's adolescent and
unthought action, a threat of economic doom as great as the hope for a different
future sparks through the air. Joe's actions do not gain him immediate communal
support. In the mix of fears, worries, and weariness, even he must be convinced—
convinced primarily by Ruby (she of great value), the community's plumber, of communal relations, who leads a petition drive, and Charlie Bloom, a burned-out, 1960s,
white, radical lawyer in whom Ruby reawakens the passion for justice.

When the infamous pig of the town drunk, Pacheco, begins to root out Joe's
beans, Joe takes a gun—first to the pig, and then, when Pacheco responds in
drunken grief, to Pacheco, shooting Pacheco in the chest in self-defense. This

seems to the Anglos the perfect chance to frame Joe in order to ease themselves out of the mounting communal pressure, the hope inspired by that measly seven-tenths of an acre of adolescent pique. First fleeing to the mountains, only to draw out a full-fledged police posse, Joe turns back and turns himself in—but under the protective watch of the unofficial Senile Brigade of "useless old men" and fat, belligerent women, headed by the amputee Onofre Martinez, along with his three-legged dog. Like an incarnation of the pack of Coyote Angels, the Senile Brigade serves as witnesses and overseers of any governmental and police interactions with citizens of the valley, showing up at a moment's notice in their fleet of 1953 Chevy pickup trucks. With attention focused elsewhere, a crew member from The Miracle Valley Development Project nevertheless attempts to raze Joe's bean field with a backhoe, only to have ninety-three-year-old emeritus sheriff Amarantee Cordova with his "peacekeeper" recommission the backhoe and run it off the gorge. With the community gathered to insist upon Joe's innocence by self-defense, the political scheme for control of the valley gets scuttled. The war for the bean field has been won by the emergent collective of the town itself.

The fable seems to invite us to think through the two distinct theological economies—and their tradition of miracles—that have been pitted against each other: the theology that supports Ladd Devine (Could that be Son of God, or one who believes in his own divine right?) and his hankering after economic progress in juxtaposition to what supports the subaltern communities of "Just Your Average Joe," attempting (if fearfully, reluctantly, inadvertently) simply to reclaim living space. As Nichols's fable makes obvious, resistance doesn't emerge single-minded and riding a ready rebel force, but must be coaxed and humored among bodies that do not always fit lovingly, but often fearfully, suspiciously, apprehensively, side by side. Bhabha, writing of a Chipati panic somewhat parallel to the ambiguous symbol of Joe's irrigated bean field, warns readers against endowing peasants with a "simplistic sense of intentionality." Nichols seems to have had such studied premonitions. At the same time, "historical agency," Bhabha reminds us, "is no less effective because it rides on the disjunctive or displaced circulation of rumor."[32] Miracles, too, appear not so much as manifesting a causal chain of power, but as sparks of insight and bursts of catalytic energy within self-organizing systems.

In Nichols's fable, miracles—everything from apparitions to timely dust devils and rainbows—seem to work similarly to rumors. Incarnations of the town's protective pack of "limping, chewed-up, noisy, useless, blind drunk, flea-bitten, tail-draggin, shifty-eyed Coyote Angels" work their magic: A Coyote Angel with a smoker's hacking jag, limping along the roadway, appears in a scene of annun-ciation to Amarante Cordova, an old man with questionable eyesight, but who miraculously becomes a straight-shooting sheriff: "Listen, cousin . . . the way things are supposed to work out, one day the struggles of all you little screwed-up underdogs will forge a permanent rainbow that'll encircle this entire earth."[33] El Brazo Onofre—the phantom arm of Onofre Martinez, which having always wandered loose among townfolk and there committed various trickster and way-ward acts—now instigates a one-handed campaign of terror by mocking Ladd Devine. Here miracle seems to invite a form of playful satire among the colo-nized who have otherwise been "reduced to a body of individuals who only find cohesion when in the presence of the colonizing nation."[34] As Nichols imagines it for us, miracles among subalterns generate just enough openness in the reason-able course of events and just enough energy for courage and collectivity until the little war is won. And so it was said that life in the valley "was all going to change now. . . . The people had been apart for a long time, and now . . . sensed a coming together. . . . Apparently the people have banded together and are not readily going to be intimidated."[35] So it was said, since no one could be sure that at the next sociopolitical and economic hurdle persons wouldn't again succumb to their fears, that a leader would emerge for the new cause. That would take another miracle, or more.

If we were to draw conclusions about how miracles play among this Crip Nation and its equally crip Coyote Angels, miracles appear to address the psy-chic reluctance to be called out, to stand out or to take a stand, as well as the loss of the indigenous economy of place. Both the psychic and the corporate, sociopolitical structures of life, which appear to be mutually reinforcing, would appear to be of interest to the subaltern telling of miracle stories. If the common lore of miracle accounts threatens "radical change" and embodies "a promise of reformation and restructuring after what appeared to be destruction," such change begins by opening out other ways of looking at the daily and mundane, when "the ground in which the most diverse ideas in the world can take root has been reconquered."[36] Miracles get below or outside of our infrastructure of tacit knowledge and may invigorate ways of thinking that escape the historipolitical realism of the reigning regime. Like sparks that ignite combustion, these ener-gies may serve to break persons out of old patterns of thought, which physicist David Bohm has called the most vital act of all creative activity.[37]

"The sorcery of the imagination" proves the power of miracle, Feuerbach suspected.[38] And I hear an echo of this in Anita Haya Goldman's summarization of Fanon's notion of freedom: "Fanon does not conceive of . . . freedom as a civil right," but rather as "taking cognizance of a possibility of existence. Rather than articulating a meaning for freedom expressed as participation within preexisting social structures, the freedom Fanon prescribes is an existential, creative, demanding freedom of consciousness, upon which any possibility of willed action or passivity with respect to social structures is predicated."[39] Among subordinated groups, the role of the imagination need not then be dismissed as mere infantile wish fulfillment. These flights of the fantastic, as Scott would add, "are not merely abstract exercises. They are embedded . . . in innumerable practices . . . and they have provided the ideological basis of many revolts."[40] Miracles, run through the rumor mill of popular imagination, thereby opening up worldviews and rerouting life economies, come in that way to "negate the existing social order," as Scott puts it. "Without ever having set foot outside a stratified society," Scott concludes, "subordinate groups can, and have, imagined the absence of the distinctions they find so onerous."[41] Without physically exiting empire, persons begin to live another social economy of life.[42] These less than triumphal occasions of transcendence may appear small, almost indiscernible, even pathetic against the scope of supernaturalisms and biotechnopower, but could occasion a transcendence that is not a mere reversal of power, but the creation of a new humanity in the land, a transformed earth.

By contrast, understanding miracle as miraculous remediation can but assign bodies back to the Ladd Divine Development Project. The notion of miracle as miraculous remediation, via supernaturalism or biotechnopower or certain forms of compassionate rescue, sides with colonial power as it rehabilitates bodies for the dominant, if unconsciously assumed, economic worldview. Diseased and disabled bodies do, to be sure, form in the wake of colonialism, as suggestively evidenced in Nichols's fable. As Nichols puts it, "If Jesus Christ himself was [present in Milagro] he'd have . . . scars from an old bullet wound in his belly and only three and a half fingers on his right hand and no more than four teeth in this mouth."[43] But the fact that colonialism occasions disease and disability, as contemporary African theologian Jean Marc Ela observes in "The Health of Those without Dignity," points precisely to the reason one must interrogate this notion of miracle as individual somatic remediation: "We must question the demagogic use of slogans like 'HEALTH FOR ALL!' within a society living on one cash crop, in poor housing, and with the dilemmas caused by development."[44] Simply put, an economy hijacked from responding to the social needs of the majority occasions disabling conditions. But the presence of such disabled and diseased bodies can then equally be read back upon society as economic critique.

As we have noted before, modern Euro-Western biblical scholars have consistently avoided the socioeconomic conditions that occasion impairment in their readings of miracle. "To explain suffering," Paul Farmer instructs us in his *Pathologies of Power*, "one must embed individual biography in the larger matrix of culture, history, and political economy," for "social forces . . . structure . . . risk for most forms of extreme suffering."[45] Such "social forces ranging from poverty to racism become *embodied* as individual experience" and are "translated into personal distress and disease."[46] Ignoring the social context of disease, "cloak[s] the violences of economic domination, of capital-labor relations."[47] Where the goal of health is not kept conceptually relevant to sociopolitical and economic systems, medical miracles simply serve the assumption of the dominant economy—to repair its labor force—as even the supernatural versions that condition modernism assume. In that sense, the modernist presumption that individual somatic restoration—named miracle—constitutes the resurrection of life may appear a rather puny and pathetic claim, if not inherently imperialistically inclined, for those who recognize in a body the overwhelming economically colonizing structures of a life.

The Figure of the Suffering Slave, the Crip Nation, and the New Earth

In that milagro valley named Palestine around the end of the first century C.E., a new innovation upon the Isaianic concept of a Crip Nation was wielded as the basis of a "theology of subversive cohabitation (Sawicki)." Miracle stories have been arranged in the Gospels so as to "replicate . . . in miniature the story of the Exodus from the crossing of the sea," explains Mack.[48] While Mack consequently wants to mount the miracle collection as evidence of explicit ecclesiological development, I instead see something like *The Milagro Beanfield War*.[49] Floated on the lore of miracles, calling the reluctant into collectivity, and "embedded in social practice" (Scott), crip bodies stage an exodus in the "withinness" of empire. "There's no outside," says sociologist Zygmunt Bauman of the imperial tentacles of contemporary globalization.[50] It must have seemed comparable to persons living in the heart of the Mediterranean region at the end of the first century C.E. If "the boundaries crossed [by those receptive to the miracle lore in this milagro valley] were social boundaries," as Mack insists, then I would say the secret to subversive cohabitation has to do with learning, as must every crip, to become (as the twentieth-century philosopher Gilles Deleuze would say) a "body without organs"—a body that deconstrues its social organizational alliances (such as our patterns of overwork) as these circulate desire through the body, both individually and communally.[51] Becoming a Crip Nation, then as now, pivots upon a critique of economic structure and demands reimagining collectivity, kinship, and interdependence.[52]

In the first century C.E., as Marianne Sawicki observes in her *Crossing Galilee: Architectures of Contact in the Occupied Land of Jesus*, the Roman Empire "disrupted virtually every material expression of divine sovereignty," beginning with relations to the land and extending through "the indigenous logic or economy governing circulation of relations, channeling of foods and water," how bodies moved through places, and so on.[53] Treating relations as patterns of flow and appropriate flow patterns as the realization of justice, Sawicki suggests that "the holiness of the Land of Israel depended on having things travel across it in the right direction: produce, labor, brides, cattle, words, and so forth."[54] But where Jews had developed such a ritual geography to remind them that they lived the land as a sacred trust, Rome treated land as commodifiable property. Where Jews assumed the waters freely and therefore equitably poured from the heavens upon the just and the unjust, Rome secularized water access with aqueducts and sewers.[55] In time, Rabbinic Judaism would "recolonize the built environment through reform of the calendar" and develop the *miqveh* (the freshwater bath) to correct and restore the just flow of water.[56] But what adaptation to Roman disruption was the Crip Nation, in terms of its concrete, material, cultural interface, in terms of its articulation of desire?

In the acts of rememoration we call the Gospels, a critique of economics, including labor, has come to appear prominent as we shake off the glamour of supernaturalism. Sawicki, for example, argues that surplus resources for Herod Antipas's recreational project of Tiberias in earlier decades, like the development of later Roman cities, had "to be created through reorganization of labor, and that entailed an upheaval of residence and kinship patterns."[57] "The roads, water lines, and city grids imposed upon Galilee," Sawicki surmises, "both advertized and accomplished the Roman intention of bringing the benefits of imperial civilization into the province." But the new infrastructure also occasioned dispersal of the local social economy: "Connection with imperial world markets, through Roman cities and roads, encouraged Galilean farm laborers to move to urban jobs, producing the kinds of social displacements experienced in other urbanizing situations. . . . The Roman alteration of the landscape increased the mobility of labor and commodified it."[58] The popular culture of the Gospels proposes a subversive flow to this Miracle Land Development Project, Sawicki suggests: "Jesus' distribution of 'free fish and bread' made sense only as a refusal of the imperial economic disruptions of local-market commodities circulation. . . . Jesus' detour out of the Jordan corridor after accepting John's baptism was a disengagement from Herodian multinational business traffic in particular and from Roman water management in general."[59]

In an ironic challenge to the empire of Caesar, the empire (*basileia*) of God practiced by the paleochurch would rechannel the flow of justice: It would "manage the distribution of food and other commodities . . . in favor the people of the land rather than for the benefit of the colonizers and their clients. . . . It would bring people together in new affinities and interests, apart from traditional kinship lines." Attacking the rationale of empire, the tendency of empire to build systemic scarcity and to raze the holds of kinship, the Gospels "affirm . . . a new intimacy among people that is already coming into being through social adaptations to the reality of the Roman occupation" and "the survival strategies that people have worked out in the midst of empire." Confessing God as sovereign of the universe would imply some form of material "refusal of the totalitarian claims of the empire that world markets and steeply stratified social classes were the best way or the only way to organize life on earth," Sawicki concludes, even as the paleochurch had to work imaginatively within the new sociopolitical conditions, including the new colonially induced context of human relations, to build sacred trusts.[60]

John Dominic Crossan insightfully connects such a subversive flow pattern with and situates the birth of Christianity within the ancient religious politics of Jubilee, where coincide the two great ancient faith declarations—"The earth is the Lord's" and "Remember that you were slaves in Egypt, but Yahweh redeemed you."[61] While Crossan recognizes the pervasive conditions of "indebtedness, enslavement and dispossession" as both occasioned by "Roman commercialization, urbanization, and monetization in the first-century Jewish homeland" and as evoking the religiopolitical agenda of Jubilee in this regard, he does not connect these to the stigmatic outcroppings of enslavement in the liturgical refrains "the blind see, the lame walk, the deaf hear" or with the figuration so prominently at the heart of the synoptics, that of the suffering slave.[62] But frankly, the economic conditions of slavery "distinctly concentrated" in the Gospels of Luke and Matthew—softened by translation to terms of *servanthood*—catch the eye of very few contemporary readers.[63] To identify with the body, as Perkins suggested Christians did, was to identify with slaves, to accept the identity of slaves: "The

Greek word *to soma*, "body," functioned as a synonym for *ho doulos*, "slave. . . . Slaves could be referred to as bodies."[64] And nothing was so true of slavery in the ancient world as its "absolute corporeal vulnerability."[65] The Jubilee agenda of economic reform seems, then, undeniably the subversive political agenda for this Crip Nation, for these bodies in pain within the contact zone, for their notions of redemption from economic colonization.[66]

Taking us into the economic underpinnings of ancient Jewish and Christian texts, economics professor Michael Hudson, in an essay titled "It Shall Be a Jubilee Unto You," writes:

> Christianity elaborated its ideas of redemption . . . on this principle of restoring freedom to debt-slaves and unburdening the land. . . . For thousands of years, redeeming people and land from debt was the primary and most concrete form of redemption. Indeed, when Christians pronounce "Hallelujah," they repeat the ritual term *alulu*, chanted upon the freeing of Babylonian debt-slaves.

Hudson then goes on to explain that the Hebrew word for "liberty," *deror*, as in Luke's charge to Jesus (Luke 4) to proclaim the Liberty Year, gleaned from Levitical law (Leviticus 25:10), implies the agility of free movement like that of undammed water, that is, "to move . . . as freely as debt-slaves liberated to rejoin their families."[67] Starkly, Hudson concludes his essay: Rome was the first society to not cancel its debts.[68] Rome's recalcitrance and its remapping of sacred geography set the scene for the synoptic gospels, their metaphoric range of disabilities, and the resort to miracles and Spirit.[69]

In the milagro valley of Palestine, bodies in pain (performatively so), when rumoring claims to miracles like those that Moses had effected before the Pharaoh (now Caesar), entered the arena of ideological and, therefore, sociopolitical contestation. The presence of crip bodies has a long history of offending national self-image. If stigma all too easily generates structures of exclusion, including the refusal of citizenship for those manifesting physiognomic impairments, crips can also perform and play with the fear that lies behind such stigmatization. In that way, performing the body in pain can be felt as a threat to nationhood—or, perhaps, then also to the Pax Romana. Christians, performing the vulnerability of the body, of the slave, may have begun to irritate imperial powers.

Comparably, the redemption of a Crip Nation required not miraculous somatic remediation but the forgiveness of debts, clean-slate legislation, living room, communal collectivity. Re-creation of the New Israel after the razing of the Second Temple moved by relational connections effected to redeem one another. In the Gospels, kinship—that "comprehensive 'social safety net'"—would be replaced by affiliations such as adoptive spiritual families and friendship.[70] So Sawicki concludes: "Reassert[ing] certain kin-based dependence relationships . . . could . . . be read as calculated resistance against colonial market pressures," which had "produced ['individuality'] for the convenience of empire."[71] Similarly, it could be read as generating affiliative relations that would allow a slave to break with obedience to his or her master, since "natal alienation isolated the slave making compliance with an owner's demands to be effected out of a desire by the slave . . . to have some type of personal connection . . . and helped to ensure the long-term loyalty of the slave."[72] Whether the Jubilee was ever fully implemented (whatever that would have meant within each new imperially capped context since the razing of the first temple), communities could and did induce rumor about Jubilee and undertake actions that intimated it, that embedded it, so as to change the economic flow, and that moved public policy toward such redemptive idealization—something like the just flow of waters through Taos, New Mexico, and the leveling of landed aristocracies.

But what if this reconstruction with the metaphoric memorialization of enslaved bodies—crip bodies always already standing in economic critique of the sociopolitical system that had effected them—was equally meant to *awaken* consciousness? Not to awaken conscience so as to practice compassion for "those poor, handicapped souls over there," but so as to loosen attachment to the enslaving economics that constricted Christians' own bodies, precisely because in those conditions they couldn't always feel imperial economics as a constraint? Remember that Isaiah's earlier liturgical refrains were trying to call forth the reluctant elite into exodus from the comforts of Babylonian exile. Set into synoptic narrations, would this Isaianic liturgical reminder of formerly enslaved bodies not again awaken persons to the binding imperial economics inscribed on their own bodies, especially when they didn't exactly feel constrained by the new imperial articulation of bodies? The liturgical refrain recalled them to mind as a Crip Nation, reminding them that bodies and desires, too, can be colonized, reminding them to deploy their bodies as building blocks of the kin-dom of God.

In first-century Palestine, living as a good slave brought one better economic prospects than being a peasant:

> Those who suffered worst were not the slaves on the *latifundia* [plantations], who were of value to their masters and were at least regularly fed,

but the mass of nominally "free" peasants, who were without means of support and who, in the provinces, often also lacked the privileged status of a Roman Citizen.[73]

Further, "Roman conquests had produced hordes of slaves as intelligent, cultured, and educated as their captors." Working with Roman householders, such slaves, with their needs met and entrusted with estate management, could earn enough profit to buy their own freedom and receive Roman citizenship. Where only 25 percent of the Roman Empire's members were citizens, all but the top 5 percent acquired that status as freed slaves.[74] It was in this regard that the prominent figuration of that heroic suffering slave in the popularized anti-epics of the Gospels was set forth.

At the heart of Christian popular culture, serving as symbol for the "transmission of rebel agency," has been the figuration of one disfigured slave.[75] Isaiah 53, with its representation of a slave despised, humiliated and rejected, was a treasure trove for New Testament authors.[76] Like the cripped figurations of contemporary postcolonial literature, Jesus—nominally proclaiming "Yahweh saves"—might well have been a "clever polemical construction," a "composite figure," assumed by many reform and anti-imperial movements consequent to the fall of the Second Temple.[77] Likely, the figuration served as a "collective reference to the Chosen People," adds Donald Akenson.[78] In a setting where the life of a holy figure could be read like a scroll of Torah, the figuration analogically evoked something parallel the Pauline Body of Christ.[79]

Figurations may be defined as "performative images that can be inhabited" or as "condensed maps of contestable worlds."[80] If this figuration would have been recognizable as the suffering slave, then might it have mapped a sacrificial path of disarticulating the flows and excising the desires of the Pax Romana? The combination of disfigurement and Spirit, performatively evoking the body in pain, might have meant to underscore "unworldliness," a wrestling with prevailing values.[81] What it called forth was the corporate incarnation of the Crip Nation, its economic disarticulation from what it could discern as enslaving, its ways of living the land as sacred trust rather than real-estate commodity, its resort to collectivity and kinship in the face of the razing of biological relations.

Crip bodies with their subversive claims to pain made something of a significant contextual power by third and fourth centuries. Enough so that collaboratively gathering up into its own grid the innovative subjectivities released by Christianity was necessary for empire by the fourth century. But equally, by the fourth century, Jesus, the Suffering Slave figuration, had also (it appears) become, Jesus the Miracle Worker with phenomenal superpowers. Christianity had developed into a religion of healing, medical anthropologist Gary Ferngren confirms. "Healing now came to be widely sought—and was often gained—by Christians through a variety of means: invocation of the name of Christ, prayer and fasting, the sign of the cross, the laying on of hands, unction, the use of amulets, and exorcism." As Ferngren puts it, referring to the further development of areatologies, reliefs, saints' lives, and scholarly defense of supernaturalist miracles, "Christians now advertised their cures."[82] If "until the time of Augustine and Ambrose, healing miracles were seldom exploited in apologetic literature," by contrast "the overwhelming and uncritical acceptance of miracles of healing in the fourth century and during the rest of late antiquity . . . and their ubiquity among all classes of society" has been well-established.[83] When Christianity's figurative identification as a Crip Nation assumed a practice of healing (third to fourth centuries), and when it appointed itself as "care-giver for the poor" (not always two distinct assumptions, when poverty occasions illness, mind you), Christianity developed therewith the specular eye and what Deleuze calls "the power to judge."[84]

As Christians receive the miracles from the fourth century on, we have moved to reading Spirit as promising wholeness—not decolonization. Since then, demonstrative miraculous remediation has been among the medicine shows of empire, of Christendom: Jesus the Miracle Worker has been a performative story, a public transcript—"a self-portrait of dominant elites as they would have themselves seen."[85] Religion and science have appeared in late modernity to be in perpetual conflict, yet their war games actually keep us from recognizing their shared vision for the modern miracle, their shared value: "Modern medicine constitutes . . . a set of practices in which the religious biases and predilections of Europe have been made merely more subterranean, more difficult to detect."[86] With that, Spirit has become an agent of normalcy and conformity, rather than creating spaces, pockets of other worlds, of Crip Nations.

Earlier Christianities, according to Perkins, asserted the body in pain as a, if not the, central icon. Although in that context pain appears to have been performed as a prophetic critique of imperial power, likely this included a multiplicity of strategies around the coincidence of the shared conceptual figuration of the suffering slave. Why would such a symbol work, if slaves were better off than peasants? Perhaps because, especially when the loss of psychic meaning overwhelms the register of material well-being, persons can come to desire the path of sacrifice. As our contemporary Sharif Abdullah, director of the Commonway

Institute, observes in today's situation of empire by globalizing capitalism, "We make our commitment to things that are not worthy of our sacrifice" because "there's no structure for meaningful, spiritual sacrifice in this society." People today do recognize that we can be deadened and flattened by economic material-ism and seek a spiritual life that involves them in ritual, in community, in beauty, in social purpose—or, call it "the realization of value."[87]

Within the reach of Enlightenment modernity, Christianity has withheld wres-tling with pain and suffering from spiritual practice, has posited them as opposed to and effacing sacred value. That precludes pain's prophetic cry and makes pain—ever more suppressed, ever more demanding—meaningless. Modernity aspired to the goals of redeeming life from the curses of the Garden, including toil and troubles. When Christianity divided life from pain and suffering and set them in opposition to life, it also evacuated the sacrificial path and reinforced the isolation and silencing of bodies in pain by squelching their socioeconomic critique. Could depression be systemically endemic in capitalism, as Deleuze and Guattari suspect? Could borderline personality disorder be the outcropping of a mediated culture? Challenging a North American Christianity which has succumbed to palliative care without attending the prophetic voice raised by bodies in pain, Canadian theo-logian Douglas John Hall writes:

> Christendom could be said to think of itself as the comforter, resolver, or even eliminator of suffering—and such a role need not be scorned. But it still presupposes a distance from the world in which God suffers in the suf-fering of God's creatures. It is better to heal suffering than to inflict it, but healing too can signify distance and usually does.

Any faith that calls itself the body of Christ, he concludes, must overcome just such a distance.[88] Spirit and sentience must be kept resonate. Pain, too, must be socioeconomically, culturally exegeted, not simply objectified and medicalized.

A review of historical, biblical, and secondary literature suggests that modern realism, inserting our values of cure to normalcy and longevity as effected by Spirit, overwrote the strands of earlier Christianities' relations to suffering. Miracles, like Ezekiel's scripting of the resurrection of bodies, had more to do with the overcom-ing of sociopolitical, economically colonizing conditions effecting body-psyches and social communities. The liturgical refrains regarding blindness, lameness, and deafness as positioned in Matthew and Luke likely did not signal an individuate sense of bodies needing healing for something they lacked—namely, health. Nor did they necessarily map the white man's burden (Rudyard Kipling). I have suggested that in a world where "Romans themselves complain of being debilitated by excessive refinements and distinctions," to quote Carlin Barton once again, this figuration could at least as likely have posed a socioeconomic analysis of bodies enslaved to the labor of empire, needing therefore the rehabilitative flow of wildness and the grotesque. The grotesque, as Wilson Yates helpfully reminds us, "refers to aspects of human experience that we have denied validity to, that we have rejected," such that "to experience grotesque realism . . . is to recover that which has been lost."[89] Or perhaps in that intriguing coincidence of disability with banquet, the Crip Nation—a nation of *derisors*—might have been loosing upon empire satire and derision and the promise of a world upside down, of world reversal.[90]

Rather than assuming that health requires individual remediation to normalcy, the transcendent template at the heart of today's empire, these traditions challenged the representations of worldly desire and wealth, challenged a romantic vision of the world. Contemporary neo-Marxist philosophers Michael Hardt and Antonio Negri have surmised that Christianity, become the machinery for the generation of new subjectivities, a "new humanity" articulated on the basis of "a completely different ethical and ontological axis," undermined the social relations and civic passion of the Roman Empire, thereby occasioning its decline.[91] North American Christians in the face of today's Pax Americana share with earliest Christians the need to do the same with empire. Our reluctance to exit globalization has rather less to do with the economic fear of persons such as those living in the Milagro Valley and more to do with the difficulty of breaking through the enchantment of economic realism. A sacrificial path may not be unwelcome, but it takes a miracle to break through our tacit understanding to generate a new circulatory pattern of justice.

Whether the language of crips figured literally, given what happens to health in imperial contact zones, or metaphorically, so as to evoke God's limping people (the slaves of God, not of Caesar), these images called for subversive living even within the belly of the beast. Subversion, however, worked not by marching army against army, but rather by excising and otherwise exciting desire so as to subvert empire from within. Such wisdom appears to have been introduced by the Crip Nation, those who knew the secrets of disarticulating desires without losing life love—or, precisely, in the name of life love. I wonder if solidarity with the Crip Nation—an awareness that "disability is a socially created category derived from labor relations, a product of the exploitative economic structure of capitalist society" and "one of the conditions that allow the capitalist class to accumulate wealth"—might be the sign by which "insurgent subjects" might today "create a collective agency."[92] Could not the Crip Nation—that is, disablement as a reminder of capitalism's choke hold on the laboring body, if also the body's desire for collectivity, for not having to go it alone—serve as symbol for the "transmission of rebel agency"?[93]

Getting Spirit on the Slant: Spirit and Spiritual Practice within the Crip Nation

His name is Brady. He's a jock of a young man. We emerged at curbside together one morning this past winter. Our windshields were caked with frost and the ground was looking like a hockey rink—not optimal conditions for an amputee on crutches, in other words. He started his car; then, using the Vancouver-based 2010 Olympics as cover conversation, he started scraping down the passenger side of my vehicle as I scraped down the driver's side. It made my day: just two humans fitting together, side by side, something like a shin bone connected to a thigh bone. To offer another the authority of our own humanness, the ability to extend our humanity to another: of such might be the kin-dom.

When I returned home from my extended hospitalization consequent to my health crisis and amputation, not all was grief and horror and trauma. There was also, perhaps shockingly, world wonder—the thrill of the song sparrow's twitter, the glorious hum of a refrigerator, the quiet of a sun-enfolded sleep on the sofa under grandma's quilt. I found myself, in the midst of it all, singing with Louis Armstrong, that child of brothels and blues, "What a Wonderful World." It seems to me that, given contemporary world disillusionment, the awareness that the era of progress (with its delusions and blessings) has come to an end, we might want to know—so as to generate world love within these conditions—how a world made wonderful can be felt within and not just as a materialist, idealist reversal of what happens to bodies in a lifetime. How do we live with disillusionment, without resentment, without progress, and yet love life? Such world made wonderful insights could be cultivated so as to challenge out our contemporary ideologies of normalcy, performance, productivity, efficiency.

Spiritual practice might begin here: Insomuch as disability might be described in Faulkner's words as "the way the majority of folks is looking at [you],"[94] spiritual practice might take up the work of what Buddhist Joan Tollifson names "open seeing," or seeing with "the innocence of a baby"—what Christians might call being born again through Spirit, perhaps.[95] Contrary to the production of Spirit via metaphysical speculation and the consequent presumption of a transcendent meaning lodged in complaint against material bodies, meditative seeing attempts to generate an inner recess so that sentience and spirit may affectionately "reside at a single location"—in the actual physical body, not in the upper room of the ideal—so that Spirit cannot be achieved at the expense of stigmatized bodies.[96] "When little babies encounter my arm," Tollifson writes—she herself born with an abbreviated upper limb— "it is seen as just another interesting shape to explore and put into their mouths. There is nothing scary or creepy or taboo about it."

"As adults we can't become babies again," Tollifson goes on to say, before concluding: "But it is possible to come upon a listening stillness that illuminates all the conditioned concepts and judgments that are superimposed by our thinking."[97] Christians in my tradition call such a listening stillness the state of grace. Meditation, Tollifson concludes, "is about . . . seeing the conceptual grid of thought, image and belief for what it is: imagination," which has elsewhere been called the insight of social construction.[98] If the eyes of all those who stare would learn to look with the eyes of a baby, with eyes that have learned to release us from social constructions, we all might be reborn out of normative idealism. Releasing me from Ladd Divine's Miracle Land Development Project would also then begin to open out the imaginal space of a postgrowth society, a society that is not teleologically driven by progress.

So what would Christianity now admit to the world if we released the delusion of normative idealism and practiced open seeing? What would Christianity admit to the world if the Sovereign of the World desired disabled persons—desired us with all God's heart, mind, and soul—without wanting to save us, or to fix us up? What if we persons with disability weren't set up theologically to found Christian mission and "the politics of rescue" (Razack)? Well, then, I think Christianity would have to admit that the world is a bit "wabi-sabi," as Japanese philosophers have put it—that is, endowed with "the beauty of things imperfect, impermanent, and incomplete."[99] Or as Tollifson concludes, "Life is the way it is, not the way we wish it was, and disability is a constant embodiment of this basic truth."[100] An idealist philosophy such as currently inflates Christian eschatological thinking has humiliated and marginalized persons with disabilities. But as the sociologist of religion Nancy Eiesland has written, "real bodies are seldom the icons of health and physical attractiveness that popular culture parades as 'normal.' Yet these [real bodies] are the bodies of desire and imagination"—even for the sovereign of the universe.[101] Say, would you "Go, Tell John?" Then again, he probably already knows.

"A Cripple on this Bridge":
Thinking Difference, Thinking Differently

What has been discussed on the slant in terms of the spiritual practice of the Crip Nation also is subject to rigorous theoretical and philosophical discussion. Twentieth-century philosopher Gilles Deleuze,

For everyone . . . must live . . . like the Zen tea box broken in a hundred places, whose every crack is repaired with cement made of gold, or like the church tile whose every fissure is accentuated by the layers of paint or lime covering it.

—Deleuze & Guattari,
Anti-Oedipus

himself suffering pulmonary disease and someone we might today call disabled, subjected "Oedipalized capitalism" to the analytic couch and found in the creative energies of schizophrenia a "line of flight" or "escape"—hence, his (along with Felix Guattari's) "schizoanalysis." Deleuze's affirmative deployment of this conceptual disfiguration—the schizo—likely evolved from the centrality of "the question of *health*," along with his consequent social revaluation of illness, in his philosophical reflections [*sic*].[1] Here, any notion of disability takes up the possible force of those who for health reasons choose paths of escape from subjective normalization, which has often during modernity been mistaken for the epitome of health.

Without wishing to deny the "modest relief of suffering effected by the Scientific Revolution" (Haraway) or the way in which formulations of pain as averse to life led to theologies of liberation from social injustices, I want to raise Deleuze's question of health in the context of the first world, where "Empire moves as bioregime."[2] How might the disfiguring discourse of Deleuze denormalize the pliability of subjects to the ideals of empire and lead to a different way of inhabiting the world?

More specific to the theological agenda: Both liberalizing and conserving Christianities, the binary, opposed theological remnants of modernity, have been based upon philosophical idealism, as we have seen. By contrast, Deleuze and his philosophical predecessors—Nietzsche, in particular—have declared metaphysical idealism to be "sick." How therefore might the question of health as posed by these Deleuzean "energetic materialists" propose a different theological agenda? What would a theology that resists the cure undertake as its work? If "the importance of minority does not reside in the fact of its relative exclusion from the majority but in the political potential of its divergence from the norm," in its potential capaciousness by providing "an element capable of deterritorializing the dominant social codes," what life could persons with disabilities possibly be said to mobilize?[3] Deleuze's "becoming minoritized" as the revolutionary posture may prove to include a strategy for Christianity itself resuming its status as "Crip Nation"—at least figuratively speaking.

Everywhere the Imperative "Be Well"

A weak, sluggish economy, the contagion of terrorism and SARS, sick buildings, people becoming dangerously obese, exercise regimes to extend one's quality of life: Each such news event, in sometimes subtle, sometimes overt ways, sets its demand upon us. "Everywhere," as Deleuzian scholar Ian Buchanan observes, "we are enjoined to get well." "Virtually every institution in our society," he continues, urges health upon us, as if in our own best interest.[4] As we reach "the end of the infinite on earth" and "health replaces salvation," we raise our cups of mineral water, seal our lips to carbohydrates, jump on our Stairmasters, and toast in celebration: To Life! If there is anything like an orthodoxy underlying Western culture, this would be it: We desire to be healthy, normal. And who would dare to reproach such an imperative wellness? Truly, have not, would not, Christian theologians, of all people, welcome this salutation, "To Life"? And yet, concludes Buchanan, "our very interest in being well needs to be explained."[5]

Today the emergent "multinational ecumenical organization"[6] that some have named empire arrives under the beguiling banner of a spiritualized valorization of life itself.[7] Health is that to which we unquestionably aspire, the key to a good life. Health, far more important today than any notion of life inside of the Pearly Gates, is the proverbial paradise in which we might enjoy the fruits of our labor. And while modernity has presented itself as the simplicity of a contract around labor (if we labor together, we can be free in all other venues of our life), using the case of disability—modernity's refuse, that zero degree of labor and libido (so it is assumed!)—as something like a rune stone might suggest how economy has been reliant upon this libidinal investment in health as a process of somatic territorialization.[8]

Our desire for health has emerged with capitalism's normalization of the body as the basic unit of labor. While disability seems to present itself as an obvious health issue and has been publicly cross-examined in terms of its quality of life, disability—like modern civilization's other already analytically engaged conditions of degeneracy, gender and race—has been, in fact, indexed to the totalizing subsumption of the body to labor value.[9] What disability impedes is the efficient flow of capital. Capitalism assumes as its basic territorial unit the abstraction called the individual worker with his or her labor power as the primary commodifiable property. Just as feminists found the construction of gender to hide a division of labor and "*ethnicizing* others" cloaked the class-ification of labor, disability names a body suffering degrees of variance from normal, which impedes the simple economic formula that a body works in order to eat.[10] Obeying the duty to health, which presumes a territorial enclosure of the body and effective, Oedipal property management thereof (hence, moral propriety), proves one of our most basic acts of economic and social compliance: Sacrificial labor (the founding social contract of modernity) and economics (the sacramental rite of consumption of the fruits of those labors) have been enfolded into the assumption to health as wholeness of individuated, abstracted bodies.

Given the insight of Max Weber from the early twentieth century, Christian theologians cannot ignore that a certain spiritual, ascetic quality also informs and reinforces this desire for the normal and, therefore, valuable body on the labor market. "Normalization," the Foucauldian sociologist Martin Hewitt instructs us, "becomes one of the great instruments of power" in late capitalist modernity. It reaches into "aspects of the body that cannot be inscribed with the exactness of law."[11] As Foucault himself put it, "A normalising society is the historical outcome of a technology of power centered on life."[12] As such, the appeal to the normal, which "demands political conformity as well as physical conformity . . . can be used as a tool for social control," as disabilities activist Marta Russell reminds us, the social Darwinism of capitalism in the front of her mind and the eugenic experiments of Nazi Germany in the back.[13] Bounded by a single, fixed perspective, which Deleuze calls the "despotic ego," the body becomes an enclosure, rather than a dynamic capaciousness. Health concerns become a border war with disease and an aesthetic war against defects. The cultural desire to be normal—as on *The Swan*, a spring 2004 television series, where "normal" means no squinty eyelids, no cellulite love handles, no ungraceful limp—has become indistinguishable from the organic desire for health. Where economics also now becomes the nexus of sociality or, variously, where sociality becomes an adjunct of the market, that "racism that is not really ethnic but biological" (as Foucault put it) becomes ever more subtly virulent.[14]

Where biomedicine treats illness as in need of cure, Deleuze, like Nietzsche, challenges the metaphysical idealism—and inherently unethical fascism—in this picture of civilization and its duty to health. "It is in the irrationality of the full body that the order of reason is inextricably fixed," Deleuze wrote.[15] From a Deleuzean perspective, we might then explicate the way in which "embodiment has become a controlling technology" in terms of the creation of a "plane of transcendence."[16] "A plane of transcendence," as Brian Massumi explains, "is a movement of abstraction, but at the same time of embodiment," since "an Idea has nowhere to be, if not in a book or on our lips or in a brain."[17] Globalizing capitalism names such a transcendent zone, the embodiment of a utopian, paradisiacal generality and the identity grid that is coextensive with it. Ideationally, each of us, by the movement of ego and/or, today, its media subsidiaries, can be drawn up into this plane of transcendence. Massumi continues:

> Rather than plunging into the fractality of the living body, [the plane of transcendence] tries with utmost dogmatism to elevate bodies to its own level of perceived stasis and putative wholeness. The plane of transcendence lifts bodies out of the uniqueness of the spatiotemporal coordinates through which they move. It abstracts them . . . demands that [bodies] live up to its abstraction, embody its glory. It disregards what is most intimate to bodies, their singular way of decaying, their tendency to escape not only from molar constraint but from themselves (illness and death, not to mention becoming).[18]

While biomedicine insists upon the cure—insists that I (as an amputee), for example, lack health and need to be made whole, Deleuze, refusing to submit illness to the totalizing symbolic of Oedipus (ego), puts out the welcome mat to illness. The schizo imports a little madness, a little chaos, into this all-too-stable because all-too-totalitarian picture of health and civilization. When Buchanan quips about Deleuze's propensity for "introducing mania into civility," we must understand that civility, from a Deleuzean perspective, has aligned itself with vertical transcendence, filial order, the fascism of ego, and the outcroppings of paranoid neurosis.[19] It is for such reasons, that Deleuze and Guattari conceptually pivot their revolutionary critique of capitalism around the figure of the schizo: "The schizo knows how to leave"—to take leave of repressive, social-desiring machines, that is.[20] More specifically, the schizo knows how to take leave of the libidinalizing machinery of Oedipalized capitalism and its maintenance of desire under the law of castration (as instantiating a sense of primordial lack) or infinite indebtedness. Or quite simply, the schizo—sharing some affinities with the practicing Buddhist here—knows how to take leave of egoic stability, which modern civilization has assumed to be preeminent in definitions of life, health, and social order.

Becoming Disabled, Becoming a Philosopher

Among the forces involved in the becoming other than oneself, what compels Deleuze's unusual "poststructuralist psychoanalytic historical materialism" may be occasioned by illness. After all, as translator and commentator Massumi observes, "Schizophrenia, like those 'suffering' from it, goes by many names. 'Philosophy' is one."[21] Indeed, "just as Deleuze was referring to Spinoza's and Nietzsche's weak state of health, from 1968 onward, Deleuze was forced to live with illness." The coincidence of the launching of his philosophical oeuvre, which "pose[d] a significant disruption to the canonical traditions," with the onset of pulmonary disease, as noted here by his interviewer Claire Parnet, would be remarked upon numerous times by Deleuze's various biographers.[22] In fact, after completing his 1968 book *Difference and Repetition*, Deleuze was hospitalized for the first time with chronic tuberculosis. By 1993, when his last book, *Critique et Clinique* (*Essays Critical and Clinical*), was released, his pulmonary disease had occasioned severe confinement and had impeded his writing, and he ended his own life shortly thereafter, in November 1995. His philosophical work was configured around persons, like his two most prominent philosophical interlocutors, Spinoza and Nietzsche, who likewise were given to "a weak constitution."[23]

The question of what Deleuze made of this relationship between health and his "disruptive" work as a philosopher was, somewhat incidentally, put to him by Parnet as she, in constructing a Deleuzian thought primer on the model of an abecedarius, prompted "M is for Maladie." Deleuze responds: "The question is whether the illness made something easier . . . specifically an enterprise of thought." While Deleuze assumed a rather surprising relationship between illness and the facilitation of thought, Deleuze's contemporary, Foucault, heralded Deleuze's work with the distinguishing epigraph "*new* thought is possible."[24] Enlightenment Reason, however, dismissed pain as a viable discursant, as, for example, in the sentiment "That's just pain talking." Deleuze continues: "Illness is not an enemy, not something that gives the feeling of death, but rather, something that gives a feeling of life . . . life in all its force, in all its beauty." Nietzsche, in a section of his *Ecce Homo* titled "Why I Am So Wise," had observed something similar: "Being sick can . . . become an energetic stimulus for life, for living *more*. This, in fact, is how that long period of sickness appears to me now: as it were, I discovered life anew . . . I tasted all good and even little things, as others cannot easily taste them—I turned my will to health, to life, into a philosophy."[25] So Deleuze's becoming disabled, like Nietzsche's becoming ill, somehow induced in him a "becoming philosopher."

Among Deleuze's figural models for becoming disabled and becoming philosopher, F. Scott Fitzgerald's trilogy of essays titled "The Crack-Up" appears paradigmatic. Fitzgerald, a writer in his late thirties, was handed what he calls a reprieve from a death sentence after six months' time. It was then, he notes, that he cracked, like an old plate in the pantry.[26] Was it, one of Fitzgerald's Jobian counselors queries, that the Grand Canyon had, still quaking, now also shaken him open, that one of its chasms had now ruptured right through him?[27] The thought initially untenable to him, he heroically shoulders the meltdown as "his own," but comes to recognize in the ensuing vacuum of illness that he has had several parallel experiences, including one such in his final semesters at Princeton, when tuberculosis occasioned his resignation of several prestigious collegiate offices. "Some old desire for personal dominance was broken and gone" thereafter, he recalls, and in that ensuing wake, he learned to write. In that early rupture, he drew the philosophical conclusion that would carry him through his current crack-up: A person "does not recover from such jolts." Rather, she or he "becomes a different person" with "new things to care about."[28] At the end of his fourth decade, this self-differentiating person finds the cracks in his mental fortress to be something like escape hatches from the walls of civility—from the fencing of obligations and assumed values, even from the mechanics and methods of his art, writing. There, finally, in the void left after the property fences have fallen away, he reports: "I was forced into a measure that no one ever adopts voluntarily: I was impelled to think. God, was it difficult! The moving about of great secret trunks."[29]

Recognizing a resemblance to his own experience of health (or would we still call it illness?) and that of others of his genealogy of orphan philosophers, Deleuze launched philosophy from the edge of such fissures and the accompanying aftershocks of "I am not yet thinking."[30] Illness shakes the compound of ego, as Fitzgerald saw it, with the consequent realization that we have quite unwittingly handed over the intellectual, ethical, aesthetic, and political work of thought without exercising the labor of ethical autonomy.[31] To become a philosopher, as Deleuze consequently also came to see it, one must leave the land of the good and always righteous and reasonable, must refuse to live by analogy or methods, and so begin to respond to immanent, differential dynamics—what Deleuze calls "intensities," "affects" and "percepts"—rather than by subject/object relations and the reductions of a philosophy of perception in which the mind has been split from the body and, like the ego-self, left attendant to the mirror of good, reasonable ideas and propriety, the foundational fantasy of neurotic normalization, yielding the hallucination of control.

Keith Ansell Pearson explains the broader, epochal background of the Deleuzean perspective:

> Deleuze holds that the themes of a reduction of difference, a uniformization of diversity and an equalization of inequalities came together in the nineteenth century to form a strange alliance between science, good sense and philosophy (and, we might add, politics). As a result, "reason" [was] installed as the power which identifies and equalizes difference, concealing the diversity of existence by subjecting it to an entropic narrative in the form of a philosophy of history, establishing a politics of identity and, finally, branding the absurd or the irrational as that which resists appropriation to the common sense of humanity.[32]

With the onset of illness, however, these restraining relations crack, and the transcendental tumbles into the wash of chaos.[33] The projects of civility and its ever urgent demand for personal transformation fall away: A person wakes like an infant, no longer trying to get somewhere, no longer having something to make of herself or himself.[34] Letting the flood of chaotic process through the cracks of consciously held territories, feelingly attending divergent sensory fluxes, sprouting rhizomes of new growth like new capillaries after a wound: This will be the Zenlike practice of "becoming impersonal," becoming a philosopher.

Fitzgerald does not necessarily tell us what his breaks with civility looked like, only that consequent to the crack-up, he refused to be "good" and efficient, to dream of being "entire."[35] I, from the crack-up of becoming disabled, could imagine some such breaches: Emergent from illness, one refuses to put life in a savings deposit, awaiting fulfillment. Where civilization holds its head high, disabilities throw class-conscious behaviors into confusion at street level.

With hands preoccupied on crutches, I must constantly unload the handbags of work, life's cosmetic coverage and the baggage of the good life. When I move to Vancouver ahead of my family, I send ahead a survival package: one sleeping bag, one pan, one spoon, one lamp, one towel—all I could manage. Every evening for two weeks, I have nothing to do but fall away into the deep quiet, to stare at the moon and listen to crickets. In daily life, I have become much more an attentive "grow light" of the waving grass, of the child in motion, of the puppy in the park. I wonder: Could such attentive witnessing express a stronger will to life than willpower? Now that would, if taken up as a cultural value, really throw off that quality of life question, wouldn't it?

I am the annoying customer who carries on personal conversations with clerks, because face-to-face relationships create the means by which my life is carried (literally). Assuming the privilege of not always carrying on and dropping the baton, I ask myself repeatedly: What really needs to get done? What would, in terms of the earth, truly matter? To be sure, these breaks transpire—other than the day when the Bohemian waxwings made bigger news than writing my dissertation—at what Deleuze would call a molar, rather than molecular, level of organization.[36] Perhaps they nevertheless begin to unfold the occasions of freedom in becoming disabled—to which even able-bodied persons can of course aspire, if you, for example, will but sit it out with me. Refuse to be counted among those worshipping (the) upright. Stop asserting transcendence on the vertical, the up-and-up.

That disability, as Fitzgerald found, suspended idealist form/alities and civil graces might be among the reasons modern rationalism put illness in philosophical suspension. The "territory of 'health'" has been equally a moral preserve: "Use your words [to express desire]," "Work in order to eat," "Keep up your appearance," "Don't show your hurts in public."[37] Frankly, on those terms, disability obviously won't always behave well. Dis/eased by the mad, the schizo, and the crip, illness and pain might rather best be dealt with as intruders, Western culture has likewise insisted. Illness, after all, can raze the best-laid plans. Why, cracking up, becoming disabled, one becomes unfamiliar even to one's self.

Deleuze might well agree. A practicing poststructuralist will recognize, however, the similarity between illness and the presence of the unannounced, the calling into abeyance of each projected goal, the instability of identity. At what might be his most distressing (even for poststructuralists, that is), Deleuze seems to insinuate (here reading Fitzgerald) that even the fluxes of illness cannot be written off as self-identical to the negative terms of civilization. Indeed, precisely when things become simply too self-identical, on this account we should be most suspicious of our mental health: "I had," observed Fitzgerald, "developed a sad attitude toward sadness, a melancholy attitude toward melancholy and a tragic attitude toward tragedy—*why I had become identified with the objects of my horror*. . . . [I]dentification such as this spells the death of accomplishment."[38] What constitutes illness, to whom it belongs, and how it works cannot be essentially assumed.

The experience of illness, whether F. Scott Fitzgerald's crack-up or Humpty-Dumpty's proverbial fall, ruptures what has passed as common sense. According to Deleuze, "The sensory-motor break makes the human a seer, who finds [her/] himself struck by something intolerable in the world, and confronted by something unthinkable in thought." "Between the two," he continues, "thought undergoes a strange fossilization, which is as it were . . . its dispossession of itself and the world."[39] A strange freedom, to be dispossessed of the territory of the body and thereby the world. Yet recuperating the facilitating difference of illness, the energy of its decon-structive rupture, the capaciousness of becoming disabled (among the affects of which recuperation could be the freedom to escape from hegemonic forms), might be the yet unarticulated, unacknowledged contribution of a Deleuzian philosophy. If "an organism is that which is organized," and "subject/ed" thereby to God and world history, then a crack-up in its organization begins to leak with creative flux.[40]

Deleuze's illness, lived simultaneously with the composing of his philosophical oeuvre, gave rise to a philosophy that set out not only to think difference, but to think differently. Deleuzian philosophy situates difference ontologically, dynami-cally, not linguistically, not in a Lacanian symbolic order, as if human culture were still somehow exceeding or superseding nature, but where life becomes unfamiliar, loses its solid foundations and its reassuring representations. It situates difference amid various waves of rising and falling intensities with which one must becom-ingly coordinate one's own "sensory-motivity."[41] There, difference must be lived in its corporeal locations. The practice of philosophy, comparably, becomes here something like aikido—an active, somatic, mindful engagement with these waves of intensity. Rather than accumulating the encyclopedic baggage of knowledge, "learning," Deleuze writes, "means composing the singular points of one's own body . . . with those of another shape or element, which tears us apart but also propels us into a hitherto unknown and unheard-of world of problems. To what are we dedicated if not to those problems which demand the very transformation of our body?"[42] Indeed. And yet, surprisingly, training in this martial art of philosophy, becoming an adept of the samurai mind, has progressed, at least for Deleuze and his orphan genealogy of philosophers, through becoming disabled.

The Great Health

Modern civilization's metropolitan and colonial health plan distinguished the degenerate (those supposedly lacking generative energies) from the wholesome. During the Enlightenment, "one of the most feared perversions of the imagination was the confusion of pain for pleasure."[43] The disabled body would consequently fall outside civilization, outside of culture—always implying, of course, high culture. Our denial of sexuality to disabled persons, let alone our refusal to desire the worn, historied, and lived-in body, may speak volumes regarding even contemporary culture's refusal to co/implicate pleasure with pain.[44] Separating pain and pleasure, like an egg white from a yolk, invariably denies a person with disability liveliness and vitality, given that the disabled body has been socially registered as in pain. Psychologically speaking, this denial seems consistent with the economy of the gratification of the body, which has become morally, politically, psychologically, and even biologically correct to the extent that any contrary conditions have been pathologized.[45] Health, or better, one's state of health, has been measured in terms of "the ideal of the undisturbed functioning of the physical organs, an existence free of conflict, and a state of general well-being."[46]

This vision of fulfillment and ingratiating wholeness was also appropriated within Christian spirituality, which has cultivated "the calm, ordered life of the soul." That life should be redeemed from suffering and restored through the romantic harmony of all things coming back together, this eschatological idealism Christian theology has preferred to the unsecured "passionate life of the soul."[47] Yet, prior to modernity, as Nietzsche reminds us in *Genealogy of Morals*, "neither for the Christian . . . nor for the naive [person] of more ancient times . . . was there any such thing as *senseless* suffering."[48] The construction of the senselessness of suffering, which publicly uses disabled bodies contrarily to prove its assertion of the quality of life, has been a most modern, utopian proposal. Stemming from an "inability to . . . 'think matter as living'" and coupled with "'a panic-stricken terror of nature,'" as Deleuzean philosopher Elliot Albert puts it, health becomes a possession, a territory to be held.[49] What theologian Catherine Keller calls "tehomaphobia"—an aversion to chaos, to the shifting of tectonic plates, and the tug of tides—has settled into our bones, our desires, into the aversions of embodied life in dynamic process.[50] Christianity has resolutely blocked affection for the world where it has found pain and suffering. Yet, rather than simply a belief to be dispensed with at will, we metabolize this dialectic of pain as averse to pleasure, of pleasure and fulfillment as absent all pain, individually and socially. It is an "interpretation inscribed in the body," a metaphysics lived out psychically within and among bodies.[51]

This is not contrarily to insinuate nihilism in concerns of well-being. Nihilism, parallel to its inverse, metaphysics, "creates the fiction of something to be valued more than life," as Deleuzean philosopher Tamsin Lorraine makes clear.[52] Rather, situated as one who bears the stigmatic mark of disability, I wish to push out the distinction between wellness and the state of health so as to begin to unhitch Christian theology from capitalism's pervasive territorialization of bodies, human and otherwise, but beginning with that most intimate process of being in possession of the body. Desire for life can be catalyzed, as disabled persons venture daily, other than as desire for wholeness, for cure. Indeed, Nietzsche insisted that "it was during the years of my lowest vitality that I ceased to be a pessimist," that the will to life "forbade me a philosophy of . . . discouragement."[53] Like Nietzsche, Deleuze himself came to assume, if not directly to pose, a definition of "the Great Health," a love of life that was not diminished by illness, that was rather, perhaps shockingly, strengthened by the experience of illness. In terms of the Great Health, even (or perhaps especially) illness or becoming disabled might be cultivated as a spiritual practice of becoming mindfully, creatively attentive to the midst of life, to difference in our midst.

Nietzsche distinguished between "The Great Health" and

> The "Bad" or sickly life . . . an exhausted and degenerating mode of existence, one that judges life from the perspective of its sickness, that devaluates life in the name of "higher" values. The "Good" or healthy life, by contrast, is an overflowing . . . form of existence, a mode of life that is able to transform itself depending on the forces it encounters, always increasing the power to live, always opening up new possibilities of life.[54]

Thinking about health in this way involves us in the broader field of life, an awareness that personal life is emergent only with this field. Considering the Great Health resituates us within the love of life in that broad landscape. Consequently, personal health, Nietzsche continues, must be considered in relation to the differentials that self enfolds and unfolds: "Health and morbidity: Be careful! The measure is the body's efflorescence, the mind's impetus, courage and exuberance."[55] One does not overcome illness, one lives with it like an ascetic, assuming it as a practice through which one might learn to cull out reactive forces and numbing habits, while staying present to being alive.[56] To assume that health could be measured by idealization of the body, one has already acquiesced to resentment against *this* life, has assumed the measure of otherworldly standards.

Assuming this Nietzschean orientation, Deleuze suggested that the impersonal or nonegoic sense of life that came into view with the experience of personal illness is our primary obligation, the grounds of creative becoming (again, not of our own becoming, but of life's). His plane of immanence, which came into view with his own chronic disability, is thus comparable to the grounds of Nietzsche's Great Health: "Immanence does not relate to a Something that is a unity superior to everything, nor to a Subject that is an act operating the synthesis of things; it is when immanence is no longer immanence to anything other than itself that we can talk of a plane of immanence. . . . A life is the immanence of immanence, absolute immanence: it is sheer power, utter beatitude."[57] Personal health, in a Deleuzean sense, might best be defined as an autopoetic creative capacity, "a becoming that escapes the *ressentiment* of persons and the dominance of established orders."[58] In our best health, we responsively—not reactively—interact with affects, intensities, and relations. Instead of ensconcing ourselves in disappointment, memory, and wistfulness, we experiment with what yet might thereby become.[59] "To become," Deleuze advises us, "is not to attain to a form," the presence of which will be indicative of the imposition of transcendental ideals. Rather, to become is "to find the zone of proximity, indiscernibility, or indifferentiation where one can . . . be . . . singularized out of a population rather than determined in a form."[60] Illness, on the other hand, is a "stopping of the process": "Neuroses or psychoses are not passages of life, but states into which we fall when the process is interrupted, blocked, or plugged up," and here Deleuze already has in mind the paranoid neurosis of the capitalist machinery of Oedipalized civility.[61]

Like Nietzsche, Deleuze assumed what he called the "clinical" rather than "critical" philosophical orientation. Attempting to fashion a process of dynamic discernment from within immanent conditions, Nietzsche, in his first essay in *On the Genealogy of Morals*, distinguishes between the sets of evaluative terms "Good and Bad" and "Good and Evil," which Deleuze would also assume as the basis of his "clinical" craft.[62] The critical enterprise he assumed to be still too enthralled to ideals and weighted with psychic resentment. Refusing to think life in transcendental ideals, Deleuze, like Nietzsche, also refused to raise sickness or illness to a question of theodicy.[63] "The renunciation of judgement," as Daniel Smith writes, when introducing Deleuze's *Essays Critical and Clinical*, "does not deprive one of the means of distinguishing . . .the becoming of Life," which "can be evaluated by criteria that are strictly immanent to the needs of existence."[64] If life cannot be discerned based on the imposition of ideal forms, then "The Philosopher as Physician of Culture" (as Nietzsche put it) must artistically craft a diagnostic and an emergent picture of health within the plane of immanence.[65] Literature, like art and music, is a form of philosophy, as Deleuze saw it. Deleuze writes: "The writer as such is . . . a physician, the physician of [her/]himself and of the world. The world is the set of symptoms whose illness merges with [the writer]. Literature then appears as an enterprise of health." Literature, as an enterprise of health and a philosophical discipline, "consists in inventing a people who are missing"—that is, it involves discerning the movement of critical freedom and fabulating the life-giving mutation.[66]

What personal illness or disability breaks open, given Deleuze and his reading of Nietzsche, is our contemporary-world fantasy, idealism—our refusal to believe in the world as it is. "Metaphysics"—Deleuze using this term to name the Platonic trajectory of asserting value as if from outside world conditions, that is, metaphysical idealism, even in its modern materialist formation—was built upon one answer to pain. Metaphysical idealism has determined a certain mode of existence. While it offers consolation, it requires one, as Nietzschean philosopher Tyler Roberts put it, to "turn against life."[67] But again, metaphysics, at least within the purview of an energetic materialist, might better be thought about as a sociopsychophysics. Metaphysics names how we feelingly organize our realities, how we invest or disarticulate desire therein. Idealism—psychically correlated to a fear of pain, of ambiguity, and of dynamic openness—could be defined as an ideation that is psychically held against the becoming of life.[68] As Nietzsche had asserted contrary to his contemporaries, pleasure and pain are not fundamental causes (identifiable with the Good and the Evil), but are rather effects of one's will to live, one's vitality, strengthened as much by way of the averse as by anything that might be called sheer pleasure.[69] As Roberts puts it: "To affirm life only in the hope that we are able to end suffering—or to affirm life only from the perspective of that goal . . . is not to affirm this life. . . . Affirmation wells from out of the body as much as from the mind, compelling one to live vibrantly rather than assuredly."[70] Becoming disabled—refusing to seam up the cracks that shatter our idealizations—could potentially cure us of belief in transcendence, and we might thereby begin the process of acquiring an exit visa from globalizing capitalism.

Of Delirium, Disability, and Other Deconstructive Moves

For an energetic materialist like Deleuze, there is no original state of health from which we have lapsed; there is only ever and again the enfolding of difference.[71]

Or as the poststructuralist theologian Mark C. Taylor, in his personal reflections on diabetes, comparably put it: "Health is not original. . . . Disease is one of the guises in which altarity approaches."[72] Like theoretical deconstruction, illness— where we do not separate the cultural symbolic from nature—has "the potential . . . to deconstruct the mental, social, and physical habits that imprison us, thereby making new perceptions, emotions and modes of mutuality possible."[73] The physiological epitome of deconstructive moves, "disability confounds any notion of a generalizable, stable, physical subject."[74] It virtually insists upon a dynamic, materialist philosophy.

But such an energetic materialism with which illness may enfold the self also challenges the protection of power, the centrality to self of the will to control, cultural and spiritual commitments to improvement, striving, autonomy, and productive work, which have all been held in place in and through modern idealistic materialism.[75] Whereas the cure reintroduces metaphysical totalizations—which always embed themselves in bodies (as per Massumi)—illness introduces the possibility of difference, the need to improvise with the givens. Parasailing the plane of transcendence, we hardly ever anymore encounter otherness. Illness puts us to the test of becoming unlike one's self. Where the elevators of wealth and reason lift us into the region of unconstrained choice, disability forces us to face limits.

Deleuze thinks with and through illness as a *schizze*, as a fissure, as a crack or rupture, through which non-Oedipalized desires flow.[76] On this point, Deleuze affirmatively cites the late twentieth-century psychoanalytic philosopher R. D. Laing, who wrote, "Madness need not be all breakdown. It may also be breakthrough."[77] Among other things, write Deleuze and Guttarri, delirium yields the sobering truth of nature as a process of production. Illness resets our cosmology, reminding us that we live within far from homeostatic conditions, that we are not distinct from nature, that the dominion of the will does not always have its way.[78] Additionally, illness cracks open and breaks through fixations so that desire can flow freely without ego's judgments. Living "the cracks in our all-too-closed minds . . . true sanity entails in one way or another the dissolution of the normal ego."[79] For health reasons, then, the cracks of illness can be followed as so many possible lines of escape or lines of flight from the little fascist of the ego-self, from modern civilization as the order of the ego.

Life, Deleuzian scholar Keith Pearson explains, proceeds "by contamination, contagion, conversion and other forms of transversal communication. . . . 'Life' or evolution only really gets interesting (inventive) when it operates within far from equilibrium conditions."[80] Rather than referring life to the Platonic mirror of perfect forms and the power of judgment established thereby, Deleuze—assuming the body to be located in something like a tidal zone or ecotone—treats illness as a productive mutation. Illness could as likely, then, be viewed as a productive phase transition.

Even a virus, given that there exists nothing so innocent as an original state of health, might prove a productive mutation. A couple examples might elucidate the point: Tulips, as the *New York Times* science editor Michael Pollan details in *Botany of Desire*, caught the human eye for beauty by surreptitiously cooperating with viruses to fashion color flares, or what were known as "breaks," on their otherwise mono-chromatic schemas.[81] Nietzsche posed similar reflections in his *Genealogy of Morals*: Just as he insisted that illness be engaged as an event for the possible invention of new values, so what he called the infection of "slave morality" occasioned soulful innova-tions. The instinctiveness and impulsiveness of the vigorous underwent mutation with what Nietzsche called the slave virtues—meekness, equality, peacefulness, and the notion of free will—so that more ascetic, martial virtues, such as ethical autonomy and the forgetting of resentments emerged. In a Nietzschean sense, as philosopher Paul Glenn concludes, "The feature which marks the superiority of the sovereign individual is the result of an infection."[82] In this vein, the creative, if now problematic liberal identity politics of the 1970s, through which were asserted the rights of persons of color, women, and gay and transgender individuals, might com-parably be traced through contestation based in resentment.[83] Deleuze and Guattari hope that schizophrenia, being "our very own 'malady,'" itself something like a virus, might mutate the character of capitalism's possessive, fascistic (because egoic) desire.[84] Again, schizophrenization names that way of taking leave of the normal by disavowing the power of judgment that fixes and prizes consciousness as a power of standing apart from nature, a practice for releasing ego, which neurotically obeys the requirements of constructed reality. It is a practice for breaching the restraining walls of individuation as territorialization or self-possession.[85]

Becoming Disabled, Becoming Revolutionary

Capitalist productive desire as desire to be well, as desire for cure, is not a Manichean other against which we can draw the immunity line so as to mount a revolt. We cannot, in other words, identify a pure reserve of natural desire as dis-tinct therefrom. Rather, insomuch as productive desire (natural, technological, social, and psychic) is singular, we metabolize this possessive desire. It subjectiv-izes us.[86] Desire being always socially formulated and circulated, we are faced not so much with the choice of choosing for or against globalizing capitalism's picture of health, but of recognizing its demands for normalization in the name of health and mutating it, by allowing other mechanic assemblages or Oedipally perverse desiring attachments.[87] Deleuze pushes the poststructuralist agenda into the psyche and cosmology: Difference is not simply linguistically, textually positioned (ala Derrida), but psychically held in mind or abjectly refused.

But really, becoming disabled as positionally becoming revolutionary? Metaphysical idealism might have a good laugh at such a preposterous fable. A Deleuzian emphasis on becoming, however, shifts the death state with which disability has been identified in the age of ego. Even persons with disability must learn to become disabled becomingly, if you will. Frankly, even Deleuze observes that one can live as a "slave to one's own illness."[88] Here the feminist Deleuzian Rosi Braidotti helpfully elaborates:

> Becoming nomadic [a.k.a., becoming revolutionary, becoming minor . . . and thus what I call "becoming disabled"] means you learn to reinvent yourself. . . . It's about the desire for . . . flows and shifts of multiple desires. Deleuze is no Romantic. Deleuze's nomadology stresses the need for a change of conceptual schemes altogether. . . . Both the majority and the minorities need to untie the knots of envy (negative desire) and domination that bind them so tightly. . . . What matters to Deleuze is to keep open the process of becoming-minoritarian and not stop at the dialectical role-reversal . . . to go beyond the logic of reversibility.[89]

As Deleuze himself wrote, "To become is not to attain a form (identification, imitation, mimesis) but to find the zone of . . . indiscernibility," to be "singularized out of a population rather than determined in a form."[90] As if composing a desiderata for becoming disabled, Deleuze and Guattari confess:

> We no longer believe in the myth of the existence of fragments that, like pieces of an antique statue, are merely waiting for the last one to be turned up, so that they may all be glued back together to create a unity that is precisely the same as the original unity. We no longer believe in a primordial totality that once existed, or in a final totality that awaits us at some future date. We no longer believe in the dull gray outlines of a dreary, colorless dialectic of evolution aiming at forming a harmonious whole out of heterogeneous bits by rounding off their rough edges.[91]

Conceptually speaking, becoming disabled *potentially* offers a line of flight for becoming revolutionary insofar as we take up our divergence from the norm not as a resistance, but as a creative edge, as a location for inventing new forms of subjectivity, rather than returning to the realm of ego and identity.[92] Here, civilization's degenerate—the ones whom modernity assumed could not generate life, those who have been taken as the opposite of life and Spirit—may shed ego and the fixations of normalization in order to regenerate Earth, to generate a new people. But saying that, let me reassure you: The point here is not to return to some Origenist practice of lopping off anatomical extremities, although revisiting his extreme practice could be interesting in this light of refusing normalization. The event of disability happens whenever any dares pass through the dizzying whirl of abjection psychically laid between disabled persons and the rest of the human community. Just try this, it's really quite simple: Become the machinic assemblage for a coffee cup, attaching it to a crip on crutches.

A Cripple on this Bridge

If we philosophers take to our work as culture's physicians and writers like good diagnosticians "who isolate a particular 'possibility of life,' a certain way of being or mode of existence," then in becoming disabled might be found the humanity that Nietzsche (in the voice of Zarathustra) evokes as "a bridge and not the goal," a humanity that never sees itself as complete, consummate, but always as yet evolving ever new values.[93] At the bridge, in the space of becoming, stands the figure of the cripple.

In a scene Nietzsche intriguingly calls "Redemption," a crowd of cripples gather to block Zarathustra's bridge crossing, posing the final challenge to his teaching: "For [the people] to believe fully in thee, one thing is still needful—thou must first of all convince us cripples!" "It matters little to me that there is one arm here, one leg there," says Zarathustra. Having traveled among humans, he continues, "I see and have seen worse things": "reversed cripples," to be precise, persons who had too little of everything and too much of one thing—one grown stalk-thin on pure envy, another all head. Having disclosed himself as "a seer" and a bridge to the future, Zarathustra teaches the crowd of cripples about redemption from the memory of the past, from the "It was" that, like a huge stone, imprisons creative life vitality in a tomb. "Something higher than all reconciliation must the Will will," Nietzsche concludes in the voice of Zarathustra.[94] He does so as himself "a cripple on this bridge."

That philosophy, like literature, has, in postcolonializing, become disabled has to do with calling forth a people yet to be, with values unable to be articulated in terms of modern civilization. Disability's "malleable and shaky foundation," as disabilities theorist Lennard Davis puts it, with Deleuze in mind, "can be the beginning of an entirely new way of thinking about identity categories."[95]

Schizos, for whom the Oedipal machine of territorial and civilized desire has been broken, "experience nature as a process of production," of ceaseless flows. With the Oedipal halls of mirrors and ideal forms and analogies left behind, desire flows, no longer disarticulated with hungry, yawning lack everywhere. Becoming disabled troubles the bounded distinction between autonomous self and other, disconcertingly mixes life's pleasure with pain. As disabilities studies philosopher Rosemarie Garland Thomson would add, "'freaks' defy the ordinary and mock the predictable . . . [they] confuse comforting distinctions between what is human and what is not."[96] Disability, an absolute refusal of disciplinary mastery (a disabled body obviously cannot pretend to high culture, cannot stand apart from nature), escapes being subject/ed and discursively relocates self as a dynamic process of enfolding difference.

To be sure, Deleuze and Guattari are most careful to distinguish between a certifiable schizophrenic and the revolutionary process of schizophrenia. "The process of schizophrenia advocated by schizoanalysis is . . . *not*," as philosopher Eugene Holland insists, "about going mad or taking merely individual lines-of-flight from institutions of social repression."[97] And yet, there's not a pure disjunct here, either. There is, after all, for Deleuze, no entertaining something purely metaphorical, so that's not the tone with which he invokes schizophrenization. Ignoring the semiotics of illness would amount to committing the same error as has modernity—pretending to a metaphysical utopianism that assumes an originary and, therefore, politically eugenic state of health. Disability, illness, and pain belong among existent conditions of chaos cosmology. Illness can give back the body's relationship to the world and bring the world back to mind.

Indeed, pain has the capacity—Linda Holler writes in *Erotic Morality*, her attempt to recoup the semiotics of pain for moral agency—"to break down dualistic thought," to dethrone the ego, to locate us within an experience of the world "in the mode of acceptance as it is."[98] By inducing the body's own cannabinoid system, pain may dissemble what Aldous Huxley called "the reducing valve of consciousness," opening out the terrain of the present moment—the rapturous experience of being alive that spiritual practitioners seek through multiple corporeal practices.[99] Sinking into chaotic immanence situates one on the edge of becoming differently, awash in a sea of sensibly felt forces. "Desiring-to-live," the cellular logic with which pain may put one in sympathy, cuts through the idealistic distortions of the mind that occasion flight from direct experience.[100]

As Deleuze himself put it, the schizo "has simply ceased being afraid of becoming mad. [S/]he experiences and lives [her/]himself as the sublime sickness that will no longer affect [her/]him."[101] For Deleuze and Guattari, "the clinical schizophrenic's debilitating detachment from the world is a quelled attempt to engage it in unimagined ways," Massumi explains. Constructively turned, "schizophrenia as a positive process is inventive connection, expansion rather than withdrawal. . . . Schizophrenia is the enlargement of life's limits through the pragmatic proliferation of concepts."[102] What the revolutionary can learn from the psychotic is "how to shake off the Oedipal yoke and the effects of power in order to initiate a radical politics of desire freed from all beliefs."[103] In other words, the question of how life escapes its moral, Oedipal straitjacket, how it escapes judgment and organismic territorialization, how its subject/ed persons might take leave of civilization, how we sidestep the conditions of the globalizing capitalist empire—these concerns have been referred to the capaciousness of becoming disabled as an image in thought. Today, the schizo is *Homo natura*," Deleuze insists. Deleuze may then open up for those of us become disabled a different way to live disability. But equally, disability may be what "we [all] need to accept about ourselves," as Russell puts it.[104] It can force recalibration of all that our Oedipalized, ascetic capitalist culture hides away in the cryptic abject.

In the end, the Deleuzean project emancipates desire to flow otherwise than needing a fix, a cure, a transformation, whether spiritual or physical, which assumes an image of wholeness toward which we are moving. He emancipates desire into the unselfconscious immediacy of direct experience unconstrained by resentment, envy, memory, promise, guilt, or indebtedness: "The task of schizoanalysis is that of tirelessly taking apart egos and their presuppositions," that of liberating "schizoid movements [from Oedipal repression]" so that these movements affect "the flows of labor and desire, of production, knowledge and creation in their most profound tendency." Like the Christian ascetic of antiquity, schizos must risk "desert-desire," which he would come to call in his later work with Guattari "nomadology."[105]

Yet Deleuze's nomadology, especially when inflected by disability, basically resembles the way in which persons with disability have been forced into begging: For most of history, disability and mendicancy have been nearly seamless, "virtually synonymous."[106] It is to be granted Deleuze that a nomad is not a Leibnizean nomad. At the same time, health, when becoming minor, cannot be found in the desert of solipsism.[107] Not only do persons with disability need socially interdependent assemblages, this need would seem equally to resonate with chaos-complexity theories' insight into self-organization.

But living the fissured, desiring self soulfully, creatively—this, admittedly, has no guarantees, offers no security states. How do we psychically, then, move into becoming? We can begin by refusing to let disability or the body be visited as a "captivity narrative."[108] Others—such as AIDS activist Mark Matousek and poet Audre Lorde—have shown us how to live illness as a "savage grace."[109] Deleuze teaches us a philosophical practice for "thinking difference, thinking differently."

Thinking Difference, Thinking Differently

Within postcolonial literature such as Anosh Irani's magical realist *The Cripple and His Talismans*, disability locates the refused matter of modernity and the ecotone of resurrection for a postcolonial postmodernity. Having mysteriously lost his arm to Baba Raku, ruler of Bombay's underworld and also, ironically, the embodiment of justice, Irani's cripple undertakes a quest to unfold why this karmic event interrupted his otherwise fine life. Encountering along his way the misfits and storytellers of Bombay's underworld, Irani's cripple soon recognizes the disease from which he has almost died—not gangrene, but civilization, its pretensions passed off as reason and moral values. Walking along, he realizes that he had in the past "used [his] hands wrongly," blindfolding himself when he should have been helping, reading his palm while ignoring "the torn elephants" along his path.[110] One day, watching a beggar boy approach a woman in the rear seat of a taxi, he realizes that civil society suffers from this same misassemblage of organs and extremities: "'In God's name,' I hear the boy say. 'Please give money.'. . . At this moment, even though the boy's words are the same as they have always been . . . I am listening through the arm I do not have. So it does not surprise me when the woman in the taxi ignores the small boy's words and shifts to the centre of her seat. She has two arms and that impairs her hearing. . . . 'Raju,' I say . . . that well is dry. . . . I dig into my pocket. . . . I feel sad, as if I have found a remedy for a disease that has already killed me."[111] Here, an amputation has become a *schizze*, a cut in the territorialization of thought and the civility of reason. Psychically laid boundaries rupture, begin to flow, and become what Deleuze calls "a line of escape," or rhizome.[112]

Fearing of all things that threat to the self called becoming disabled or falling ill, modernity could hardly notice in the rearview mirror that we have held life in transcendental, if paranoid suspension. The ego and its plane of transcendence have in common this dialectically aversive and dismissive relation to pain and its related conditions, illness, fatigue, disabilities. The imagination captured by ego's mirror image, rather than by the ethical interplay with difference (including mutation and transmutation), can only experience heterogeneous flux as a constant affront to its hallucinatory picture of the whole and of the peaceful equilibrium it promises. Where time is money, the body is labor, and its intactness is correlative with moral uprightness; malady can only then be a lapse, a lack. Like Irani's proprietorial woman, transcendentals (including those schooled in systematic theology) need to flee the scene of dis/ease, to seek out (at all costs) the security states of the harmonious, the whole. In a Deleuzean mode, however, philosophy, rather than divining metaphysics and setting up transcendentals with their well-established (if delusional) identities "must approach the immanent conditions of that which it is trying to think." But where thinking becomes "physical . . . rather than metaphysical," there we may well have arrived, personally delivered—like Irani's cripple—by pain, illness, or disability. [113]

Thinking begins, Deleuze insists, only when "the world . . . loses its reassuring power of familiar representations."[114] Philosopher Tamsin Lorraine describes her Deleuzian improvisation on this practice of "thought without image," as "visceral philosophy"—a concept that helpfully distinguishes between philosophical idealism, based in perception, and the Deleuzean corporeal practice of thinking the fluxes and flows of molecular processes.[115] Instead of leaping with the ego to the transcendent ideal or settling for the moment of categorical recognition selected from among the gallery of representations, then jumping into the power play of subject over object, Deleuzean thinking transpires in and as the skillful interplay of a field of always multiple dynamic forces and affects, without assuming to power, but rather by sensibly discerning vitality. Living disability persistently poses unthought of, unexpected, noninhabituated encounters: "Excuse me," I say to the complete stranger in the coffee line, "would you please retrieve my thermos and my wallet from the pack on my back?" Throwing trust at the tombs of our contemporary security states, I wonder what might kindle. Whereas knowledge compiled and carried as answers and truths introjects, Deleuze insisted, "an inaccurate notion of the instance,"[116] visceral philosophy moves from such idealistic and objectifying "thinking about" (this is a table, that is a chair) to "thinking within" the maelstrom, from knowledge as setting foundational piers to justify life on the plane of transcendence to thinking as a skillful practice of sensible immediacy—a practice that must anticipate, as Nietzsche did, distortions of desire such as envy and resentment.[117]

Here thinking articulates not the interiority of self, but "the process whereby a multiplicity of . . . forces establish connections with one another."[118] Deleuze's meditative commentary on Cezanne, who "spoke of the need to always paint at close range, to be too close to . . . see the wheat field" and the forms, "but only forces, densities, intensities," suggests the autopoetic quality and immediacy to experience of this way of thinking: "Not a 'minute of the world passes' . . . that we will preserve if we do not 'become that minute.' We are not in the world, we become with the world. . . . Everything is . . . becoming."[119] When Deleuze consequently defines philosophy as a "theory of multiplicities that refer to no subject as preliminary unity," disability—that site of refusal (of attention and value), even amid identity politics—locates the demodernizing move, the mutating edge that idealist theories of subjectivity, world, and reason attempted to foreclose.[120]

Self, in this cosmology, designates "an intensive, multiple and discontinuous process."[121] Cracking up, the body opens out as a "play of forces, affects and a surface of intensities," in sharp contrast to modernity's construal of the body as the material substratum of the self (identified with consciousness), as territory enclosed by the projections of the ego. Illness, sickness, fatigue, pain, disability: All of these can be among the sensory quakes that strike below the belt of the general habits of stereotype, category, recognition, and representation. "Something in the world forces us to think," Deleuze writes. "This something is an object not of recognition but of a fundamental encounter. . . . It may be grasped in a range of affective tones: wonder, love, hatred, suffering. In whichever tone, its primary characteristic is that it can only be sensed."[122] Thinking disability "without recognition"—thinking disability through the "language of life, rather than of law"—reintroduces into discourse a vital figurative concept of human life dipping its feet back in the tidal pool of the mutational sea.[123] By thinking the lines that cut through us, rather than by playing in the stultifying hall of mirrors of representation, we might, Deleuze hoped, "become something other than what history has made us and wishes to make of us."[124] Breakdowns of conventional structures of subjectivity—just as Irani's cripple found two arms to be insufficient organs for the capacity of hearing the world—can become, in this way, creative breakthroughs. Becoming disabled thus involves transcending oppositional reactions, morality, identity forms, and the climb to perfection so as to become with earth.[125]

Thinking about Zarathustra, Nietzsche's cripple on the bridge, Deleuze writes: "To affirm [life] is not to . . . harness oneself to that which exists, but on the contrary to unburden, unharness and set free that which lives. It is not to burden life with the weight of higher or even heroic values, but to create new values that would be those of life."[126]

9

NEVER QUITE HERSELF AGAIN:
FRIDA KAHLO'S DOCTRINE OF CREATION

To put it paradoxically, what matters most in a human life may in some sense be one's specific form of disorientation, the idiomatic way in which one's approach to and movement through the world is "distorted."

—Eric L. Santner,
The Psychotheology of Everyday Life

Like one become disabled, philosophy, Deleuze suggests, must invent new forms of life. Constructive theology shares that work. In that vein, "to write philosophically involves inventing conceptual personae—characters or perspectives like Nietzsche's Zarathustra," Tamsin Lorraine explains. "Conceptual personae can enable the embodied philosopher to engage in thinking that goes beyond the thinking of a molar subject"—that is, a subject already territorialized by sociality.[1] Here I turn to the work of artist Frida Kahlo, who mapped one way of thinking the critical freedom of becoming disabled, indeed, of becoming postcolonial.[2] How does one stop living like a capitalist transcendental, since "capitalism is like the Christian religion" (that is, "constantly cutting off flows") and its holy family works like a machine of Oedipalization?[3] By learning to become, as did Kahlo, "unlike one's self."

Rather than rehearse a reading of Kahlo's art through Deleuzean philosophy, I would like to work with Kahlo as a fabulating machine for our becoming disabled—for "thinking difference, thinking differently," as opposed to pathologically steeling ourselves to overcome our sufferings and reterritorializing the body for the ego. It would seem, in light of contemporary interest in her, that our desires have lead us to Kahlo—perhaps evidencing yet again our appropriation and commodification of exotic cultural icons (e.g., playing Indian) or, perhaps, evidencing that we cannot, despite the cultural credo regarding the meaninglessness of suffering, do without some account thereof. Featured in the recent exhibit *Carr, O'Keefe, Kahlo: Places of Their Own* (Vancouver Art Gallery, 2003), Kahlo has also been the subject of recent biographies, for example, Sarah Lowe's *Frida Kahlo* (1991), Hayden Herrera's *Frida, A Biography of Frida Kahlo* (1983) as well as her 1991 collection of Kahlo's paintings, at least one historical novel, Barbara Mujica's *Frida*, and a movie based on Herrea's biography (2003). *The Diary of Frida Kahlo* was itself published in 1995. At a popular level, Kahlo has also been iconically inlayed on kitsch art (necklaces, bracelets, shopping bags). In their display window, Barneys (the famous New York City department store) interpolated her image with that of her primary contemporary collector, Madonna.

I want to address, through our longing for Kahlo, the viability of a pedagogy of pain linked to becoming politically, culturally creative at this time.[4] Clinically speaking, transcendentals or globals, awash with life resentment, are in tremendous pain, "owing to the sclerosis or hardening of . . . consciousness."[5] Chronic, if hidden pain, depression, and anxiety are among the big secrets of our lives. Further, "a truly just society," writes David Morris, concluding his study of Sade in his *The Culture of Pain*, "would need to construct a new understanding of pain: an understanding that did not disavow but rather accepted and transformed the tendency in pain to isolate the individual."[6] We would need a way of living pain without putting the ego in charge of it, I would imagine Deleuze to add by way of qualification. Sentient pain, when not referred to the ego, may not necessarily be dialectically opposed to desire's fulfillment. In this way, we may even learn to suffer—that is, have enduring patience with and equanimity in—the presence of difference.

In situating ourselves next to Kahlo, I encourage us to ask what Deleuze calls the "clinical" question of literature, art, and philosophy, "What mode of existence does it [she] imply?"[7] "Each of Kahlo's portraits maps . . . a way to exist, a way to position herself in the world," comments Sarah Lowe, Kahlo's most astute biographer.[8] The event of becoming disabled transpires in how we thus position ourselves, how we assemble ourselves around and in relation to those sites that social normalization has marked as the ground zero of labor and of libido, as there being nothing of value there.

For Deleuze, fabulating or "metamorphosis machines"—the conceptual means for mutating desire—are events of art, literature, and science or the concepts of philosophy that differently metabolize social life, especially accessing anOedipal desires.[9] Social formations, in a Deleuzian dynamic sense, name specific machines of desire, desire always then being psychosociohistorically determined. Literature, philosophy, and art each take clinical responsibility for analyzing such operative social machines, for appraising the vitality of desire as well as its symptoms, and for fabulating new modes of existence that free desire from what imprisons it.[10] "A metamorphosis machine would then be one that does not simply support the repetition of the same [course of desire, which is causing the present symptom] but rather engenders the production of something altogether different."[11] Iterating our desire with and through a work of art—as a metamorphosis machine—can help us respond to local symptoms by producing new ways of acting upon the present.[12]

Kahlo figuratively, through her performance art, models the critical freedom of becoming disabled—models, that is, *"a new way of experiencing pain,"* a way of experiencing pain other than by standing outside the skin.[13] How could experiencing pain in a new way possibly lead to critical, creative freedom? "Distancing ourselves from the world's flesh-and-blood reality," observes Linda Holler,

> is part of everyday life when bureaucratic systems and technologies of mass production take us away from the sources of our material existence and therefore the consequences of our actions. To the dissociated ego of the bourgeois world . . . the consequences of action appear insubstantial. . . . Consumers stand outside of the flesh, living in a vast commodification of reality, one that eventually turns their own bodies into things in need of modification and perfection.[14]

In one sense, as Holler observes, in such a world, pain isn't counted as real: We try to keep pain out of consciousness and secret it away from culture. Yet in such a situation we easily become manipulated by our fear of pain—such fears are readily provoked and manipulated in our culture. Further, such dissociation generates the worst kind of suffering—excruciating psychic pain, to say nothing of broader environmental damage, our paralysis around social injustices, and the ethical insensitivities occasioned by such dissociation from the flux and flows of sentient life. Of this broad capitalist landscape, Deleuze wrote: "Whenever a physical relation is translated into logical relations, a symbol into images, flows into segments, exchanged, cut up into subjects and objects, each for the other, we have to say that the world is dead, and that the collective soul is in turn enclosed in an ego, whether that of the people or a despot."[15] The transcendent, if despotic ego, an immature and truncated relation with the world, asserts its regime of power by using pain as a threat.

Following Deleuze, I have suggested that becoming disabled might be a site for opening out what he calls the room of critical freedom—the freedom

to refuse replication in and through the copy machine of dissociative idealism, the possibility of becoming with the Earth, the freedom to practice what
Holler calls "erotic morality." So I welcome the reader to take this excursion
through "becoming Frida Kahlo" as an invitation to critical freedom, as an
invitation to what Nietzsche also called the Great Health.

"The Disquieting Muse"

Frida Kahlo, born in 1907 just outside Mexico City, became one of Mexico's
preeminent artists of the twentieth century. Her works, considered sometimes
shocking, even indecent, seem to provide a rather straightforward chronicle
of disability, of immense personal, physical and emotional suffering. To be
sure, Kahlo contracted polio at age six. More recently, it has been surmised
from her diaries that she may, in fact, have been born with cerebral palsy. In
1925, at the age of nineteen, coming home from a carnival day in the city, she
and her *novio* (boyfriend), Alejandro, were among those in a bus that collided
with a streetcar. Kahlo was impaled on a metal rod, which passed through her
pelvis, chest, and spine. Her right leg was crushed. Complications of these
conditions, along with several miscarriages, occasioned chronic pain and more
than two dozen surgeries throughout her life. Her right leg was amputated
due to gangrene about a year before her death in 1954.

With her suffering in full view, even splashing out into several frames,
Kahlo's work has often been treated dismissively. Her "stark disclosure of
intimacies"—as in the painting *My Birth*—seems almost to dare viewers to
declare them publicly inappropriate. As biographer Sarah Lowe comments,
"Her work was deemed so excessively personal and self-referential that it
was thought incapable of expressing . . . the human condition."[16] To be sure,
approximately two-thirds of Kahlo's works appear to be self-portraits—thus
the charge of self-absorption, especially given the hermeneutic of indulgent
narcissism to which the disabled and ill are often treated in our culture.[17]
Kahlo, however, was a philosophically astute and politically engaged woman.
Intending to become a doctor, Kahlo was one of only a few women accepted
into Mexico's National Preparatory School in 1922. Introduced to the arts
early in life through her photographer father, she took up painting while lying
prone and convalescing after the streetcar accident. First thinking to become
a medical illustrator, Kahlo rather became something more of a performance
artist-activist in the social revolution convulsing Mexico following the removal
of the last European-influenced, imperial-style dictator, Porfirio Diaz.[18]

Like Deleuze, Kahlo was an avid reader of Nietzsche and D. H. Lawrence and a critical reader of Freud. While recruited under the canopy of the Surrealist movement of Artaud (another key figure for Deleuze) and Breton as an example of exotic otherness, she likely used Breton's display of her to get her art noticed.[19] Kahlo's creativity came from an interface with her own hybrid and revolutionary location: Child of a German Jew of Austro-Hungarian descent and a Catholic Mexican mestiza, she would artistically combine Christian and Aztec symbolism with indigenous sources, ancient mythologies, and socialist political philosophy.[20] In this way, Kahlo became a figurative fabulation—a performance artist—for a Mexico throwing off colonialism.

Given her immersion in the cultural and political milieu of Mexico and her saturation in vitalist philosophy, mythology, and indigenous culture, I, too, would argue, along with Sharyn Rofhlsen Udall, curator of *Carr, O'Keefe, Kahlo: Places of Their Own*, that Kahlo's art was truly not about the person, was not necessarily, then, self-portraiture, but rather was an attempt—like that of her contemporaries Emilie Carr and Georgia O'Keefe—to "paint something beyond the visible subject itself."[21] Further, her sharp ironic sensibilities allowed her to use the body in pain persistently to disrupt common sensibilities. Kahlo consistently "overturns expectations of the image of women in art" (of women fashioned according to male standards of beauty, that is) by painting herself as sensuous *and* suffering.[22] In apparent mimesis of Giorgio de Chirico's 1924 painting titled *The Disquieting Muse* (itself hardly a study of stylized feminine beauty, though still fashioning female forms as divinatory repositories for man), she retorts to the public charge that she is but a muse for men of genius by painting herself in (and as) *The Broken Column* (1944). Her chest cavity split open from head to hips to expose her cracked spine, Kahlo appears held together by only a surgical corset.[23] Even her partner, Diego Rivera, was subjected to her artistic retorts, his apparently affirmative incorporation of industrialism answered by her 1933 painting *My Dress Hangs There* (The dress hangs on a clothesline strung between a toilet and a sports trophy, each set on a pillar in front of the Lincoln Memorial, the clothesline keeping her dress from dragging in the accumulating garbage and from being trodden underfoot by the armies of anonymous workers.) Rivera's grand revolutionary, if still romantic murals are answered by her postcard-size *retablos* and *ex votos*, insistently posing pain front and center.[24] Never quite "herself" (entire, integrated, transparent, and self-identical from one moment to the next), Kahlo simply refused to be a decent woman, either as a painter or socially, practicing cross-dressing and artistic gender innovation (as with her unibrow and mustache) and undertaking multiple sexual liaisons. Her self-portraits stare back and splash the viewer with her iconoclastic imagery of bloody births, deaths, fetuses, corpses, and disembodied organs.[25] Yet in painting after painting, Kahlo's earthquake-riddled, surgically sliced or disintegrating body was simultaneously the provocative location of continuous creation—new bloody capillaries, new green rhizomes, each intriguingly flowing into the other.

Always devotional, Kahlo simultaneously frames and voids miracle.[26] Her *ex voto* paintings are exemplary in this regard. An *ex voto* was supposedly something like "a receipted bill for spiritual or physical boons received," each one painted to commemorate miracles.[27] Yet the *ex voto* inscription of her painting *Remembrance of an Open Wound* (1938) says it all: She lifts her leg, disclosing her right thigh to display the splayed flesh. "Kahlo's *retablos* disturb in part because they depict unrelieved pain, as they commemorate actual events for which there is no outside intervention depicted, no miracle to stop the wounding," Paula M. Cooey observes—at least no miracle that we can apparently see, no supernatural intervention as we have been trained to expect (supernaturalism in the Christian West has assumed a defining distance from nature, a guarded affiliation with the angels, the expectation to changed reality).[28] If Kahlo ironically plays us against our own assumptions regarding supernaturalism, however, she also offers us a view of that most excellent miracle—the rapture of being alive. No interventions, just a doctrine of creation, of chaosmic creativity, where once again out of the wound new growth sprouts.

"Don't Stare!?"

One approaches Kahlo's work by entering and passing through the stare. In civil society, we have been instructed not to look at bodies in pain ("Don't stare," every parent instructs their protesting three-year-old, assessing the obvious: I have but one leg.). Kahlo insists otherwise. If the stare is illicit, for Kahlo it is also mutual. Kahlo's paintings do not have demure, averted, feminine eyes (inviting objectification), but eyes that insistently dare the viewer to hold her gaze, to move through the pain. If the world stares at the disabled, Kahlo's stare dares us to move into regions of life that we don't want to see. Why don't we want to see this region? What would happen to us emotionally as a culture if we did not presume to close our eyes to it? Kahlo refuses to bear disability shrouded in guilt, refuses to invite pity. Her desire thus exceeding, refusing standards of beauty, she tempts, attempts, invites desire—even in that condition.[29] Eyes do not need to stare; they, too, can open out to touch upon and hold each other.   ·

In her paintings, animals—parrots, deer, her dogs, and especially her monkey Fulang-Chang—often surround her body. These animals, biographers of a Freudian bent have suggested, were for Kahlo child substitutes. I wonder: When I'm not feeling well, my daughter's cats refuse to leave me, even seeming to know the onset of illness ahead of (my) time. In an earlier stage of my rehab, my family and I walked at the Watchung Park Reserve early on Sunday mornings, one morning taking with us a young golden retriever we met in the parking lot—his elderly owner wary of suffering a heart incident with exertion in the New Jersey winter cold. Less than a quarter-mile away, the dog—her head anxiously looking back for her domestic companion, appearing more and more compromised as we gained distance from him—finally lay down on the path, unable to proceed. But when my daughter tried to run the dog back to its human familiar faster than I could move, the dog again laid on the path, now caught in compassion between the two of us, proceeding only as I was able to catch up with her. If we humans presumed to look at pain, might we, as animals, find ourselves caught up in compassion? And then what? According to Nietzsche we—like "that profound physiologist, the Buddha"—would have to yield our resentment: "To liberate the soul from this [resentment] is the first step toward recovery."[30] That we should make looking at pain, touching upon it with our eyes, illicit: Might this be one of the ways we mark and hold our resentment against life, keep ourselves from dwelling in the midst of life? Is that not, as Nietzsche first suggested, the great illness from which our civilization must recover?

Kahlo invites erotic desire for life even as she lets pain bleed through—reflecting "her general resistance to romanticization."[31] She perhaps paints compassion, the animal energy folding body round body—"*not* morality," but "physiology," Nietzsche insisted.[32] Certainly, Kahlo invites a passionate equanimity in relation to suffering—never acquiescence, never permitting her life to be summed up in suffering, but also unremittingly present, without supernatural assuagements. Yet such recognitions keep suffering all too private, within the territory of the personal self, when life for Kahlo—the lover of Trotsky and women unnamed, the political artist-activist—was anything but that. "From her diaries it is clear that [Kahlo] identified herself, her body, its appearance, her pain, and her pleasure metaphorically with Mexico. . . . [H]er mixed heritage and the events of her life reflected the history of struggles and suffering as well as the hoped for destiny of Mexico itself."[33] She was no more immune in illness than in imagination and sustenance from the "vitality-sustaining ground."[34] Her paintings "bring together sentience and nature with history, psychology and spirituality with politics."[35] Her suffering could not consequently be so narrowly conceived as but a biomedical phenomenon.

When we move out of the Cartesian worldview, with its singularly agential, human subject, desire's prodigal quality circulating through this "vitality-sustaining ground" comes into focus. *New York Times* science writer Michael Pollen, standing in his garden, explains: "All these plants, which I'd always regarded as the objects of my desire, were also . . . subjects, acting on me, getting me to do things for them they couldn't do for themselves. . . . Seeing these plants instead as willing partners in an intimate and reciprocal relationship means looking at ourselves . . . as the objects of other species' designs and desires, as one of the newer bees in Darwin's garden."[36] So when we comparably stand within the complex, dynamic life field, the subject or object of pain may be as difficult to isolate as desire in Pollen's garden: If "plants evolved by stirring human desires and values," then does the earth ache through us?[37] In *Roots* (1943) as also in *Tree of Hope* (1946), the chasm that opened out the length of Kahlo's reclining body resembles the quakes opening out in the surrounding earth, the wounds then appearing to be of a kind. Unexpectedly, in an otherwise apparently barren picture, the region's new growth sprouts from the crevices of her fractured spinal column. A somewhat similar phenomenon can be noted in *The Dream* (1940), where Frida's bed sheets sprout rhizomes while Judas, the death figure, bunks on the upper berth. Rather than thinking of health as a lost object to be recovered, health might be calculated rather by the rhizomatic growth in the nurse log of the body's fissures. "The world," Deleuze wrote, "is the set of symptoms whose illness merges" with humanity.[38]

Her wound was intensely her own, and Mexico's, the body but a "landscape in the first person."[39] Was not that place—Mexico—creatively suffering regeneration consequent to the rejection of colonial culture, but also in and through her? Might we actively suffer desires' creative, inpersonal, though also political and cultural endeavors and their redemptions? Pain during modernity has been kept individuated and subjectively personalized. Deleuze instructed: "The statement is individuated, and the enunciation subjectified, only to the extent that an impersonal collective assemblage requires it and determines it to be so."[40] So does Oedipalized capitalist civility keep us from adding one plus one, preventing the awareness that our pains—depression, let's say, chronic anxiety, or back pain—might be produced in, through, and by this particular social assemblage?

Kahlo wrote, in her 1940 application for a Guggenheim Foundation Fellowship, that "my subjects have always been my sensations, my states of mind and the profound reactions that life has been producing in me."[41] Deleuze endorses this "kind of thinking that does not subordinate difference to an identity logic," that moves "beyond representational thought in order to approach imperceptible happenings."[42] What becomes socially significant, Deleuze contends, must first be discerned, not as strategies among always already complete human agents, but from within a field of affects and percepts, as Kahlo suggests she did. Something of a Zenlike physiotherapy practice, attention to these genetic, preconscious elements of life, allows us to slip under the rabbit-proof fence of always already Oedipally organized civility. Refusing the subjective framing of persons who assume force as their own, becoming a Body without Organs (BwO), as Deleuze calls it, humans access that plane of immanence where "the landscape is no longer an external reality but . . . a 'passage.'"[43] "Pure affects," Deleuze explains, "imply an enterprise of desubjectivation."[44] Passing from the heights of egoic consciousness into the landscape, humans who become imperceptible might also affect the becoming new of Earth.

Becoming a Body without Organs—a puzzling term, itself redolent of the disarticulation that is (for some of us) the experience of becoming disabled—is our critical freedom. Deleuze explains this phenomenon, which I have elsewhere referred to as living the self like an ecotone, as like "the strength of life in a baby, before the body has been properly organized." Rather than conceiving of strength as like that of a man of war, think of strength as the vitality of the will to life, the newborn body, "which concentrates in its smallness the same energy that shatters paving stones."[45] But if there's a certain, curious theologic here of being born again, there's also something about this infant body traversed with vitality, but without— because prior to—a socially mapped, libidinal organization that, even in Deleuze's mind, resonates with becoming disabled. Recalling D. H. Lawrence's literary evocations of the vital, if organically defective bodies, Deleuze concludes: "The way to escape judgment is to . . . find yourself a body without organs. This had already been Nietzsche's project: to define the body in its becoming, in its intensity, as the power to affect or to be affected," not as the power to seize force so as to make it one's own (again, the possessive power of ego), but as power that is an enriching vitality.[46] This "immanent life" of the BwO, explains translator and commentator Daniel Smith, functions for Deleuze "as an ethical principle"—a teaching about creativity, a doctrine of creation, if you will.[47]

If it was Kahlo's practice to be but a passage of the landscape, "Kahlo's paintings, especially her self-portraits, created a rupture in the history of art by overturning expectations of the image of women in art," Lowe observes. Kahlo's self-portraiture "marks a resistance to objectification rarely seen in art. . . .

She perpetually embodies the condition of 'the other'—not male, not Anglo, not whole, not verifiably heterosexual—an artistic curiosity."[48] Gambrell, not one schooled in Deleuzean philosophy, astutely concludes her study of Kahlo by noting her paintings' ability to carry the touch of the spoilative without exhausting the exquisiteness of life as also the continuum of the animal and the human, the organic and inorganic: "We can . . . begin to sense within Kahlo's autobiographical impulse a slightly different effort—one directed towards the creation of 'a being [*un*]like oneself,' rather than towards a fully knowable, coherent self" [*sic*].[49]

Kahlo's meditative attention to the fluxes and flows broke through Oedipalized desire and the sclerosis of consciousness: "Speaking for yourself, in your own name . . . doesn't at all come with seeing yourself as an ego or a person or a subject," Deleuzes instructs. "Individuals find a real name for themselves only through the harshest exercise in depersonalization, by opening themselves to . . . the intensities running through them. . . . Experimentation on ourself is our only identity."[50] In a Deleuzean sense, Kahlo exemplifies the practice of critical, because creative, freedom. But how shall we live our desire for her—this incomplete yet excessive being? Especially given that she so completely refuses the burden of shame and indulges so many guilty pleasures, even in a simple plate of fruit (see *Fruits of the Earth*, 1938). We'll have to let her out of our own frames of judgment. After all, "Judgment prevents the emergence of any new mode of existence," when what is needed, considering some of the destructive vectors of globalization, is to "go . . . beyond that which may be, or has been, lived."[51]

Intriguingly, this ability to become unlike one's self—encountered in Kahlo as the freedom of becoming disabled, if also the freedom of becoming postcolonial—seems comparable to the innovative technologies of the self, the ascetic disciplines of dissembling normalized subjectivity, practiced among ancient Christianities. In her work *The Sex Lives of the Saints: An Erotics of Ancient Hagiography*, historian Virginia Burrus explains that in Christianity, sacrifice, rather than an affirmative positivism of self-identity, "was the condition for the opening of the self as field of indefinite interpretation."[52] That such a "hagiographical erotics" emerged as a creative, revolutionary, subjective technology among those "within the charged and contested transculturalism of a late Roman Empire" she finds hardly accidental.[53] While scholar David Helperin retrieves "Greek and Roman styles of self-cultivation" to define the subjective stylistics of his *Saint Foucault* as (echoing what was said of Kahlo) one who exercised "the [erotic] capacity to 'realize oneself' by becoming other than what one is," Burrus finds this a promising way to read ancient discourse.[54] The saints, Burrus explains, "steadfastly reject both the comforts and the confinements of conventional roles and relationships (swapping and discarding 'identities' like so many threadbare cloaks)."[55] She continues:

> Saintly love begins with resistance to the temptations of 'worldly eroticism' . . . to perduring familial and political hierarchies, institutionalized relations of domination and submission. . . . Yet such resistance to cultural norms . . . does not take an anti-erotic turn, proffering the sterile safety of a desexualized 'agape' in exchange for the firm repression of sexual desire. Rather, it gives rise to an exuberant art of eroticism in which the negativity harbored within resistance is eclipsed by the radical affirmation of desire also conveyed in resistance.[56]

Sacrifice, implying the release by transcendence of the positive, fixed frame of self-identity, moves within an erotic, nature mysticism that does not avoid the coincidence of pleasure and pain in the becoming unlike one's self, in the becoming new of the Earth.[57]

Kahlo lived what might be called an "ecstatic naturalism."[58] Instead of "containing the spiritual within as a personal property," mysticism—here according to Deleuze's pivotal predecessor, Henri Bergson—"provides an opening to the process of life itself, to a spiritual dimension wholly immanent to life in which processes of creation and differentiation, virtualisation and actualisation are continually taking place."[59] Backgrounded by Aztec vegetation rites in which a representation of the goddess Coatlicue was sacrificed as a symbol of the rejuvenation of nature and assimilated with the Christian belief that life emerges from death, Kahlo's suffering takes on an undeniably sacrificial aspect.[60] Kahlo lived her pain as a sacrificial suffering with the land, as becoming Mexico. At the same time, Kahlo refused to transpose "the primordial experience of suffering into the theistic problem of evil."[61] But if we unhitch pain from life and death as also good and evil, then we must let go our resentment held against life, allowing pain to reach into and activate our emotional brain, our love for the world. "Learning to transform pain and pleasure into moral action," comments Holler, "is the heart of emotional intelligence and moral wisdom."[62] Burrus described a comparable ascetic sensibility: "When *jouissance* is understood as 'a mode of ascesis,' the ascetic emerges into view as an erotically *joyful* 'body in pain,' disclosing suffering as the vehicle of the ongoing unmaking and remaking of worlds" [*sic*].[63] Like

Christianities' sacrificially, self-transcending subjectivities of the early Common Era, becoming disabled and postcolonial (or per Deleuze, this becoming a BwO) may be among the innovative technologies for taking leave of empire—at the very least, for taking leave of the empire of the ego. The dissembling of normalized self-hood when reiterated begins likewise to swerve the structures of worldhood.

Kahlo painted herself, observes her biographer Sarah Lowe, time and again "standing in the field of cosmic phenomenon."[64] "Chaosmos" (as Deleuze and Guattari designate this plane of immanence) suggests a different energy in relation to which to live one's pain, a different narrative line than rounding each body back toward an enclosed whole.[65] Where the body is folded down to "where the roots and the stems and the flowers begin,"[66] where "an emancipation of dissonance" transpires that is "not brought into a tonality,"[67] there Kahlo paints the dove. The dove—appearing in such diverse paintings as the still life *Fruit of Life* (1954), imposed upon her unibrow, or as the shape of her necklace, painted in the margins of her diary, and as the wings of *Who Needs Legs When One Has Wings to Fly*—was yet another of Kahlo's delicious and semiotically laden puns. The partnership between Diego Rivera and Kahlo was sometimes publicly evoked as that of "The Elephant and the Dove." Whether assuming that public image as personal glyph and/or connecting the dove of peace of political demonstrations, if also of Marian devotional imagery, with her name Frida (assuming as its etymological root "*frei-*" or peace, freedom), the dove became Kahlo's personal icon. Spirit, the dove, Kahlo—all nestled in relation to sentience, sliced, dismembered, fleshy, even with a touch of spoilation.

Her still-life paintings, not unlike her self-portraits and her *ex votos*, never deny wounds, the underbelly of the life cycle, never deny a certain sacrificial quality to human life. Yet where the sweetness of fruit appears only at the knife edge of dismemberment, Spirit (Frida, the dove) appears nestled with a certain equanimity. A Kahloesque humor ripples off the portrait: "Still life," Kahlo laughs, poking us from the bed of her supposedly vegetative state. Ever punning with us, her last paintings with the dove were a series of O'Keefe-like still lifes, including *Still Life* (1951), *Naturaleza Viva* (1952), and *Fruit of Life* (1954) in which plates of juicy, fleshy, sensuous, if also cut, fruit make her final testimony. Both of her very last of these Spirit-attended still lifes, *Still Life with Legend* (1953) and her final painting, *Viva La Vida* (1954), bear that painting's title inscribed in the sliced flesh of the watermelon: Long live life.

The dove as vibrational vortex of chaosmic becoming suggests a sacramental appreciation of the wondrous commonplace events of the present. It announces what Deleuze calls "becoming mortal" and what he describes by citing Maurice Blanchot: "Something happens . . . that they can only recapture by relinquishing their power to say 'I.'"[68] Passionate equanimity, let this be Spirit's name. To be sure, "Equanimity is not indifference but a passion for life that comes from gratitude rather than the need to control."[69] Where "immanent life functions as an ethical principal," there theology might mutate into a way of learning entrustment to the midst of life, "openness to the unbidden," and an "ethics of becoming" that might themselves be inseparable from a doctrine of creation.[70]

CHAPTER 10

WISDOM TO MAKE THE WORLD GO ON

"Neither one nor two." Luce Irigaray did not have an amputee in mind when she penned that evocation of the catastrophic crisis that woman presents for phallomorphic discourse.[1] But likewise to discourse stands this disabled body—not merely on one foot, nor wholly on two, but catastrophically creased. One day I trip, turn an ankle. In that slight fracture of the integrity of natural communities that materialize the fragile contours of a body, tragedy tears the seams. I lie on the threshold of death. I lose a leg. In one slight stumble, any belief in reasonable proportions is shredded. No perpetrator, no victim. No act of God. No story of tragedy to triumph. No trajectory ascending from grave to glory. To these grand narratives, the disabled body postures as a doubter. At least in this account, there is neither a spiritual superhero nor a technologically endowed cyborg overcoming the odds. Disability precisely refuses to be overcome. This, then, is an attempt to pick up the traces of a religious hope that stays honest to corporeality—that knows how to traverse the tears in a tragic, transient, sentient nature—a religious hope that does not abandon its basic trust in life when proportions are ruptured, when causal relations are suspended, when chaos exceeds control.

To love is to bear with the chaos.

—Catherine Keller,
Face of the Deep

This chapter explores the wisdom, even authority, of bodies that admit suffering, the socially abject bodies of the disabled. What seems to the cultural eye the physical obstinacy of disability suggests, rather, a religious, philosophical, and/ or cultural rejection, an undigested or inadmissible awareness that to live will involve us, at some time and at some level, in physical and/or psychic suffering. In a religiocultural philosophy undergirded by idealism, where the perduring reality of suffering has been severely denied, where, during the Enlightenment, physical suffering's legitimacy was curtailed, survival wisdom has likewise been suppressed. As we emerge into a postmodern consciousness of discontinuities, fragmentation (here I refer not simply to the postmodern philosophical pastiche,

but to the *ecological* ramifications of our unrepented idealism), and even an awareness of irredeemability (that is, of uranium mines, genocides, amputations, and
so on), the disabled can be counted among those who have lost innocence and
who, therefore, might be able to offer wisdom to make the world go on. Contrary
to how Darwin has been read against the survival of the disabled, and contrary
to how Christianity wraps us in its petition on behalf of "the weak and handicapped," we "weaklings" may prove most adept at surviving a less than physically
perfect world as the rest of nature acts back upon humanity.

I hope, however, to work both sides of disabled persons' claim to abject
authority. As just noted, in a culture that represses suffering, disabled persons
may best know how to survive in less than ideal circumstances—a wisdom that
may become all the more necessary as we realize the repercussions of the ecological crises on our bodies, water, and land. Yet—and here is my second point—if
the disabled have such wisdom or authority, it seems to me to be the result of a
a cultural disavowal of suffering that keeps the disabled socially marginalized. If
that is true, then social-spiritual acceptance of the disabled must include removing the projections of mortality, that is, intense physicality, from the disabled,
and making each person accountable for carrying the psychic weight of their
own mortality.[2]

The Disabled Body as Icon of a Culture's Abjection of Pain

"Physical pain has no voice": With that starkly conclusive insight from her
phenomenological study of *The Body in Pain*, Elaine Scarry alerts us to the tre-
mendously difficult yet vital necessity of bringing pain to discourse, of "making
religions," those practices situated at this torsion point between the destructive
capacity of pain and the turning of that suffering body back toward rebirth.[3] Not
just playing resistively with language, pain actively destroys the voice of those
who are suffering, Scarry observes. Set this phenomenological propensity in our
Western culture, which has been materially successful at insulating the power
of the proper and propertied from the frustrations of the sentient body, and one
can hear Scarry's assessment exponentially multiplied with cultural repression:
"Nothing sustains [pain's] image in the world; nothing alerts us to the place it has
vacated."[4] Nothing, I would add, except the bodies of the disabled.

Where language cannot hold open a place of remembrance, where religions
allow pain to flee into immaterial and otherworldly eschatologies, that is, into
the hope of a world where "death will be no more," where "sorrow and sighing
shall flee away," there in your path you will encounter the iconic presence of the

disabled body. Disability acts, in such scenarios, as the unprocessable stigmata of mortality—the disabled body seen as if it were a cultural reject from the mills of transcendental transubstantiation to which all other bodies could and did aspire. The catastrophic crease of disability does not allow those of us so marked to pass as anything but mortal.

"*See, I betray you to your mortality.*" Fury fires my lips. Having just worked out in the gym, I traverse the parking lot without prosthetic veil. "*See,*" my angry and locked chin responds to those invasive, starring eyes, "*I betray that little secret which we had agreed to keep 'hush-hush'—suffering and death. No, my body doesn't evoke whispers; you gasp, clench your guts, as if the horror of me would make you spill out, as if the sight of me would rip you open. It does, mortal!*"

Normates can either vicariously suffer the wound with me and recover, or they can revulsively project on me that from which they do not know how to recover—mortality.[5] Where bodies flee their material tethers, where religions evasively displace the frustrations of sentience, where peoples refuse to "feel the great sorrows everywhere," there cultures sink into horror of the disabled.[6] Where life is transcendentalized by romantic naturalisms, religious holisms, secular idealisms, or technological virtual reality, there the disabled body will become a culture's deject, the object of its abjection of pain and transience. Where life is lifted, lofted, into the idealistic, material sublime, there—because sorrow will not cease, because pain will not disappear—the body of the disabled will be made to carry the hostility that we consequently feel toward the contours of sentience. Think, if you will: No Wailing Wall, no keening wakes, no psalms of lament in our public worship, no Mexican Day of the Dead, no Navajo "sing" to calm the percussive violence of trauma and illness. Rather, in this Western region, we are left with just the iconic disabled body, which we culturally bury in mobile crypts of silence and alienation.

"By Our Wounds. . . ."

"Most grown-ups didn't look right at Trudi; they acted as if she were invisible and said things they would never say around other children."[7] So Ursula Hegi begins Trudi's story, *Stones From the River*, a fictional account of a *zwerge* (dwarf) living in the town of Burgdorf, Germany, during World War II. Sitting at the circulation desk of the library, that confluence of a community's life stories, Trudi—a confessor more fearfully incisive than the town's ideologically blinded priest—carries the burdens of all that the town would wish to conceal from themselves, especially the failed loyalties that now implicate them in the horrors of war. Just as if they were throwing stones into the deeps of a river, these secrets of their mortality they throw toward Trudi—making their confessions to the one from whom they can in turn shield themselves by cloaking her in oversight. She carries the weight of their secrets. She learns, via observation, to divine how secrets, like stones, change the course of the river, the stream of a conversation, the flow of a body's energies.

With the catastrophic crease acting like clerical authorization of a cultural confessor, into the laps of the disabled are poured the cries and crises of mortal flesh.[8] We, the disabled, who are "all body" and "no-body"—overdetermined by the gaze and yet also constantly overlooked and seen through—are inscripted to carry the weight of corporeal abjection: the reminders and remainders of mortality, the rocks thrown into the secreting deeps.[9] Though pain may fall below language, the groaning and sighing, the moaning and mourning, these prelingual gasps are all too frequently delivered into our ears. We hear the hidden sorrows of flesh that reveal themselves as implicated in mortality—because "I," the confessee announces, "just knew *you* would understand." (This although the relation between an amputation of a leg and, for example, issues of infertility are less than obvious to me.) By keeping us marginalized and by using us as confessors, culture is kept clean of the moaning and mourning, the crying and sighing, of the awareness of transient and temporal conditions. This is culture's way of making sacrificial wisdom of our wounds: By our wounds, they are healed. Pain—by which I here refer to the incursions of transience, the sorrows of a mortal life, the humblings of the flesh—can be culturally, spiritually secreted by concealing disability, by preventing the disabled from being present to public culture, by making the "invalid" in/valid.[10]

If relief is found by bringing pain to voice, as Scarry has asserted, then, culturally speaking, justice for the disabled will require a change in our undergirding cultural philosophy. Quite specifically, we will need a discourse that holds corporeal contours—finitude, limits, transience, and mortality, as well as the suffering and pain associated with such—in cultural consciousness. This would further involve turning our fearful and therefore zealous energies away from the cultural, even scientific goal of the eradication of all suffering, a goal that obviously works aversively against the presence of the disabled, and toward the spiritual wisdom of composing ourselves with equanimity before the shifting tectonics of a lifetime, since all bodies must sometime deal with the fall from grace/fulness. Further, a religion that offers hope to the disabled would have much less to do with promising a future where tears will be no more than with promising the physical space where we, the disabled, can limp or wheel up to or lie at the table without encountering the alienating social gaze, because all bodies present have metabolized their own mortality; that is, they have learned to hold the body humbly in mind.

Holding Corporeal Contours in Cultural Consciousness

While Christianity holds the incarnation of Spirit in flesh as its defining paradigm, Christianity has also written histories qualifying just how much and precisely what kind of *carnis* ("flesh") Spirit will tolerate in term of, gender, race, sexuality. Undergirded with Platonism, Paul mapped out Christianity's trajectory of transcendent hope by generating a psychic aversion to transience and the terrestrial, "the bondage to decay" (Romans 8), and Athanasius the fear of dissolution back into chaos. (And could that be the fear triggered by the sight of disability?) If Elaine Pagels's account has been justly criticized for its oversimplificiation of the argument between Augustine and Pelagius regarding the ontological status of mortality, that is, "the nature of nature," it seems obvious, nonetheless, that much of Western Christianity has been written as if mortality, as Pagels suggests Augustine would have it, were not natural.[11] Consequently, we Christians have a tendency to read all suffering, not just social injustice, as if it were oppressive, as if it were inhuman and, therefore, as if it had to be resisted. Sometimes, in the course of a human life, suffering just happens. A religion that refuses the life-death-fertility-spoilation cycles—and their attendant sorrows—will not tolerate the value of disabled subjects, but will rather insist on our cure or, when that fails—inasmuch as "disability defies correction . . . resist[s] . . . cure"—will demand our silent submission to serving as exemplars of Christianity's benevolent charity.[12]

Where corporeality is construed as oppression, where freedom promises the supersession of sentience, where justice is colored with idealism and eschatology as holism, we, the disabled, are and will remain the unrepentant and irredeemable heretics. Our bodies, though we may not be and often are not in physical pain, will not stop confessing their transient contours. Yet this supposed captivity of the flesh, the bondage to transience, is precisely what the disabled body calls into question with its—with our—love of life.

Think of it, if you will: how disconcerting the presence of a disabled person who enjoys their life. How surprised the public is when my daughter, Sarah, practices her parade wave while seated on my lap in the wheelchair . . . when we dance, twirling round and round, in my wheelchair until we succumb to fits of giggles. How shocked, even offended, are others when we meet along the rim of Kittatiny Ridge—with me obviously having hiked in on my crutches. Would you be surprised to learn that my days are pretty normal, pretty ordinary—getting my daughter up and off to school, work, then workouts at the gym, then running . . . well, limping fast . . . to play chauffeur for my daughter's violin rehearsals? While disability may limit the range and extension of the flesh (though not necessarily of the psyche, which is also organically constituted), it does not necessarily hold the flesh in captivity, in bondage. Social and religious attitudes do.

Consequently, I am proposing a discourse that takes up the challenge of "hold(ing) traumatic reality in consciousness"—and even more specifically, of writing religious hope, that is, love of the world (John 3:16), of a "world without end," even "resurrection of the body," without evacuating corporeality.[13] I am interested in tracing out a religious hope that recognizes that finitude and mortality and transience are conditions for the everlastingness of the world—are conditions that "permit an infinite becoming within the finite."[14]

By insisting that discourse—cultural, theological, and philosophical—stay consonant to corporeal contours, we turn abjection back to what Kristeva calls its zero point, to the responsibility of each to carry their own mortal weight. To get the weight of abjection off the backs of the disabled, the humors and humiliations, the anger and agitations of sentient flesh must be brought into public discourse, spiritual conversation, and religious ritual. In this way, we pose the possibility of psychically renegotiating our inherent dependence on earth, a dependence that we currently attempt to deny by abjecting those bodies that bear the brush strokes of mortality.

Out of a more honest acquaintance with our sentient situation, we can reinstitute subjective economies that recognize that bodies have needs, that communities are woven together among people who need each other, that everyone has needs—not just the community of the disabled. *"Excuse me,"* I say, *"I need some help here."* In that moment, the frozen wall between us topples. In your converted countenance, I discern that, as if in the twinkling of an eye, *you* have been changed. For the forty-five seconds I needed you, you did not feel extraneous to the world. Sometimes I will ask for help just to save you, the nondisabled, from superficiality and irrelevance . . . just to save us from your own worst fear.

Nevertheless, I am beginning to acknowledge that I live vicariously through the nondisabled. . . . I mean, I positively enjoy you in all new ways—the shoes that I will never wear, but that I can put on through how you move in them, the dance that I will not dance, the morning run that I will not undertake, but through you. Vicarious feeling allows me to turn cartwheels with my daughter and land on the feet of my memory. Such sympathetic exchange makes me wonder if normates also try me on, vicariously speaking. Does that offensive gaze also, underneath it all, pose the question: How do you do it? How do you traverse the tragic tears, without the promise of triumph and without sinking into inconsolable disappointment, without dissociation and without despair? This is, I would suggest, the wisdom of an abject authority, the one who can navigate the passage from horror to hope, the one who can teach us to balance on the undulating surface of sentience in a posture I might call "keeping trust" with the spirit of life.

While the goal of bringing suffering into cultural and/or religious discourse is to remove the weight of social abjection from the bodies of the disabled and to return it to zero point, the individual, nevertheless, what has been abjected (as Kristeva also notes) has an authoritative potency. I therefore propose a double-braided discourse on the abjection of our transient tissue. In the upcoming section, I will undertake the first strand of this braided discourse by welcoming the wisdom of those who, admitting their mortality, can teach us to traverse the tragic tears in sentient existence with some measure of equanimity. Specifically, I will be attending to Hildegard of Bingen, who saw a connection between her own disability and her spiritual visions that gave her both political and ecclesial authority, and to contemporary writer Lucy Grealy's reflections on her disfigurement due to bone cancer. In the latter section, I attempt to reacquaint each person with not only the pain, but with the promise of holding our bodies in mind.

From Horror to Hope: Navigating the Passage

Hildegard of Bingen, a twelfth-century visionary theologian, recognized that her disability kept her close to what the poet Mary Oliver describes as the "porous line, where body is done with and the roots and the stems and the flowers begin."[15] In concluding her last book, *The Book of Divine Works*, Hildegard observed of herself that "from the day of her birth," she had "lived with painful illnesses as if caught in a net."[16] Disabled by what may have been recurrent bouts of rheumatic fever, Hildegard maintained that this instability provided access for the influx of divine authority. The divine voice itself explains to her: "thoroughly seared, so to speak, by countless grave sufferings of the body, the depth of the mysteries of God has completely permeated you."[17] A "humble" woman is she, she says: dust of dust. But laid low to the earth, she there encounters the ironic contours of divine potency: scandalous humility, a divine power in, with, and under the earth to which the humble—those maintaining sympathetic knowledge of earth ("humus")—have access. Precisely in straddling the balance of life's tenuousness, Hildegard learned to harvest the taproot, the "Life of life."

While Scarry has asserted that pain "by its aversiveness, makes most pressing the urge to move out and away from the body," and while Scarry suggests that there is an inverse relation of pain and the imagination such that pain must create a Presence outside itself, abject authorities like Hildegard bear witness to other hopeful passages through pain that include ways of sinking deeply into the sentient body.[18] Admittedly, to a culture that makes war on pain, dissociation into ecstatic rationalism is a well-traveled passage. Yet, as Caroline Walker Bynum has noted in her study of medieval women saints, there is another way of "saving life" that proceeds by plumbing the possibilities of the flesh itself.[19] Recovering from numerous bone-cancer surgeries, Lucy Grealy writes, in her *Autobiography of a Face*, of this way of becoming "ever more intimate with my body."[20] "A sort of physical awareness would take hold of me," she writes. "Each breath was an important exchange with the world around me, each sensation on my skin a tender brush from a reality so beautiful and so mysterious that I would sometimes find myself squealing with the delight of being alive."[21]

For Scarry, what brings pain to voice is the language of weapon-become-tool. "The point here is not just that pain can be apprehended in the image of the weapon . . . but that it almost cannot be apprehended without it," Scarry insists. "Even the elementary act of naming this most interior of events entails an immediate mental somersault out of the body into the external social circumstances that can be pictured as having caused the hurt," she writes, commenting on the shared etymological root of pain and punishment.[22] Thus, she positions her phenomenology of pain on a pendulum that swings between the deconstructive capacity of pain and the constructive potential of the imagination, seemingly prolific at generating images of weaponry and warfare, so as to create language and religion as bridges over the chasm carved by pain.

Grealy, like Hildegard, provides a phenomenologically thick description of the threshold (not, for them, a chasm) between pain and imagination. Each swims in a deep semiotic reservoir of ecstatic exchange with her environment. The same sentient disposition that can and does register pain for both Hildegard and Grealy nevertheless also provides for their renewal through an influx of sensuous life energies: the birds outside the window, the erotic brush of air on skin, the bosomy clouds of the sky, the bedewed, thus bejeweled bushes and branches of morning in the orchard—even, in Grealy's case, the smells of decaying flesh. Such observations would suggest that dissociation, the movement out and away from the body, for example Scarry's mental somersault out of the aversive body, is not the only traversable path through pain. Hildegard and Grealy plumb the sentient reservoir and carry energy back into the reconceptualization of their worlds.[23]

A strange maternity this, but just as surely as Spirit overshadowed Mary's womb, thus conceiving Jesus, so sure was Hildegard that Spirit overshadowed her wound, thus leading to her own incarnational (self-)conception. Setting herself as if in reminiscence of that other nativity, she seated herself under the cloister/stable roof, attended by her male secretary and emerging, as if out of and so off to the side her spiritual daughter, Richardis. From the overshadowing cloud, as that of the Exodus, she is "bedewed" with the moist breath of God, breast fed the milk of wisdom and visions of justice. Laid low to her bed by illness, lying down like an initiate in spirit rituals, sensuous energy rushes through her body to the wound.[24] As if the wound were the chamber of a harp, these energies play across her until a new song awakens a new body, attuned and activated by the dynamic reverberations of that harmony. Born from this semiotic steeping of her wound was a prophetic preacher, the first Christian female writing theologian, a musician, an herbal healer and natural scientist, a founder of two women's communities.

A strange maternity, this maternity of the mortal wound. And yet, is this not the poetic maternity that Kristeva sanctions when she calls for the privileged psychotic breaks through which artists and analysts, as practitioners of "the maternal function," transport semiotic motility across the border on which the symbolic order is founded?[25] These who traverse the threshold, the mortal passage, accessing what Kristeva terms "the archaic base and the particular *jouissance* it gives rise to," sketch out for us a kind of second birth.[26] Though subject to death, or precisely because they recognize themselves as subjects related to death, these practitioners of the maternal function, Hildegard and Grealy, are also, as Kristeva has insisted, subject to rebirth.

A Wisdom as Common as the Common Cold?

But let us lay aside the elitism that has overtaken art and analysis—those privileged sites of this maternal function, as Kristeva sees it. These who traverse this passage between death and birth, who recognize their subjectivity in terms of mortality: Who are these but the wounded, if all too eccentric healers and abject authorities of ordinary suffering? Is not Kristeva's "poetic revolution" comparable to what Virginia Woolf simply called "the spiritual change that common illness brings?" In her essay titled "On Being Ill," Woolf observes that "in illness, we become deserters. They march to battle. We float with the sticks on the stream . . . able for the first time for years to look round, to look up."[27]

Much as the artist serves to open out revelation, the semiotic baptism generated by trauma, by ripping open the veil between worlds, may initiate the calling of an apocalyptic prophet. As an apocalyptic event, trauma can reveal the world of the powers and principalities that currently subjectivate the body and an/other world to which the initiate can emigrate. A visionary, Hildegard sensed, through the social implications of her body, the hopes and fears of her surroundings. These she apparently translated into diagnostic images, or *scivias* ("showings"). As if the site of her wound were as disclosive as the rings of a fallen tree, she read out, from the apocalypse of her body, vivid sociopolitical critiques.

Let me suggest what I think it might mean to read cultural critique from the site of a wound. As if my amputation functioned like a heresy, my body resists the habits of capitalist subjective machinery. It even dissents from our culture's infatuation with the technological sublime. Where capitalism privileges efficiency of time, space, and money, I get in the way, slow the pace, presume too large a buffering presence—the enviable margins of a handicap parking space, if nothing else. "You walk like an Indian!" I'm told, you'll remember, because the normal and, thus, the technologically necessary prosthetic gait requires one to dig in their heels. Digging in one's heels: What religious posture toward the earth is this, I have asked myself, if not the incessant grinding away at any sympathetic relation, when instead we might be always on our toes to catch knowledge of humus, human mortality, and even the ironic divine potency of humility (see Gen 3:15)? In such ways, the disabled body might serve as site for prophetic critique.

Seared by trauma, the prophet of daily life also foresees, as Woolf would have it. Deserters of everyday warfare—an "outlaw" stance, as Woolf herself called it, they are yet emigrés to a world revisioned by the mortal wound.[28] Dropped off the edge of one world, they have dropped into a world experienced as more vital than that of the pretentious posturing that our disabled bodies can no longer afford. "In a strange way," Hegi observed of Trudi, "she had more freedom than other women: the freedom to make her own decisions, to provide for herself with her work at the library, to listen to her own counsel" (207). Though first ejected from the inhabitations of normative daily life with a tragic shove of physical trauma and social forgetfulness, the deep background—or Woolf's cinematic sky—yields the disabled revelations of new inhabitations. Neither one nor two, neither one world nor the other: never wholly free of the pain of the alienating shove, yet active deserters of world wars, discovering spacious openings for the reconception of life.[29]

Resurrection of the body neither begins nor ends with the transcendence of sentience, but rather starts with discerning the powers that quicken and sub-jectivate the body—globalization and its very corporeal stimulation of desires, the industrial capitalization of the body, individualism, materialism—and also possibly humility, solidarity, contentment. Postmodern discourse, discipled by Foucault, has learned to read the pneumatic webs of power coursing through the body, a knowledge that, among abject authorities such as Hildegard, used to be called "discernment of spirits." But who is it that can move beyond Foucaldian archaeology to healing and transfiguring these powers that be? Who knows how to raise up life energies that have been colonized into apathy? Who knows how to handle this horrific passage of rebirthing the self and reconceiving the world? Studying the point of quickening by straddling the porous line, Hildegard learned to cull out deadly powers and to raise up life energies in the corporate bodies that intersected and materialized her body: community, ecclesia, and empire. Yet couldn't such abject authority be as common, as Woolf would have it, as ordinary illness and as democratic as mortality?

Neither Tragedy nor Triumph, but Trust . . . as Equanimity

Straddling the porous line, plumbing the semiotic reservoir, while reconciling ourselves with the contours of corporeality: This is the nature of trust in the Spirit of life. Trust includes a certain sympathy for Spirit, which suffers the cataclysm of vital communities of livelihood coming to tragic intersections. Such sympathy does not silence the mourning or the anger. But neither does trust theologize our frustration with dependence on the earth as a transcendent longing for elsewhere. Trust, rather, is a way of abiding with our mortality, where sentience not only confirms the registration of pain, but bedews the body, baptizes it unto life.

How do you traverse the tears in a tragic nature? In the age of ecstatic ratio-nalism, we have had few teachers. The narrated passages of tragedy to triumph, from grave to glory—these ways of overcoming—continue to scandalize the sentient nature in which we live and move and have our being. The tragic tears must rather be traversed—as with the energy of a blue heron, picking its way through a marsh edge, its feet finding a path through that space where life and death course, lose their distinction, yield to transfigurations. Nothing can stabilize the risk in existence; justice can provide a clearing for livelihood. Yet the equanimity of trust offers itself as wisdom for life. Trust offers proximity to divine potency, to the Spirit's presence to life. So, to quote again Irigaray:

"I am returning this forgotten property to you: mortal. If you should die from this discovery, then you had not yet begun to be born."[30]

Endnotes

Preface

1 Augustine, *Against Julian*, trans. Matthew A. Schumacher, in *The Fathers of The Church: A New Translation*, ed. Hermigild Dressler, vol. 35 (Washington, D.C.: Catholic University Press, 1957), 118, 115. Peter Brown supports this reading: "For in the last resort, there was much that Augustine had refused to accept in the life around him: areas of experience had become unbearable to him. . . . He will react with horror to the suggestion of Julian, that life in Paradise would have been much like life as it was now lived. If this was so, Augustine repeatedly insisted, terrible things would have to be admitted into that encapsulated, unviolated area of past innocence. It would include the inexplicable sufferings of small children, the horrors of the deformed and the mentally defective." See Brown's *Augustine of Hippo: A Biography* (Berkeley: University of California Press, 1967), 396.

2 Cited in Paul Ricoeur, *The Symbolism of Evil*, trans. Emerson Buchanan (Boston: Beacon, 1967), 330 (1969 ed.).

3 Headlines of *The Globe and Mail*, Canada's national newspaper, for Saturday, October 21, 2006, suggest the broader cultural horizon of my own experience. "Do it, push him in there or I'll beat you up," the story banner reads, the story itself then detailing how children in the alleys of Winnipeg—not even yet adolescents—push a disabled teen into a burning shed and lock it fast.

4 Ato Quayson, *Postcolonialism: Theory, Practice or Process?* (Cambridge and Malden, Mass.: Polity/Blackwell, 2000), 153.

5 Franz Fanon, *Black Skin, White Masks*, trans. Charles Markmann (New York: Grove, 1967), 19, 23, 110–112.

6 Guy Debord, *Society of the Spectacle*, trans. Donald Nicholson-Smith (New York: Zone, 1995), 13, 12.

7 Debord, *Society of the Spectacle*, 13.

8 Debord, *Society of the Spectacle*, 14.

9 Debord, *Society of the Spectacle*, 17–18.

10 Debord, *Society of the Spectacle*, 20, 24.

11 Harlan Hahn, "Advertising the Acceptably Employable Image," in *The Disability Studies Reader*, ed. Lennard J. Davis (New York: Routledge, 1997), 176.

12 Quayson, *Postcolonialism*, 149.

13 Morton Schoolman, "Introduction to William Connolly," in *The Augustinian Imperative: A Reflection on the Politics of Morality* (Newbury Park, Calif.: SAGE, 1991), xviii.

14 J. Joyce Schuld, *Foucault and Augustine: Reconsidering Power and Love* (University of Notre Dame Press, 2003), 151.

15 Lennard Davis, "Nude Venuses, Medusa's Body, and Phantom Limbs: Disability and Visuality," in *The Body and Physical Difference: Discourses of Disability*, eds. David T. Mitchell and Sharon L. Snyder (Ann Arbor: University of Michigan Press, 1997), 54.

16 Zygmunt Bauman, *Liquid Modernity* (Cambridge and Malden, Mass.: Polity/Blackwell, 2000), 38.

17 Zygmunt Bauman, *Wasted Lives: Modernity & Its Outcasts* (Cambridge: Polity, 2004), 19.

18 Cited in Bauman, *Wasted Lives*, 18.

19 Bauman, *Wasted Lives*, 7.

20 The biblical story of the blinding of King Zedekiah (2 Kings 24:17—25:7) illustrates the imperial practice of mutilation—including also hobbling, punching out eardrums, and leaving persons blind, deaf, and lame—so as to prevent the flight of prisoners of war and/or slaves.

21 John Caputo, *The Weakness of God: A Theology of the Event* (Bloomington: Indiana University Press, 2006).

22 Keith Ansell Pearson, "Pure Reserve: Deleuze, Philosophy, and Immanence" in *Deleuze and Religion*, ed. Mary Bryden (New York: Routledge, 2001), 144.

23 Gilles Deleuze and Felix Guattari, *What is Philosophy?* (New York: Columbia University Press, 1994), 75.

Introduction

1 Barbara Kingsolver, *The Poisonwood Bible* (New York: HarperCollins, 2003), 483.

2 Kingsolver, *The Poisonwood Bible*, 40.

3 Kingsolver, *The Poisonwood Bible*, 88, 68.

4 Kingsolver, *The Poisonwood Bible*, 591.

5 Gilles Deleuze and Felix Guattari, *What is Philosophy?* (New York: Columbia University Press, 1991), 23.

6 Deleuze and Guattari, as cited in Paul Patton, *Deleuze and the Political* (New York: Routledge, 2000), 3.

7 Elizabeth Johnson, *She Who Is* (New York: Crossroad, 1992), 266.

8 Jay McDaniel, *Living from the Center: Spirituality in an Age of Consumerism* (St. Louis: Chalice, 2000), 5.

9 See Marcella Althaus-Reid, *Indecent Theology: Theological Perversions in Sex, Gender and Politics* (London: Routledge, 2000).

10 Benjarmin R. Barber, *Jihad vs. McWorld: How Globalism and Tribalism are Reshaping the World* (New York: Ballantine, 1996), 59–61.

11 Harlan Hahn, "Disability and the Reproduction of Bodily Images: The Dynamics of Human Appearances," in *The Power of Geography: How Territory Shapes Social Life*, eds. Jennifer Wolch and Michael Dear (Boston: Unwin Hyman, 1989), 382.

12 Thomas De Zengotita, *Mediated: The Hidden Effects of Media on People, Places, and Things* (London: Bloomsbury, 2005), 4, 7, 6.

13 Lennard Davis, "Nude Venuses, Medusa's Body, and Phantom Limbs: Disability and Visuality," in *The Body and Physical Difference: Discourses of Disability*, eds. David T. Mitchell and Sharon L. Snyder (Ann Arbor: University of Michigan Press, 1997), 54.

14 Donna Haraway, "Ecce Homo, Ain't (Ar'n't) I a Woman, and Inappropriate/d Others: The Human in a Post-Humanist Landscape," in *Feminists Theorize the Political*, eds. Judith Butler and Joan W. Scott (New York: Routledge, 1992), 86.

15 Trinh T. Minh-ha, "She, the Inappropriate/d Other," *Discourse* 8 (1986): 87.

16 Haraway, "Ecce Homo," 87.

17 Herman Daly and John Cobb, *For the Common Good: Redirecting the Economy Toward Community, the Environment, and a Sustainable Future* (Boston: Beacon, 1994), 108.

18 Faulkner, cited in Paul W. Hollenback, "Jesus, Demonics, and Public Authorities: A Socio-Historical Study," *The Journal of the American Academy of Religion* 49, no. 4 (1981): 567.

19 Rosemarie Garland Thomson, *Extraordinary Bodies: Figuring Physical Disability in American Culture and Literature* (New York: Columbia University Press, 1997), 6.

20 Frantz Fanon, *Black Skin, White Masks*, trans. Charles Markmann (New York: Grove, 1965), 116.

21 Frantz Fanon, *Wretched of the Earth*, trans. Constance Farrington (New York: Grove, 1965), 45.

22 Thomson, *Extraordinary Bodies*, 26.

23 Fanon, *Black Skin, White Masks*, 11.

24 Lennard J. Davis, *Bending over Backwards: Disability, Dismodernism and Other Difficult Positions* (New York: New York University Press, 2002), 26–32.

25 Thomson, *Extraordinary Bodies*, 6.

26 Fanon, *Black Skin, White Masks*, 19, 23, 110–112.

27 Robert C. Anderson, "Infusing the Graduate Theological Curriculum with Education about Disability" in *Theological Education* 39, no. 1 (2003):136.

28 Davis, *Bending over Backwards*, 31.

29 While the terminology *persons with a disability* (pwd) makes the point that impairment is not the central, organizing principle of life experience, most of us simply use the term *disabled* challenging instead the ideology of normalcy and social shame. The language of *physically challenged* may sound politically correct, "but it is loaded with the faulty notion that it is the individual who is challenged to 'overcome' his or her disability, rather than society's

responsibility to overcome its prejudice." See Marta Russell, *Beyond Ramps: Disability at the End of the Social Contract* (Monroe, Maine: Common Courage, 1998), 14. That said, there is no unanimity among those of us society tends to group as the disabled. Many in the Deaf World, for example, would hardly be conducive to thinking deafness as disability, since the term popularly denotes incapacity. The Deaf World sees deafness as something rather like another ethnicity. The term *Crip*—or, variously, *Crip culture* or the *Crip Nation*—simply queers the terms of social exclusion—*crip* for crippled. The term was used by David Mitchell and Sharon Snyder in the video *Vital Signs: Crip Culture Talks Back*.

30 Mary Louise Pratt, *Imperial Eyes: Travel Writing and Transculturation* (New York: Routledge, 1992), 7.

31 Harlan Lane, *The Mask of Benevolence: Disabling the Deaf Community* (San Diego: DawnSign, 1992), 38.

32 Henri Nouwen, "Contemplation and Ministry" in *Simpler Living, Compassionate Life: A Christian Perspective*, ed. Michael Schut (Denver: Living the Good News/Division of The Morehouse Group, 1999), 57.

33 Percussionist Evelyn Glennie challenges such restrictive notions of deafness as lacking a receptive modality. The first and only full-time performing classical percussionist became profoundly aurally impaired ("deaf") at age 12, yet she performs as a musician by feeling sound.

34 Zygmunt Bauman, *Globalization: The Human Consequences* (New York: Columbia University Press, 1998), 53.

35 Bill Ashcroft and others, *Post-Colonial Studies: The Key Concepts* (New York: Routledge, 2000), 116.

36 Ato Quayson, "Looking Awry: Tropes of Disability in Postcolonial Writing" in *Relocating Postcolonialism*, eds. David Theo Goldberg and Ato Quayson (Oxford: Blackwell, 2002), 228. Sanjeev Kumor Uprety has also drawn attention to the coincidence of the tropes of disablement as a frame of reference for postcolonial histories. Uprety, more psychoanalytically akin to Fanon, follows a Lacanian trajectory to hold up—amidst the celebrative capaciousness of hybridity—the memory of the colonial experience as that feeling of "being deformed or deviant." See Uprety, "Disability and Postcoloniality in Salman Rushdie's *Midnight's Children* and Third-World Novels." *The Disability Studies Reader*, ed. Lennard J. Davis (New York: Routledge, 1997), 366.

37 Quayson, "Looking Awry," 228.

38 Quayson, "Looking Awry," 228.

39 Ato Quayson, *Postcolonialism: Theory, Practice or Process?* (Cambridge and Malden, Mass.: Polity/Blackwell, 2000), 2.

40 Quayson, *Postcolonialism*, 9, 6, 11.

41 Mikhail Bakhtin, *Rabelais and His World*, trans. Helene Iswolsky (Bloomington: Indiana University Press, 1984), 317.

42 The sentiment that we are sick of ourselves is owed to Mark Seem, "Introduction" to Gilles Deleuze and Felix Guattari, *Anti-Oedipus: Capitalism and Schizophrenia* (Minneapolis: University of Minnesota Press, 1983), xxi. In introducing the concept of "becoming disabled" here, I play with the Deleuzean sensibility of "becoming minoritized." Paul Patton, *Deleuze and the Political* (New York: Routledge, 2000), 7.

43 Patton, *Deleuze and the Political*, 7.

44 *Globalization* can be heard, as Christian communities may have intended in earlier phases of missional and ecumenical outreach, as a term of planetary solidarity. However, the term today tends to connote the problematic means through which the planet is being yoked via corporately managed economic interests, which recede from democratic, including internal nation-state, negotiation. Richard Falk, *Predatory Globalization: A Critique* (Cambridge: Polity, 1999), sees the net effects of "globalization from above," that is, via neoliberal ideology, as social and economic injustice, environmental degradation, and heightened materialism leading to cultural and spiritual decay. The understanding of globalization with which I work in this book is based primarily on readings of Zygmunt Bauman, Jeremy Seabrook, and Anthony Giddens.

45 Homi Bhabha, cited in Quayson, *Postcolonialism*, 140.

46 Ashcroft, *Post-Colonial Studies*, 116.

47 Robert Young, *White Mythologies: Writing History and the West* (New York: Routledge, 1999), 159.

48 Michael Hardt and Antonio Negri, *Empire* (Cambridge, Mass.: Harvard University Press, 2000), xv.

49 Jean Comaroff and John Comaroff, *Of Revelation and Revolution: Christianity, Colonialism, and Consciousness in South Africa* (Chicago: University of Chicago Press, 1991), 2.

50 Quayson, "Looking Awry," xvii.

51 Young, *White Mythologies*, 159, 160.

52 Russell, *Beyond Ramps*, 57–68.

53 See Barbara Ehrenreich, *Fear of Falling: The Inner Life of the Middle Class* (New York: Pantheon, 1989).

54 Thomson, *Extraordinary Bodies*, 12.

55 Linda Holler, *Erotic Morality: The Role of Touch in Moral Agency* (New Brunswick, N.J.: Rutgers University Press, 2002), 206.

56 The December 2002 meeting of the Modern Language Association had a session devoted to "Cripping Globalization." I have not been able to access any of the papers presented at this conference.

57 Harlan Hahn, "Can Disability be Beautiful?" *Social Policy*, Winter (1988): 31, 28.

58 Russell, *Beyond Ramps*, 57.

59 Russell, *Beyond Ramps*, 44, 47.

60 Russell, *Beyond Ramps*, 28.

61 Lennard J. Davis, "Bodies of Difference: Politics, Disability, and Representation" in *Disability Studies: Enabling the Humanities*, Sharon Snyder and others (New York: Modern Language Association of America, 2002), 104-05; Russell, *Beyond Ramps*, 61.

62 Russell, *Beyond Ramps*, 68.

63 Russell, *Beyond Ramps*, 59, 83.

64 Russell, *Beyond Ramps*, 70.

65 Russell, *Beyond Ramps*, 13, 50.

66 Hahn, "Disability and the Reproduction of Bodily Images," 553. In North America, more than two-thirds of pwd are unemployed, even after the United States implemented the Americans with Disabilities Act (ADA). As economic globalization sweeps the planet, and as countries are brought into the patterns of industrial and postindustrial capitalism, the body count of pwds swells. Because of the way in which the economy reorients relational communities, it has been estimated that upward of 90 percent of pwds worldwide are unemployed.

67 Pwds want the insights of science, even as we seethe at its incessant, obsessive need to fix us, to eradicate our kind. We seek facilitation, not eradication. Nor do persons with disabilities form a we, a community of belonging. Not only are pwds dispersed among the general population, not only are we merely united by the stare (while each of our physiological givens are incredibly particular), we require interdependence with a human community of multiple and diverse capacities. Here I recognize something similar to the awareness within postcolonial studies that cultures in contact, even when those cultures are as unevenly paired as empire/colony, not only become unwittingly inserted into signs and values not their own, but appropriate the other's technologies, if even by remaking them in the process.

68 David D. Yuan, "Disfigurement and Reconstruction in Oliver Wendell Holmes's 'The Human Wheel, Its Spokes and Felloes'" in *The Body and Physical Difference: Discourses of Disability*, eds. David T. Mitchell and Sharon L. Snyder (Ann Arbor: University of Michigan Press, 1997), 71.

69 Physical disability has been actively effected in and through the brutality of wars, including their aftereffects, for example, land mines, religiocultural and international politics (the use of physical dismemberment by the Taliban), and the international creation of poverty zones within formerly colonized countries. More amputees reside among the combined populations of three small countries—El Salvador, Cambodia, and Bosnia—than in the entire United States.

70 Davis, *Bending Over Backwards*, 110.

71 Bauman, *Globalization*, 75–76; Kelly Oliver, *Witnessing: Beyond Recognition* (Minneapolis: University of Minnesota Press, 2001), 15.

72 Anyone from the North American middle class must, I would argue, think ourselves from this location—despite how we feel just barely able to hang on, as if we were just making it, and despite how many richly resourced others we can count as better off than ourselves on the economic rungs. First-world-class "membership," if you will, would include our food procurement system, our singular reliance on cash economy (based somewhere in property ownership), reliance upon the energy grid, waste accumulation, and means of transport (only 8 percent of the planet's citizens own cars, while many North American households own at least two). Despite how powerless we each feel, assuming such a location also steps us into responsibility and accountability.

73 "Glocalization" names the insight that, while modernity tended to distinguish the local from the global as also the city from the country or the rural from the urban, the local has been interpolated by the global. People's dreams, their sense of self and hopes for a life, are resourced by representations and imaginations that do no respect local resources. Conversely, global economic forces as well as media, e.g., television and news sources, shape local politics. *A Political Space: Reading the Global through Clayoquot Sound*, eds. Warren Magnusson and Karena Shaw (Montreal: McGill-Queen's University Press, 2002) provides an excellent analytic study of this phenomenon.

74 Winona LaDuke, "Power is in the Earth," in *Talking About a Revolution* (Cambridge, Mass.: South End, 1998), 77.

75 Gayatri Chakravorty Spivak, "Three Women's Texts and a Critique of Imperialism" in *Critical Inquiry* 12 (Autumn 1985): 244–248.

76 Carlin Barton, *The Sorrows of the Ancient Romans: The Gladiator and the Monster* (Princeton. N.J.: Princeton University Press, 1993), 3, 108. Anne McClintock, *Imperial Leather* (New York: Routledge, 1995), uses a similar methodology. McClintock there calls for a "situated psychoanalysis that is simultaneously a psychoanalytically informed history" (72). This use of psychoanalysis as intervention within the politics of representation in the metropolitan center follows the pattern of decolonizing philosophers who have used psychoanalysis as a privileged site of resistance. Homi Bhabha, in his foreward to Frantz Fanon's *Black Skin, White Masks*, explains the privileged role of psychoanalysis in the work of Fanon: "It is a mode of negation that seeks not to unveil the fullness of Man but to manipulate his representation" (Cited in Young, *White Mythologies*, 155). An analogy might also be found in the work of Spivak, who "reorients subaltern history away from the retrieval of the subalterns' consciousness and will . . . towards the location and reinscription of subject-positions which are instrumental in forms of control and insurgency" (Young, *White Mythologies*, 160).

77 Barton, *Sorrows of the Ancient Romans*, 87, 132. For the Romans, to be fascinated or transfixed by something monstrous was at once to be caught up in the circuit of curiosity where the spectator easily became conversely the benumbed, stupified spectacle (87, 89, 91 n. 34). Ironically, the only cure for such paralysis became, in turn, the horror of it all—to be rehabilitated by the monstrous, here comparable to the "noble savage" (130–132). So, Barton concludes, "It is not surprising that, in a period where Romans themselves complain of being debilitated by excessive refinements and distinctions, when the wealthy build 'pauper's huts,' sleep on boards, eat the black gruel of the despised rustic, and write bucolic poetry, they would be attracted to the virile wilderness of grotesques" (132).

78 Davis, "Bodies of Difference," 101.

79 James I. Porter, "Forward," in *Body and Physical Difference*, Mitchell and Snyder, xiv.

80 Linda Tuhiwai Smith, *Decolonizing Methodologies: Research and Indigenous Peoples* (London: Zed Books, 1999), 25–26.

81 Amy O'Brian, "Residents in Fear After Beating Death: East Vancouver Man Found in Middle of Road," *Vancouver Sun*, Section B1, April 12, 2004. James Byrd Jr., a black American, was murdered by three white supremacists on June 7, 1998, in Jasper, Texas. After being beaten, he was chained to the back of a truck and dragged three miles, his body deposited in front of a cemetery. While race was quickly identified as the basis for the hate crime, disability activists wonder how Byrd's impairments played into the crime and why our critical public analytics continue to ignore such insight.

82 Patton, *Deleuze and the Political*, 33.

83 Scott Lash, "Genealogy and the Body: Foucault/Deleuze/Nietzsche," in *The Body: Social Process and Cultural Theory*, eds. Mike Featherstone, Mike Hepworth, and Bryan S. Turner (London: Sage, 1991), 273.

84 Michel Foucault, *Power/Knowledge: Selected Interviews and Other Writings: 1972-1977*, ed. Colin Gordon (New York: Pantheon, The Harvester, 1980), 166.

85 James C. Scott, *Domination and the Arts of Resistance: Hidden Transcripts* (New Haven, Conn.: Yale, 1990), 55.

86 Hahn, "Disability and the Reproduction of Bodily Images," 377.

87 Ivone Gebara, *Longing for Running Water: Ecofeminism and Liberation* (Minneapolis: Fortress Press, 1999), 102.

88 Tamsin Lorraine, *Irigaray and Deleuze: Experiments in Visceral Philosophy* (Ithaca, N.Y.: Cornell University Press, 1999), 18, 14.

89 Lorraine, *Irigaray and Deleuze*, 15–16.

90 Haraway, "Ecce Homo," 87.

91 Elaine Graham, *Representations of the Post/Human: Monsters, Aliens and Others in Popular Culture* (New Brunswick, N.J.: Rutgers University Press, 2002), 12.

92 While "making" could be heard to herald an idealist philosophy (with a Cartesian mentalist modality), I invite the reader to hear the invitation to "make the world go on" within the immanentist philosophy and energetic materialism of Gilles Deleuze and Felix Guattari. Within this philosophical stream "production as process overtakes all idealistic categories and constitutes a cycle whose relationship to desire is that of an immanent principle." See their *Anti-Oedipus: Capitalism and Schizophrenia*, trans. Robert Hurley, Mark Seem, and Helen R. Lane (Minneapolis: University of Minnesota Press, 2003), 5. This "constructivist conception of philosophy," explains Deleuzean scholar Paul Patton, invites philosophers to "make and create [concepts]" and in this way "to invent new possibilities of life." See his *Deleuze and the Political*, 12, 23. In this mode, making has more to do with the process of composition by the activation of potentials and possibilities than with a development plan.

93 Kathleen Sands, *Escape from Paradise* (Minneapolis: Fortress Press, 1994), 2.

94 Sands, *Escape from Paradise*, 4–5.

95 Mark Thompson, Exposition in "Matthew 15:21-28" in *Interpretation*, Vol. 35.03: 279.

96 Laura Donaldson, "Joshua in America: On Cowboys, Canaanites and Indians" (Lecture within the series "Title in the Text: Biblical Hermeneutics, Colonial and Postcolonial Pre/Occupations" at Green College, Vancouver, BC, September 2002). This presentation is to be published in the forthcoming anthology, *The Calling of Nations* (University of Toronto Press).

97 Sands, *Escape from Paradise*, 16. See also 166–169.

98 Lois Keith, "Tomorrow I'm Going to Rewrite the English Language," in *Mustn't Grumble*, ed. Lois Keith (London: Women's, 1994), 57.

99 Luce Irigaray, *I Love to You: Sketch of a Possible Felicity in History*, trans. Alison Martin (New York: Routledge, 1996), 15.

100 Rosenzweig, as summarized by Eric Santner, *On the Psychotheology of Everyday Life: Reflections on Freud and Rosenzweig* (Chicago: University of Chicago Press, 2001), 22.

101 Edith Wyschogrod, "The Howl of Oedipus, the Cry of Heloise: From Asceticism to Postmodern Ethics," in *Asceticism*, ed. Vincent L. Wimbush (New York: Oxford University Press, 2002), 27.

102 Cited in Tyler Roberts, *Contesting Spirit: Nietzsche, Affirmation, Religion* (Princeton, N.J.: Princeton University Press, 1998), 14–15.

103 Santner, *On the Psychotheology of Everyday Life*, 21.

104 Zygmunt Bauman, *Liquid Modernity* (Malden, Mass.: Polity/Blackwell Publishers, 2000), 28.

105 Donna Haraway, "The Promise of Monsters: A Regenerative Politics for Inappropriate/d Others" in *Cultural Studies*, eds. Lawrence Grossberg, Cary Nelson, and Paula A. Treichler (New York: Routledge, 1992), 297–298, 300, 303.

106 Thandeka, *Learning to be White* (New York: Continuum, 2002), 118–119.

107 Bauman, *Globalization*, 39. Certainly, there are telling differences among narrative theologies. Barbara Christian insists, in her "The Race for Theory" (*Cultural Critique*, No. 6 [Spring 1987]: 51–63), that multiple cultures deploy narrative forms to do the work of critical consciousness. Admittedly so. But narrative theology as it has been presented in the pulpits of North American Protestant and Anglican communities, that is, telling our stories, car-

ries forward the problematics of modern, post-Reformation individualism without significant social insight.

108 Marcella Althaus-Reid, *Indecent Theology: Theological Perversions in Sex, Gender and Politics* (London: Routledge, 2000), 18, 27.

109 de Certau, cited in Comaroff and Comaroff, *Of Revelation and Revolution*, xii.

110 Deleuze and Guattari, cited in Patton, *Deleuze and the Political*, 3.

Chapter One

1 Eli Clare, *Pride: Disability, Queerness, and Liberation* (Cambridge, Mass.: South End, 1999), 94.

2 Chrystos, cited in Sherene Razack, *Looking White People in the Eye: Gender, Race, and Culture in Courtrooms and Classrooms* (Toronto: University of Toronto Press, 1998), 56.

3 The term *ugly laws* refers to former municipal codes that prevented persons with disabilities from "exposing themselves" in public. Here, for example, is one such from the Municipal Code of the City of Chicago: "No person who is diseased, maimed, mutilated or in any way deformed so as to be an unsightly or disgusting object or improper person to be allowed in or on the public ways or other public places in this city, shall therein or thereon expose himself to public view." If one wants to think such sentiment well in the past, Simi Linton also cites several letters to Ann Landers from spring 1987 that suggest a still quite intact social-psychic reserve about the public presence of disabled persons: "I have the right when I go out and pay good money for a meal to enjoy it. The sight of a woman in a wheelchair with food running down her chin would make me throw up. I believe my rights should be respected as much as the rights of the person in the wheelchair . . . maybe even more so, because I am normal and she is not." See Simi Linton, *Claiming Disability: Knowledge and Identity* (New York: New York University Press, 1998), 34.

4 Steve Burgess, "It Don't Mean a Thing if It Ain't Got that Bling: The Bling Crowd," *Vancouver Magazine*, November 2003: 44–45.

5 Ato Quayson, *Postcolonialism: Theory, Practice or Process?* (Cambridge and Malden, Mass.: Polity/Blackwell, 2000), 153.

6 Naomi Klein, *No Logo* (New York: Picador 1999), 57–61.

7 Lennard J. Davis, "Bodies of Difference: Politics, Disability, and Representation," in *Disability Studies: Enabling the Humanities*, Sharon Snyder and others (New York: The Modern Language Association of America, 2002), 100–101.

8 Klein, *No Logo*, 121.

9 Harlan Hahn, "Can Disability be Beautiful?" *Social Policy*, Winter (1988): 29.

10 Quayson, *Postcolonialism*, 133.

11 Quayson, *Postcolonialism*, 145, 146, 147.

12 Jeremy Seabrook, "The Metamorphoses of Colonialism," *Globalisation* 1 (2001), http://www.thecore.nus.edu.sg/post/poldiscourse/seabrook1.html (accessed April 11, 2006).

13 Cited and summarized by Donna Haraway, "The Promise of Monsters: A Regenerative Politics for Inappropriate/d Others" in *Cultural Studies*, eds. Lawrence Grossberg, Cary Nelson, and Paula A. Treichler (New York: Routledge, 1992): 329–330 n6.

14 Linda Holler, *Erotic Morality: The Role of Touch in Moral Agency* (New Brunswick, N.J.: Rutgers University Press, 2002), 140.

15 Rosemarie Garland Thomson, "Introduction: From Wonder to Error–A Genealogy of Freak Discourse in Modernity," in *Freakery*, ed. Rosemarie Garland Thomson (New York: University Press, 1996), 12.

16 Quayson, *Postcolonialism*, 148.

17 Quayson, *Postcolonialism*, 149. Even today "the hallucination of limitless wealth," as that purported by versions of growth economics, "is sustained by importing carrying capacity from elsewhere." See Thomas Prugh and Erik Assadourian, "What is Sustainability, Anyway?" in *Worldwatch*: 16.5 (Sept-Oct 2003), 20.

18 Thomson, *Extraordinary Bodies: Figuring Physical Disability in American Culture and Literature* (New York: Columbia University Press, 1997), 40.

19 Thomson, "Introduction: From Wonder to Error," 12.

20 Seabrook, "The Metamorphoses of Colonialism."

21 Harlan Hahn, "Disability and the Reproduction of Bodily Images: The Dynamics of Human Appearances," in *The Power of Geography: How Territory Shapes Social Life*, eds. Jennifer Wolch and Michael Dear (Boston: Unwin Hyman, 1989), 382.

22 See Harlan Hahn, "Advertising the Acceptably Employable Image," in *The Disability Studies Reader*, ed. Lennard J. Davis (New York: Routledge, 1997), 174–176.

23 Lennard J. Davis, *Bending over Backwards: Disability, Dismodernism and Other Difficult Positions* (New York: New York University Press, 2002), 14.

24 Thandeka, *Learning to be White* (New York: Continuum, 2002). Wendy Brown, *Wounded Attachments: States of Injury: Power and Freedom in Late Modernity* (Princeton, N.J.: Princeton University Press, 1995) recognizes that the idealized identities born of modern liberalism, which I argue avoid the way in which Euro-Western modernism conflated them as "degenerate types," "specifically abjur[e] a critique of class power and class norms precisely insofar as these identities are established vis-à-vis a bourgeois norm of social acceptance, legal protection and relative material comfort" (60).

25 Holler, *Erotic Morality*, 142.

26 Thomson, "Introduction: From Wonder to Error," 12.

27 The phrase "spectacular spectacular" comes from the postmodern movie, *Moulin Rouge*, denoting the fantastical excess of the show, even as the courtesans, show girls, and theatrical workers could never but assume such roles except upon the stage. When writing this elsewhere as "the specular spectacular," I underscore the gazing or staring, the espying of image, within this spectacular. "Spectacle," explains Guy Debord in his *The Society of Spectacle* (New York: Zone, 1995), names "a social relationship between people that is mediated by images" (12). As I play throughout the text with various innovations on this phrase, the specular spectacular suggests the surveilling function that attends this culture mediated by images.

28 Zygmunt Bauman, *Liquid Modernity* (Cambridge and Malden, Mass.: Polity/Blackwell, 2000), 32.

29 Marcella Althaus-Reid, *Indecent Theology: Theological Perversions in Sex, Gender and Politics* (London: Routledge, 2000), 1. See also Nancy Mairs, *Waist-High in the World: A Life Among the Nondisabled* (Boston: Beacon, 1996).

30 Robert Young, *White Mythologies: Writing History and the West* (New York: Routledge, 1999), summarizing, then citing Bhabha, 143.

31 Christopher Lasch, *Haven in a Heartless World: The Family Besieged* (New York: Basic, 1977), 140.

32 Paul K. Longmore, "Conspicuous Contribution and American Cultural Dilemmas: Telethon Rituals of Cleansing and Renewal," in *The Body and Physical Difference: Discourses of Disability*, eds. David T. Mitchell and Sharon L. Snyder (Ann Arbor: University of Michigan Press, 1997), 153.

33 Quayson, referencing Baudrillard, in *Postcolonialism*, 141.

34 Thomson, *Extraordinary Bodies*, 6; Thomson, "Introduction: From Wonder to Error," 17.

35 Sander L. Gilman, *Disease and Representation: Images of Illness from Madness to AIDS* (Ithaca, N.Y.: Cornell University Press, 1988), 1.

36 Augustine, *City of God*, Book XX, Chap. 14, 16.

37 Eli Clare explains: "My CP simply is not a medical condition. I need no specific medical care, medication, or treatment for my CP; the adaptive equipment I use can be found in a computer catalog, not a hospital. . . . Having particular medical needs differs from labeling a person with MS as sick, or thinking of quadriplegia as a disease. . . . Rather than a medical cure, we want civil rights, equal access . . . , a redefinition of values" (*Pride*, 106). Postcolonial theorist Trinh Minh-ha explains the stigmatic overlay of "handicap" upon the colonized and the way in which the colonized have been represented by imperial helpers/ saviors. See the epigraph of chapter 5 of this work.

38 William Stringfellow, Epigraph in *Simpler Living, Compassionate Life: A Christian Perspective*, ed. Michael Schut (Denver: Living the Good News/Division of The Morehouse Group, 1999), 58.

39 United Church of Canada, "Mending the Creation" (see section "Theological Foundations.") and "Faith Talk II" (12, 15, 18, 19) at http://www.united-church.ca/mtw/05.shtm. Thanks to Minnie Hornidge for bringing these to my attention.

40 Ato Quayson, "Looking Awry: Tropes of Disability in Postcolonial Writing," in *Relocating Postcolonialism*, eds. David Theo Goldberg and Ato Quayson (Oxford: Blackwell, 2002), 220. Rosemarie Garland Thomson created the word *normate*, now commonly used within disability studies, to designate the nondisabled in a culture that assumes a normative or idealized body over against which it then measures our disabled bodies as lacking or as too physically encumbered.

41 Quayson, "Looking Awry," 219.

42 Robert F. Murphy, *The Body Silent: The Different World of the Disabled* (New York: W.W. Norton, 2001), 100.

43 Homi K. Bhabha, *The Location of Culture* (New York: Routledge, 1994), 76.

44 Rosi Braidotti, *Nomadic Subjects: Embodiment and Sexual Difference in Contemporary Feminist Theory* (New York: Columbia University Press, 1994), 67, 64.

45 Lacan, cited in Teresa Brennan, *Exhausting Modernity: Grounds for a New Economy* (New York: Routledge, 2000), 34.

46 Brennan, *Exhausting Modernity*, 9.

47 Franz Rosenzweig suggested that, during modernity, metaphysical thinking (a kind of lure to withdraw from presence to life and into the fantasmatic) took over. He calls idealist metaphysics "a kind of fantasmatic defense against our being in the midst or flow of life." See Eric Santner, *On the Psychotheology in Everyday Life: Reflections on Freud and Rosenzweig* (Chicago: University of Chicago Press, 2001), 21.

48 J. Joyce Schuld, *Foucault and Augustine: Reconsidering Power and Love* (Notre Dame, Ind.: University of Notre Dame Press, 2003), 149.

49 Anne McClintock, *Imperial Leather: Race, Gender and Sexuality in the Colonial Contest* (New York: Routledge, 1995), 46.

50 Schuld, *Foucault and Augustine*, 151.

51 Lennard J. Davis, "Constructing Normalcy: The Bell Curve, the Novel, and the Invention of the Disabled Body in the Nineteenth Century," in *The Disability Studies Reader*, 26.

52 M. Miles, "Martin Luther and Childhood Disability in 16th Century Germany: What Did He Write? What Did He Say?" *Journal of Religion, Disability & Health*, Vol. 5, No. 4 (2001): 9.

53 Schuld, *Foucault and Augustine*, 143.

54 Schuld, *Foucault and Augustine*, 147, 149, 148.

55 I find the epitome of this in the writings of Jean Vanier, founder of the l'Arche communities, communities established to sanctuary persons living with nonnormate capacities. In his book *The Broken Body: Journey to Wholeness* (Toronto: Anglican Book Centre, 1988), he writes of being led by Jesus "to men and women who have a mental handicap," sensing "the primal cry coming from their broken bodies" (71). Vanier recognizes that the ancient tradition of Christianity intended the term *brokenness* to refer to "a world of war and despair, a world governed by fear, . . . a chaotic world of greed and oppression, of lust for power, for pleasure and for security" (15). The loss of local structural analysis, even evidenced in this definition, becomes endemic to a way of impugning the world, to despairing of, if also equally aggressively remediating existence—as did modernity with its persistent invocation of modernization and progress.

56 Jean Comaroff and John Comaroff, *Of Revelation and Revolution: Christianity, Colonialism, and Consciousness in South Africa*, Vol. 1 (Chicago: University of Chicago Press, 1991), 105.

57 Seabrook, "The Metamorphoses of Colonialism."

58 On the fall as reference to "geopolitical storms," see Catherine Keller, *Face of the Deep* (New York: Routledge, 2003), 160, 184, 186.

59 Trinh T. Minh-ha, *Woman-Native-Other* (Bloomington: Indiana University Press, 1989), 61.

60 Jean-Francois Lyotard, *The Postmodern Condition: A Report on Knowledge, Theory and History of Literature*, Vol. 10, trans. Geoff Bennington and Brian Massumi (Minneapolis: University of Minnesota Press, 1984), 80–81.

61 Uma Narayan, *Dislocating Cultures: Identities, Traditions, and Third World Feminism* (New York: Routledge. 1997), 16.

62 Gayatri Spivak, *A Critique of Postcolonial Reason: Toward a History of the Vanishing Present* (Cambridge: Harvard University Press, 1999), 6.

63 John D. Caputo, ed., *Deconstruction in a Nutshell: A Conversation with Jacques Derrida* (New York: Fordham University Press 1997), 59.

64 Kathleen Sands, *Escape from Paradise* (Minneapolis: Fortress Press, 1994), 2.

65 Benson Saler, "Supernatural as a Western Category," *Ethos* 5, no.1 (Spr. 1977): 42, 45.

66 Consequent to postmodern, poststructural critique of totalities has come a reification of fragments, as, for example, in certain theological works pertaining to Spirit—Mark Wallace, *Fragments of Spirit*; Peter Hodgson, *God in History: Shapes of Freedom*, and Mark C. Taylor, *Fragments*. Fragments, while breaking up the totality of wholesomeness, resonate all to well with dismemberment (which is not the experience of disability), then simply reversing, rather than subverting, modernity's relation to defects. Disabilities theorist Lennard Davis contends that such postmodernisms are still based on humanist identities and its politics of equality. He rather invokes "dismodernizing" so as to call into play the malleability of identity, the awareness that interdependence, even dependence is the rule, that "difference is what all of us have in common." See *Bending Over Backwards*, 26.

67 Cultural theorist Robert Young, for one, suspects that, during the nineteenth century, the obsessive innovation named "modernity" pumped up its adrenal response by scaring itself with a fear of falling that was projected into history, science, and colonial encounters: As science discovered the Second Law of Thermodynamics—the law of entropy, pertaining to dissipating energies and increasing chaos—Europeans feared they could, through miscegenation, fall away to blackness, the supposed inert and earthlike ones feared that colonial encounters could result in going native or primitive. If Europe was seen as evidence of the origin and universal mean of humanity, then the dark continents were read as symptoms of the decline and fall of civilizations—consequently to be foreclosed from speech/knowledge, as Spivak has observed. Consistently, however—as Young notes—the threat of deterioration works back upstream in a subcritical flow to exalt European cultural formation, cultural normalization, and cultural superiority (*White Mythologies*, 99–101). As disability theorists have noted, onlookers or spectators are offered an icon of physical difference that reinforces their own secretly shared common identity. See Thomson, *Extraordinary Bodies*, 17.

Political essayist Barbara Ehrenreich has found another tenacious rhizome of this fear of falling still mobilizing the North American middle class of the late 1980s, that class whose business is the proliferation of ideas and whose interests tend to dictate political, economic, social, media, and intellectual agendas. In her book titled *Fear of Falling: The Inner Life of the Middle Class* (New York: Pantheon, 1989), Ehrenreich details how this middling, managerial-professional class, which is conceptualized as the "universal class," is bound on both sides by fears of deterioration—by fears of falling either into financial and moral decadence, if aspiring too high, or destitution, if not working hard enough (4–6).

68 Theodore Hiebert, *The Yahwist's Landscape: Nature and Religion in Early Israel* (New York: Oxford University Press, 1996), 17.

69 Carolyn Merchant, *Earthcare: Women and the Environment* (New York: Routledge, 1996), 28.

70 Gerald P. McKenney, *To Relieve the Human Condition: Bioethics, Technology and the Body* (Albany: State University of New York Press, 1997), 19.

71 Dr. Francis S. Collins, cited in Hans S. Reinders, *The Future of the Disabled in Liberal Society: An Ethical Analysis* (Notre Dame, Ind.: University of Notre Dame Press, 2000), 1. Liberation theologies, to be sure, used a similar mandate to breach the social conditionedness to suffering of certain populations—women, the poor of Latin America, blacks. As a person with a disability, I nevertheless have several reasons for disturbing the way this mandate is applied: First of all, physiological variations—and not all of them would be conducive to inclusion under the category "disablement" (as for example, members of Deaf World)—are not inherently a suffering, not even always necessarily a incapacity. Nevertheless, persons with disabilities carry the weight of modernity's aversion to suffering. Why, precisely, does it seem so unthinkable that there might be, personally as well as culturally, positive qualities in living with a disability, if we even submit all the physiological variables so quarantined to be a "disability" (15)?

Second, while construed as mere medical conditions and often statistically used to override ethical precautionary principles in the haste to find a biotech cure, a significant number of us, if asked, would say that "a cure is not high on our list of goals" (Clare, *Pride*, 106). Or, like Audre Lorde, who lived with cancer, we would refuse to have our scars "hidden or trivialized," to be "reduced . . . from warrior to mere victim, simply because it might render [us] a fraction more acceptable or less dangerous to the still complacent, those who believe if you cover up a problem it ceases to exist" (Cited in Holler, *Erotic Morality*, 181). Or at the least, we might refuse to be biotechnoscience's voiceless poster children: "The strategy of biotech firms is to use sympathy for the sick to get genetic modification techniques approved, then go for the real profits—selling traits to people who aren't particularly sick"—especially since "the poor [a category that often includes "the sick"] are no one's market." See Pat Mooney, "Making Well People 'Better,'" *World Watch* 15.4 (July/August 2002): 13.

Access to health resources (or their lack) threatens to iterate the global divide between poor and rich into a genetic split between what Princeton professor Lee Silver calls "the Natural class" and "the GenRich." (See Tom Athanasiou and Marcy Darnovsky, "The Genome as a Commons," *World Watch* 15.4 [July/August 2002]: 33-34.) Given that, I would like to pose the question Plato posed: Might there be a point beyond which a health regime itself becomes enslaving? When does normalization become incapacitating? Could we, citizens of the metropolitan centers of empire, find ways to be resolved to the love of life other than that trajectory presuming we must "be made whole?"

72 Holler, *Erotic Morality*, 91; McKenney, cited in Reinders, *The Future of the Disabled in Liberal Society*, 159.

73 David B. Morris, *The Culture of Pain* (Berkeley: University of California Press, 1991), 1–2, 66.

74 Jean Baudrillard, as cited in Zillah Eisenstein, *Global Obscenities: Patriarchy, Capitalism and the Lure of Cyberfantasy* (New York: University Press, 1998), 45.

75 Thomson, "Introduction: From Wonder to Error," 2.

76 Hahn, "Disability and the Reproduction of Bodily Images," 377.

77 Ivan Illich, cited in Harlan Lane, *The Mask of Benevolence: Disabling the Deaf Community* (San Diego: DawnSign, 1992), 299.

78 Terrence Fretheim, Hebrew Testament scholar, suggests that Gen 2–3 can be read from the beginning, if you will, as evidencing "fall out." Yet, while the social angst of aggravated mistrust and alienation of affections "is a beginning of no little consequence," that familiar interpretation of these chapters which we name the doctrine of the fall depends upon the social circumstances from approximately second century B.C.E. (Eccl 25: 24) through Augustine in the fourth century C.E. See "Is Genesis 3 a Fall Story?" in *Word and World*, Vol. XIV, No. 2 (Spring 1994), 153. Similarly, Carol Meyers observes in her work, *Discovering Eve: Ancient Israelite Women in Context* (New York: Oxford University Press, 1988), that "we tend to see these pivotal texts of the Hebrew canon [namely, Gen 1–3] through the interpretive eyes of the early Jewish and Christian sages. . . . [T]he exegetical contributions of early Judaism and Christianity tend to tell us more about the particular needs of the latter groups than about the meaning of a text at the time when it first emerged"(72). Even so, neither Meyers nor Fretheim account for the translational-interpretative hand of the editor-redactors and their social situation for retelling these stories.

79 Ivone Gebara, "The Face of Transcendence as a Challenge to the Reading of the Bible in Latin America," in *Searching the Scriptures*, Vol. I, ed. Elisabeth Schüssler Fiorenza (New York: Crossroad Herder, 2000), 183.

80 Denise Nadeau, "Restoring Sacred Vitality: Reconnection and Regeneration with Women who Suffer Routinized Violence" (Doctor of Ministry Thesis, San Francisco Theological Seminary, 2003), 36.

81 This surprising designation of Israel as "the limping people," as then essentially the first Crip Nation, follows upon Israel taking its national identity from Jacob, the one who limps after wrestling with God. See Holmes Rolston, III, "Does Nature Need to be Redeemed?" in *Zygon*, Vol 29.02: 220. A second track of thought follows the verb pasach, which typically is translated as "to be lame, to limp." This same word, however, is translated as "passover" in Exod 12:13, 23, and 27 as well as Isa 31:5. Might there be some pun at work here? Could a nation who thought of themselves as former slaves—recalling now that hobbling and blinding often were strategies used to prevent slaves from running—define divine efficacy as comparable to their own mobility, that is, "limping"? Adding to such an intrigue, in the Vulgate pasach is translated as transcendere. Further, 1 Kgs 18:26 refers to a ritual involving a limping dance. Was a limping nation protected by a crooked walker who leapt or danced over the people? I'll play—and am admittedly playing with and inventing from traces—with this further in chapter six.

82 In calling for "theological archaeology," I'm suggesting that theologians recuperate not just an idea or concept or doctrine, but how a belief worked within its world-time. That is, What ecclessial and/or sociopolitical effects were released? I take my cues from Gordon Kaufman who taught that "religious myths, symbols and rituals, rather than possessing a univocal meaning, assume their meaning and function in particular contexts," such that "their interpretation and critique demand careful attention to their embodiment within a particular time and place." Cited in Linnel Cady, "Resisting the Postmodern Turn: Theology and Contextualization," in *The Theology at the End of Modernity*, ed. Sheila Greeve Davaney (Philadelphia: Trinity International, 1991).

83 I obviously wish differently to calibrate sacred presence to life, Spirit's power to resurrect life: When I, as an amputee, or my sisters, the "Clan of One-Breasted Women" can be held in sacred regard, then perhaps we all can be resurrected from the confines of normativity. See the essay of this name in Terry Tempest Williams, *Refuge: An Unnatural History of Family and Place* (New York, Vintage Books, 1992).

84 Ivone Gebara, "The Face of Transcendence," 175.

85 Oona Eisenstadt, "Making Room for the Hebrew: Luther, Dialectics and the Shoah" in *JAAR* (Sept 01), Vol. 69:3: 552.

86 Oona Eisenstadt, "Making Room," 551.

87 Virginia Burrus, *"Begotten, Not Made": Conceiving Manhood in Late Antiquity*. (Stanford, Calif.: Stanford University Press, 2000), 190.

88 Zygmunt Bauman, *Globalization: The Human Consequences* (New York: Columbia University Press, 1998), 17.

89 Cited in Robert C. Anderson, "Infusing the Graduate Theological Curriculum with Education about Disability," *Theological Education* 39, no. 1 (2003): 138.

90 Michael Hardt and Antonio Negri, *Empire* (Cambridge, Mass.: Harvard University Press, 2000), 207, 393.

91 Bauman, *Liquid Modernity*, 3, chapter 1.

92 Caputo, *Deconstruction in a Nutshell*, 68.

93 Sands, *Escape from Paradise*, 29.

94 Sands, *Escape from Paradise*, 28–29.

95 Bauman, *Globalization*, 52–54.

Chapter Two

1 Donna Haraway, *Simians, Cyborgs, and Women: The Reinvention of Nature* (New York: Routledge, 1991), 153.

2 Michel Foucault, *The Birth of the Clinic: An Archaeology of Medical Perception* (New York: Vintage, 1994), 31–32.

3 Foucault, *The Birth of the Clinic*, 32.

4 Donna Haraway, *Modest_Witness@Second_Millennium.FemaleMan_Meets_OncoMouse: Feminism and Technoscience* (New York: Routledge, 1997), 102.

5 Michael Hardt, and Antonio Negri, *Empire* (Cambridge, Mass.: Harvard University Press, 2000), 23–27; Michel Foucault, *The History of Sexuality: An Introduction*, Vol. 1, trans. Robert Hurley (New York: Vintage/Random House, 1990), 139–144.

6 Carolyn Abraham, "Gene Pioneer Urges Wakening to Dream of Human Perfection," in *The Globe & Mail*, Toronto, 10/26/2002, A1.

7 Wendy Brown explains that "without recourse to the white masculine middle class ideal, politicized identities would forfeit a good deal of their claims to injury and exclusion, their claims to the political significance of their difference." Yet insomuch as they "require this ideal for the potency and poignancy of their political claims," such idealism likely forecloses a critique of capitalism. See Brown, *Wounded Attachment: States of Injury: Power and Freedom in Late Modernity* (Princeton, N.J.: Princeton University Press, 1995), 61, 65. See also Lennard J. Davis, *Bending over Backwards: Disability, Dismodernism and Other Difficult Positions* (New York: New York University Press, 2002).

8 Sherene Razack, *Looking White People in the Eye: Gender, Race, and Culture in Courtrooms and Classrooms* (Toronto: University of Toronto Press, 1998).

9 Franz Fanon, *Black Skin, White Masks*, trans. Charles Markmann (New York: Grove, 1967), 11.

10 Gayatri Chakravorty Spivak, *A Critique of Postcolonial Reason, Toward a History of the Vanishing Present* (Cambridge, Mass.: Harvard University Press, 1999), 6.

11 George Aichele and others. *The Postmodern Bible* (New Haven, Conn.: Yale University Press, 1995), 120.

12 Sharon Snyder, Brenda Jo Brueggemann, and Rosemarie Garland Thomson, eds., *Disability Studies: Enabling the Humanities* (New York: The Modern Language Association of America, 2002), 2.

13 Davis, *Bending over Backwards*, 34.

14 Hardt and Negri, *Empire*, 275–276.

15 Homi K. Bhabha, *The Location of Culture* (New York: Routledge, 1994), 154.

16 Robert Young, *Colonial Desire: Hybridity in Theory, Culture and Race.* (New York: Routledge, 1995), 180.

17 Martha C. Nussbaum, *Hiding from Humanity: Disgust, Shame and the Law* (Princeton, N.J.: Princeton University Press, 1994), 98.

18 Nussbaum, *Hiding from Humanity*, 74, 87, 92.

19 Zygmunt Bauman, *Liquid Modernity* (Cambridge and Malden, Mass.: Polity/Blackwell, 2000), 38.

20 Young, *White Mythologies*, 167–168.

21 Bhabha, *The Location of Culture*, 148.

22 Stephen D. Moore, *God's Beauty Parlor: And Other Queer Spaces in and Around the Bible, Contraversions* (Stanford, Calif.: Stanford University Press, 2001).

23 Augustine, *City of God*, Book XVI, chap. 8, 663–664.

24 Ibid., 662.

25 Augustine, *City of God*, Book XXI, chap. 8, 982–983.

26 Augustine, *Enchiridion*, chap. 87.

27 Augustine, *On the Gospel of John*, 8.2.1.

28 Ian Wood, "'The Ends of the Earth': The Bible, Bibles, and the Other in Early Medieval Europe." Paper presented within the lecture series "Title in the Text: Biblical Hermeneutics, Colonial and Postcolonial Pre-Occupations" (lecture, Green College, Vancouver, BC, 24 October 2002), 19.

29 Wood, "The Ends of the Earth," 26.

30 Foucault, cited in Sherene Razack, "Gendered Racial Violence and Spatialized Justice: The Murder of Pamela George," in *Canadian Journal of Law and Society* 15, No. 2 (2000): 94n7.

31 Sherene Razack, "Race, Space, and Prostitution: The Making of the Bourgeois Subject," in *Canadian Journal of Women and Law* 10 (1998): 361.

32 See Razack, "Gendered Racial Violence and Spatialized Justice."

33 Rosemarie Garland Thomson, *Extraordinary Bodies: Figuring Physical Disability in American Culture and Literature* (New York: Columbia, 1997), 5.

34 Robert F. Murphy, *The Body Silent: The Different World of the Disabled* (New York: W.W. Norton, 2001), 124–125.

35 Sherene Razack, *Looking White People in the Eye: Gender, Race, and Culture in Courtrooms and Classrooms* (Toronto: University of Toronto Press, 1998), 362.

36 Razack, *Looking White People in the Eye*, 362–363.

37 Davis, *Bending over Backwards*, 45.

38 Razack, *Looking People in the Eye*, Chap. 5.

39 Gayatri Chakravorty Spivak in Razack, *Looking People in the Eye*, 89.

40 David T. Mitchell and Sharon L. Snyder, *The Body and Physical Difference: Discourses of Disability, The Body, in Theory: Histories of Cultural Materialism* (Ann Arbor: University of Michigan Press, 1997), 17.

41 Ashis Nandy, *The Intimate Enemy: Loss and Recovery of Self under Colonialism* (Delhi: Oxford, 1988), x–xi.

42 Gerald P. McKenney, *To Relieve the Human Condition: Bioethics, Technology and the Body* (Albany: State University of New York Press, 1997), 204; Michel Foucault, *Power/Knowledge: Selected Interviews and Other Writings: 1972-1977*, ed. Colin Gordon (New York: Pantheon, Harvester, 1980), 172.

43 Gerald P. McKenney, *To Relieve the Human Condition*, 207, 209.

44 Ato Quayson, *Postcolonialism: Theory, Practice or Process?* (Cambridge and Malden, Mass.: Polity/Blackwell, 2000), 133. See also Gerald P. McKenney, *To Relieve the Human Condition*.

45 Bauman, *Liquid Modernity*, 4.

46 See Hardt and Negri, *Empire*. 194–195; Anne McClintock, *Imperial Leather: Race, Gender and Sexuality in the Colonial Context* (New York: Routledge, 1995), 38.

47 In the same way that Karen King insightfully quipped that "men use women to think with," Christianity and Judaism may have analogically engaged disabled bodies. King's insight was cited by Elizabeth A. Castelli, "Romans," in *Searching the Scriptures, Vol. 2: A Feminist Commentary*, ed. Elisabeth Schüssler Fiorenza (New York: Crossroad, 1994).

48 Paul Tillich, "Aspects of a Religious Analysis of Culture," in *Theology of Culture*, ed. Robert C. Kimball (New York: Oxford University Press, 1959), 42.

49 David T. Mitchell, "Narrative Prosthesis and the Materiality of Metaphor" in Sharon Snyder and others. *Disability Studies: Enabling the Humanities* (New York: The Modern Language Association of America, 2002), 16.

50 Bauman, *Liquid Modernity*, 16.

51 Cynthia D. Moe-Lobeda, *Healing a Broken World: Globalization and God* (Minneapolis: Fortress Press, 2002), 2, 9.

52 Moe-Lobeda, *Healing a Broken World*, 1.

53 Based upon Moe-Lobeda's rhetorical refrain, the story of the healing of the paralytic appears to provide the not so covert scrim for the remediation of the incapacitation of Christian agency in the face of globalization. She writes, echoing Jesus' command to the paralytic in Matt 9 and Mark 2, "The moral crisis . . . is the failure to get up and walk" (4). And again, "The purpose of all that I have said is . . . that we might rise up and walk away from compliance with economic violence and toward resistance, new vision and rebuilding" (133). To be sure, Moe-Lobeda appears to be using one biblically familiar method of working disablement as a spiritual analytic—namely, discursive reversal. The Revelation to John (3:17-18) uses such a sense of reversal: "You say, 'I am rich' . . . not realizing that you are wretched, pitiable, poor, blind and naked." Yet, such reversal does nothing to displace the demand for normalcy. It simply differently weights it, still leaving persons with disabilities declassified and silenced subjects.

Further, the use of the disability metaphor seems to undercut Moe-Lobeda's intent: she unwittingly bases her spiritual remediation of incapacitated citizens upon the "desire towards wholeness" with which globalization girds itself and that likely also contributes to the enervation of the public, civic nexus. At its best, Moe-Lobeda's use of the metaphor of disablement here can echo the awareness of postcolonial writers who find in these physiological differences a language for the pain and for the dismembering effects of colonization. At the same time, given the controls Moe-Lobeda sets around the use of her terms, disability must be read as brokenness and incapacity. And note again the way in which, given the title of her book , disability continues to serve as the quintessential paradigm of brokenness in Christian discourse. This condition, in Christianity's redemptive plot line, specifically requires spiritual remediation—as if disability were ever and always then lacking that energetic infusion or enthusiasm.

54 While extermination of the deviant other may seem like an antiquated and primitive solution, disability activists have suggested that certain acts of euthanasia or mercy killing be reconsidered in this light, for example, the Tracy Lattimer case, as well as the voluntary suicide of disabled persons. In 1993, farmer Robert Lattimer of Saskatchewan killed his twelve-year-old daughter, Tracy. His police confession stated that he loved his daughter and could not bear to watch her suffer from cerebral palsy. But let it also be noted that Lattimer's action interrupted yet another planned surgery. In terms of the supposed voluntary suicide, the lack of communal, relational, and economic support along with the insistent individualism of our culture can pressure disabled individuals and/or their families to read their quality of life as minimal—the social construction of what makes for life thereby condoning the elimination of the life of a disabled person. Other disability activists view

the human genome project as itself a project of cultural genocide in regard to differently enabled persons.

55 Harlan L. Lane, *The Mask of Benevolence: Disabling the Deaf Community*, 1st ed. (New York, 1992), 10, 33.

56 Lane, *The Mask of Benevolence*, 40.

57 Snyder, Brueggermann, and Thomson, *Disability Studies*, 24.

58 Jean Comaroff, "The Diseased Heart of Africa: Medicine, Colonialism and the Black Body," in *Knowledge, Power, and Practice: The Anthropology of Medicine and Everyday Life*, ed. Shirley Lindenbaum and Margaret M. Lock, Comparative Studies of Health Systems and Medical Care, no. 36 (Berkeley: University of California Press, 1993), 313.

59 Thomson, *Extraordinary Bodies*, 6.

60 James C. Scott, *Domination and the Arts of Resistance: Hidden Transcripts* (New Haven, Conn.: Yale University Press, 1990), 49–50.

61 Scott, *Domination*, 67.

62 Thomson, *Extraordinary Bodies*, 6.

63 Martha Minow, cited in Razack, *Looking White People in the Eye*, 21.

64 Thomson, *Extraordinary Bodies*, 40.

65 Spivak, *A Critique of Postcolonial Reason*, 6.

66 Spivak, *A Critique of Postcolonial Reason*, 4, 5.

67 Spivak, *A Critique of Postcolonial Reason*, x.

68 Michael Lodahl, *Shekhinah/Spirit: Divine Presence in Jewish and Christian Religion* (Mahwah, N.J.: Stimulus/Paulist, 1992), 186.

69 Lennard J. Davis, "Nude Venuses, Medusa's Body, and Phantom Limbs: Disability and Visuality," in *The Body and Physical Difference: Discourses of Disability*, eds. David T. Mitchell and Sharon L. Snyder (Ann Arbor: University of Michigan Press, 1997), 54.

70 Musa W. Dube, *Postcolonial Feminist Interpretation of the Bible* (St. Louis: Chalice, 2000), 116.

71 Dube, *Postcolonial Feminist*, 40.

72 Dube, *Postcolonial Feminist*, 116.

73 Dawn DeVries, "Creation, Handicappism, and the Community of Differing Abilities," in *Reconstructing Christian Theology*, Rebecca S. Chopp and Mark L. Taylor (Minneapolis: Fortress Press, 1994), 137.

74 Murphy, *The Body Silent*, 116–117.

75 Mary Oliver, "Whelks," in *New and Selected Poems* (Boston: Beacon, 1992), 30.

Chapter Three

1 When I speak of the physics or efficacy of Spirit, I speak of the valuation of divine power, or variously, the trajectories of transcendence we write into our religious symbolic, our way of holding value within world conditions, the contours we hold open for relational encounter, and, therefore, social authority and power, within the world. Crediting to Spirit notions of miraculous remediation of disablement has authorized patterns of relation that hide their interests in paternalistic benevolence.

2 Donna Haraway, "The Promise of Monsters: A Regenerative Politics for Inappropriate/d Others" in *Cultural Studies*, eds. Lawrence Grossberg, Cary Nelson, and Paula A. Treichler (New York: Routledge, 1992), 311.

3 Rita Nakashima Brock, *Journeys by Heart: A Christology of Erotic Power* (New York: Crossroad, 1992), 34.

4 Rosemarie Garland Thomson, *Extraordinary Bodies: Figuring Physical Disability in American Culture and Literature* (New York: Columbia, 1997), 5.

5 Sherene Razack, *Looking White People in the Eye: Gender, Race, and Culture in Courtrooms and Classrooms* (Toronto: University of Toronto Press, 1998), 10.

6 William R. LaFleur, "Body," in *Critical Terms for Religious Studies*, ed. Mark C. Taylor (Chicago: University of Chicago Press, 1998), 41.

7 Lennard J. Davis, *Enforcing Normalcy: Disability, Deafness, and the Body* (New York: Verso, 1995), 45.

8 Davis, *Enforcing Normalcy*, 24.

9 Davis, *Enforcing Normalcy*, 28.

10 Davis, *Enforcing Normalcy*, 30, 31.

11 Sigmund Freud, "The Uncanny," *Studies in Parapsychology* (New York: Collier 1963), 240.

12 Lee Davis Creal, "The 'Disability of Thinking' the 'Disabled' Body," http://www.normemma.com/artcreal.htm (accessed 14 February 2006).

13 Paul Longmore, "Conspicuous Contribution and American Cultural Dilemmas," in *The Body and Physical Difference: Discourses of Disability*, eds. David T. Mitchell and Sharon L. Snyder (Ann Arbor: University of Michigan Press, 2000), 153.

14 Davis, *Enforcing Normalcy*, 4.

15 Davis, *Enforcing Normalcy*, 23.

16 Marcus J. Borg, *Jesus, A New Vision: Spirit, Culture, and the Life of Discipleship* (San Francisco: Harper San Franscisco, 1987), 61. Both Borg and Crossan insist on the "fact" that Jesus was a healer. Intriguingly, both sidestep the fact that the miracle stories actually seem to effect "cure." Eric Eve, *The Jewish Context of Jesus' Miracles* (Sheffield, UK: Sheffield Academic Press, 2002), might suggest that this seems a move in accord with modern rationalism, but it is in the end a move that obscures the function of miracles in the text and in social life. Unlike shamanic healing, Eve notes, these synoptic accounts do not include inquiry into the wider social, emotional, or family situations of patients. "Each reported healing is far too rapid for effective psychotherapy—including folk psychotherapy—to have taken place... . [Further] the miracle stories focus on the cure of disease, not the healing of illness: blind people see, deaf people hear, lame people walk, but we learn little about other aspects of their life situation" (355–356). I address the disconnection of miracle and healing in a later section, "A Crip Nation."

17 Borg, *Jesus, A New Vision*, 59–60.

18 Borg, *Jesus, A New Vision*, 59.

19 Brock, *Journeys by Heart*, 72.

20 Brock, *Journeys by Heart*, 1.

21 Borg, *Jesus, A New Vision*, 67.

22 Joan Tollifson, *Bare-Bones Meditation: Waking Up From the Story of My Life* (New York: Bell Tower/Harmony, 1996), 106.

23 Adolf Von Harnack, *The Mission and Expansion of Christianity in the First Three Centuries*. Vol. I, trans. James Moffatt (New York: G. P. Putnam's Sons, 1908), 101–109.

24 Von Harnack, *The Mission and Expansion of Christianity*, 121.

25 Von Harnack, *The Mission and Expansion of Christianity*, 109.

26 Michel Foucault, *The Birth of the Clinic: An Archaeology of Medical Perception*, trans. A. M. Sheridan Smith (New York: Vintage, 1994), 107.

27 Stephen D. Moore, *God's Beauty Parlor and Other Queer Spaces in and around the Bible* (Stanford, Calif.: Stanford University Press, 2001).

28 Lennard J. Davis, *Bending over Backwards: Disability, Dismodernism and Other Difficult Positions* (New York: New York University Press, 2002), 95–98.

29 In "A Postcolonial Exploration of Collusion and Construction in Biblical Interpretation," R. S. Sugirtharajah explains that "the emergence of many missionary societies in the eighteenth and nineteenth centuries led exegetes to impose a missionary journey structure on the Acts. This missionary-tour scheme has been used to sustain and legitimize mission activity." *The Postcolonial Bible*, ed. R.S. Sugirtharajah (Sheffield, UK: Sheffield Academic Press, 1998), 100.

30 Eve, *The Jewish Context of Jesus' Miracles*, 1.

31 Davis, *Bending over Backwards*, 82.

32 Davis, *Enforcing Normalcy*, 44.

33 Barry W. Henault, "Is the 'Historical Jesus' a Christological Construct?" in *Whose Historical Jesus?* eds. Wm. E. Arnal and Michel Desjardins (Waterloo, Ont.: Wilfred Laurier University Press for Canadian Corporation for Studies in Religion, No. 7, 1997), 243.

34 Henault, "Historical Jesus," 265.

35 Zygmunt Bauman, *Liquid Modernity* (Cambridge and Malden, Mass.: Polity/Blackwell, 2000), 38.

36 Bauman, *Liquid Modernity*, chs. 1–2.

37 Paul Rabinow, "Introduction" in *Foucault Reader*, ed. Paul Rabinow (New York: Pantheon Books, 1984), 21.

38 Elizabeth Stuart, "Disruptive Bodies," in *The Good New of the Body: Sexual Theology & Feminism*, ed. Lisa Isherwood (Sheffield, UK: Sheffield Academic Press, 2000), 169.

39 Burton L. Mack, *A Myth of Innocence: Mark and Christian Origins* (Philadelphia: Fortress Press, 1988), 211.

40 Gerd Theissen, *The Miracle Stores of the Early Christian Tradition*, trans. Francis McDonagh (Edinburgh: T&T Clark, 1983), 276.

41 Theissen, *The Miracle Stores*, 289.

42 Theissen, *The Miracle Stores*, 302.

43 John Dominic Crossan, "Open Healing and Open Eating: Jesus as Jewish Cynic," *Biblical Research* 36 (1991): 7.

44 Jean Comaroff, "The Diseased Heart of Africa: Medicine, Colonialism, and the Black Body," in *Knowledge, Power, and Practice: The Anthropology of Medicine and Everyday Life*, eds. Shirley Lindenbaum and Margaret Lock (Berkeley: University of California Press, 1993), 307.

45 Gayatri Chakravorty Spivak, "Can the Subaltern Speak?" in *Marxism and the Interpretation of Culture*, eds. Cary Nelson and Lawrence Grossberg (Chicago: University of Illinois Press, 1988), 301.

46 Ashis Nandy, *The Intimate Enemy: Loss and Recovery of Self Under Colonialism* (Delhi: Oxford, 1988), x–xi, 11, x. Nandy also enumerated hypermasculinity and progress as psychopathologies.

47 Rabinow, "Introduction," 8.

48 Mitchell and Snyder, eds., *The Body and Physical Difference*, 19.

49 Rey Chow, *Writing Diaspora: Tactics of Intervention in Contemporary Cultural Studies* (Bloomington: Indiana University Press, 1993), 112, 114.

50 Haraway, "The Promise of Monsters," 311.

51 Jean Comaroff and John Comaroff, *Of Revelation and Revolution: Christianity, Colonialism, and Consciousness in South Africa*, Vol. 1, (Chicago: University of Chicago Press, 1991), 15.

52 David Mitchell, "Modernist Freaks and Postmodernist Geeks," in *The Disability Studies Reader*, ed. Lennard J. Davis (New York: Routledge, 1997), 348.

53 Marcus J. Borg, *Jesus in Contemporary Scholarship* (Valley Forge, Penn.: Trinity International, 1994), 26.

54 Marcus J. Borg, *Meeting Jesus Again for the First Time* (San Francisco: Harper San Franscisco, 1995), 15, 17, 31–32.

55 Borg, *Jesus, A New Vision*, 67, 65–66, 70–71.

56 Borg, *Jesus, A New Vision*, 100–102, 130–142. See also Borg, *Meeting Jesus Again for the First Time*, 46–68 and *The God We Never Knew* (San Francisco: Harper San Francisco, 1998), chap 6.

57 Borg, *Jesus, A New Vision*, 65–66.

58 Borg, *Meeting Jesus Again for the First Time*, 46. Borg cites Luke 6:36.

59 Borg, *Jesus, A New Vision*, 130.

60 Borg, *Jesus in Contemporary Scholarship*, 53.

61 Borg, *Jesus in Contemporary Scholarship*, 53.

62 Borg, *Jesus in Contemporary Scholarship*, 55-6.

63 Borg, *The God We Never Knew*, 142, 150–152.

64 Sharene Razack, "Race, Space, and Prostitution: The Making of the Bourgeois Subject," in *Canadian Journal of Women and Law* 10 (1998): 362–363.

65 John Dominic Crossan, *Jesus, A Revolutionary Biography* (New York: HarperCollins, 1994), 196, 198.

66 Crossan, *Jesus, A Revolutionary Biography*, 198, 196; John Dominic Crossan, *Birth of Christian-*

ity: Discovering What Happened in the Years Immediately After the Execution of Jesus. San Francisco: Harper San Francisco, 1998), 331, 335.

67 Crossan, *Jesus, A Revolutionary Biography*, 196.

68 John Dominic Crossan, "Open Healing and Open Eating: Jesus as Jewish Cynic," *Biblical Research* 36 (1991): 7.

69 Crossan, *Jesus, A Revolutionary Biography*, 31–32, 67, 198.

70 John Dominic Crossan, *Essential Jesus* (San Francisco: Harper San Francisco, 1995), 12.

71 Crossan, "Open Healing and Open Eating," 11.

72 John Dominic Crossan, *The Historical Jesus: The Life of a Mediterranean Jewish Peasant* (New York: HarperCollins, 1992), 304, 323–324.

73 Crossan, *Jesus, A Revolutionary Biography*, 83–84; Crossan, *The Historical Jesus*, 323.

74 Crossan, *Jesus, A Revolutionary Biography*, 55–56.

75 Sherene Razack, "Gendered Racial Violence and Spatialized Justice: The Murder of Pamela George," in *Canadian Journal of Law and Society* Vol. 15, No. 2 (2000): 94 n7.

76 Lennard Davis, "Constructing Normalcy: The Bell Curve, the Novel, and the Invention of the Disabled Body in the Nineteenth Century," in *The Disability Studies Reader*, ed. Lennard Davis (New York: Routledge, 1997), 10–11.

77 Edward Said, "Jane Austen and Empire," in *Culture and Imperialism* (New York: Vintage/Random House, 1993), 91–93.

78 Mitchell and Snyder refer to this literary phenomenon in terms of "narrative prosthesis"— that is, the disabled or defective always serves the character development of the protaganist. A person with a disability becomes a prosthesis for developing the sympathetic, humanitarian character of the nondisabled protagonist. This tends to preserve the outlook of the eye of the beholder—not to renegotiate social understanding and sacred value.

79 To be sure, Crossan's work does profess interest in the ways in which imperial power and ambition cut through religious communities of the first century, their assertion of values and articulation of bodies. In his *Jesus, A Revolutionary Biography*, Crossan writes that where "body is society and its rules writ small," healing—not simply a scenario of the private and individuated body—refers to disruption of the social systems of value used to interpret the body (77). One might then imagine that what would follow might include an allowance for those who have been marginalized to describe what constitutes health. If, for example, the disabled body were not at all statistically abnormal in the ancient world, might persons rather then define health as the strength to be humane—to behave with passionate equanimity, given what can happen to bodies in a lifetime? In the face of his promising comments, Crossan's latter statements about Jesus' purported healing by negation of social ostracism appear as at odds with his constructivist insights—the latter set actually suggesting he is unable to get the individual sick or defective body off the eyeball, rather than paying attention to disrupting the social system descriptor, as the first set of definitions seemed to promise.

In his more extensive chapters on healing in *Birth of Christianity* and in *The Historical Jesus*, Crossan recognizes that imperial social structures may well occasion disease and illness. In a subsection titled "Possessed by Demonic Imperialism" (Historical Jesus 313), he concludes that "Roman imperialism meant that God's people were possessed by demons on the social level." (318). Physical illness, he there observed—given his reading of several cultural anthropologists and social scientists, including Franz Fanon, the early psychologist of decolonization—may sometimes represent a somatic protest, a safer form of resistance than open public actions (Historical Jesus, 324; Birth of Christianity, 295). Consequently, "colonial exorcisms are at once less and more than revolution; they are, in fact, individuated symbolic revolution" (Jesus, a Revolutionary Biography, 91). Despite his psycho-philosophical insights, it's the social level—the broad, corporate politics of culture and cultural knowledge formation—that never quite gets addressed by Crossan's attention to healing. Crossan yet again reverts to a modern medicalized or biological essentialism of the body in his definition of health. But has he not then merely allowed for the repair of and/or reinsertion of bodies into Rome's economic agenda—instead of challenging that system and its values, given what it does to bodies?

80 Henault, "Historical Jesus," 268.

81 While Talmudic scholar Susannah Heschel's concern revolves around implicit Chris-

tian supersessionism, her observation resonates with my own about the optics of modern realism: "Almost every study of Christian origins includes a contrasting description of a degenerate first-century Judaism." See her *Abraham Geiger and the Jewish Jesus* (Chicago: University of Chicago Press, 1998), 21. Comparably, portraits of Jesus as healer require a cadre of disabled—read as degenerate—bodies. After Heschel shows how liberal Protestant Christianity was able to undertake historical-critical methodology while avoiding the Jewishness of Jesus, specifically by evoking a "degenerate Pharisaism" as that against which Jesus reacted, Heschel writes: "Schleiermacher presents Jesus as the founder of a new religion who had an extraordinary awareness of the presence of God, resulting from his unique religious consciousness. . . . Schleiermacher's insistence on the theological significance of Jesus' unique religious consciousness functioned as a metaphysical escape from historical criticism" (144, 129). Comparably, I am interested in the way in which modern, liberal Christianity, identifying with that higher [than historical, material] consciousness, a neurotic structure to be sure, could then hide the socioeconomic technology of normalcy within our practices of healing. That this higher consciousness has been theologized again suggests an enmeshment of spiritual thought and practice with the ideology of normalcy.

82 Dieter Georgi, "The Interest in Life of Jesus Theology as a Paradigm for the Social History of Biblical Criticism," *Harvard Theological Review* 85, no. 1 (1992): 56, 83.

83 Kwok Pui-lan, "Jesus/The Native: Biblical Studies from a Postcolonial Perspective," in *Teaching the Bible: The Discourses and Politics of Biblical Pedagogy*, eds. Fernando F. Segovia and Mary Ann Tolbert (Maryknoll, N.Y.: Orbis, 1998), 78, 75.

84 Kwok Pui-lan, "Jesus/The Native," 69.

85 LaFleur, "Body," 41. A 1999 ad campaign for Mysap.com—a software package suite that is marketed to businesses as capable of being customized to specific needs while "enhancing collaboration and creating efficiencies across supply chains" (http://www.microsoft-sap.com/pr1_05-04.html)—sells its technotopian "NetWeaver" supported space as next in the generation of such humanitarian concerns. In one particular ad, a young white female doctor sits in a warehouse in Africa filled with black patients. The doctor taps into her computer for access to the global marketplace of pharmaceuticals, thereby saving time, money, and a life. In an essay on this advertisement entitled "Virtual Colonialism, or Dr. Schweitzer Gets Wired," the author notes that "though the ad's message is that the virtual . . . creates a new and more efficient linkage between core and periphery, the commercial leaves intact the moral economy of colonial relations. The doctor is empowered to act upon the powerless, and does so for their own good. . . . The virtual city is still the colonial city in which the developed world acts upon the underdeveloped. . . bringing health care to the dark continent." (See http://www.lclark.edu/~soan370/global/jungledoctor.html. Accessed June 6, 2002.)

86 Ronald Niezen, "Medical Evangelism," in *Spirit Wards*, ed. Ronald Niezen (Berkeley: University of California Press, 2000), 94, 95.

87 So, for example, the Western scientific paradigm undercut taste for available food sources and dietary habits, trust in available plant medicines, and faith in local wisdom. It disrupted systems of reciprocity among persons as well as between persons and the land community.

Chapter Four

1 Donna Haraway, *Simians, Cyborgs, and Women: The Reinvention of Nature* (New York: Routledge, 1991), 249.

2 Elizabeth Grosz, *Volatile Bodies: Toward a Corporeal Feminism* (Bloomington: Indiana University Press, 1994), 219.

3 Donna Haraway, "The Promise of Monsters: A Regenerative Politics for Inappropriate/d Others," in *Cultural Studies*, eds. Lawrence Grossberg, Cary Nelson, and Paula A. Treichler (New York: Routledge, 1992), 296. While Haraway is generally referred to in the category of postmodernism, she herself prefers to think in terms of the "amodern" so as to move yet another step away from salvation histories. "The amodern refers to a view of the history of science as culture that insists on the absence of beginnings, enlightenments, and endings: the world has always been in the middle of things" (304).

4 Haraway, "The Promise of Monsters," 86; Haraway, *Simians, Cyborgs, and Women*, 212.

5 David T. Mitchell and Sharon L. Snyder, eds., *The Body and Physical Difference: Discourses of Disability* (Ann Arbor: University of Michigan Press, 1997), 1.

6 Herman Melville, *Moby Dick* (New York: Signet Classic/New American Library, 1961), 447.

7 Haraway, "The Promise of Monsters," 87.

8 See "1990 Law Has Not 'Accommodated' All People with Disabilities," *Sunday Star-Ledger of New Jersey*, August 23, 1998, section 1, 23. This article summarizes a poll conducted by Louis Harris and Associates for the National Organization on Disability and an MIT study coauthored by Joshua Angrist.

9 See, for example, "Technology Aids Disabled: Hi-tech Devices Are Leveling the Playing Field for the Disabled," *CNNfn* (9/28/1998) at http://cnnfn.com/digitaljam/9809/28/disabled_pkg/.

10 Haraway, "The Promise of Monsters," 311.

11 Donna Haraway, *Modest_Witness@Second_Millennium.FemaleMan_Meets_OncoMouse: Feminism and Technoscience* (New York: Routledge, 1997), 24, 28, 29, 31, 32.

12 Gabriel Brahm Jr. and Mark Driscoll, *Prosthetic Territories: Politics and Hypertechnologies*, Politics and Culture Series, No. 3. (Boulder, Colo.: Westview, 1995).

13 Haraway, *Modest_Witness@Second_Millennium*, 45.

14 Haraway, *Modest_Witness@Second_Millennium*, 119.

15 Haraway, *Modest_Witness@Second_Millennium*, 119.

16 Susan Wendell, *The Rejected Body: Feminist Philosophical Reflections on Disability* (New York: Routledge, 1996), 44–45; Haraway, "The Promise of Monsters," 149.

17 Haraway, *Simians, Cyborgs, and Women*, 7, 8.

18 Elizabeth Grosz, *Volatile Bodies*, chaps. 3, 4.

19 Haraway, *Modest_Witness@Second_Millennium*, 47.

20 *enable: Official Magazine of the AAPD*, 2, no. 4 (August-September-October 1998): 89.

21 Pierre Bourdieu, *The Logic of Practice* (Stanford, Calif.: Stanford University Press, 1995), 52–65.

22 Donna Haraway, "Cyborgs at Large: Interview with Donna Haraway," with "Introduction" by Constance Penley and Andrew Ross and postscript, "The Actors are Cyborg, Nature is Coyote, and the Geography is Elsewhere" by Donna Haraway, in *Technoculture*, eds. Penley and Ross, Cultural Politics Series, Vol. 3: 1–20 (Minneapolis: University of Minnesota Press, 1991), 178.

23 For some of us who become disabled through traumatic midlife events, this sense of lack will be a self-defining trap. According to anecdotal reports within the disability rights movement, this is much less the case for those who are congenitally differently abled. Congenitally differently abled persons tend to have a sense of themselves as whole without prostheses. Within western culture, traumatically disabled persons arrive at this much more slowly and complexly, since many of us cannot deny the loss and its tragic ramifications, yet refuse to be defined by the dizzying donut hole of abjection spinning loose in the social psyche.

24 Timothy V. Kaufman-Osborn, *Creatures of Prometheus: Gender and the Politics of Technology* (Lanham, Md.: Rowman & Littlefield Publishers, 1997), 15.

25 Haraway, "The Promise of Monsters," 190.

26 Haraway, "The Promise of Monsters," 195.

27 Haraway, *Simians, Cyborgs, and Women*, 151.

28 Haraway, *Simians, Cyborgs, and Women*, 71.

29 David D. Yuan, "Disfigurement and Reconstruction in Oliver Wendell Holmes's 'The Human Wheel, Its Spokes and Felloes,'" in *Body and Physical Difference*, Mitchell and Snyder, 81, 75.

30 Yuan, "Disfigurement and Reconstruction," 92, 74–75.

31 Haraway, *Modest_Witness@Second_Millennium*, 12.

32 Donna Haraway, "Ecce Homo, Ain't (Ar'n't) I a Woman, and Inappropriate/d Others: The Human in a Post-Humanist Landscape," in *Feminists Theorize the Political*, eds. Judith Butler and Joan W. Scott (New York: Routledge, 1992).

33 Haraway, "Cyborgs at Large," 6.

34 Haraway, *Simians, Cyborgs, and Women*, 193.

35 Rosi Braidotti, *Nomadic Subjects: Embodiment and Sexual Difference in Contemporary Feminist Theory* (New York: Columbia University Press, 1994), 3.

36 Rosi Braidotti, "Becoming Woman: or Sexual Difference Revisited," *Theory, Culture and Society*, Vol. 20, No. 3 (2003): 62.

37 Haraway, "The Promise of Monsters," 115.

38 Haraway, "The Promise of Monsters," 150.

39 Haraway, "The Promise of Monsters," 152–155.

40 Virginia Burrus, *"Begotten, Not Made": Conceiving Manhood in Late Antiquity* (Stanford, Calif.: Stanford University Press, 2000), 47.

41 Judith Z. Abrams, *Judaism and Disability: Portrayals in Ancient Texts from the Tanach through the Bavli* (Washington, D.C.: Gallaudet University Press, 1998), 8.

42 Haraway, "The Promise of Monsters," 330–331.

43 Haraway, *Modest_Witness@Second_Millennium*, 102.

44 Jürgen Moltmann, *The Spirit of Life: A Universal Affirmation* (Minneapolis: Fortress Press, 1992), 88.

45 Nicolas Berdyaev, *The Meaning of History* (New York: Charles Scribner's Sons, 1936), 116–117.

46 Haraway, "Cyborgs at Large," 16.

47 Catherine Keller, "No More Sea: The Lost Chaos of the Eschaton," an unpublished paper delivered at the Christianity and Ecology Conference in Boston (April, 1998), 12.

48 Keller, "No More Sea," 3; David F. Noble, *The Religion of Technology: The Divinity of Man and the Spirit of Invention* (New York: Alfred A. Knopf, 1998), 3, 9–20.

49 Haraway, "The Promise of Monsters," 152; Haraway, "Ecce Homo."

50 Haraway, "The Promise of Monsters," 153.

51 Haraway, "The Promise of Monsters," 193, 150–151.

52 Haraway, *Modest_Witness@Second_Millennium*, 16; Haraway, "The Promise of Monsters," 192.

53 Haraway, *Simians, Cyborgs, and Women*, 198; Haraway, *Modest_Witness@Second_Millennium*, 40.

54 See Terry Tempest Williams, *Refuge: An Unnatural History of Family and Place* (New York, Vintage, 1992).

55 Haraway, *Simians, Cyborgs, and Women*, 296.

56 Simi Linton, *Claiming Disability: Knowledge and Identity* (New York: New York University Press, 1998), 3.

57 Haraway, *Simians, Cyborgs, and Women*, 249.

58 Kate Soper, "Nature/'nature,'" in *Future Natural: nature/science/culture*, eds. George Robertson, and others (New York: Routledge, 1996), 28, 23.

59 Catherine Keller, *Apocalypse Now and Then: A Feminist Guide to the End of the World* (Boston: Beacon, 1996), 24.

60 Haraway, *Simians, Cyborgs, and Women*, 178.

61 Haraway, *Simians, Cyborgs, and Women*, 249.

62 Barbara Hillyer, *Feminism and Disability* (Norman: University of Oklahoma Press, 1993), 173.

63 *Active Living Magazine* 7, no. 4 (September-October 1998): 11. Kitty Lunn—actor, dancer, and founder of the Infinity Dance Theater of New York City—is another such figure. See *Enable* 2, no. 3 (May-July 1998).

64 Haraway, *Simians, Cyborgs, and Women*, 193.

65 Haraway, *Modest_Witness@Second_Millennium*, 15.

Chapter Five

1 Albert Memmi, cited in Harlan Lane, *The Mask of Benevolence: Disabling the Deaf Community* (San Diego: DawnSign, 1992), 75.

2 Trinh T. Minh-ha, *Woman-Native-Other* (Bloomington: Indiana University Press, 1989), 54.

3 Gayatri Chakravorty Spivak, "Can the Subaltern Speak?" in *Marxism and the Interpretation of Culture*, eds. Cary Nelson and Lawrence Grossberg (Chicago: University of Illinois Press, 1988), 294, 296.

4 Sherene Razack, *Looking White People in the Eye: Gender, Race, and Culture in Courtrooms and Classrooms* (Toronto: University of Toronto Press, 1998), 138.

5 Bhabha, cited in Robert Young, *White Mythologies: Writing History and the West* (New York: Routledge, 1999), 143.

6 Meyda Yegenoglu, "Sartorial Fabrications: Enlightenment and Western Feminism," in *Postcolonialism, Feminism and Religious Discourse*, eds. Laura Donaldson and Kwok Pui-lan (New York: Routledge, 2002), 93.

7 Spivak, "Can the Subaltern Speak?" 294, 298.

8 Frantz Fanon, *Black Skin, White Masks*, trans. Charles Markmann (New York: Grove, 1965), 41.

9 David T. Mitchell, "Narrative Prosthesis and the Materiality of Metaphor," in Sharon Snyder and others *Disability Studies: Enabling the Humanities* (New York: The Modern Language Association of America, 2002), 17, 20; Mitchell, "Modernist Freaks and Postmodern Geeks," *The Disability Studies Reader*. Edited by Lennard J. Davis (New York: Routledge, 1997), 350.

10 Michael Lackey, "Frantz Fanon on the Theology of Colonization," *Journal of Colonialism and Colonial History* 3 (2). http://muse.jhu.edu/journals/journal_of_colonialism_and_colonial_history/v003/3.2lackey.html (accessed November 5, 2005).

11 Young, *White Mythologies*, 125.

12 Gayatri Chakravorty Spivak, "Righting Wrongs," *The South Atlantic Quarterly* 103, no. 2 (2004): 524, 532–535.

13 Kelly Oliver, *Witnessing: Beyond Recognition* (Minneapolis: University of Minnesota Press, 2001), 45–46.

14 Oliver, *Witnessing*, 39–40.

15 Lackey, "Frantz Fanon on the Theology of Colonization."

16 D. H. Lawrence, cited in Gilles Deleuze, "To Have Done with Judgment," in *Essays Critical and Clinical* (Minneapolis: University of Minnesota Press, 1997), 127.

17 Mitchell, "Narrative Prosthesis," 20.

18 Mitchell, "Narrative Prosthesis," 20.

19 Ashis Nandy, *The Intimate Enemy: Loss and Recovery of Self Under Colonialism* (Delhi: Oxford, 1988), x.

20 Marcus Borg, *Meeting Jesus Again for the First Time* (San Francisco: Harper San Franscisco, 1995), 55–56.

21 Rita Nakashima Brock, *Journeys by Heart: A Christology of Erotic Power* (New York: Crossroad, 1992), 9, 23. Crossan explains at the end of his *Jesus, A Revolutionary Biography* (New York: Harper Collins, 1994) that "the structure of a Christianity will always be: this is how we see Jesus-then as Christ-now. Christianity must repeatedly, generation after generation, make its best historical judgment about who Jesus was then and, on that basis, decide what that reconstruction means as Christ now" [*sic*] (200).

22 Brock, *Journeys by Heart*, 29.

23 Preceded by the television show *Extreme Makeover*, which concentrated on identified bodily deficiencies, the 2006 spin-off was to be called *Miracle Works*, featuring further corrective surgeries. "The mask of philanthropy," Harlan Lane, *The Mask of Benevolence*, suggests, protects the majority from deviation and conceals their "selfish interests" in detection and correction (85). "Paternalism evades responsibility for its failure by affirming the biological inferiority of the beneficiary," he explains (38).

24 James C Scott, *Domination and the Arts of Resistance: Hidden Transcripts* (New Haven, Conn.: Yale, 1990), 49–50.

25 Scott, *Domination and the Arts of Resistance*, 67.

26 Gerd Theissen, *The Miracle Stories of the Early Christian Tradition*, trans. Francis McDonagh (Edinburgh: T & T Clark, 1983), 277–278; This reading of miracles as proleptic experiences of resurrection remains exceedingly consistent, extending from at least Augustine to some

believers in biotech miracles who purport that medical miracles promise our return to an original state of health. During modernity, a millennialist type of hope gravitated to science and medicine such that the role of biotechnology becomes itself the miracle worker.

27 Theissen, *Miracle Stories*, 281–223.

28 Theissen, *Miracle Stories*, 283.

29 Jean Comaroff, "The Diseased Heart of Africa: Medicine, Colonialism, and the Black Body," in *Knowledge, Power, and Practice: The Anthropology of Medicine and Everyday Life*, eds. Shirley Lindenbaum and Margaret Lock (Berkeley: University of California Press, 1993), 319.

30 Paul Longmore, "Conspicuous Contribution and American Cultural Dilemmas," in David T. Mitchell and Sharon L. Snyder, *The Body and Physical Difference: Discourses of Disability* (Ann Arbor: University of Michigan Press, 1997), 146, 154.

31 Longmore, "Conspicuous," 154.

32 Longmore, "Conspicuous," 146, 154.

33 Kwok Pui-Lan, "Com/Promised Lands: The Colonial, the Postcolonial, and the Theological" (Lecture, Drew University, Madison, N.J., 28-29 September 2002).

34 Marianne Sawicki, *Seeing the Lord: Resurrection and Early Christian Practices* (Minneapolis: Fortress Press, 1994), 30.

35 Sawicki, *Seeing the Lord*, 297.

36 Dieter Georgi, "The Interest in Life of Jesus Theology as a Paradigm for the Social History of Biblical Criticism," *Harvard Theological Review* 85, no. 1 (1992): 56, 76.

37 Georgi, "The Interest in Life of Jesus," 83.

38 Razack, *Looking White People in the Eye*, 20.

39 Razack, *Looking White People in the Eye*, i.

40 Razack, *Looking White People in the Eye*, 10.

41 Razack, *Looking White People in the Eye*, 4.

42 Nandy, *The Intimate Enemy*, xi, 1.

43 Nandy, *The Intimate Enemy*, 30, 34.

44 Lennard Davis, cited in Mitchell and Snyder, *The Body and Physical Difference*, 54.

45 Rey Chow, *Writing Diaspora: Tactics of Intervention in Contemporary Cultural Studies* (Bloomington: Indiana University Press, 1993), 10. Each of these trajectories can be employed as a psychological screen for the helper—what Rey Chow calls "the sanctification of the subaltern, an idealization of the subaltern position, for example, the noble savage, the spirituality of the poor, the inspiration of a supercrip, and so on.

46 Gayatri Chakravorty Spivak, "Three Women's Texts and a Critique of Imperialism," *Critical Inquiry* 12 (Autumn 1985): 269

47 Razack, *Looking White People in the Eye*, 135, 132,152.

48 Wendy Brown, *Wounded Attachments: States of Injury: Power and Freedom in Late Modernity* (Princeton: Princeton University Press, 1995), 55.

49 Rey Chow, *The Protestant Ethnic and the Spirit of Capitalism* (New York: Columbia University Press, 2002), 11.

50 Chow, *The Protestant Ethnic*, 14.

51 Brown, *Wounded Attachments*, 55.

52 Gayatri Chakravorty Spivak, "Righting Wrongs" *The South Atlantic Quarterly* 103, No. 2 (2004): 534.

53 Spivak, "Righting Wrongs," 545.

54 Kelly Oliver, *Witnessing: Beyond Recognition* (Minneapolis: University of Minnesota Press, 2001), 15.

55 Spivak, "Righting Wrongs," 531, 545.

56 Spivak, "Righting Wrongs," 541, 537.

57 Spivak, "Righting Wrongs," 534, 531, 533.

58 Spivak, "Righting Wrongs," 531, 561.

59 Oliver, *Witnessing*, 15.

60 Oliver, *Witnessing*, 42–43.

61 Oliver, *Witnessing*, 42, 43, 44.

62 Spivak, "Righting Wrongs," 567 n16.

63 Spivak, "Righting Wrongs," 524.

64 Mitchell and Snyder, *Body and Physical Difference*, 6.

65 Spivak, "Righting Wrongs," 559, 551.

66 Jürgen Moltmann, *The Spirit of Life: A Universal Affirmation* (Minneapolis: Fortress Press, 1992), 8.

67 Moltmann, *The Spirit of Life*, 37, 42, 43.

68 David Abram, *The Spell of the Sensuous: Perception and Language in a More-than-Human World* (New York: Pantheon, 1996), 13, 7.

69 Abram, *The Spell of the Sensuous*, 7.

70 Christopher Hill, *The World Turned Upside Down: Radical Ideas During the English Revolution* (London: Penguin, 1975), 129.

71 Helen Meekosha and Leanne Dowse, "Enabling Citizenship: Gender, Disability and Citizenship in Australia" *Feminist Review* 57 (Autumn 1997): 49, 58, 67.

72 Brock, *Journeys by Heart*, 91, 105.

73 Brock, *Journeys by Heart*, 99, 73.

74 Musa Dube, *Postcolonial Feminist Interpretation of the Bible* (St. Louis: Chalice, 2000), 195.

75 Brock, *Journeys by Heart*, 52.

76 Brock, *Journeys by Heart*, 87, 90.

77 Martha L. Edwards, "Constructions of Physical Disability in the Ancient Greek World: The Community Concept," in Mitchell and Snyder, *Body and Physical Difference*, 38.

78 Gregory J. Riley, *One Jesus, Many Christs: How Jesus Inspired not one true Christianity, but Many: The Truth about Christian Origins* (Minneapolis: Fortress Press, 2000), 55–56.

Chapter Six

1 Lynn Manning, "The Magic Wand," in *Staring Back: The Disability Experience From the Inside Out*, ed. Kenny Fries (New York: Plume/Penguin, 1997), 165.

2 Thomas F. Mathews, *The Clash of Gods: A Reinterpretation of Early Christian Art* (Princeton, N.J.: Princeton University Press, 1993), 65.

3 Mathews, *The Clash of Gods*, 65, 62.

4 Burton L. Mack, *A Myth of Innocence: Mark and Christian Origins* (Philadelphia: Fortress Press, 1988), 209.

5 Gary Ferngren, "Early Christianity and Healing," *Bulletin of the History of Medicine* 66 (1992): 2, 4, 8, 12.

6 Mathews, *The Clash of Gods*, 59, 62.

7 Cited by Elizabeth A. Castelli, "Romans," in *Searching the Scriptures, Vol. Two: A Feminist Commentary*, ed. Elisabeth Schüssler Fiorenza (New York: Crossroad, 1994), 281.

8 Peter L. Hays, *The Limping Hero: Grotesques in Literature* (New York: New York University Press, 1971), suggests that the limping hero—from Oedipus and Achilles to Herman Melville's Ahab—has been something of a Western literary archetype.

9 Simon Horne, "'Those Who are Blind See': Some New Testament Uses of Impairment, Inability, and Paradox," in *Human Disability and the Service of God: Reassessing Religious Practice*, eds. Nancy Eiesland and Don E. Saliers (Nashville, Tenn.: Abingdon, 1998), 89–90.

10 S. J. David Hamm, "Sight to the Blind: Vision as Metaphor in Luke," *Biblica* 67 (1986): 465.

11 Carlin Barton, *The Sorrows of the Ancient Romans: The Gladiator and the Monster* (Princeton, N.J.: Princeton University Press, 1993), 107–108, 145.

12 Barton, *The Sorrows of the Ancient Romans*, 132.

13 David Ray Griffin, *God and Religion in the Postmodern World: Essays in Postmodern Theology* (Albany: State University of New York Press, 1989), 85.

14 Norman Cohn, *Cosmos, Chaos and the World to Come: The Ancient Roots of Apocalyptic Faith* (New Haven, Conn.: Yale University Press, 1993), 162.

15 Catherine Keller, *Face of the Deep* (New York: Routledge, 2003), 20–21.

16 Gerda Lerner, *The Creation of Patriarchy* (New York: Oxford, 1986), 81.

17 Lerner, *The Creation of Patriarchy*, 81.

18 Timothy Taylor, "Believing the Ancients: Quantitative and Qualitative Dimensions of Slavery and the Slave Trade in Later Prehistoric Eurasia," *World Archaeology* 33, no.1:36, 38.

19 J. Gelb, "Prisoners of War in Early Mesopotamia," *Journal of Near Eastern Studies* 32, no. 1/2 (January-April 1973): 87.

20 Lerner, *The Creation of Patriarchy*, 82.

21 K. Neumann, *Die Hellenen im Skythenlande* (Berlin 1855), cited in Stephanie West, "Introducing the Scythians: Herodotus on Koumiss (4.2)," *Museum Helviticum* 56 (1999): 78n10.

22 Cited in Rav Elchanan Samet, "Parashat Mishpatim" in "The Israel Koschitzky Virtual Beit Midrash," http://www.vbm-torah.org/parsha.63/18 (Accessed 28 November 2004), 8–9.

23 Stephanie West, "Introducing the Scythians," 78n11.

24 W. D. Dunsmuire and E. M. Gordon, "The History of Circumcision," *BJU International* 83, sup. 1 (1 January 1999): 1, http://www.cirp.org/library/history/dunsmuir1/ (May 24, 2004).

25 Samet, "Parashat Mishpatim," 2.

26 Paul D. Hanson, *The Dawn of Apocalyptic* (Philadelphia: Fortress Press, 1975), 128; Joseph Blenkinsopp, *Isaiah 1-39: A New Translation with Introduction and Commentary. The Anchor Bible* (Toronto: Doubleday, 2000), 454–457.

27 Hanson, *The Dawn of Apocalyptic*, 25. Cohn, *Cosmos, Chaos and the World to Come*, argues that "in the days of Second Isaaiah the notion that Yahweh created the world was ... taking on more importance than it had possessed for the pre-exilic prophets" (152).

28 Cohn, *Cosmos, Chaos and the World to Come*, 157.

29 The movement of imagery in Pauline literature, progressing from slavery to the status of "servants of God/Christ," might suggest something like this.

30 Hays, *The Limping Hero*, 32n36.

31 Robert Graves, *The White Goddess: A Historical Grammar of Poetic Myth* (London: Faber and Faber Limited, 1948), 327.

32 Hays, *The Limping Hero*, 126.

33 Modern high civilization presumed a certain pure surface intactness of the flesh as desirable. Prosthetics thus are presumed to cover over cosmetically the physical stigmata of disability. Similarly, Western high culture presumed painting, tattooing, and scarification of the body to be primitive. I'm suggesting here that humans do not always want to eliminate the marks life makes on the flesh. Indeed, religious meaning has often included marking the flesh and inducing pain—for example, the sun dance. Somaticizing and marking pain on the body, wearing that pain as the history of the body, seems psychically important to persons—whether piercing, tattooing, or refusing to wear cosmetic prostheses.

34 Donald Akenson, *Surpassing Wonder: The Invention of the Bible and the Talmuds* (Chicago: University of Chicago Press, 1998), 213.

35 Morrison, cited in Homi K. Bhabha, *The Location of Culture* (New York: Routledge, 1994), 198.

36 Bhabha, *The Location of Culture*, 198.

37 Bhabha, *The Location of Culture*, 199.

38 Marianne Sawicki, *Crossing Galilee: Architectures of Contact in the Occupied Land of Jesus* (Harrisburg, PA: Trinity Press International, 2000), 155.

39 Akenson, *Surpassing Wonder*, 250.

40 Hanson, *The Dawn of Apocalyptic*, 177, 179.

41 Akenson, *Surpassing Wonder*, 245.

42 Cohn, *Cosmos, Chaos and the World to Come*, 156–157.

43 Judith Perkins, *The Suffering Self* (New York: Routledge, 1995), 16.

44 Bhabha, *The Location of Culture*, 199.

45 Perkins, *The Suffering Self*, 3, 13.

46 Peter Brown, *The Body and Society: Men, Women, and Sexual Renunciation in Early Christianity* (New York: Columbia University Press, 1998), 2.

47 Perkins, *The Suffering Self*, 76–77, 90.

48 Perkins, *The Suffering Self*, 3.

49 "The Acts of Peter," cited in Perkins, *The Suffering Self*, 137.

50 Perkins, *The Suffering Self*, 169.

51 Elaine Scarry, *The Body in Pain: The Making and Unmaking of the World* (New York: Oxford, 1985), 137.

52 Perkins, *The Suffering Self*, 115.

53 Perkins, *The Suffering Self*, 26–27, 115.

54 Perkins, *The Suffering Self*, 3.

55 Perkins, *The Suffering Self*, 8.

56 Perkins, *The Suffering Self*, 109.

57 Perkins, *The Suffering Self*, 140.

58 Perkins, *The Suffering Self*, 64, 1–2. Perkins and Riley do seem to differ on Christianity's calibration of the body-soul split. Riley insists that "a body-soul dualism is the contribution of Christianity," that it "makes Christianity possible," while Perkins seems to suggest that body-soul dualism was a Stoic and aristocratic commitment that produced among this economic strata a sense of the charmed and romantic life.

59 Gregory J. Riley, *One Jesus, Many Christs: How Jesus Inspired not one true Christianity, but Many: The Truth about Christian Origins* (Minneapolis: Fortress Press, 2000), 26.

60 Riley, *One Jesus, Many Christs*, 199, 139.

61 Dennis R. MacDonald, *The Homer Epics and the Gospel of Mark* (New Haven, Conn.: Yale University Press, 2000), contends that "the earliest evangelist was not writing a historical biography, as many interpreters suppose, but a novel, a prose anti-epic of sorts" (7). In its context, Jesus would have been recognizable as a transvalued, figural redeployment of Odysseus, MacDonald argues—an action figure more virtuous, more compassionate, more noble and inured to suffering than Odysseus, a model of what was expected of his followers. MacDonald works specifically with the Gospel of Mark, but Marianne Palmer Bonz does the same with Luke. Her text, *The Past as Legacy: Luke-Acts and Ancient Epic* (Minneapolis: Augsburg Fortress, 2000), interprets the Jesus of Luke-Acts likewise as an adaptation of the heroic epic, but with a concluding, intriguing twist: "At the center of Luke's theological reflections is the conviction that the divine solution for human salvation involves not just the death of the beloved Son but also the rebirth of the people of God" (193). Riley, *One Jesus, Many Christs*, asserts that Jesus was modeled on Achilles (20) in Virgil's *Aenid*, that reconstruction of Homer's *Illiad* and his hero, Odysseus.

62 "Acts of Polycarp," cited in Perkins, *The Suffering Self*, 33.

63 Riley, *One Jesus, Many Christs*, 55–56, 47, 209.

64 Riley, *One Jesus, Many Christs*, 29.

65 Cohn, *Cosmos, Chaos, and the World to Come*, 156–157.

66 Perkins, *The Suffering Self*, 27, 290, 39, 191.

67 Perkins, *The Suffering Self*, 211, 26, 192.

68 Riley, *One Jesus, Many Christs*, 41.

69 Perkins, *The Suffering Self*, 12.

70 Peter Brown, *Poverty and Leadership in the Later Roman Empire* (Hanover, N.H.: University Press of New England, 2002), 8–9.

71 Brown, *Poverty and Leadership in the Later Roman Empire*, 15.

72 Brown, *Poverty and Leadership in the Later Roman Empire*, 14.

73 Perkins, *The Suffering Self*, 213.

74 Perkins, *The Suffering Self*, 142, 214, 213.

75 Marcus J. Borg, *Meeting Jesus Again for the First Time* (San Francisco: Harper San Francisco, 1995), 55–56.

76 Gary Lee Alley Jr., in "'Good News to the Poor': Demarcating Disabilities within the Synoptic Gospels and Qumran's Messianic Schemas," a paper delivered at Society of Biblical Literature, San Antonio, TX, 2004, suggested that the synoptics' use of disablement countered the Qumran community's purity ethos regarding the exclusion of disabled poor.

77 Elaine Scarry, *The Body in Pain: The Making and Unmaking of the World* (New York: Oxford, 1985), 4.

78 See Paul Farmer, *Pathologies of Power* (Berkeley: University of California Press, 2002).

Chapter Seven

1 Burton L. Mack, *A Myth of Innocence: Mark and Christian Origins* (Philadelphia: Fortress Press, 1988), 208.

2 Gregory J. Riley, *One Jesus, Many Christs: How Jesus Inspired not one true Christianity, but Many: The Truth about Christian Origins* (Minneapolis: Fortress Press, 2000), 18, 21, 80–81.

3 Laura E. Donaldson, in "Native Women's Double Cross: Christology from the Contact Zone," a presentation at First Nation's House of Learning, University of British Columbia, September 2003, describes the contact zone (a term originally used by Mary Louise Pratt) as "the space of colonial encounters where people divided both geographically and historically come into contact with each other, usually under conditions of severe inequality and intractable conflict. . . . The contact zone also foregrounds the interactive, improvisational dimensions of colonial encounters"(2).

4 Mack, *A Myth of Innocence*, 217. Mack asserts that this "set of stories on the model of epic prototypes was composed to portray the origins of a most unlikely congregation in the process of formation. . . . Miracle stories served some Jesus movement as its myth of origins" (219, 215). Mack and I differ with reference to the figuration versus realism in regard to Jesus. He asserts that "Jesus is the founder of the new society" (223). I can agree with "Jesus" as the figural pattern thereof, the figural "Torah scoll." With feminists, I would assert that we need no hero, but rather a model of community (see Brock).

5 David T. M. Frankfurter, "The Origin of the Miracle-List Tradition and Its Medium of Circulation," in *Society of Biblical Literature*, Seminar Papers (Atlanta: Scholars Press, 1990), 346.

6 Frankfurter, "The Origin of the Miracle-List," 349.

7 James C. Scott, *Domination and the Arts of Resistance: Hidden Transcripts* (New Haven, Conn.: Yale University Press, 1990), 80–81.

8 The Sibylline Oracles, dated circa second century B.C.E., had repeated the reversal message previously encoded in Isaiah, integrating with it the resurrection tradition of Elijah: "There will be a resurrection of the dead / and most swift racing of the lame, / and the deaf will hear, / and blind will see, / those who cannot speak will speak, / and life and wealth will be common to all" (Frankfurter, "The Origin of the Miracle-List," 347–48).

9 Cited in Homi K. Bhabha, *The Location of Culture* (New York: Routledge, 1994), 200.

10 Frankfurter, "The Origin of the Miracle-List," 346n6.

11 Frankfurter insists that "the Mosaic prophet paradigm was one of the first 'christologies' in the Jesus movement. . . . [A] Mosaic araetology for demonstrating someone's status as this prophet actually determined the collection and publication of miracle stories attributed to Jesus" ("The Origin of the Miracle-List," 350–351). I am less inclined to jump immediately to the presumption of a historical Jesus who fits this job description. Robert Price adds the insight that "the northern kingdom (Israel) did not dream of a messiah but of a Moses-like restorer," concluding that "the chains of Moses—and Elijah-like miracles" made their way from northern Israel into southern gospels (64, 65).

12 Scott, *Domination and the Arts of Resistance*, 144. Persons within social conditions of domination, Scott reminds us, cannot always safely employ direct speech without recrimination and thus develop hidden paths of communication. The African American song "Follow the Drinking Gourd"—meaning, use the North Star as the directional map of freedom—is one such example. The Isaianic vision that "the blind see, the lame walk, the deaf hear" may serve something of that purpose in the synoptic narratives.

13 Bhabha, *The Location of Culture*, 203.

14 Bhabha, *The Location of Culture*, 200.

15 Eric Eve, *The Jewish Context of Jesus' Miracles* (Sheffield, UK: Sheffield Academic Press, 2002),

196; Kvalbein, cited in Eve, 196n62.

16 Frantz Fanon, *A Dying Colonialism*, trans. Haakon Chevalier (New York: Grove, 1965), 96. Thanks to Barbara Boruff, research assistant, for bringing this quote to my attention.

17 Eve, *The Jewish Context of Jesus' Miracles*, 377.

18 Mack, *A Myth of Innocence*, 217.

19 Thomas F. Mathews, *The Clash of Gods: A Reinterpretation of Early Christian Art* (Princeton, N.J.: Princeton University Press, 1993), 76.

20 Mathews, *The Clash of Gods*, 76.

21 Mathews, *The Clash of Gods*, 76.

22 Mack, *A Myth of Innocence*, 11.

23 Gerd Theissen, *The Miracle Stories of the Early Christian Tradition*, trans. Francis McDonagh (Edinburgh: T & T Clark, 1983), 291.

24 Theissen, *The Miracle Stories*, 291, 302.

25 Theissen, *The Miracle Stories*, 299.

26 Luis Leal, "Magical Realism in Spanish American Literature (1967)," in *Magical Realism: Theory, History, Community*, eds. Lois Parkinson Zamora and Wendy B. Faris (Durham, N.C.: Duke University Press, 1995), 119–123.

27 Alego Carpentier, "On the Marvelous Real in America (1949)," in Zamora and Faris, *Magical Realism*, 85–86.

28 Angel Flores, "Magical Realism in Spanish American Fiction (1955)," in Zamora and Faris, *Magical Realism*, 113–116; also see David Mikics, "Derek Walcott and Alejo Carpentier: Nature, History and the Caribbean Writer," in Zamora and Faris, *Magical Realism: Theory, History, Community*, 372. In a sense, magical realism might be seen to protest any idealist metaphysics, which then confines the excess, the ambiguous, the heterogeneous. As Garcia Marquez contends, "realism is a kind of premeditated literature that offers too static and exclusive a vision of reality. . . . Disproportion is part of reality too. Our reality is in itself all out of proportion. . . . the magic text is, paradoxically, more realistic than the realist text" (Scott Simpkins, summarizing Marquez in "Sources of Magic Realism," in Zamora and Faris, *Magic Realism*, 148).

29 Jean Comaroff and John Comaroff, *Of Revelation and Revolution: Christianity, Colonialism, and Consciousness in South Africa*, Vol. 1 (Chicago: University of Chicago Press, 1991), 31–32.

30 Kenneth Orona, "Locating the Milagro Beanfield War in Early Twentieth Century New Mexico," *DES: A Scholarly Journal of Ethnic Studies*, www.colorado.edu/EthnicStudies/ethnicstudiesjournal/Current%20Issue/milagro_beanfield_war.htm (7 March 2006).

31 John Nichols, *The Milagro Beanfield War* (New York: Owl Books, 2000), 293.

32 Bhabha, *The Location of Culture*, 208.

33 Nichols, *The Milagro Beanfield War*, 292.

34 Frantz Fanon, *The Wretched of the Earth*, trans. Constance Farrington (New York: Grove, 1963), 293–294.

35 Nichols, *The Milagro Beanfield War*, 421, 431; Judith Perkins, *The Suffering Self* (New York: Routledge, 1995), 140.

36 Franz Roh, "Magic Realism: Post-Expressionism," in *Magical Realism*, Zamora and Faris, 15–32.

37 David Bohm and F. David Peat, *Science, Order and Creativity*, 2nd edition (London: Routledge, 2000), 32.

38 Feuerbach, cited in Gerd Theissen, *The Miracle Stories*, 288.

39 Anita Haya Goldman, "Comparative Identities: Exile in the Writings of Frantz Fanon and W.E.B. DuBois," in *Borders, Boundaries, and Frames: Essays in Cultural Criticism and Cultural Studies*, ed. M. G. Henderson (New York: Routledge, 1995), 122.

40 Scott, *Domination and the Arts of Resistance*, 80.

41 Scott, *Domination and the Arts of Resistance*, 80–81.

42 As Nandy has pointed out, even the binarization of resistance can be an account more true for the colonizer than the colonized, for whom life might just, at least in many terrains of the daily, go on—even while suffering effects of and making/poking fun of the regime.

Not to deny the decimating impact of a colonial presence, but to think of colonial power as all pervasive may merely flatter the colonizer.

43 Nichols, *The Milagro Beanfield War*, 424.

44 Jean Marc Ela, *My Faith as an African*, trans. John Pairman Brown and Susan Perry (Maryknoll, N.Y.: Orbis, 1988), 70–71.

45 Paul Farmer, *Pathologies of Power* (Berkeley: University of California Press, 2002), 7, 41.

46 Farmer, *Pathologies of Power*, xiv, 30.

47 Francoise Heritier, cited in Farmer, *Pathologies of Power*, 7.

48 Mack, *A Myth of Innocence*, 222–223.

49 Mack, *A Myth of Innocence*, 215. It is likely that, given the razing of the temple, people were creating a congregation, but equally, then, a nation. I worry, in other words, that modern Western notions demarcating religious life keep us from seeing the socioeconomic and political material culture of New Israel. Mack, like others, assumes the modern realist structure of exclusion: "The selection of extreme cases (blind, lame, deaf, incurable hemorrhage, etc.) accentuates the point that the new congregation was not formed by attention to Jewish rituals, for these people are impossible cases and need something more. They are figures chosen to represent the unthinkable aspect of the new social arrangement, its difference from the prevailing models. Jesus heals and cleanses them . . . without any precondition based on social status governed by the laws of purity. . . . Those without any claim to membership in Israel are nevertheless included" (223).

50 Zygmunt Bauman, "Living and Dying in the Planetary Frontier-Land," *Tikkun* 17.2 (March/April 2002): 42.

51 Mack, *A Myth of Innocence*, 223. On the concept of the "body without organs," see Gilles Deleuze and Felix Guattari, *Anti-Oedipus: Capitalism and Schizophrenia* (Minneapolis: University of Minnesota Press, 1983), 8.

52 Helen Meekosha and Leanne Dowse, "Enabling Citizenship: Gender, Disability and Citizenship in Australia," *Feminist Review* 57 (Autumn 1997): 49.

53 Marianne Sawicki, *Crossing Galilee: Architectures of Contact in the Occupied Land of Jesus* (Harrisburg, Penn.: Trinity Press International, 2000), 178. Sawicki is well aware that "there is no way to recover a baseline 'indigenous' or pure culture" in Palestine beneath the influences of economic and cultural contact promoted by the previous empires. "But we can talk about the persistence of kinship practices and strategies, insofar as these were an intentional effort to constitute Israelite identity in the midst of these incursions" (9).

54 Sawicki, *Crossing Galilee*, 37.

55 Sawicki, *Crossing Galilee*, 24.

56 Sawicki, *Crossing Galilee*, 24, 120.

57 Sawicki, *Crossing Galilee*, 92.

58 Sawicki, *Crossing Galilee*, 116–117, 127.

59 Sawicki, *Crossing Galilee*, 173.

60 Sawicki, *Crossing Galilee*, 179, 184, 175.

61 John Dominic Crossan, *The Birth of Christianity: Discovering What Happened in the Years Immediately After the Execution of Jesus* (San Francisco: Harper San Francisco, 1998), 196.

62 Crossan, *The Birth of Christianity*, 182–183.

63 Jennifer A. Glancy, *Slavery in Early Christianity* (New York: Oxford University Press, 2002), 122, 103, 107.

64 Perkins, *The Suffering Self*, 2–3; Glancy, *Slavery in Early Christianity*, 10, 12.

65 Glancy, *Slavery in Early Christianity*, 114.

66 Jennifer A. Glancy, by breaching our contemporary religious euphemisms of servanthood, illuminates the multiple references to slavery within the Synoptic Gospels. See her *Slavery in Early Christianity*. More problematically, however, Glancy—ignoring the Jubilee agenda of the Gospels and how that would have meant for slaves—assumes that metaphoric usage of terms and conditions of slavery in a mimetic context (for example, the empire of God versus the empire of Caesar,) leaves the practice of slavery intact—as an unquestioned assumption about the nature of the world. So, for example, she concludes, "As with Paul's deployment of slave metaphors, Matthew 'depends on the reality of slavery to convey . . .

[his] meanings and therefore reinscribes the relation[s] of slavery'" (120). I can not deny that Christians owned slaves at least into the nineteenth century; nor can I deny that such mimetic reversals can and have endorsed "slave mentality," that is, obedience, among Christians, as Nietzsche appropriately assessed. But I equally cannot deny that Jubilee sat at the front of the Gospels and that it implied economic reform especially pertaining to debt slavery. The figuration of Jesus was likely a composite built up around "the suffering slave" imagery of Isaiah 52–53, intending, as I understand it, to map or to swerve response to the economics of empire.

67 Michael Hudson, "It Shall be a Jubilee Unto You," *Yes! A Journal of Positive Futures* (Fall 2002): 39.

68 Hudson, "It Shall be a Jubilee Unto You," 39.

69 Parallel this with New Testament scholar Hyun Ju Bae's work on Paul's "war of myths" with the values of Hellenistic-Roman society. See her dissertation *The Symbolism of Evil Powers in 1 and 2 Corinthians: Power, Wisdom and Community* (Casperson School of Graduate Studies, Drew University, Madison, N.J., 2001), 264. While "Paul's concern with the language of omnipotence and the ownership of the earth resembles the preoccupations of the imperial power, Paul's apocalyptic thought world moves beyond a scenario of reversal toward a menace not only to the imperial power, but also to the very logic of retribution and triumphalism inherent in the divine judgment" (187–188).

70 Sawicki, *Crossing Galilee*, 91.

71 Sawicki, *Crossing Galilee*, 91.

72 John Byron, *Slavery Metaphors in Early Judaism and Pauline Christianity: A Traditio-Historical and Exegetical Examination* (Tübingen, Ger.: Mohr Siebeck, 2003), 39–40.

73 Geza Alfoldy, cited in Crossan, *The Birth of Christianity*, 178–179.

74 Crossan, *Birth of Christianity*, 181.

75 Bhabha, *The Location of Culture*, 200.

76 Donald Akenson, *Surpassing Wonder: The Invention of the Bible and the Talmuds* (Chicago: University of Chicago Press, 1998), 248.

77 Robert Price, *Deconstructing Jesus* (Amherst, Mass.: Prometheus, 2000), 13, 15.

78 Akenson, *Surpassing Wonder*, 249.

79 Marianne Sawicki, *Seeing the Lord: Resurrection and Early Christian Practices* (Minneapolis: Fortress Press, 1994), 273; Akenson, *Surpassing Wonder*, 249.

80 Donna Haraway, *Modest_Witness@Second_Millennium. FemaleMan_Meets_OncoMouse: Feminism and Technoscience* (New York: Routledge, 1997), 11.

81 Price, in his *Deconstructing Jesus*, compares what scholars have called the "Q-material" or "the Lost Gospel" with Cynic philosophy and Sufi wisdom. In Sufi transmitted saying 67, a blind, leprous, crippled paralytic with elephantiasis recognizes that he is of "the Spirit of God," that his disabilities align him with the itinerant asceticism and "unworldliness" of "the Spirit of God" (143). Here Spirit is evoked due to the irrelevance of outward form, of human figure. In the Q-like material of the Sufi-type sayings of Jesus, Jesus is frequently addressed "O Spirit of God," which denotes not the divine nature of Jesus (an impossibility in Islam), but rather his unworldliness and itinerant asceticism (115).

82 Gary Ferngren, "Early Christianity and Healing," *Bulletin of the History of Medicine* 66 (1992): 14.

83 Ferngren, "Early Christianity and Healing," 8n43, 11.

84 Gilles Deleuze, *Essays Critical and Clinical*, trans. Daniel W. Smith and Michael A. Greco (Minneapolis: University of Minnesota Press, 1997), 126–127.

85 Scott, *Domination and the Arts of Resistance*, 18.

86 William R. LaFleur, "Body," *Critical Terms for Religious Studies*, ed. Mark C. Taylor (Chicago: University of Chicago Press, 1998), 48.

87 Larry Daloz, "Interview with Sharif Abdullah," *Earth, Spirit and the Human Future: The Newsletter of the Whidbey Institute* 5, no. 1 (Spring 2003): 11; Sue Fishkoff, "Out of the Wilderness: Jewish Converts Are Sprouting across the American Heartland," *Utne Reader* (March-April 2001): 14–15.

88 Douglas John Hall, *The Cross in our Context* (Minneapolis: Fortress Press, 2003), 172, 175.

89 Wilson Yates, "An Introduction to the Grotesque: Theoretical and Theological Considerations," in *The Grotesque in Art and Literature: Theological Reflections*, eds. James Luther Adams and Wilson Yates (Grand Rapids, Mich.: Eerdmans, 1997), 40, 26.

90 Carlin Barton, *The Sorrows of the Ancient Romans: The Gladiator and the Monster* (Princeton, N.J.: Princeton University Press, 1993), 132.

91 Michael Hardt and Antonio Negri, *Empire* (Cambridge, Mass.: Harvard, 2000), 21, 373.

92 Marta Russell and Ravi Malhotra, "The Political Economy of Disablement: Advances and Contradictions," http://www.yorku.ca/socreg/RusMal.htm (Accessed March 7, 2006), 1; Bhabha, *The Location of Culture*, 199.

93 Bhabha, *The Location of Culture*, 200; Sawicki also rightly cautions us that "colonized people may devise various strategies of resistance, ranging from outright avoidance" to "collaboration" (118).

94 Faulkner, cited in Paul W. Hollenbach, "Jesus, Demoniacs, and Public Authorities: A Socio-Historical Study," *Journal of the American Academy of Religion* 49, no. 4 (1981): epigraph.

95 Joan Tollifson, "Imperfection is a Beautiful Thing: On Disability and Meditation," in *Staring Back: The Disability Experience From the Inside Out*, ed. Kenny Fries (New York: Plume/Penguin, 1997), 111.

96 Elaine Scarry, *The Body in Pain: The Making and Unmaking of the World* (New York: Oxford University Press, 1985), 219.

97 Tollifson, "Imperfection is a Beautiful Thing," 111.

98 Tollifson, "Imperfection is a Beautiful Thing," 108.

99 Leonard Koren, *Wabi-Sabi for Artists, Designers, Poets and Philosophers* (Berkeley, Calif.: Stone Bridge 1994), 7.

100 Tollifson, "Imperfection is a Beautiful Thing," 110.

101 Nancy Eiesland, *The Disabled God: Toward a Liberatory Theology of Disability* (Nashville, Tenn.: Abingdon, 1994), 110.

Chapter Eight

1 Gilles Deleuze, *Nietzsche and Philosophy* (New York: Columbia University Press, 1983), 135, 131; Daniel W. Smith, "Introduction" to Gilles Deleuze, *Essays Critical and Clinical*, trans. Daniel W. Smith and Michael A. Greco (University of Minnesota Press, 1997), xv.

2 Donne Haraway, *Modest_Witness@Second_Millennium. FemaleMan_Meets_OncoMouse: Feminism and Technoscience* (New York: Routledge, 1997), 3; Michael Hardt and Antonio Negri, *Empire* (Cambridge: Harvard, 2000), xiii, xv. See also chap. 1 (22–41) and 364–365.

3 Paul Patton, *Deleuze and the Political* (New York: Routledge, 2000), 7.

4 Ian Buchanan, *Deleuzism: A Metacommentary* (Edinburgh: Edinburgh University Press, 2000), 110.

5 Michel Foucault, *The Birth of the Clinic: An Archaeology of Medical Perception* (New York: Vintage, 1994), 198; Buchanan, *Deleuzism*, 110. Given government cuts to social programs in Canada and the United States and the consequent lack of national as well as state or provincial health resources, raising this critique feels risky. My concern here, however, has to do with the distinction between health and the normalization of the body—a distinction not easily made, of course. Yet health, as I hope to make clear, can never be so individuated, personalized, and achieved as a "state of health," as we have been led to accept. Health is as much about the environment of bodies (ecologically, sociopolitically, and culturally speaking) as it is about what takes place within the immunized borders of a body, the latter being the apparent orientation of Western culture and biomedicine. Nor is health about the intactness of a body, but about what Nietzsche calls its "efflorescence," its courage to be not the consummate, integrated end-all and be-all of humanity, but a bridge to the evolution of new values, new peoples. Nietzsche, cited in G. M. Danzer, M. Walter Rose, and B. F. Klapp, "On the Theory of Individual Health" *Journal of Medical Ethics* 28, no. 1 (2002): 18.

6 Gilles Deleuze and Felix Guattari, *Anti-Oedipus: Capitalism and Schizophrenia*, trans. Robert Hurley, Mark Seem and Helen R. Lane (Minneapolis: University of Minnesota Press, 2003), 453–454.

7 Rey Chow, *The Protestant Ethnic and the Spirit of Capitalism* (New York: Columbia University Press, 2002), 10.

8 Nick J. Fox, "Refracting 'Health': Deleuze, Guattari and Body-Self," *Health: An Interdisciplinary Journal for the Social Study of Health, Illness and Medicine* 6, no. 3 (2002): 355.

9 "Modern civilization," the periodization of Enlightenment views on rationality, history, and subjectivity, set itself over against not simply what it called the primitive, but against degeneracy, a term that included peoples whom we now distinctly analytically engage in discourses of race, ethnicity, sex, gender, and disability, people whose generative capacities were put in question, given assumptions to the transcendentalist (objectifying) epistemology of Euro-Western modernism and its modes of desiring production. As Guy Hocquenghem observed in this regard, "The homosexual can only be a degenerate for he does not generate." See *Homosexual Desire*, trans. Daniella Dangoor (London: Allison and Busby, 1978), 93. Think also of the forced sterilization of persons with disability, even the refusal to extend desire thereto as if we were not a generative interface.

10 Tamsin Lorraine, *Irigaray and Deleuze: Experiments in Visceral Philosophy* (Ithaca, N.Y.: Cornell University Press, 1999), 5; Chow, *The Protestant Ethnic and the Spirit of Capitalism*, 41, 33.

11 Martin Hewitt, "Bio-Politics and Social Policy: Foucault's Account of Welfare," in *The Body: Social Process and Cultural Theory*, eds. Mike Featherstone, Mike Hepworth, Bryan S. Turner (London: Sage, 1991), 229.

12 Foucault, cited in Hewitt, "Bio-Politics and Social Policy," 229.

13 Marta Russell, *Beyond Ramps: Disability at the End of the Social Contract* (Monroe, Maine: Common Courage, 1998), 16–17.

14 Polyani, cited in Russell, *Beyond Ramps*, 68; Foucault cited in Chow, *The Protestant Ethnic and the Spirit of Capitalism*, 11.

15 Deleuze, *Nietzsche and Philosophy*, 367.

16 Gerald P. McKenney, *To Relieve the Human Condition: Bioethics, Technology and the Body* (Albany: State University of New York Press, 1997), 201, 222.

17 Brian Massumi, *A User's Guide to Capitalism and Schizophrenia: Deviations from Deleuze and Guattari* (Boston: MIT Press, 1994), 111.

18 Massumi, *A User's Guide to Capitalism and Schizophrenia*, 111–112.

19 Deleuze, *Nietzsche and Philosophy*, 99.

20 Deleuze and Guattari, *Anti-Oedipus*, 131.

21 Massumi, *A User's Guide to Capitalism and Schizophrenia*, 1.

22 "Gilles Deleuze," European Graduate School, http://www.egs.edu/resources/deleuze.html (8 March 2006).

23 Smith, "Introduction." xv; Deleuze, *Essays Critical and Clinical*, 3.

24 Foucault, cited in Constantin V. Boundas and Dorothea Olkowski, *Gilles Deleuze and the Theatre of Philosophy* (New York: Routledge, 1994), 1.

25 Freidrich Nietzsche, *Ecce Homo*, trans. Walter Kaufmann (New York: Vintage/Random House, 1989), 224.

26 F. Scott Fitzgerald, "The Crack Up," in *The Crack Up*, ed. Edmund Wilson (New York: New Directions Paperback), 75.

27 Fitzgerald, "The Crack Up," 74.

28 Fitzgerald, "The Crack Up," 76.

29 Fitzgerald, "The Crack Up," 78.

30 Gregg Lambert, *The Non-Philosophy of Gilles Deleuze* (New York: Continuum, 2002), 130.

31 Lambert, *The Non-Philosophy of Gilles Deleuze*, 79.

32 Lambert, *The Non-Philosophy of Gilles Deleuze*, 11.

33 Kelly Oliver, *Witnessing: Beyond Recognition* (Minneapolis: University of Minnesota Press, 2001), 171.

34 Deleuze and Guattari, in *A Thousand Plateaus: Capitalism and Schizophrenia*, trans. Brian Massumi (Minneapolis: University of Minnesota Press, 2002), use the experience of the dissembled infant—with its burps and smiles not yet schematically organ/ized—to teach their conceptual notion of the "Body without Organs" (BwO) (79). Their critique of the organic and the organism, as also their use of what appear at first to be the ecologically troubling terms of the *inorganic* or the *nonorganic* (These terms refer to the refusal to organize relations,

either mentally or libidinally, into a "world under God."), are offshoots of this concept. Resonances between Deleuze's and Fitzgerald's writings suggest to me that illness, among other things, do to some extent return us to this preorganizational experience of the body.

35 Fitzgerald, "The Crack Up," 84.

36 In *Anti-Oedipus*, Deleuze and Guattari distinguish the molar (that is, large social or desiring-machines, for example, the economic, the political), from the molecular, the microphysics of desire, "the parts and wheels of desiring-machines" (183).

37 Hocquenghem, *Homosexual Desire*, 15; Nick J. Fox, "Refracting 'Health,'" 355.

38 Fitzgerald, "The Crack Up," 80, 81.

39 Deleuze, cited in Lambert, *The Non-Philosophy of Gilles Deleuze*, 127.

40 Judith Poxon, "Embodied Anti-Theology: The Body without Organs and the Judgement of God," in *Deleuze and Religion*, ed. in Mary Bryden (New York: Routledge, 2001), 45, 47.

41 Inna Semetsky, "Deleuze's New Image of Thought, or Dewey Revisited," in *Educational Philosophy and Theory* 35, no. 1 (January 2003): 18–19.

42 Gilles Deleuze, *Difference and Repetition*, trans. Paul Patton (New York: Columbia University Press, 1994), 192.

43 Vernon A. Rosario, *The Erotic Imagination: French Histories of Perversity* (New York: Oxford University Press, 1997), 15.

44 What do I mean by cultural denial of erotic pleasure to persons with disabilities? Recall the sterilization projects of previous decades. More pervasive still, the view of persons with disabilities as nondesirable, nonsexual.

45 Karmen MacKendrick, *Counterpleasures* (Albany: State University of New York Press, 1999), 71.

46 Jürgen Moltmann, *The Spirit of Life: A Universal Affirmation* (Minneapolis: Fortress Press, 1992), 271.

47 Patton, *Deleuze and the Political*. 33.

48 Friedrich Nietzsche, *On the Genealogy of Morals*, trans. Walter Kaufmann (New York: Vintage/Random House, 1989), 68.

49 Eliot Albert, "Deleuze's Impersonal, Hylozoic Cosmology: The Expulsion of Theology," in Brydon, *Deleuze and Religion*, 193.

50 Catherine Keller, *Face of the Deep*, (New York: Routledge, 2003), 26–27.

51 Tyler Roberts, *Contesting Spirit: Nietzsche, Affirmation, Religion* (Princeton, N.J.: Princeton University Press, 1998), 92.

52 Lorraine, *Irigaray and Deleuze*, 150.

53 Nietzsche, *Ecce Homo*, 224.

54 Smith, "Introduction," xiv–xv.

55 G. M. Danzer, Rose M. Walter, and B. F. Klapp, "On the Theory of Individual Health," *Journal of Medical Ethics* 28, no. 1 (2002): 18.

56 Paul F. Glenn, "The Great Health: Spiritual Disease and the Task of the Higher Man," *Philosophy and Social Criticism* 27 no. 2 (2001): 110; Linda Holler, *Erotic Morality: The Role of Touch in Moral Agency* (New Brunswick, N.J.: Rutgers University Press, 2002), 157–159.

57 Gilles Deleuze, "Immanence, A Life," *Theory, Culture and Society* 4, no. 2 (1997): 4.

58 Smith, "Introduction," xi.

59 Fox, "Refracting 'Health,'" 360.

60 Deleuze, *Essays Critical and Clinical*, 1.

61 Deleuze, *Essays Critical and Clinical*, 3.

62 Nietzsche, *On the Genealogy of Morals*, see section 17; Smith, "Introduction." xv; Deleuze, *Essays Critical and Clinical*, 105.

63 As pertaining to Nietzsche, see William E. Connolly, *Identity/difference: Democratic Negotiations of Political Paradox* (Ithaca, N.Y.: Cornell University Press, 1991), Introduction, esp. ix and xxii, 164–171.

64 Smith, "Introduction," liii.

65 Freidrich Nietzsche, "The Philosopher as Cultural Physician," in *Philosophy and Truth: Selections from Nietzsche's Notebooks of the early 1870's*, trans. Daniel Breazeale (Atlantic Highlands, N.J.: Humanities Press, 1979) 69–76.

66 Deleuze, *Essays Critical and Clinical*, 3–4.

67 Roberts, *Contesting Spirit*, 36.

68 Michael Goddard, "The Scattering of Time Crystals: Deleuze, Mysticism and Cinema," in Brydon, *Deleuze and Religion*, 59.

69 MacKendrick, *Counterpleasures*, 106.

70 Roberts, *Contesting Spirit*, 14–15, 16.

71 Patton, *Deleuze and the Political*, 34.

72 Mark C. Taylor, "The Betrayal of the Body: Live Not," in *Nots* (Chicago: University of Chicago Press, 1993), 216. While on this point Deleuze and Taylor would be in agreement, Taylor distances himself from Deleuze, contending that Deleuze "romanticizes" illness. Taylor, intriguingly, refers illness to the Freudian death drive.

73 Holler, *Erotic Morality*, 133.

74 Rosemarie Garland Thomson, *Extraordinary Bodies: Figuring Physical Disability in American Culture and Literature* (New York: Columbia, 1997), 24.

75 Mikhail Bakhtin's notion of "the grotesque" with its power to "unsettle the ascendant order" is suggestively comparable. Bakhtin himself, intriguingly enough, was an amputee. Cited in Thomson, *Extraordinary Bodies*, 38, 150n48.

76 Here I am assuming some continuum between disability and illness, which is telling of my own experience of becoming an amputee at the age of thirty-seven. Those differently abled from birth rightly do not wish to be misconstrued as sick. As Davis points out, "the idea of birth 'defect' comes to us direct and unaltered from a eugenic model of the human body" (Bending Over Backwards, 20). I am hoping through this book to loosen both notions—of disability and illness—or rather to call attention to the culture that emplots both of them as disadvantageous to its self-image and interruptive of its goals. "If a physical condition is widespread enough in a community and does not interfere substantially with the community achieving its goals, it will be seen as an illness [or disability] only by outsiders with a different cultural frame of reference and different goals." (See Lane, *The Mask of Benevolence*, 210.)

77 R. D. Laing, cited in Deleuze and Guattari, *Anti-Oedipus*, 131.

78 Deleuze and Guattari, *Anti-Oedipus*, 4, 2.

79 Laing, cited in Deleuze and Guattari, *Anti-Oedipus*, 131–132.

80 Keith Ansell Pearson, ed., "Deleuze Outside/Outside Deleuze: On the Difference Engineer," in *Deleuze and Philosophy: The Difference Engineer* (New York: Routledge, 1997), 5, 6.

81 Michael Pollan, *The Botany of Desire: A Plant's-Eye View of the World* (New York: Random House, 2002), 87–91.

82 Paul F. Glenn, "The Great Health: Spiritual Disease and the Task of the Higher Man," *Philosophy and Social Criticism* 27, no. 2 (2001): 108.

83 Wendy Brown, *Wounded Attachments: States of Injury: Power and Freedom in Late Modernity* (Princeton, N.J.: Princeton University Press, 1995), 60.

84 Deleuze and Guattari, *Anti-Oedipus*, 130; Massumi, *A User's Guide to Capitalism and Schizophrenia*, 119; How does the schizophrenization or de-Oedipalization of capitalism help us take a variant line of flight from the conditions of capitalism? Oedipalization creates "territory," "possession" (the body being among the territories captured by ego), and a sense of infinite indebtedness. Schizophrenizing opens flows of desire to perverse and prodigal couplings that can exit the Oedipal/ego regime. Without ego/Oedipus in play, where might desire flow? Wouldn't its improvising tendencies exit the territories of monetary capital? What would happen to labor? In what would desire invest itself? Not necessarily in "having and appearing."

85 Smith, "Introduction," xx–xxix.

86 Mark Seem, "Introduction" to Deleuze and Guattari, *Anti-Oedipus*, xiv.

87 There is no "Man" as distinct from "nature," insist Deleuze and Guattari (1983). And there is no desire that is a pure reserve, that is, other than that now being circulated as the

desire for health. Globalizing capitalism's "desire for health" does not confront us with a "take it or leave it" option, but rather as a situation of "take it" *and* sidestep it, schizophrenize it.

88 Patton, *Deleuze and the Political*, 63.

89 Rosi Braidotti, "Becoming Woman: or Sexual Difference Revisited," *Theory, Culture and Society* 20, no. 3 (2003): 55.

90 Deleuze, *Essays Critical and Clinical*, 1.

91 Deleuze and Guattari, *Anti-Oedipus*, 42.

92 Patton, *Deleuze and the Political*, 7. Admittedly, Deleuze was not expressly interested in disability theory. In fact, Deleuze insists on the primacy of "becoming woman" to "becoming revolutionary." And yet, that ignores both his insistence upon philosophy as clinical work and the way in which degeneracy has been the abject bottom line for the project of modern civilization. Further, Deleuze himself slipped through the crack of becoming disabled, as did many in his genealogy of orphan philosophers. So becoming disabled could, in fact, be Deleuze's default position, his own unconscious working concept. The feminist Deleuzian philosopher Rosi Bradotti insinuates as much as she refutes his notion of becoming woman: "Deleuze becomes caught in the contradiction of postulating a general 'becoming-woman' which fails to take into account the historical and epistemological specificity of the ... feminist standpoint." A truly "Deleuzian approach calls on us to relinquish this quest for identity ... to activate instead multiple becomings, away from identity. Some of these transitions are happening already in the fact that so many bodies are malfunctioning [or ceasing?] to produce the programmed codes, of which the use of Prozac, the spreading of anorexia and bulimia are clear symptoms" (Braidotti, "Becoming Woman," 51, 53).

Fabulating a people yet to be, given modernity, current conditions, and existent standards of health, Deleuze seems then almost unconsciously to insist, will unfold as becoming disabled. Indeed, he decisively marked this turning away from history in his reading of D. H. Lawrence: Christianity did not so much renounce power and empire "as invent a new form of power as the power to judge," Deleuze reads Lawrence to say (*Essays Critical and Clinical*, 127). As an ideal projection of this "power to judge," God has been the keystone to a romantic view of nature as inherent harmony (whereas cosmos proves "chaosmic") and to organism ("organized" under the dominion of or "subject/ed" to the ego, that is) such that the despotic ego and its God hold the key to authorized libidinal investment and allowable assemblages. In other words, "The unity and finality of nature as a whole and the organism as a microcosm have always been patterned on God" (John Protevi, "The Organism as the Judgement of God: Aristotle, Kant and Deleuze on Nature That Is, on Biology, Theology and Politics," in Brydon, *Deleuze and Religion*, 30). What next caught Deleuze's attention was the conceptual force of disruption in disability; for against this power of judgment, Lawrence posed something like a teratological catalog. Lawrence, observes Deleuze, "ceaselessly describes bodies that are organically defective or unattractive ... but that are nonetheless traversed by this intense vitality that defies organs and undoes their organization. This inorganic vitality is the relation of the body to the imperceptible forces and powers that seize hold of it or that it seizes hold of" (*Essays Critical and Clinical*, 131). To those bodies cross-examined by modernity and found wanting in terms of quality of life, Lawrence, and now apparently Deleuze, return to reconsider a humanity yet to be.

Becoming disabled introduces the dissolution of modernity's idealist subjective stance. Disability theory thus has a profound choice to make—to adhere to the neurotic pathology of civilized reason in which we have been viewed as lacking health (and within which we have been proposing something like an identity politics), or to abandon that as structure and "introduce mania into civility" (Buchanan), or to work some dynamic conjunctions thereof. That seems to be the point of Lennard Davis's opening essay in *Bending over Backwards: Disability, Dismodernism and Other Difficult Positions* (New York: New York University Press, 2002). Second, disability as a concept turns postcoloniality, in a Deleuzian style, "clinical." It refuses, even the critic's penchant "to reterritorialize, to redo the photos, to remake power and law." See Gilles Deleuze and Felix Guattari, *Kafka: Toward a Minor Literature*, trans. Dana Polan (Minneapolis: University of Minnesota Press, 1986), 86.

93 Smith, "Introduction," li; Freidrich Nietzsche, *Thus Spake Zarathustra*, trans. Thomas Common (Mineola, N.Y.: Dover, 1999), 5.

94 Nietzsche, *Thus Spake Zarathustra*, 93–97.

95 Davis, *Bending over Backwards*, 5, 31.

96 Rosemarie Garland Thomson, "Introduction: From Wonder to Error–A Genealogy of Freak Discourse in Modernity," in *Freakery*, ed. Rosemarie Garland Thomson (New York: University Press, 1996), 1.

97 Eugene Holland, *Deleuze and Guattari's Anti-Oedipus: Introduction to Schizoanalysis* (New York, Routledge, 1999), 121.

98 Holler, *Erotic Morality*, 159, 161.

99 Pollan, *The Botany of Desire*, 155, 169, 162; Holler, *Erotic Morality*, 133.

100 Process theologian Charles Hartshorne describes pain as sympathy with cellular life. *Omnipotence and Other Theological Mistakes* (Albany: State University of New York Press, 1984), 61.

101 Deleuze and Guattari, *Anti-Oedipus*, 131.

102 Massumi, *A User's Guide to Capitalism and Schizophrenia*, 1.

103 Seem, "Introduction," xxi.

104 Deleuze and Guattari, *Anti-Oedipus*, 5; Russell, *Beyond Ramps*, 16–17.

105 Deleuze and Guattari, *Anti-Oedipus*, 123, 321, 378; Deleuze and Guattari, *A Thousand Plateaus*, 351–352.

106 Thomson, *Extraordinary Bodies*, 35.

107 Lorraine, *Irigaray and Deleuze*, 163.

108 See Chow, *The Protestant Ethnic and the Spirit of Capitalism*, chap. 1.

109 Mark Matousek, "Savage Grace," *Utne Reader* Vol 62 (Mar/Apr 94), pp. 104-112.

110 Anosh Irani, *The Cripple and His Talismans* (Vancouver: Raincoast Books, 2004), 157.

111 Irani, *The Cripple and His Talismans*, 76–77.

112 Deleuze and Guattari, *Anti-Oedipus*, 366–367.

113 Jane Gallop, *Thinking through the Body* (New York: Columbia University Press, 1988), 1. See http://www.egs.edu/resources/deleuze.html.

114 Semetsky, "Deleuze's New Image of Thought," 18–19.

115 Semetsky, "Deleuze's New Image of Thought," 19.

116 Gilles Deleuze, *Difference and Repetition*, trans. Paul Patton (New York: Columbia University Press, 1994), 192.

117 Patton, *Deleuze and the Political*, 19.

118 Constantin V. Boundas and Dorothea Olkowski, eds., *Gilles Deleuze and the Theatre of Philosophy* (New York: Routledge, 1994), 11.

119 Smith, "Introduction," xxv; Gilles Deleuze and Felix Guattari, *What is Philosophy?* (New York: Columbia University Press, 1991), 169.

120 Peter Canning, "The Crack of Time and the Ideal Game," Boundas and Olkowski, *Gilles Deleuze and the Theatre of Philosophy*, 73; Deleuze, cited in Boundas and Olkowski, *Gilles Deleuze and the Theatre of Philosophy*, 73; See Davis, *Bending over Backwards*.

121 Boundas and Olkowski, *Gilles Deleuze and the Theatre of Philosophy*, 10–11.

122 Deleuze, *Difference and Repetition*, 134.

123 Gregg Lambert, "On the Uses and Abuses of Literature for Life: Gilles Deleuze and the Literary Clinic," Online at http://www.jefferson.villiage.virginia.edu/pmc/text-only/issue.598/8.3lambert.txt (Accessed March 12, 2004).

124 Pearson, "Deleuze Outside/Outside Deleuze," 2.

125 Deleuze, *Essays Critical and Clinical*, 105, 100.

126 Deleuze, *Essays Critical and Clinical*, 100.

Chapter Nine

1 Tamsin Lorraine, *Irigaray and Deleuze: Experiments in Visceral Philosophy* (Ithaca, N.Y.: Cornell University Press, 1999), 138.

2 In terms of her performance art, take for example her choice of dressing as a Tehuana. Tehuana women maintained a "sharp and sustained resistance to European colonization" (Alice Gambrell, "A Courtesan's Confession: Frida Kahlo and Surrealist Entrepreneur-

ship," in *Women Intellectuals, Modernism and Difference: Transatlantic Culture, 1919-1945* [New York: Cambridge University Press, 1997], 53). Kahlo was herself a hybrid of that colonial phase, even as she attempted resistance and the reinvention of Mexico.

3 As Mark Seem points out in his "Introduction" to Gilles Deleuze and Felix Guattari's *Anti-Oedipus: Capitalism and Schizophrenia*, trans. Robert Hurley, Mark Seem and Helen R. Lane (Minneapolis: University of Minnesota Press, 2003) one cannot but hear this text as a sequel to Nietzsche's *The AntiChrist* (xvi), surmising then that Oedipalization and Christianity (as well as school, family, and nation) must be coimplicit in this production of desire (Seem, "Introduction," xvii). As Deleuze and Guattari suggest, "Oedipus presupposes a fantastic repression of desiring machines" (3). That such repression has been significantly shaped by Christianity is overtly suggested by the title of Chapter 2, "Psycho-Analysis and Familialism: The Holy Family" (51).

4 Linda Holler, *Erotic Morality: The Role of Touch in Moral Agency* (New Brunswick, N.J.: Rutgers University Press, 2002), 206.

5 Lorraine, *Irigaray and Deleuze*, 153.

6 Lorraine, *Irigaray and Deleuze*, 242.

7 Daniel W. Smith, "Introduction" to Gilles Deleuze, *Essays Critical and Clinical*, trans. Daniel W. Smith and Michael A. Greco (Minneapolis: University of Minnesota Press, 1997), xiv.

8 Sarah M. Lowe, *Frida Kahlo* in Universe Series on Women Artists (New York: Universe Publishing, 1991), 34.

9 Deleuze and Guattari actually call these "war-machines." I follow philosopher Paul Patton transposition of their concept into "metamorphosis machines" because of the problematic misunderstanding occasioned by Deleuze and Guattari's naming: "The real object of Deleuze and Guattari's war-machine concept is not war but the conditions of creative mutation and change" (110). The historian of science Donna Haraway works with a similar concept, "figuration," in *Modest_Witness@Second_Millennium. FemaleMan_Meets_OncoMouse: Feminism and Technoscience*. She defines figurations as "performative images that can be inhabited." Sounding much like Deleuze, though with no obvious intertextual discourse, she continues: "Verbal or visual, figurations can be condensed maps of contestable worlds. All language, including mathematics, is figurative, that is, made of tropes, constituted by bumps that make us swerve from literal-mindedness. . . . To read such maps with mixed and differential literacies and without the totality, appropriations, apocalyptic disasters, comedic resolutions, and salvation histories of secularized Christian realism is the task of the mutated modest witness" (11).

10 In his introduction to Deleuze's *Essays Critical and Clinical*, Daniel Smith explains: "The symptomatological method is only one aspect of Deleuze's [clinical] project. The deeper philosophical question concerns the conditions that make possible this production of new modes of existence, that is, the ontological principle of Life as a nonorganic and impersonal power" (li).

11 Paul Patton, *Deleuze and the Political* (New York: Routledge, 2000), 110.

12 Patton, *Deleuze and the Political*, 133.

13 Antonio Saborit, "Iztaccíhuatl in the Valley of Anáhuac," in Luis-Martín Lozano and others, *Frida Kahlo*, trans. Mark Eaton and Luisa Panichi (Boston: Bulfinch, 2000), 191.

14 Holler, *Erotic Morality*, 140.

15 Deleuze, *Essays Critical and Clinical*, 52.

16 Sarah M. Lowe, "Essay and Commentaries," in *The Diary of Friday Kahlo: An Intimate Self-Portrait* (New York: Abradale, 1995), 28, 26.

17 Tobin Siebers, "Tender Organs, Narcissism, and Identity Politics," in Sharon Snyder and others. *Disability Studies: Enabling the Humanities* (New York: The Modern Language Association of America, 2002), 41.

18 Martha Zamora, *Frida Kahlo: The Brush of Anguish*, trans. Marilyn Sode Smith (San Francisco: Chronicle Books, 1990), 19.

19 While frequent references note Artaud's travels to Mexico during the early middle decades of the twentieth century, I have not noted direct contact with Kahlo. Breton, rather, was the direct liaison with Kahlo, generating a show for her in Paris. See Gambrell, "A Courtesan's Confession," 42–43.

20 Lowe, *Frida Kahlo*, 10.

21 Sharyn Rohlfsen Udall, *Carr, O'Keefe, Kahlo: Places of Their Own* (New Haven, Conn.: Yale University Press, 2000), 3.

22 Lowe, *Frida Kahlo*, 10.

23 Gambrell, "A Courtesan's Confession," 68–73.

24 *Retablos* and *Ex Votos* were popular, religious art forms during the nineteenth century in Mexico. *Retablos*—literally meaning "behind the altar"—were small iconographic oil paintings, often executed on tin, portraying individuals of the Christian Holy Family (Jesus, Mary) as well as recalling scenes from the lives of other Christian saints. These were typically set up on people's home altars, inviting supplication. *Ex Votos*—literally meaning "out of thankfulness"—were of similar form in sizes of six inches by fourteen inches to fourteen inches by eighteen inches, but were commissioned by individuals to commemorate a person's recovery from some grave danger. These "offerings" were sometimes placed around a saint's shrine or pinned to her or his statuary. Often the ex-voto incorporated—in a written banner or text—the circumstances of the miraculous cure, intervention, or rescue. See Gloria Kay Giffords, *Mexican Folk Retablos: Masterpieces on Tin* (Tucson: University of Arizona Press, 1974), 19–20, 119–122. Kahlo and Rivera had a collection of several hundred of such pieces of popular art. See Zamora, *Frida Kahlo*, 110.

25 Lowe, *Frida Kahlo*, 11.

26 Arguments to the contrary that Kahlo adopted "the spatial and temporal organization of the *ex-voto* without carrying over any specific religiosity," that her work was "ultimately bereft of any theological content" (See Lowe, *Frida Kahlo*, 54–55.), I find myself in agreement with philosopher of religion, Paula Cooey: "While she was in no way religious in any conventional sense . . . her constant return to various religious art forms as well as symbols suggests a sensibility that might be called religious insofar as it is a ritualistic sacralization of the ordinary that reflects a deeply held faith." See "Mapping the Body through Religious Symbolism: The Life and Work of Frida Kahlo as Case Study" in *Faithful Imagining*, eds. Song Hyun Lee, Wayne Proudfoot, Albert Blackwell (Atlanta: Scholars, 1995), 124. Kahlo consistently paints in sacred frame—ex-votos, retablos. Indeed (I would claim) she paints herself as saint, martyr, and free spirit within hagiographic tradition. If two-thirds of her works figurally appear to be self-portraits, we might rather see them as iconographic—Kahlo framed in the familiar Mexican retablos as "Ecce Homo" (Note the crown of thorns here around her neck in *Self-*Portrait, 1940.), "Mater Delorosa" (overseeing *My Birth* [1932], but also note the dagger torn breast in *Memory* [1937], among others). Beyond Christian tradition, she also appeared in iconic shadows of Isis (note the watery venue and miniature shoe boat in *Memory*, 1940), Egyptian Queen Nefertiti (The Diary of Frida Kahlo, 220–21), and the Aztec goddess Coatlicue (*Self-Portrait with Braid* [1941]) (see Udall). But what, then, is the "deeply held faith" (Cooey) of this woman who canonizes herself as saint, martyr, the mother of the incarnation, ancient goddess, and wild woman? Pray tell, how dare she at/tempt the sacred with this [dismembered, if daringly differentiating] body (of faith)?

27 Giffords, *Mexican Folk Retablos*, 119.

28 Cooey, "Mapping the Body through Religious Symbolism," 112; Michael Pollan, *The Botany of Desire: A Plant's-Eye View of the World* (New York: Random House, 2002), 172.

29 Lowe, *Frida Kahlo*, 38.

30 Freidrich Nietzsche, *Ecce Homo*, trans. Walter Kaufmann (New York: Vintage/Random House, 1989), 230–231.

31 Cooey, "Mapping the Body through Religious Symbolism," 115.

32 Nietzsche, *Ecce Homo*, 231.

33 Cooey, "Mapping the Body through Religious Symbolism," 109, 110.

34 David Michael Levin, "Painful Time, Ecstatic Time," *Eastern Buddhist* 11 (1978): 92.

35 Levin, "Painful Time, Ecstatic Time," 117.

36 Pollen, *The Botany of Desire*, xv, xxv.

37 Pollen, *The Botany of Desire*, xviii.

38 Deleuze, *Essays Critical and Clinical*, 3.

39 Udall, *Carr, O'Keefe, Kahlo*, 81.

40 Deleuze, cited in Ian Buchanan, *Deleuzism: A Metacommentary* (Edinburgh: Edinburgh University Press, 2000), 110.

41 Lowe, *Frida Kahlo*, 64.

42 Lorraine, *Irigaray and Deleuze*, 127.

43 Deleuze cited in Daniel W. Smith, "Introduction," xxxiv.

44 Deleuze, cited in Smith, "Introduction," to *Essays Critical and Clinical*, xxxiii.

45 Deleuze, *Essays Critical and Clinical*, 176n15.

46 Deleuze, *Essays Critical and Clinical*, 131–132.

47 Smith, "Introduction," xiv.

48 Lowe, *Frida Kahlo*, 10–11.

49 Lowe, *Frida Kahlo*, 55.

50 Deleuze, cited in Smith, "Introduction," xxxvi–xxxvii.

51 Deleuze, *Essays Critical and Clinical*, 135; Mary Bryden, ed., *Deleuze and Religion* (New York: Routledge, 2001), 11.

52 Virginia Burrus, *The Sex Lives of Saints: An Erotics of Ancient Hagiography* (Philadelphia: University of Pennsylvania Press, 2004), 5. Setting terms of sacrificial subjectivity in resonance with "sex lives" hardly accords with common sense ("Thankfully!" Deleuze sighs); in such terms, Burrus nevertheless takes the ancients out of our imposed frames of ascetic ideals. A phenomenon of moral prohibition, those ascetic ideals Nietzsche also earlier rejected as punishing, excruciating forms of proprietarian enclosure that reduce life to reactive forces (summarized in Deleuze, *Essays Critical and Clinical*, 101). "Religious sacrifice is about taking life in a serious and moral way without the emotional deadening typical of the sadist and mechanist," instructs Holler (see *Erotic Morality*, 53).

53 Burrus, *The Sex Lives of Saints*, 18.

54 Burrus, *The Sex Lives of Saints*, 8, 11.

55 Burrus, *The Sex Lives of Saints*, 2.

56 Burrus, *The Sex Lives of Saints*, 14. Scholar Karmen MacKendrick explains that "Self-mastery can itself be transcended in a self-defiance that overcomes the self in the discipline of restraint and the delight of pain. This is the defiance of *telos*. . . . Asceticism, binding, bondage, discipline in the non-Foucauldian sense, restraint, chosen pain . . . these . . . are strategically deployed forces of power through which the body resists . . . the social restraints that constitute the good subject" (see *Counterpleasures* [Albany: State University of New York Press, 1999] 108–109). But this forgets the "non-chosen" experience of pain, which one should not overwrite in considering Nietzsche's life. To speak of choice is a properly modernist strategy in regard to practicing justice. Yet if pain is not presumed to be the repression of desire, could that not necessarily chosen pain also be, if not mastered, then harnessed?

57 Burrus, *The Sex Lives of Saints*, 7.

58 See Robert Corrington, *Nature and Spirit: An Essay in Ecstatic Naturalism* (Bloomington: Indiana University Press, 1994).

59 Michael Goddard, "The Scattering of Time Crystals: Deleuze, Mysticism and Cinema," in Brydon, *Deleuze and Religion*, 57, 62–63.

60 Udall, *Carr, O'Keefe, Kahlo*, 19; Cooey, "Mapping the Body through Religious Symbolism," 110.

61 William E. Connolly, *Identity/difference: Democratic Negotiations of Political Paradox* (Ithaca, N.Y.: Cornell University Press, 1991), 2.

62 Holler, *Erotic Morality*, 162.

63 Burrus, *The Sex Lives of Saints*, 15.

64 Lowe, *Frida Kahlo*, 43.

65 Smith, "Introduction," xxvi.

66 Mary Oliver, "White Flowers," in *New and Selected Poems* (Boston: Beacon, 1992), 59.

67 Smith, "Introduction," xxvii.

68 Deleuze, *Essays Critical and Clinical*, 2.

69 Holler, *Erotic Morality*, 192.

70 Smith, "Introduction," xiv; Ato Quayson, "Looking Awry: Tropes of Disability in

Postcolonial Writing," in *Relocating Postcolonialism*, eds. David Theo Goldberg and Ato Quayson (Oxford: Blackwell, 2002), xii; Deleuze would tolerate nothing like a notion of creation. Here I am simply trying to name the previous rhizomatic tip from which this theology springs.

Chapter Ten

1 Luce Irigaray, *This Sex Which Is Not One*, trans. Catherine Porter (Ithaca, N.Y.: Cornell University Press, 1985), 26.

2 Lois Bragg notes that while other cultural milieus have "constructed aberrancy as the mark of an outstanding person," Western culture has, by and large, socially marginalized the disabled. See her "Oedipus Borealis," *Disability Studies Quarterly* 17 (Fall 1997): 258–263. I disagree with Bragg to the extent that I find the enthronement of the disabled subtly and perversely available in Western culture, for example, the spiritual inspiration consumed by normates observing the disabled. I would nevertheless agree with Bragg that even this is secondary to our culture's social suppression of the disabled's subjective value. I, however, personally find this nomination for sainthood, that is, "aberrancy as the mark of the outstanding person," the obverse side of social marginalization. This chapter seeks neither to read my physical disability as the stigmata of a saint nor as to serve as provocation for social taboo.

3 Elaine Scarry, *The Body in Pain: The Making and Unmaking of the World* (New York: Oxford University Press, 1985), 3. In *Religious Imagination and the Body: A Feminist Analysis* (New York: Oxford University Press, 1994), Paula Cooey extends Scarry's observation about the primary function of religions in the resolving and/or curing of suffering. Cooey writes: "I argue that religious traditions provide a pedagogical context for the sociocultural transfiguration of human pain and pleasure in ways that continually recreate and destroy human subjectivity, the world within which it emerges, and the transcendent realities with which the subject seeks relation" (9). If we agree with such assertions concerning the role of religions/theologies, the lack of any hermeneutic based on disability would seem to challenge the ethical quality of our contemporary religions.

4 Scarry, *The Body in Pain*, 60.

5 Because my disability came midlife, I will refer to it as traumatic and as a wound—since I do not wish to invalidate the catastrophic conditions surrounding my amputation either for myself or for my family and friends. Those with congenital disabilities are less likely to use either term and rather speak of themselves as differently abled.

6 Ursula Hegi, *Stones From the River* (New York: Poseidon, 1994), 460.

7 Hegi, *Stones From the River*, 69.

8 John Hockenberry, a reporter for National Public Radio, in *Moving Violations* (New York: Hyperion, 1994), notes the way in which his disability acts as a key to opening out intimacy and to the unloading of burdensome secrets specifically not accessible to nondisabled journalists. While Hockenberry has learned to use this "authorization" to his own advantage, his experience still validates my point.

9 Abjection, Julia Kristeva writes, is what a subjective economy sets aside so as to create the borders of subject/object relations. Abjection, the psychic ridges generated by cultural taboos, lays the foundations of the imaginary, of the psychic map of the (acceptable or sacred) world. See *Powers of Horror* (New York: Columbia University Press, 1982), 5. Jettisoned to the side, these abject remains continue to haunt the subject, acting as a "vortex of summons and repulsion" (1). In Western Christianity, the transient character of mortal life has quite typically served as the foil for the transcendent imaginary, for life "in the Spirit."

10 While a reader might protest that civil rights legislation has brought about the mainstreaming of the disabled, several startling statistics need to be considered: Despite the passage of the Americans with Disabilities Act (ADA) in 1990 and nearly a decade of enforcement, unemployment of the disabled has actually increased from 66 percent to 71 percent; 69.1 percent of disabled persons in the United States live below the poverty line. See David T. Mitchell and Sharon L. Snyder, "Introduction," in *The Body and Physical Difference: Discourses of Disability* (Ann Arbor: University of Michigan Press, 1997), 1–9.

11 Elaine Pagels, "The Nature of Nature," in *Adam, Eve and the Serpent* (New York: Vintage/Random House, 1988), chapter 6.

12 Mitchell and Snyder, "Introduction," 3.

13 Judith Herman, *Trauma and Recovery* (New York: Basic/HarperCollins, 1992), 9.

14 Luce Irigaray, *Sexes and Genealogies*, trans. Gillian C. Gill (New York: Columbia University Press, 1993), 133.

15 Mary Oliver, *New and Selected Poems* (Boston: Beacon, 1992), 59.

16 Hildegard of Bingen, *Book of Divine Works*, ed. Matthew Fox (Santa Fe, N.M.: Bear and Company, 1987), 265.

17 Hildegard, *Book of Divine Works*, 5.

18 Scarry, *The Body in Pain*, 162.

19 Caroline Walker Bynum, *Holy Feast, Holy Fast* (Berkeley: University of California Press, 1987), 249.

20 Lucy Grealy, *Autobiography of a Face* (Boston: Houghton Mifflin, 1994), 57.

21 Grealy, *Autobiography of a Face*, 91.

22 Scarry, *The Body in Pain*, 16.

23 Recent scientific work has suggested that life is most prolific at "the edge of chaos," during the phase transition between order and chaos. See, for example, the work of Stuart Kauffman in *At Home in the Universe* (New York: Oxford University Press, 1995). For relating this to illness and life-onset disability, see Tobi Zausner, "When Walls Become Doorways: Creativity, Chaos Theory, and Physical Illness," *Creativity Research Journal* 11, No. 1 (1998): 21–28.

24 Karen McCarthey Brown, in *Mama Lola: A Vodou Priestess in Brooklyn* (Berkeley: University of California Press, 1991), describes the initiation of a vodou priestess (often one who has herself passed through illness), a process interestingly called *kouche*, or lying down—a position thus not unlike that of illness. Through a profusion of herbs, foods, baths, and so on, the initiate is brought through a rebirth. These baths, which immerse the senses, appear to me similar to the sensuous physicality that both Hildegard and Grealy have described amid their illnesses. Hildegard's sense of music reminds me also of the Navajo healing ritual called "holding a sing." In my text, I am calling this sensuous threshold the sentient, semiotic reservoir—based upon my reading of Kristeva.

25 Julia Kristeva, "The Maternal Body," in *m/f* 5-6 (1981): 161. Kristeva's notion of "the maternal body" or "maternal function" names not so much our biological mothers, but the "field" of life shared with our mothers—the sheltering womb space that constituted our first experience of the body. In other words, "the maternal body/function" belongs to/with each of us and is the libidinally charged and psychophysically affective memory field of that material-maternal space-time fold. Or said in another way, it is the sheltering energy field of the body. It constitutes the outer perimeters of our body. In a culture that abjects the material-maternal, this somatic memory has been cut off, yet accessing this, according to Kristevan theory, provides for our personal sense of security in life and now our hope for cultural renewal.

26 Kristeva, "The Maternal Body," 161.

27 Virginia Woolf, "On Being Ill," in *Collected Essays*, Vol. 4 (New York: Harcourt, Brace, and World, 1925), 193 and 197.

28 Woolf, "On Being Ill," 200. Judith Herman, *Trauma and Recovery* (New York: Basic/HarperCollins, 1992), in writing on trauma survivors, fittingly describes this passage between worlds—one world tragically foreclosed and another world positively disclosed—as "immigration" (196).

29 See also Rosemarie Garland Thomson's essay "Disabled Women as Powerful Women in Petry, Morrison and Lorde," in *The Body and Physical Difference*, Mitchell and Snyder, eds., for a parallel analysis—here drawn from African-American women's literature in which disabled bodies come to oppose the dominant order and offer physical alternatives to it from not an intellectual, but "an immutable ontological state" (247).

30 Luce Irigaray, *Elemental Passions*, trans. Joanne Collie & Judith Still (New York: Routledge, 1992).

Index